ANGER'S PAST

8 ↓ Title
2 ↓ Text

Intro 1
Pt 1 22
1 23
2 39
Pt 2 76
3 57
4 77
5 95
Pt 3 134
6 116
7 135
8 151
9 177
Conclusion 197
Biblio 208
VA 225

a

ANGER'S PAST

The Social Uses of an Emotion in the Middle Ages

EDITED BY

BARBARA H. ROSENWEIN

CORNELL UNIVERSITY PRESS

ITHACA AND LONDON

First published 1998 by Cornell University Press.
First printing, Cornell Paperbacks, 1998.

Printed in the United States of America.

Cornell University Press strives to utilize environmentally responsible suppliers and materials to the fullest extent possible in the publishing of its books. Such materials include vegetable-based, low-VOC inks and acid-free papers that are also either recycled, totally chlorine-free, or partly composed of nonwood fibers.

Library of Congress Cataloging-in-Publication Data

Anger's past : the social uses of an emotion in the Middle Ages / edited by Barbara H. Rosenwein.
p. cm.
Includes index.
ISBN 0-8014-3266-9 (cloth : alk. paper).—ISBN 0-8014-8343-3 (pbk. : alk. paper)
1. Anger—History. 2. Social history—Medieval, 500–1500. I. Rosenwein, Barbara H.
BF575.A5A55 1998
152.4'7'0902—dc21

97-39493

Cloth printing 10 9 8 7 6 5 4 3 2 1
Paperback printing 10 9 8 7 6 5 4 3 2 1

Contents

Illustrations

Acknowledgments

The present collection began as a session at the American Historical Association in January 1995 organized by Sharon Farmer, who deserves special thanks here. Entitled "The Social Construction of Anger," the session consisted of papers by Lester K. Little, Richard Barton, and Paul Freedman, with a comment by the present editor. Subsequently, Peter Stearns suggested that the session be expanded into a book. Although the particular publication scheme he proposed turned out to be unfeasible, his initiative is much appreciated. John G. Ackerman, Director of Cornell University Press, gave the project much encouragement. To all of these "facilitators" I wish to record my debt of gratitude.

I want also to thank the contributors. Normally authors of essays in collections have nothing to do with one another. The authors of these essays, however, read the entire collection in draft, and they wrote to each other and to me by e-mail, fax, and letter, commenting on, criticizing, and applauding various points. It was Zouhair Ghazzal who suggested that we might profit from an e-mail forum. Through this electronic discussion list, set up by John W. Corliss of Loyola University's Information Technologies, contributors with access to e-mail were able to communicate with the others in the "Anger group." I have made reference to some of the issues raised by these messages in my concluding chapter, but I would here like to thank the "Anger group" as a whole for making e-mail as close to a fireside chat as one might hope.

I am grateful to Research Services of Loyola University Chicago for providing a generous subvention to help defray the cost of this book's illustration program.

Finally, I thank my husband, Tom, who not only expressed no anger at his preoccupied wife, but materially aided and abetted this project with all the lawyerly skills and devices at his disposal.

BARBARA H. ROSENWEIN

Evanston, Illinois

Abbreviations

Annales ESC = *Annales: Économies-sociétés-civilisations*
CSEL = Corpus Scriptorum Ecclesiasticorum Latinorum
DPI = Gerald of Wales, *De Principis Instructione,* ed. George F. Warner, in Giraldus Cambrensis, *Opera* (London: Rolls Series, 1891), vol. 8
JWCI = *Journal of the Warburg and Courtald Institutes*
M = al-Ḥajjāj b. Muslim, *Ṣaḥīḥ Muslim,* 5 vols. (Beirut: Mu'assassat 'Uzz al-Dīn, 1987)
MGH = *Monumenta Germaniae Historica*
AA = *Auctores antiquissimi* (15 vols., 1877–1919)
DD = *Diplomata regum et imperatorum Germaniae* (10 vols., 1879–1975)
Dt Chron = *Deutsche Chroniken* (6 vols., 1892–)
LL = *Leges nationum Germanicarum* (6 vols., 1892–1969)
Poet = *Poetae Latini medii aevi* (6 vols., 1881–1951)
SS = *Scriptores* (32 vols., 1826–1934)
SSrG = *Scriptores rerum Germanicarum in usum scholarum* (1839–1965)
SSrerMerov = *Scriptores rerum merovingicarum* (7 vols., 1884–1920)
MIÖG = *Mitteilungen des Instituts für österreichische Geschichtsforschung*
Erg. Bd. = Ergänzungsband
PL = *Patrologiae cursus completus. Series latina,* ed. J.P. Migne (222 vols., Paris, 1844–64)
TRHS = *Transactions of the Royal Historical Society*
SE = *The Standard Edition of the Complete Psychological Works of Sigmund Freud,* ed. James Strachey, 24 vols. (London: Hogarth Press, 1966–74)
VsG = *Vita sanctae Geretrudis abbatissae Nivialensis,* ed. Bruno Krusch, MGH SSrerMerov 2: 453–64.

ANGER'S PAST

Introduction

BARBARA H. ROSENWEIN

"The history of anger has yet to be written," wrote Theodore Zeldin in 1977.[1] The comment could still be made today. Apart from a few studies, pursued mainly by the husband-and-wife team of Carol and Peter Stearns, very little attention has been given to the history of anger or, for that matter, most emotions other than love.[2] This is the first book explicitly devoted to the history of anger in the medieval West and (in two essays) on its Islamic and Celtic fringes. We might—indeed we do—congratulate ourselves on the breakthrough. But in the writing of it we have come to understand more clearly the reasons why Zeldin's observation remains true.

For writing about anger is not merely a matter of isolating a topic and setting out to research it; the history of anger does not follow an "agenda" for research the way, for example, the history of women has done.[3] This is

[1] Theodore Zeldin, *France, 1848–1945*, vol. 2, *Intellect, Taste and Anxiety* (Oxford: Clarendon, 1977), p. 1120.

[2] Carol Zisowitz Stearns and Peter N. Stearns, *Anger: The Struggle for Emotional Control in America's History* (Chicago: University of Chicago Press, 1986), pp. 30–31. See also Peter N. Stearns, "Historical Analysis in the Study of Emotion," *Motivation and Emotion* 10 (1986): 185–93. On love in the Middle Ages: John C. Moore, *Love in Twelfth-Century France* (Philadelphia: University of Pennsylvania Press, 1972).

[3] In 1993 Nancy Partner could write that "the reasons which account for the recorded history of the political, social, religious, and aesthetic strivings of our mammalian species being so overwhelmingly dominated by only one of its two sexes have turned out, on repeated examination, to be so shamelessly thin and brittle that there is almost something comical about it" (introduction to the

so for two reasons. First, we don't know what anger is.[4] The essays in this book reflect, in the way that they sometimes disagree with one another, a serious and ongoing theoretical debate among professionals in psychology and anthropology. To pose the problem in its starkest form: some scholars view emotions as innate whereas others consider them to be "social constructions." Readers interested in this controversy will find it discussed in some detail in the concluding chapter. At this point, however, it is simply important to know that this debate is implicit in all the essays presented here. Of course, no one writing for this book thinks that anger is simply the uncontrolled welling up of feeling; or if anyone does, he or she is not prepared to assert that we can know about this sort of anger from a medieval text. Indeed, many of the contributors are concerned first and foremost with the *representation* of anger and attitudes toward it, rather than its *nature.* Yet nature cannot be avoided entirely. Thus there is a fundamental difference between, for example, Richard Barton—who in Chapter 7 speaks of anger as a social "signaling device"—and Lester Little—who in Chapter 1 speaks of restraints and controls on anger's surge.

Second, anger begets anger. That is, it is an emotional subject, tied directly to the ways in which people (including historians) think about themselves, their societies, and their values. These concerns are reflected in a second and related debate in this book: whether (to simplify radically) anger is "good" or "bad." No contributor, of course, poses the matter so starkly, though each finds clear evidence that *medieval* sources did so; rather, the debate centers on the concept of the "civilizing process." This term refers in the first place to Norbert Elias's book by that name, which was written before the Second World War but began to earn critical acclaim only in the 1980s. Elias contrasted the "violent" expression of the emotions in the Middle Ages with the delicate, embarrassed, ashamed expression of feeling in his own time.[5] The turning point, in his view, came with the development of princely power and the imposition of the absolute state in the sixteenth century. Within this context, "courtly forms of conduct" were adopted by the middle classes as they strove to find a place in the new order. By setting up a standard of emotional repression, the state both enhanced its own social control and monopolized

---

special issue, "Studying Medieval Women: Sex, Gender, Feminism," *Speculum* 68 [1993]: 305). The reasons not to write about emotions are neither thin nor brittle; they have to do with our unwillingness to touch what we cannot see or know clearly and to deal with what is (or seems) irrational.

[4] Of course, some would say that "women" also constitute an arbitrary category, socially constructed; in that case, they too would present a problematic research agenda.

[5] Norbert Elias, *The Civilizing Process: The History of Manners and State Formation and Civilization,* trans. Edmund Jephcott, 2 vols. (Oxford: Blackwell, 1994). This work was originally published in 1939.

expressions of violence. The transformed context eventually effected a "long-term change in human personality structures."[6] To be "civilized" meant to repress anger.

More generally, the idea of the "civilizing process" retains its potency even when it does not refer specifically to Elias's formulation. Indeed, part of the appeal of his view is that it accords with at least two common current assumptions: (1) that people who cannot control their anger, or who are violent, are acting in "uncivilized" ways; and (2) that, as Carol Tavris argues, "we" (i.e., members of the middle class) have repressed our emotions and forgotten how to be angry.[7] In this latter view, although anger is "good," the repressive nature of our society renders it "unavailable."

In this collection only the chapter by Zouhair Ghazzal accepts Elias's scheme without modification, but that is because he seeks to contrast the development of the West with Islamic society, where princely courts never transmitted notions of "courtly behavior" to a wider circle. Other chapters, such as those by Paul Hyams and Lester Little, though demurring on particular points, accept as fundamental the notion that anger is less civilized than its repression or sublimation. Still other contributors, Stephen White and Richard Barton, for example, swim upstream against Elias and modern "common sense," arguing for anger's key role in medieval society not because that society was "uncivilized" but, on the contrary, because it was sensitive, adaptive, and attuned to possibilities of adjustment.

These fundamental differences over the nature and value of anger inform, to greater and lesser degrees, each of the chapters in this book. The undercurrent of debate should help to quicken the reader's own emotional involvement in the volume, inviting him or her to assent or degree. Nevertheless, scholarly inquiry, not argument, dominates the book as a whole. Each historian writing here gives a deep analysis of anger in one particular context. Taken together, the essays provide a wide survey of the role of anger in the social lives and conceptual universes of a varied and significant cross-section of medieval people: monks, saints, kings, lords, peasants.

The book begins with holy men and women. Lester Little sets the parameters of subsequent discussions with a review of teachings about anger (*ira* in Latin) in patristic and other learned texts. God could express righteous anger, but human anger was conceived as part of a system of vices: it was one of the seven deadly sins. In pictorial and sculptural images, anger

[6] Ibid., p. 223.
[7] Carol Tavris, *Anger: The Misunderstood Emotion* (New York: Simon and Schuster, 1982).

was a woman (*ira,* being feminine in grammatical gender, was considered female) so full of her own wrath that she was doomed to turn it against herself in suicide. Countering this fury was monastic patience (*patientia*). Even when monks cursed, as they did in their liturgy when threatened by enemies, their cursing was drained of anger. Among other things, Little's piece shows graphically how slippery the topic of "anger" is: while in our own culture cursing is clearly associated with anger, in the monastic culture of the eleventh century cursing was connected precisely with "lack of anger."

Still within a monastic context comes a text that makes its point by stressing the anger of a saint. In Chapter 2, Catherine Peyroux explores anger (in this case the Latin word is *furor,* a masculine noun) in the *Life of Saint Gertrude,* written ca.670. Peyroux shows how crucial is the exploration of context and culture to understand what anger meant in this literary text. She shows as well some gender dimensions of anger: the saint who acts "as if filled by fury" is a young woman. Her fury signals that the expectations of adults about her availability to marry must give away to another reality: her celestial marriage to Christ.

Thus human anger was sometimes warranted. And if saints could sometimes be angry, even more so could kings. The topic of royal anger was much commented upon in the Middle Ages and receives corresponding emphasis in this collection. In Chapter 3, Gerd Althoff shows that in the context of royal power, "anger" was the opposite of "favor." Nevertheless the full potential of royal disfavor was not exploited by royal theoreticians until the twelfth century. Indeed, in Althoff's view, the celebration of royal anger had to overcome a long tradition, going back to the Carolingians, which associated the king's anger with injustice.

In Chapter 4, Geneviève Bührer-Thierry shows how ideas about the very acts that constituted royal anger and injustice could change over time. Whereas the punishment of blinding was originally seen as an abuse of power, the fruit of tyrannical fury, it later came to be associated with royal clemency in the Visigothic Kingdom and then with the very luster of imperial rule in the Carolingian Empire.

Paul Hyams in Chapter 5 traces a different trajectory for the career of royal anger. He emphasizes the way in which royal anger in England was invoked and praised by commentators who looked upon fury as a useful adjunct to power. In the twelfth and thirteenth centuries, however, kings, advisers, and chroniclers were taking very seriously a new ethic of restraint. Henry III was inspired by courtesy and clemency: he dreamed of being "debonaire."

From kings, who were themselves lords, we turn to lesser lords. In

Chapter 6 Stephen White challenges the view that medieval warriors were prey to their impulses. He suggests, on the contrary, that there were well-understood rules and conventions for lordly anger. Displays of anger were—not always, but often enough—played out and interpreted as political statements in a feuding culture where competition for honor was paramount.

In Chapter 7 Richard Barton provides examples of how such conventions were used and manipulated in specific instances of disputing. He speaks of anger as a "social signal" which, paradoxically enough, helped keep the peace. The anger of lords was nicely calibrated to show that something was wrong in a relationship, to get mechanisms of change underway, and to produce a new (generally more amicable) relationship. Theologians and other commentators explicitly recognized the constructive uses of wrath; they elaborated the notion of "zealous anger."

While lords might express anger righteously, peasants—nonwarriors and therefore by definition without honor—could not be rightly or even truly angry. In Chapter 8, Paul Freedman shows how medieval writers refused to recognize peasant anger. Rather, peasants were depicted as largely docile; if they became "warlike," their feeble attempts were only risible. This view changed at the end of the Middle Ages, during the various peasants' revolts: now the peasants were seen as not docile but violent. However, their violence was depicted as deriving not from human anger but from animal rage.

Thus anger in the Latin West had a privileged place: it was a sin, but a sin that could be turned into a virtue, monopolized by an aristocracy. What of the world beyond? In Chapter 9, Wendy Davies stresses some differences between medieval Celtic society and the Latin West. In the first place, she denies that Celtic cursing was evidence of anger, even anger drained of affect: it was, rather, the way in which holy men upheld the honor and status of God within a legal system that was itself based on finely calculated degrees of status and honor. Anger did exist in the Celtic world; but it was recognized primarily in the case of lay warriors, whose rage was meant to get them up and fighting. It was a form of energy rather than a moral stance.

In the Islamic world, as Zouhair Ghazzal shows, anger (at least as it was revealed in Islamic texts) was monopolized by the ruler himself. It was, for example, an integral part of the heroic personality of the Prophet in ninth-century *ḥadīth* literature (texts about the sayings and doings of the Prophet). As such, anger was a key element in structuring narratives of acceptance into and rejection from the *umma,* the community of believers. In *adab* literature (the poetry and prose of courtly, polite society), anger was more clearly a political concern. Indeed, it was the key to power: the caliph's role was to contain and control anger in both himself and others.

In sum, anger had an important place in a panoply of subjects, ideas, roles, discourses, and gestures in the Middle Ages. We are just beginning to learn about it.

PART I

MONKS AND SAINTS

CHAPTER ONE

Anger in Monastic Curses

Lester K. Little

The histories of individual monks and nuns are seasoned with instances of anger; these range from mild and momentary pique to bitter, enduring vengefulness. In like fashion monasteries, being this-worldly institutions with corporate interests to defend and advance, provide fertile ground for a range of tensions from polite difference of opinion to all-out assault. Monastic communities, no less surprisingly than individuals, therefore, have on occasion to express displeasure. Between the tenth and thirteenth centuries they often did so through formal complaints by the abbot or abbess, or some surrogate such as an advocate, but also at times through the cursing of enemies in their corporate worship. It is to the component of anger in such formal, collective cursing that I wish here to give attention, first by noting expressions of anger in the liturgy, then by examining the monastic theology of both anger and its virtuous counterpart, patience, next by considering curses formally as speech acts, and finally by considering liturgy itself as an agent of restraint on anger.

Anger in Liturgical Curse Formulas

Maledictory formulas in monastic liturgy called for a dazzling array of

In the preparation of this essay, I was ably assisted at the outset by Tracey L. Billado, a senior at Smith College in 1994. My thanks go to her and also to the Cornell Quodlibet Society, the Yale English Department Colloquium, and the seminar of Jean-Claude Schmitt at the École des Hautes Études en Sciences Sociales, Paris, for opportunities to discuss these matters.

terrible afflictions to befall alleged malefactors: to be cursed not just by God Almighty but by angels and archangels as well, by the prophets and the patriarchs, the apostles, the martyrs, the confessors, the virgins, and all the saints; to be cursed, moreover, while asleep and while awake, while sitting or standing, while eating or drinking or performing other bodily functions (listed in some detail); cursed, too, in town or countryside, field or forest, at home or away, and entering or leaving home. The families and retinues of malefactors were to share these fates, some of which were more specific than merely to be cursed: for example, to be cursed in all parts of the body (these, too, extensively catalogued), to suffer terrible illnesses, or to suffer hunger and thirst, intense heat and cold. "May the sky above them be made of brass," says one formula, "and the earth they walk on iron. May the Lord toss their bodies as bait to the birds of the sky and the beasts of the land. May their homes be deserted and may no one inhabit them. May the sword devastate them on the outside and fear on the inside. May they be damned with the devil and his angels in hell and may they burn in eternal fires with Dathan and Abiron. Amen. Amen." For good measure, even after the double "Amen," comes this postscript: "Thus may all memory of them be extinguished for ever and ever."[1]

"Multiple jeopardy" may serve as a name for this game, amusing in those variants that list so many different kinds of death for the evildoers but end by specifying that they be alive when they descend into hell, the better to suffer its torments there forever. These compound calamities were spelled out in the vernacular for the lay faithful to ponder. And they could be repeated day after day until some satisfaction were gained. The effect of such spoken series—of cursing agents, of dispositions for receiving curses, of bodily parts that are cursed, as well as of specific curses—is one of cumulative power; repetition builds upon itself in an escalation of rhetoric that transcends by far the phrases naming particular afflictions and eventually signifies the most appalling apocalypse imaginable.

Yet however terrible these curses were, no malefactor could really claim that he had not been warned of them. Everywhere in Latin Christendom ecclesiastical possessions and privileges were attested by written instruments—charters—and these typically contained sanction clauses warning of dire consequences for anyone who contravened their terms. Thus at Rochester in 1103, for example, King Henry I confirmed all the possessions, rights, customs, and privileges of Rochester cathedral; then Anselm of Canterbury confirmed the royal confirmation and promised the fate of Judas the traitor to any who attempted to diminish the belongings of this

[1] Lester K. Little, *Benedictine Maledictions: Liturgical Cursing in Romanesque France* (Ithaca: Cornell University Press, 1993), pp. 12–13.

church; and finally the bishop of Rochester added that the names of any violators would be struck from the book of the living and that on the day of just and eternal retribution they would be placed on the left-hand side and receive a sentence of severe punishment. The reference for this last scene is Jesus' foretelling of the Day of Judgment (Matt. 25:31–46), where the saved gather at his right hand and he praises them and invites them to receive as their inheritance the kingdom that has been prepared for them, after which he turns to those gathered on the left side and says: "Depart from me, you that are cursed, into the eternal fire prepared for the devil and his angels."

Sanction clauses are perhaps most readily traced to Roman law, an example being the clause in a contract establishing a fine for violating the terms of the contract itself. But early conciliar deliberations on doctrine constitute another source, for they usually ended with an anathema against those considered to be heretics. The earliest examples of ecclesiastical charters in most regions have fines for sanctions, and while fines never disappeared completely from sanction clauses, by the ninth century their place had been taken nearly everywhere by the anger of God (*ira Dei*) or some related form of spiritual sanction. A charter of Sauxillanges from about 1000 says: "May he incur the anger of God almighty and of the holy apostles and of all the saints, and may he remain damned in hell with Dathan and Abiron and with Judas the traitor of the Lord." The transition from material to spiritual sanctions was prepared already in the books of formulas, starting in the seventh century, where we find in the formulary of Marculf this sanction: "May he incur the anger of the triune majesty, and may he be summoned before the court of Christ." Whereas a sanction's formulaic and repetitious nature may weaken its vitality, an occasionnal local reference may give it bite. Take, for example, a sanction clause from Saint-Martial of Limoges, where the liturgical clamor calls for curses upon the malefactors from the standard panoply of spiritual characters, such as apostles, martyrs, and confessors, "but especially Saint Martial, whom they are treating so badly."[2]

The substitution of spiritual for material sanctions points to a weakened monetary economy for sure, but more especially to a weakened system of public justice. When monastic authors claimed that their monasteries had fallen prey to the unrestrained violence of the *milites,* they showed also that their leaders were frequently frustrated in their quest for justice. Unable to make their complaint, called a *clamor,* before a magistrate, one with the authority to summon an accused malefactor and with police power sufficient to enforce his resolution of the case, religious

[2] Ibid., p. 12.

leaders and indeed entire religious communities knelt before their altars to plead their cases before God and the patron saints, the constituted authorities who still commanded respect. The name of the liturgical order for this pleading, *clamor ad deum,* demonstrates how precisely liturgy had come to serve a function of judicial practice.

Monastic Spirituality of Anger and Patience

The standard view of anger developed by Christian theologians distinguished between a vice that was self-indulgent and could be recklessly destructive and a righteous zeal that could marshal passion and thus focus energy to fight constructively against evil. In the *City of God,* Augustine says that "in our ethics we do not so much inquire into whether a pious soul is angry as to why he is angry . . . I am not aware that any right thinking person would find fault with anger at a wrongdoer who seeks his amendment."[3] And Gregory the Great, in the *Moralia,* distinguishes between two sorts of anger: one stirred up by impatience, the other by zeal. The former, generated by vice, renders one blind, while the latter, generated by virtue, sharpens one's vision. The former, being unrestrained, can bring one to catastrophe, while the latter, subservient to reason, can be of vital assistance.[4] These distinctions were still holding strong in the time of Aquinas (*Disputed Questions on Evil,* q. 12).[5]

Martin of Braga, on the other hand, does not grant either the acceptability or utility of anger. In his tract on anger, he says, "One need not be angry to correct wrongdoers. Since anger is a sin of the soul, one must not correct a sinner with a sin." The person who does become angry at one who has done him wrong merely "places one vice against another."[6]

John Cassian, a key figure in the organization of thought about virtues and vices, and no less important for the formation of monastic ideals, prescribes a similarly restricted view of anger for monks and nuns. In eight of the twelve books of his *Institutes,* he treats of the principal vices. Anger he presents as a deadly poison to be rooted out utterly from the innermost corners of the soul. While he grants it can be useful to rage against the lustful emotions in our hearts, and cites instances from sacred history in which wrath was rightly felt (these are among the usual underpinnings of

[3] Augustine, *De civitate dei* 14.15, PL 41, col. 260.
[4] Gregory, *Moralia in Job* 5.33, PL 75, col. 726.
[5] Léon J. Elders, "Les *questions disputées sur le mal* de s. Thomas," *Divinitas* 36 (1992): 154–55.
[6] Martin of Braga, *De ira* 6.8, PL 72, cols. 46–47.

justifiable, zealous anger), he is uncompromising in insisting that a monk free himself from all anger. The charge is stated in Ephesians 4:31: "Have done with spite and passion, all angry shouting and cursing, and bad feelings of every kind." Cassian comments that this text allows for no exceptions: no anger or wrath may be considered either necessary or useful for a monk. "As long as [anger] remains . . . we cannot be partakers of life, nor can we become partakers of wisdom, nor can we attain immortal life."

On a more practical level, Cassian teaches monks not to let the day end while they still feel anger within. He teaches in addition that monks who do have anger in them are not to pray. And since the monks' vocation is to pray without ceasing, an angry monk either does not carry out his vocational obligation or else deceives himself by pouring forth prayers that are not valid. It is insufficient, moreover, not to be angry against other persons, for a monk must also not allow himself to become angry over situations or inanimate objects. A monk, in yet another elaboration of this doctrine, must not allow himself to be the object of someone else's anger, for the prayers of a monk in such a situation are rejected by God.

The positive side to this negative admonition is the cultivation of patience, which Lactantius had already counterposed to anger in his tract on the anger of God. Indeed for Cassian, as the monk succeeds in expelling anger from his heart, its place therein is taken by none other than the virtue of patience. The monk's very goal is patience and perfection. Cassian then continues: "Wherefore the athlete of Christ who strives lawfully ought thoroughly to root out the feeling of wrath," but while he yet feels any, he ought not pour out any prayer to God.[7]

In Benedict's *Rule for Monasteries,* with its pointed and exceptional advice to read the works of Cassian, the tools for good works include an exhortation "not to act in anger or nurse a grudge."[8] The conclusion of the prologue to the *Rule* emphasizes the importance of patience: "We shall through patience share in the sufferings of Christ that we may deserve also to share in his kingdom." And in the chapter on the mutual obedience that all the brothers owe one another, the *Rule,* in keeping with a passage from Cassian cited a moment ago, says: "if a monk gets the impression that one

[7] For Cassian, see *A Select Library of Nicene and Post-Nicene Fathers of the Christian Church,* ed. Philip Schaff and Henry Wace, 2d series, XI (New York: Christian Literature Co., 1894; repr., Grand Rapids, Mich.: W. B. Eerdmans, 1982), pp. 257–64, 350, 455. For Lactantius, *De ira dei* 20.5, see *La colère de Dieu,* ed. and trans. Christiane Ingremeau, Sources Chrétiennes 289 (Paris: Editions du Cerf, 1982), pp. 192–93.

[8] Benedict, *Rule for Monks* c. 4, vv. 22–23, in *RB 1980: The Rule of St. Benedict in Latin and English with Notes,* ed. Timothy Fry et al. (Collegeville, Minn.: The Liturgical Press, 1981), pp. 182–83; cf. *Rule of the Master* 3.24–25, in *La règle du Maître,* ed. Adalbert de Vogüé et al., 3 vols., Sources Chrétiennes 105–7 (Paris: Éditions du Cerf, 1964–65), 1:366–67.

of his seniors is angry or disturbed with him, however slightly, he must, then and there without delay, cast himself on the ground at the other's feet to make satisfaction, and lie there until the disturbance is calmed by a blessing."[9]

The pairing of certain virtues and vices was further solidified by the conflicts described in the *Psychomachia* of Prudentius. Building upon the Pauline idea that the Christian must arm himself with spiritual weapons in order to face the forces of evil (Ephesians 6:11–17) and the parable of Tertullian about the victory of the virtues over the vices, Prudentius constructed his epic poem of seven battle scenes between pairs of personified virtues and vices. Humility forthrightly decapitates the fallen figure of Pride; so also Chastity pierces the throat of Lust. Patience, however, with Job at her side, practices nonviolence, for when Anger and Patience square off, Ira unleashes "a lethal pike" and then "a shower of javelins" at Patientia, but as these slide harmlessly off the latter's helmet and armor, Ira explodes in uncontrollable fury, becomes desperate, and commits suicide.[10]

The earliest extant illustrated versions of this poem date from the ninth century. One of these, thought to have been produced in southern Germany and now located in Bern, devotes four pages to the struggle between Anger and Patience. On the first page (Fig. 1), Anger, according to the text "foaming at the mouth" and taunting her adversary, attacks Patience first with a stave and then with a spear. On the second (Fig. 2), Anger's spear bounces off the ever-serene, unruffled Patience, and a sword that Anger thrusts at her shatters on her shield. On the third page (Fig. 3), Anger lands a blow on the helmet of Patience with a heavy sword, which on the final page (Fig. 4) is shown falling to pieces. Thus utterly frustrated, and with passion urging her to end her life, Anger is then shown impaling herself on one of her own weapons, and shown a last time as a corpse, which Patience gently pokes with the end of a spear, as if to be sure she is dead.[11]

The influence of the illustrated versions of the *Psychomachia* is evident in subsequent representations of virtues and vices that are not specifically related to Prudentius's poem. On sculpted capitals of the twelfth century at both Clermont and Vézelay, for example, the figure of Ira is disheveled

[9] Benedict, *Rule for Monks,* prologue and c. 71, vv. 6–8 (pp. 166–67, 292–93).

[10] *Aurelii Prudentii Clementis Carmina,* ed. Johannes Bergman, CSEL 61 (Vienna: Hoelder, 1926), pp. 175–77; *The Poems of Prudentius,* trans. M. Clement Eagan, The Fathers of the Church 43, 52 (Washington, D.C.: Catholic University Press, 1965), 2:85. Adolf Katzenellenbogen, *Allegories of the Virtues and Vices in Mediaeval Art, from Early Christian Times to the Thirteenth Century* (New York: W. W. Norton, 1964), pp. 1–3.

[11] Otto Homburger, *Die illustrierten Handschriften der Burgerbibliothek Bern* (Bern: Burgerbibliothek, 1962), pp. 136–58.

Figure 1. Anger attacks Patience. Anger lunges at Patience from behind with a large stave and then launches a spear at Patience. These scenes appear on the first of four pages devoted to the battle between Anger and Patience in a ninth-century manuscript of Prudentius's *Psychomachia,* a poem on the struggle between the virtues and the vices that was composed in the fifth century. MS, Bern, Burgerbibliothek, cod. 264, f. 38v; by permission of the Burgerbibliothek Bern.

Figure 2. Patience rebuffs Anger's attacks. On the second page of this sequence, the spear thrown by Anger gets bent out of shape and bounces off Patience; similarly, other weapons thrown or shot by Anger at Patience fall away blunted or broken. MS, Bern, Burgerbibliothek, cod. 264, f. 39r; by permission of the Burgerbibliothek Bern.

Figure 3. Anger escalates the attack on Patience. By a gesture of the left hand, Anger seems to be putting aside the useless spears, while with the right hand lands a blow with a heavy sword to the head of Patience. But the latter's helmet is unyielding "and thwarts unharmed the striker's vicious thrust." MS, Bern, Burgerbibliothek, cod. 264, f. 39v; by permission of the Burgerbibliothek Bern.

Figure 4. The death of Anger. On the final page of the sequence, there are three scenes. The first shows the follow-through from the previous page, where the sword wielded by Anger (now holding a scabbard) falls to pieces. In the second, Anger, driven to despair by frustration and passion, is fatally pierced by a spear that she holds in place and upon which she has fallen. And finally, Patience ascertains with a spear handle that Anger is indeed dead. MS, Bern, Burgerbibliothek, cod. 264, f. 40r; by permission of the Burgerbibliothek Bern.

by rage, her features distorted and her hair standing on end, and she runs a sword through herself (see Figs. 5 and 6).[12] This way of depicting Ira had been bolstered in the meantime by texts associating Anger's appearance with that of the Devil. There is a "Sermon on Conscience," for example, a brief work purportedly by St. Augustine but now thought to date from about the time of Charlemagne, which was subsequently absorbed into some of the canonical collections assembled for the defense of ecclesiastical property. This sermon includes a gathering of biblical injunctions against speaking ill of others, against not forgiving others, and against cursing other people, "who are made in the image of God" (James 3:9). It exhorts the faithful to renounce their sins, to be peaceful in relating to others, and to look to Christ so that nothing will seem burdensome, "because patience is the image of Christ (quia patientia imago est christi). Whoever, though, is impatient becomes angry and stirs up strife. This is the image of the Devil (Haec imago diaboli est)." The details of this image are then made explicit, including the fierce look of the eyes and the trembling lips (see Fig. 7 for the contrast between Patience and Anger, and, for the similarity of the Devil to Anger, Figs. 8 and 9). Then the text repeats: "This is the image of the Devil (Haec imago diaboli est). Therefore let us cast away the image of the Devil and assume the image of Christ, that by it we might deserve to be saved."[13]

This pairing of opposites, Christ and the Devil, is also alluded to in Romanesque iconography. In the tympanum of Conques, there is of course no figure that balances or matches the central figure of Christ the Judge. In the lower register on the side of the damned, the section featuring the seven deadly sins, however, there is a central, dominant figure, namely the Devil, with grotesque, distorted features, whose position in this small

[12] Jennifer O'Reilly, *Studies in the Iconography of the Virtues and Vices* (New York: Garland, 1988), pp. 8–12, 49–51; pls. 1b, 5b, 6a, 7b, 8a, 8b. For Ira at Clermont, see Bernhard Rupprecht, *Romanische Skulptur in Frankreich,* 2d ed. (Munich: Hirmer, 1984), p. 102; pl. 126. For Ira at Vézelay, see Peter Diemer, "Stil und Ikonographie der Kapitelle von Vézelay" (dissertation, University of Heidelberg, 1975), pp. 290–92; and Kristen M. Sazama, "The Assertion of Monastic Spiritual and Temporal Authority in the Romanesque Sculpture of Sainte-Madeleine at Vézelay" (Ph.D. dissertation, Northwestern University, 1995), pp. 148–50. My thanks to Kristen Sazama for these last two references and for discussing Vézelay with me. I wish to express my sincere thanks to Barbara Deimling of the Index of Christian Art for assisting me in locating materials on the iconography of Ira.

[13] Roger E. Reynolds, "The Pseudo-Augustinian *Sermo de conscientia* and the Related Canonical *Dicta sancti gregorii papae," Revue Bénédictine* 81 (1971): 310–17. On the iconography of the devil, see Jeffrey B. Russell, *Lucifer: The Devil in the Middle Ages* (Ithaca: Cornell University Press, 1984), pp. 128–33. On the monastic discipline of the body and the relationship of bodily gestures to inner states of mind, see Jean-Claude Schmitt, *La raison des gestes dans l'Occident médiéval* (Paris: Gallimard, 1990), pp. 173–205. For Patientia and Ira at Autun, see Denis Grivot and George Zarnecki, *Giselbertus, Sculptor of Autun* (New York: Orion Press, 1961), p. 70; pls. 19a, 19b; for the hanging of Judas, p. 70, pl. 17a.

Figure 5. Anger commits suicide. Here, on this capital in the choir of Notre-Dame-du-Port at Clermont-Ferrand, a rather crudely carved figure (early twelfth century) holds a large blade to its chest. Any doubts about the figure's identity or purpose are dispelled by the inscription above the scene, which reads: *Ira se occidit* (Anger kills herself). Foto Marburg/Art Resource, N.Y.

Figure 6. Anger commits suicide. A totally wild representation of Anger, with open mouth, distended tongue, wide-open eyes, and hair standing on end, thrusts a sword through her chest. It is found on a twelfth-century capital in the nave of Sainte-Madeleine at Vézelay. Foto Marburg/Art Resource, N.Y.

Figure 7. Patience dominating Anger. A calm and collected Patience stands on the head of a squatting and grimacing figure of Anger on one of the twelfth-century capitals from the church of Saint-Lazare at Autun. Anger clutches a sword that transfixes her torso. Foto Marburg/Art Resource, N.Y.

Figure 8. Hanging of Judas. Judas, according to Matthew 27:5, hanged himself, but some Romanesque artists externalized interiority and turned passivity into vivid action, as on this twelfth-century capital from the church of Saint-Lazare at Autun, where demons, with characteristics similar to those of Anger, participate eagerly in the execution of the archtraitor. ©Lefèvre Pontalis/Archives photographiques, Paris/CNMHS, Paris.

Figure 9. Struggle between Good and Evil. The polarities of Christ and the Devil and of Patience and Anger have their parallel in this representation of Good and Evil on a capital (twelfth century) from Sainte-Madeleine et Vézelay. The figure of Evil is notable for its resemblance to contemporary representations of Anger. Foto Marburg/Art Resource, N.Y.

subsection of the whole mimics that of Christ in the composition of the entire tympanum (Fig. 10).[14]

Later on, in Hugh of Saint-Victor's handbook for novices, a direct association is made between certain kinds of gesture and particular vices and virtues. Based on the Ambrosian principle that the comportment of the body reveals the state of the soul, Hugh's scheme identifies one of the six reprehensible modes of movement, turbulence, or violent agitation (*turbidus*) with impatience, irascibility, or anger.[15] Thus while it might always have struck us as obvious that the Devil should appear to us as disheveled, with distorted features and gesticulating, there are quite precise cultural reasons for the similarity of Romanesque representations of Ira and Diabolus.

In addition to the theological and iconographical programs, the penitentials played an important role in perpetuating and propagating western society's prevailing views of the vice of anger. Their purpose, to be sure, was not theoretical, but to measure out penances appropriate to various faults including crimes. Thus anger is present as a problem to be dealt with in many of these texts. In several cases, a fault is considered greater if committed in anger; similarly, it is greater if committed by a cleric instead of a layman, and greatest of all if by a monk. Anger prevents a monk from praying and thus has to be expelled.[16]

To conclude this brief typology of sources that speak to the issue of anger and patience, there is the virtuous monastic model portrayed in John of Salerno's life of Odo of Cluny (ca. 878–942). As a young monk at Baume, Odo had to face the provocation of false accusations; he did so by bearing up patiently, in conscious imitation of Jesus: Jesus who did not sin and did not have guile in his mouth, who when he was cursed did not curse, and who when he suffered did not threaten but handed himself over to those judging unjustly. Later on, as abbot, Odo governed with patience, both resolving petty feuds within the monastery and overcoming the armed opposition of the monks of Fleury.[17]

There is nothing astonishing about monks and nuns being held to a higher standard than were lay believers; it is enough to recall the obligation of chastity that separated their ways of living. In this traditional,

[14] Jean-Claude Bonne, *L'art roman de face et de profil: Le tympan de Conques* (Paris: Le Sycamore, 1984), pp. 8, 296–97, figs. 9, 10.

[15] Schmitt, *La raison des gestes*, pp. 173–205, 388–91. For Ambrose, see *De officiis ministrorum* 1.18.71, PL 16, col. 44; for Hugh of Saint-Victor, see *De institutione novitiorum*, c. 12, "De disciplina servenda in gestu," PL 176, cols. 938–40.

[16] *Medieval Handbooks of Penance*, ed. and trans. John T. McNeill and Helena M. Gamer (New York: Columbia University Press, 1938), pp. 92, 107, 165–66, 177, 234, 280, 307, 327.

[17] Barbara H. Rosenwein, *Rhinoceros Bound: Cluny in the Tenth Century* (Philadelphia: University of Pennsylvania Press, 1982), pp. 89–93, 108.

Figure 10. Devil presiding over the damned. In a way that parallels and mimics the dominant position of Jesus at the very center of the entire tympanum, an imposing figure of the Devil holds the center position of just a portion of the tympanum, the side of the damned, which is to Jesus' left (the viewer's right). While such an arrangement does not in any way give the Devil equal standing with Jesus (indeed it gives a dramatic reminder of hierarchy), it does suggest the parallel, even if done in mockery. Abbey church of Sainte-Foy, Conques-en-Rouergue, second quarter of the twelfth century. Foto Marburg/Art Resource, N.Y.

hierarchic warrior society, whose Christianity had a decidedly Old Testament stamp, the religious formed a caste charged with fulfilling the entire spiritual obligation of that society. As holy people they were special, above all in their virtually exclusive access to divine authority. Although anger, like sex, was not absent from the monastic experience, the virtue of patience was so characteristic of the monastic ideal that the occasional layperson who exemplified it was perceived by others as being in some way monastic. That is the way Odo of Cluny viewed the saintly career of Count Gerald of Aurillac, who in one light was the epitome of a powerful warrior. In writing his biography of Gerald, Odo, whose own spirituality had patience at its core, stressed the central role of that same virtue in his subject. Gerald could not avoid the use of force in putting down injustice and in punishing the wicked, but he exercised restraint that minimized bloodshed and above all he bore with patience (following the model of Job) all the attacks and persecutions and other provocations directed at him. Although he fought on battlefields and presided in courts, Gerald was not one who fueled his aggression on behalf of good causes with controlled and channeled anger; he just did not get angry. He was something more, and perhaps less, than an ideal knight: he was a monk in knight's clothing. In the eleventh century, just as the chaste behavior of King Edward the Confessor gave him the aura of a holy man, so, too, did the patience and humility of King Robert the Pious lead others to regard him as a royal monk.[18]

Thus the Christian traditions about anger developed into a double standard. For the laity, anger was an accepted aspect of the human condition that could have legitimate origins and could be made to serve legitimate ends, while for the *oratores* (those who pray) it had to be eliminated altogether to permit the right practice of religion.

Liturgical Curses as Speech Acts

The very nature of liturgical curses tends to drain them of emotional energy. It is in their nature to be speech acts, or as John Austin, author of *How to Do Things with Words,* preferred, "performative utterances."[19] In

[18] Ibid., pp. 73–81. For Edward, see *The Life of King Edward, Who Rests at Westminster,* ed. and trans. Frank Barlow (London: Nelson, 1962), pp. 56–81. For Robert, see Helgaud de Fleury, *Vie de Robert le Pieux (Epitoma vitae regis rotberti pii),* ed. and trans. Robert-Henri Bautier and Gillette Labory (Paris: CNRS, 1965), pp. 58–65, 74–75, 78–81, 84–85, 100–101, 138–39. Cf. Brian Stock, *The Implications of Literacy: Written Language and Models of Interpretation in the Eleventh and Twelfth Centuries* (Princeton: Princeton University Press, 1983), pp. 481–89.

[19] John L. Austin, *How to Do Things with Words,* 2d ed. (Cambridge: Harvard University Press, 1975), and Little, *Benedictine Maledictions,* pp. 113–18.

uttering them, speakers are thought of as doing something rather than, as Austin put it, "merely saying something." Utterances that contain the word "hereby," such as "I hereby crown you emperor," are considered not as reports whose veracity can be challenged or certified, but as accomplishments of the very acts they name. In addition to the present, active, indicative form of this particular example, speech acts can be in the subjunctive mood, either active ("May the fun begin") or passive ("Let the children be excused"); parallel examples of curses would be "May he fall from his horse" and "May he be killed in a fall."

What actually happens when a person is cursed is not the specific action named (such as the recipient's fall or death) but the cursing of that person. The person's state has been altered by the fact or, better, the act (the use of "mere words") of being cursed. But if all it took were mere words to put someone in these circumstances, we need ask whether it would not be equally easy for just anyone to do likewise. The answer is no, for in order for any speech act to be valid, according to Austin's scheme, it must meet a set of conditions he called the "conditions of felicity." The first of these is that there be a generally accepted, conventional procedure for the type of utterance in question. The second is that the persons and circumstances involved be appropriate for its invocation. And the third is that the performer of the procedure be in the proper frame of mind for carrying it out. The lack of any of these requisite conditions gives an infelicitous result.[20]

Seen in this light, for a clamor or formal malediction to be effective in the period between the tenth and twelfth centuries, a time when Western Europe might be said to have had a shared culture of speech acts, it clearly had to be carried out, just like an excommunication, (1) in accordance with a carefully prescribed liturgy, (2) by a duly authorized religious person, and (3) by a person who, following upon a prolonged fast, felt free of personal animosity and adopted an attitude of humility. For the same reasons and just as clearly, a spontaneous outburst of hostile curses would not qualify as a speech act.

But here we need take account of those matchless champions of the art of the spontaneous, hostile, and efficacious curse, namely the Celtic, especially the Irish, saints. Gerald of Wales called attention in his *History and Topography of Ireland* to their "vindictive cast of mind": "just as the men of this country are during this mortal life more prone to anger and revenge than any other race, so in eternal death the saints of this land that have been elevated by their merits are more vindictive than the saints of any other region." Their curses flowed freely in response to provocation, and

[20] Austin, *How to Do Things with Words*, pp. 12–38.

these followed no particular formulas. But since by all accounts these appear to have worked, one could ask whether they were speech acts. Even if not formulaic, the curses were uttered by people of great spiritual prestige, that is, people who had inherited from the druids the power to manipulate with words the forces governing the natural world. As legitimate heirs to such an ancient tradition, Christian holy people had a power that was universally recognized within that society, and hence their curses, conceived and launched in an anger that was considered legitimate because it was theirs, can be said to have met the conditions of felicity.[21]

To return, though, to liturgical curses: for these to work, so many conditions had to be met that virtually all elements of passion—that explosive mix of unthinking feeling and unplanned speech—were removed. But let us now turn from such theoretical considerations to historically documented cases.

Liturgy as a Restraint on Anger

The accounts of property disputes between monastic communities and laymen in which the former resorted to liturgical maledictions—accounts, we need to recall, that were recorded almost invariably by monks—demonstrate emotional control in the face of apparent provocation. At the Abbey of the Holy Trinity at Vendôme in 1074, the monks claimed they were being put upon by a knight named Odo of Blazon, who with his men simply took over the church of Cheviré, which the monks claimed was theirs. Odo was doing these things with the apparent consent of Fulk Rechin, the count of Anjou. Whatever he thought of Odo's behavior, Fulk was submerged in constant warfare, which circumstance kept him from dealing properly with the "persecutors of holy church."

The monks had to face the double problem of seeing many of their vital crops carried off while knowing they had no hope of receiving help from any human source. And so, convinced there would be no help from "the very one who ought to acquire justice for them," they turned with contrite hearts to making a clamor. They took down from its high place the image of the crucified Lord and placed it upon a bed of thorns on the church floor. This gesture was undertaken, the text explains, not out of disrespect or disdain for this symbol of the Lord, but so that the malefactors would be frightened and would cease their unlawful invasions and theft.[22]

[21] Gerald of Wales, *The History and Topography of Ireland,* trans. John J. O'Meara (Harmondsworth, England: Penguin, 1982), p. 91. For further, and rather different, reflections on Celtic curses, see Chapter 9 by Wendy Davies in this volume.

[22] Little, *Benedictine Maledictions,* pp. 137–38.

"With no hope of justice from men" was a phrase employed at the Abbey of Marchiennes in Flanders, with its precious relics of Saint Richtrude, to justify the monks' use of a clamor with the sounding of bells and launching of anathemas. The object of these complaints was a knight named Hilouin, who, safe in his castle surrounded by water, continually raided a possession of Saint-Richtrude's, the villa of Gouy. The monks became involved when they heard of the complaint of the "little people" of Gouy to Saint Richtrude. The author of the *Miracles of Saint Richtrude* laced his telling of this story with rhetorical questions. He said that the monks could find neither mercy nor consolation nor clemency. "So what? The abbot was depressed; his congregation was depressed. But what should they do? Wait for vengeance? But from whom?" At the end of this series of questions, in which the malefactor has been denounced as a "tyrant" and a "second pharaoh," the author asks: "What then? Did he go unpunished? No way (nullo modo)." Then the author tells of the clamor. It took that clamor a year to take effect, a year to the very day and hour when Hilouin died of a wound. The community took note of this great miracle, acclaimed God, and extolled the virtues of Saint Richtrude.[23]

The miracles of Saint Bavon of Ghent that were recorded in the eleventh century include the story of one Siger of Meerbeke, who pillaged the hamlet of Houtem. He and his men took away everything they could lay their hands on, including the work animals. Houtem belonged to the Abbey of Saint-Bavon, and when Siger heard that the peasants were complaining about his behavior, he added insult to injury by "vomiting up sarcastic comments" about the abbey's patron saint. The peasants undertook the thirteen-mile trek to Ghent to bring their complaint directly to the saint. At the saint's tomb they were in tears when they exclaimed: "Bavon, soldier of God, where are you? Siger, this follower of the devil has injured you and your servants." The women among them let out with a *vero femineo clamore,* as if to wake up Saint Bavon, who, they lamented, seemed to be asleep during their time of tribulation.

When the peasants had exhausted their complaint, the monks took over. They placed the bodies of the saints on the floor. Although they were saddened by the terrible happenings at Houtem, they were "much more saddened by the deposition of the saints." They warned Siger, then they excommunicated him. In the meantime they advised the aggrieved peasants to be patient (i.e., to imitate them) in awaiting the divine response. Siger did not change his ways either soon or willingly, but in another of his raids he received a wound that brought him to his death. The account leaves little doubt that it was the formal and learned clamor of the monks,

[23] Ibid., pp. 138–39.

carried out in the calm and deliberate manner appropriate to the liturgy, rather than the chaotic commotion stirred up by the peasants, that obtained the desired results. Clearly the abbot had been wise to allow the peasants into the church to register their complaint; had they found the door closed or the abbot blocking it, they almost surely would have directed their anger against him.[24]

And to turn once more to Marchiennes, we see that the clamor there became intertwined first with the suppression and then with the unleashing of a knight's fury during the chaos that followed the assassination of Count Charles the Good in 1127. In this instance, there was a knight, unnamed throughout the story, who had been preying upon the monks' lands. The monks in turn "struck him and his whole family with a horrendous anathema." Furthermore, the abbot went to court to complain to the count about this knight. The next time the knight was at court, Count Charles reproached him severely for maltreating the monks. Thus humiliated, the knight became enraged, but there was nothing he could do until that fateful day when conspirators murdered the count in his chapel. The knight then went wild. He burned a mill that belonged to the monks, and he threatened to burn down their whole monastery as well. The "horrendous anathema" was renewed many times, and a priest repeated the daily clamor, with the whole community prostrate and the bells ringing. One day the knight rode by the church, heard the bells, and learned what their ringing signified. The next day he was dead.[25]

In these few cases the main guarantor of public order and of restraint in social interaction was supposed to be the law, as enforced by powerful figures such as the counts of Anjou and of Flanders. But if these authorities were uncooperative, or simply absent, then *milites* were not restrained from depredating as they pleased. This is not to say that knightly activity was always based on whim or fueled by anger; often enough, knights were fully confident of being in the right, and their capacity on occasion to restrain or cease their violence when they had achieved all or just some of what they wanted testifies to their self-control. The peasants who were on the front lines of depredation, meanwhile, were certainly not obliged either to suppress their outrage or to express it in polite terms. Between the peasants of Houtem and the monks of Saint-Bavon there was of course a considerable social gap, but the peasants and monks were also separated by a no less significant gap in cognitive development. Even between groups of people of similar social standing, such as the religious (nuns as well as monks) and others of the knightly class (the religious mostly came

[24] Ibid., pp. 135–36.
[25] Ibid., p. 139.

from this class), it is above all the differences in cognitive development, due mainly to monastic schooling, that separate them. Without the external restraints of legal authority, and in the absence of strong social conventions or expectations that called upon them to curb their expressions of affect, laypeople of whatever social level were relatively free to act out their emotions.[26] Monks and nuns meanwhile, in the same situation of weak restraints but with their virtual monopoly on literacy and an iconographic as well as bookish cultural inheritance that idealized the virtue of patience over the vice of anger, were expected to remain within the bounds set by religious discipline, in theory internalized but in fact bolstered by the vow of obedience and an awesome array of sanctions.[27]

Only to the religious, then, did it fall to remain calm: not just to restrain their anger, but not to be angry in the first place. "In the spirit of humility and with a contrite soul," begins the clamor or malediction prayer, "we come before your sacred altar, Lord Jesus, and we acknowledge ourselves guilty against you on account of our sins, for which we are justly afflicted." Where can there be space for anger if one acknowledges all afflictions as just punishments for one's own sinful behavior? The prayer continues: "To you, Lord Jesus, we come; to you, prostrate, we clamor because iniquitous and proud men invade, plunder, and lay waste the lands of this your sanctuary. They compel your poor ones who till these lands to live in pain and hunger and nakedness."[28] The contrasts between the monks, who proclaimed themselves poor, and these poor ones who till their lands are most clear in the Saint-Bavon incident, where the latter express themselves in their disorderly shouting and the former patiently suffer this boorish behavior until they can carry out their decorous, liturgical order. Take note also that one utterance of these liturgical formulas usually did not suffice. Sometimes it took a whole year of daily recitations—not the stuff of passion—to bring down, or bring around, a malefactor.

[26] This point is essential for understanding a *New Yorker* cartoon of some years back in which there is an after-battle scene in a medieval setting. Against a backdrop showing a castle reduced to rubble and smouldering beams and a field strewn with the bodies of dozens of knights, horses, and footsoldiers, two knights, who appear to be the only survivors, stand in the foreground and one says: "I want to apologize for some of the remarks I made during the heat of battle."

[27] In a perceptive (and generous) review of my *Benedictine Maledictions* (*Times Literary Supplement,* April 14, 1995, p. 25), Janet Nelson calls my talk of disparate levels of cognitive development "not helpful," adding, "*Milites* may often have been young men but they were not children." I should have made clear that I was not discussing either child development or age. I was, and am here, referring to the socially and culturally determined higher level of cognitive development arrived at by many adult religious, chiefly through schooling, and quite apart from their individual differences of intellectual capacity, as distinguished from the levels reached by illiterate lay adults. See Charles M. Radding, *A World Made by Men: Cognition and Society, 400–1200* (Chapel Hill: University of North Carolina Press, 1985), pp. 28–29, 258, an instructive and stimulating work, which, however, deals only sporadically and briefly with cognitive differences among historical contemporaries.

[28] Little, *Benedictine Maledictions,* p. 25.

The expressions of anger we saw in maledictory liturgies at the outset, while formulaic and perhaps lacking in personal affect, were nonetheless tremendously forceful. The monks' authority to curse as well as their capacity for doing so effectively were part of their virtual monopoly on all forms of prayer. No one knew this better or was more convinced of it than they. But one should not discount the corporate fervor that threats to their community provoked, a fervor that they were able to direct into a collective ritual hostility, witness their tears at Saint-Bavon, their fierceness and persistence at Marchiennes, or their rejoicing, once triumphant, at Holy Trinity of Vendôme.[29]

Moreover, the monks' carefully measured, liturgical anger had a purpose, which was to bring about a change of behavior in the *potentes.* It was a tool used in negotiation with these powerful antagonists; it was a self-consciously and skillfully manipulated tool, or force, which was summoned to confront the more conventional force of heavily armed, mounted warriors.[30]

In the heyday of liturgical cursing, then, there appears to have been a correlation, or at least balance, between the monks' individual control of anger and the effectiveness of their corporate liturgy; and when their monopoly on the religious life weakened, it was their discipline rather than their liturgical powers that had the longer-lasting influence. It was as a result of the successes of the many reform groups of the twelfth century that the monks lost their monopoly on the religious life. But as their own role diminished, their spiritual heritage remained strong within the religious life, at first among the canons and later on among the friars, as well as outside it among the laity. The regular devotions, mainly prayers, performed daily by some laypeople starting in the fourteenth century attest most concretely to this heritage. Similarly, the control of emotions, which became a theme in the handbooks of proper social comportment for the upper strata of lay society in the later Middle Ages, owes much to monastic discipline.[31]

[29] Cf. Barbara H. Rosenwein, "Feudal War and Monastic Peace: Cluniac Liturgy as Ritual Aggression," *Viator* 2 (1971): 128–57; and Little, *Benedictine Maledictions,* pp. 131–46.

[30] Patrick J. Geary, "Living with Conflicts in Stateless France: A Typology of Conflict Management Mechanisms, 1050–1200," in his *Living with the Dead in the Middle Ages* (Ithaca: Cornell University Press, 1994), pp. 125–60. In his lectures at Princeton, J. R. Strayer used to suggest that the mounted warrior, particularly from the point of view of the unarmed, "was the medieval equivalent of a tank."

[31] Dilwyn Knox, "*Disciplina:* The Monastic and Clerical Origins of European Civility," in *Renaissance Society and Culture: Essays in Honor of Eugene F. Rice, Jr.,* ed. John Monfasani and Ronald G. Musto (New York: Italica, 1991), pp. 107–35; cf. Jonathan Nicholls, *The Matter of Courtesy: Medieval Courtesy Books and the Gawain-Poet* (Woodbridge, Suffolk: D. S. Brewer, 1985), pp. 22–44; see also Schmitt, *La raison des gestes,* p. 361. For connections between monastic spirituality and the religious life of merchants in the fourteenth century, see Lester K. Little, *Religious Poverty and the*

In his great work of historical sociology completed in the 1930s, Norbert Elias gave special attention to Renaissance handbooks of courtly etiquette for their crucial role in the early stages of what he called "the civilizing process." This work can be criticized for its Euro-centrism, its implied teleology, its evolutionary explanation of change, and its dated historiography (especially as concerns the "Middle Ages"), and yet Elias's insight into the history of comportment remains an essential, stimulating lesson. Others have pointed to different social settings and earlier time periods for examples more important than those Elias believed crucial to the civilizing "process." Even if we reject the notion of an orderly process itself, we can acknowledge a considerable debt to Elias while directing attention to the major role of monastic discipline in the history of European social behavior.[32]

By way of conclusion I turn to two counterexamples in which religious women combined anger with liturgy, just barely in the first case but with abandon in the second. Both incidents occurred considerably later, and both, I believe, may be exceptional. It is highly likely that there were other incidents of this sort, but until evidence of them is brought forth it would be premature to ascribe particular significance to the details, such as the date, the region, or the gender of the protagonists, in these two examples. Both involved the reactions of comfortably well-off religious to a visitor who was intent upon reforming their lives and who, to be sure, was the author of both the accounts that have come to us. In 1455 Johan Busch, a member of the Brethren of the Common Life who worked tirelessly at religious reform, visited the canonesses of Wenigsen (near Hannover) accompanied by the duke of Brunswick. The prioress, upon learning the reason for Busch's visit, announced to the visitors that she and her sisters had sworn not to change their ways and thus begged these visitors not to force them to perjure themselves. She then repeated this request in the chapel, where in the choir the canonesses were lying face down, their

---

Profit Economy in Medieval Europe (Ithaca: Cornell University Press, 1978), pp. 195–96.

[32] Norbert Elias, *The Civilizing Process,* trans. Edmund Jephcott, 2 vols. (New York: Pantheon, 1982). See also C. Stephen Jaeger, *The Origins of Courtliness: Civilizing Trends and the Formation of Courtly Ideals, 939–1210* (Philadelphia: University of Pennsylvania Press, 1985), although Jaeger pushes his thesis about the key role of German bishops so hard as to leave little room for other influences. Recent studies of the early modern state, kindly pointed out to me by my colleague Joachim W. Stieber, give much attention to the long-range influence of religious discipline. In this connection, see *Disciplina dell'anima, disciplina del corpo e disciplina della società tra medioevo ed età moderna,* ed. Paolo Prodi, Annali dell'Istituto storico italo-germanico (Bologna, 1994); Heinz Schilling, "Confessional Europe," in *Handbook of European History, 1400–1600: Late Middle Ages, Renaissance, and Reformation,* ed. Thomas A. Brady, Heiko Oberman, and James Tracy (Leiden: Brill, 1995) 2:641–70; and William V. Hudon, "Religion and Society in Early Modern Italy—Old Questions, New Insights," *American Historical Review* 101 (1996): 783–804, esp. pp. 788–89.

arms stretched out to make the form of the cross, and singing in a loud voice the anthem *Media vita in morte sumus.* This humble Lenten devotion, with a moving reflection upon mortality and salvation, had become by the thirteenth century an incantation widely understood to be a curse. The duke understood perfectly the canonesses' intention, for he reacted in fright, fearing that his entire territory would be brought to ruin by this curse. Yet the learned cleric assured him that the curse would turn back against the holy women, and so they left.

Later in the same year, the reformer and the duke went to visit the Cistercian nuns of Mariensee, also supposedly much in need of reform. For a time Busch thought he had gained a settlement, but then, according to his account: "when we were leaving the church, the nuns began the antiphon *Media vita* and they sang it at us at the tops of their voices. Then, following us through the church with this chant, they threw lighted candles at us." One young nun followed them into the churchyard and sang three times one of the phrases of the anthem, and then, says Busch, "she knelt, and three times scooped up dirt in her mouth as a sign of malediction against us; then she threw dirt and stones at us."[33] Perhaps these religious women would have reacted in the same way to a pastoral visit from John Cassian himself; at least their way of life as depicted by one of the Brethren of the Common Life seems to have been as different from the *imitatio Cassiani* as it was from the *imitatio Christi.*

[33] Lester K. Little, "*Media vita* between Maas and Weser," in *Pauvres et riches: Société et culture du moyen-âge aux temps modernes. Mélanges offerts à Bronislaw Geremek à l'occasion de son soixantième anniversaire* (Warsaw: Wydawnictwo Naukowe PWN, 1992), pp. 223–29. On eating dirt, cf. Geoffrey Koziol, "The Making of Peace in Eleventh-Century Flanders," in *The Peace of God: Social Violence and Religious Response in France around the Year 1000,* ed. Thomas Head and Richard Landes (Ithaca: Cornell University Press, 1992), p. 251; and on throwing stones, cf. Jacques Eveillon, *Traité des excommunications et monitoires avec la manière de publier, exécuter et fulminer toutes sortes de monitoires et excommunications,* 2d ed. (Paris: Couterat, 1672), pp. 378–79.

CHAPTER TWO

Gertrude's *furor:* Reading Anger in an Early Medieval Saint's *Life*

CATHERINE PEYROUX

In a work written around the year 670 for the monastery of Nivelles, situated in what was then northeastern Francia and is now modern Belgium, an anonymous religious told a vivid and curious tale about a moment of anger that had taken place perhaps some thirty years previously, during the childhood of Gertrude, the first abbess and patron saint of Nivelles. The writer recorded that according to the account of a "just and truthful man" who had been present, the young Gertrude's "election to the service of Christ" began thus:

> When Pippin, her [Gertrude's] father, had invited King Dagobert to a noble banquet at his house, there came also a noxious man, son of a duke of the Austrasians, who requested from the king and from the girl's parents that this same girl be promised to himself in marriage according to worldly custom, to satisfy earthly ambition as well as for a mutual alliance. The request pleased the king and he urged the girl's father that she be summoned with her mother into his presence. Without their knowing why the king wanted the child (infantem),

This essay has benefited profoundly from the generous attention and criticism of Barbara Rosenwein, Jennifer Thorn, Susan Thorne, Matthew Price, David Ganz, Stephen White, Wendy Davies, Monica Green, Lester Little, William Reddy, Philippe Buc, and the anonymous readers of Cornell University Press; I thank them heartily for their readings and suggestions, and for making so sociable the process of thinking about anger's socially fractious potentialities.

> she was asked by the king, in between courses [of the banquet], if she would like to have that boy dressed in silk trimmed with gold for a husband. But she, as if filled with *furor* (quasi furore repleta), rejected him with an oath, and said that she would have neither him nor any earthly man for husband but Christ the lord. Whereupon the king and his nobles marveled greatly over these things, which were said by the little girl (parva puella) under God's command. The boy indeed left disturbed, filled with anger (iracundia plenus). The holy girl returned to her mother and from that day her parents knew by what manner of king she was loved.[1]

This compact narrative, structured around the revelation of a noble maiden's true and royal spouse, has an abstract, almost stylized quality resonant equally of folkloric motif and hagiographical cliché. The protocols of composition and selection that govern biographies of early medieval saints have here preserved the traces of a dynamic, living culture in the restricted medium of exemplary legend. Nonetheless, there are reasons to read this story with eyes more closely attuned to the "what happened" and, indeed, the "how it felt" than to the "once upon a time" of early medieval Europe. The text from which this passage comes is among the immediate witnesses for the history both of seventh-century Frankish monasticism and of the early fortunes of the family who were to emerge as the Carolingians.[2] Its protagonist, Gertrude (who lived 625/26–659), was a

[1] "Primum electionis sibi in Christi servitio initium fuit, sicut per iustum et veracem hominem conperi, qui praesens aderat. Dum Pippinus, genitor suus, regem Dagobertum domui sue ad nobilem prandium invitasset, adveniens ibidem unus pestifer homo, filius ducis Austrasiorum, qui a rege et a parentibus puellae postulasset, ut sibi ipsa puella in matrimonium fuisset promissa secundum morem saeculi propter terrenam ambitionem et mutuam amicitiam. Placuit regi, et patri puellae suasit, ut in sua praesentia illa cum matre sua fuisset evocata. Illis autem ignorantibus, propter quam causam rex vocaret infantem, interrogata inter epulas a rege, si illum puerum auro fabricatum, siricis indutum voluisset habere sponsum, at illa quasi furore repleta, respuit illum cum iuramento et dixit, nec illum nec alium terrenum nisi Christum dominum volebat habere sponsum, ita ut ipse rex et proceres eius valde mirarentur super his, quae a parva puella Dei iussione dicta erant. Ille vero puer recessit confusus, iracundia plenus. Sancta puella ad suam convertit genetricem, et ex illa die parentes eius cognoverunt, a quali Regi amata fuerat." *Vita sanctae Geretrudis abbatissae Nivialensis* 1, ed. B. Krusch, MGH SSrerMerov 2:453–64, hereafter *VsG.* Krusch provides both the Merovingian (A) and Carolingian (B) versions of this text in parallel columns; note that I have used the earlier, grammatically more awkward version A of the *Life* of Gertrude; translations are my own. For an English translation of the whole life based on version B, see *Sainted Women of the Dark Ages*, ed. and trans. Jo Ann McNamara, John E. Halborg, and E. Gordan Whatley (Durham, N.C.: Duke University Press, 1992), pp. 220–28. Since this paper was written, a new translation of version A with an excellent historical commentary has appeared in Paul Fouracre and Richard A. Gerberding, eds., *Late Merovingian France: History and Hagiography, 640–720* (Manchester: Manchester University Press, 1996).

[2] On the historical value of the *VsG*, see Krusch's introductory commentary to his editions of the *Life* in MGH SSrerMerov 2:447–49; J.J. Hoebanx, *L'Abbaye de Nivelles des origines au XIVe siècle*

daughter of the materially and politically preeminent household formed by the marriage of the heiress Itta (d. 650) and Pippin I (d. 639), a noble magnate and the sometime mayor of the palace of the eastern Frankish kingdom of Austrasia.[3]

Most important for our purposes in exploring this record of anger, the dead saint's biography originated in the community that had, until only a decade before its composition, surrounded the living abbess Gertrude; the quality of the presentation should not distract us from indications of the author's first-hand experience embedded in the text. Scattered throughout the *Life* are multiple references to personal and immediate knowledge of the events depicted: the prologue claims to set forth the "example and conduct" of the holy Gertrude according to "what we saw ourselves or heard through witnesses"; in chapter 4 the narrator is figured among those to whom Gertrude herself related a wondrous vision; the closing chapter includes an account of the narrator's own presence at the monastery on the day of Gertrude's death and implies the narrator's participation in the saint's funerary rites.[4] Some debate is possible over whether the *Vita sanctae Geretrudis* (hereafter *VsG*) was written by a monk or a nun.[5]

(Brussels: Palais des Académies, 1952), pp. 23–30; Alain Dierkens, "Saint Amand et la fondation de l'abbaye de Nivelles," *Revue du Nord* 68 (1986): 326.

[3] For a brief chronology of Gertrude's life, see Dierkens, "Saint Amand," pp. 330–31; for a careful consideration of early Pippinid chronology in the light of the widowed Itta's monastic patronage, see J.-M. Picard, "Church and Politics in the Seventh Century: The Irish Exile of Dagobert II," in *Ireland and Northern France,* A.D. 600–850, ed. J.-M. Picard (Dublin: Four Courts, 1991), pp. 27–52, esp. pp. 34–36. The origins and politically precarious career of Pippin I are recounted by Pierre Riché, *The Carolingians,* trans. Michael Idomir Allen (Philadelphia: University of Pennsylvania Press, 1993), pp. 15–19, and more closely chronicled by Richard Gerberding, *The Rise of the Carolingians and the "Liber Historiae Francorum"* (Oxford: Clarendon, 1987), esp. pp. 6–7, 120–21. For Pippin's landbase, see Matthias Werner, *Der Lütticher Raum in frühkarolingischer Zeit* (Göttingen: Vandenhoeck & Ruprecht, 1980), pp. 342–54 (but see Gerberding, *Rise of Carolingians,* p. 121, for cautions about Werner's estimates). For Itta's disposition of family wealth, see Alexander Bergengruen, *Adel und Grundherrschaft im Merowingerreich* (Wiesbaden: F. Steiner, 1958), pp. 109–10; and Hoebanx, *Abbaye de Nivelles,* pp. 86–95. In a text filled with proper names, the identity of the (conspicuously?) unnamed "son of a duke of the Austrasians" seems deliberately vague. McNamara speculates that the young man might be either the brother of the early seventh-century saint Glodesind of Metz or else Ansegisel, later husband of Gertrude's sister Begga (*Sainted Women of the Dark Ages,* p. 223 n. 13). Both men were sufficiently well connected to Gertrude's family to merit a proper name and a more positive characterization than "pestifer homo" in the text. See Werner, *Lütticher Raum,* p. 44 n. 56, for a judicious refusal of the sure identification of the *VsG*'s "dux Austrasiorum" with the Duke Adalgisel named by Dagobert I in 633–34 as regent for his son Sigibert III, infant king of Austrasia. But see also Bergengruen, *Adel und Grundherrschaft,* p. 118 n. 73, for possible connections between Gertrude's family and Adalgisel.

[4] *VsG,* prologue: "exemplum vel conversationem . . . quod vidimus vel per idoneos testes audivimus"; c. 4: "quod ipsa Dei famula . . . nobis narravit"; c. 7 (at the death of Gertrude, on March 17): "Deo desideratum amisit spiritum. Dum ibidem ego et alius frater Rinchinus . . . fuimus evocati propter sororum consolationem."

[5] The dominant assumption has been that the *Life* was composed by a monk; see Krusch, MGH SSrerMerov 2:448; Hoebanx, *Abbaye de Nivelles,* pp. 31–36; Dierkens, "Saint Amand," p. 326 n. 5. A

Nonetheless, the closing episode of the *Life,* in which the author is summoned "with another brother . . . to console the sisters" (*VsG,* c. 7: ego et alius frater . . . evocati propter sororum consolationem) at Gertrude's death, indicates to me that we are right to read this voice as that of a monk, possibly even that of a priest.[6] Debate is likewise possible concerning whether the author had originally come from or was yet a member of the nearby monastery of Fosses, a community that had been founded under Itta's sponsorship around an Irish monk named Foillan.[7] The connection between the two houses is evident in the *VsG* itself: in the seventh chapter of the *Life,* Gertrude's deathday (and thus, presumably, her cult) is markedly entwined with that of St. Patrick by the prophetic words of the Irish abbot of Fosses, who is named in some manuscripts as Ultan. The abbot of Fosses predicts correctly that Gertrude's death will take place on Patrick's feast day, March 17, and that "blessed Bishop Patrick" is prepared to receive her "with the elect angels of God and with great glory."[8] In any case, there is every reason to believe that the author was either a member of, or had intimate knowledge of, the double monastery of Nivelles during Gertrude's abbacy and that he was writing for a community with a still vivid memory of significant episodes in the saint's life, and so was constrained by the principles of verisimilitude in reporting the events of Gertrude's history. Thus we may take it that, if the story of Gertrude's anger is not "true" by whatever standards we might wish to apply to something so subjective as emotional experience, it was nevertheless composed so as to seem well imagined and essentially plausible to Gertrude's contemporaries.[9]

---

caution against so easy and automatic an ascription has been made by Ian Wood, who has suggested that the author could as easily have been a female member of the community of Nivelles; Wood, "Administration, Law, and Culture in Merovingian Gaul," in *The Uses of Literacy in Early Medieval Europe,* ed. Rosamond McKitterick (Cambridge: Cambridge University Press, 1990), pp. 63–81, 70 n. 50.

[6] This is the ascription made by Rosamond McKitterick, "Women and Literacy in the Early Middle Ages," in *Books, Scribes, and Learning in the Frankish Kingdoms, 6th–9th Centuries* (Aldershot: Variorum, 1994), XIII, p. 26.

[7] For the foundations of Fosses and its ongoing connections with Gertrude's family, see Alain Dierkens, *Abbayes et chapitres entre Sambre et Meuse* (Sigmaringen: J. Thorbecke, 1985), pp. 70–76. Hoebanx, *Abbaye de Nivelles,* p. 30, considered the author to be an Irish monk of the community of Nivelles. Ludwig Bieler ascribed the *VsG* with startling confidence to an Irish author, calling the *Life* "one of the oldest monuments of Irish hagiography"; Bieler, *Ireland: Harbinger of the Middle Ages* (London: Oxford University Press, 1963), p. 101.

[8] "Beatus Patricius episcopus cum electis angelis Dei et cum ingenti gloria parati sunt eam recipere" (*VsG,* c. 7).

[9] On contemporaries' memory as a constraint for hagiography, see Paul Fouracre, "Merovingian History and Merovingian Hagiography," *Past and Present* 127 (1990): 3–38, p. 11; Fouracre argues that much of the awkward hagiography produced in the seventh century has a strong claim to be read as history. For a refusal of the very categories of 'hagiography' vs. 'history' before the twelfth century,

But how are we to read the fact of a little girl getting—or appearing to get—very angry in this anecdote? What does Gertrude's evident anger mean, and what will we see when we can parse it appropriately? I shall argue that within the space of the text Gertrude's angry reaction is made to function as a site where one realm of knowledge (the saint's certainty about her heavenly husband) is translated into another (the expectations that her parents, King Dagobert, and potential earthly marriage partners have about her eligibility). Her manifest anger is itself fundamental to that translation because it naturalizes the authority of her perception of herself and her true identity. I shall suggest that for the author of her *Life,* and presumably for that writer's intended audience, the instance of her evident anger itself was interpreted as evidence that demonstrated the certain and indubitable facticity of the supervening reality Gertrude asserted. As the text has it, her apparent rage, *as* rage, inflected her vow to refuse an earthly husband in favor of the divine one, interrupting and nullifying the normal and ordinary patterns of marriage previously marked out for her as a well-born and richly landed woman in seventh-century Frankish society.

In seeking to make sense of the place of emotion in this tale, we should first note that the saint's anger is incidental to the anecdote's larger narrative of Gertrude's rejected betrothal to the son of a duke of the Austrasians. The story could be told without reference to Gertrude's ire and yet still convey in substantially the same form the little girl's refusal of an earthly spouse in favor of a marriage to Christ.[10] The anger, incidental to the basic betrothal plot, marks a deliberate inclusion on the part of the author and was presumably intended to shape readers' perceptions of the event depicted. Moreover, precisely because the narrator did not step outside the frame of the drama to explain how Gertrude's anger was to be understood, the episode of Gertrude's rage becomes all the more interesting as an issue for historical exploration. Not least because of its unselfconscious rendition of emotionality in the context of a marital negotiation, this story would appear to bring us tantalizingly close to the realm of the "unspoken everyday" upon which social interaction is built. The very absence of explanatory markers that might seek to qualify, explain, defend, or otherwise direct a further interpretation of Gertrude's anger sug-

---

see Felice Lifshitz, "Beyond Positivism and Genre: 'Hagiographical' Texts as Historical Narrative," *Viator* 25 (1994): 95–113.

[10] The phenomenon of a female saint's mystical marriage to Christ was well developed in the hagiographical imagination even by the time of the *VsG,* and the topos of her rejection of an earthly suitor in favor of Christ is well attested; but this is the only early medieval example that I have been able to discover in which the anger of the female saint is figured. See Réginald Grégoire, "Il matrimonio mistico," in *Il matrimonio nella società altomedievale,* Settimane di Studio 24 (Spoleto: Presso la sede del Centro, 1977), pp. 701–94; my thanks to David Ganz for this reference.

gests that such behavior was assumed to be readily intelligible and even normal, if not normative, to the *Life*'s intended audience. The passage thus presents an opportunity to explore an aspect of the affective world of the Frankish nobility so as to discover something about how people in Merovingian society processed an experience in terms of a feeling.[11]

Although the presence of Gertrude's emotion in this text warrants consideration, it presents immediate and slippery problems of interpretation. The hagiographer has framed the tale to assert a primary literal meaning by invoking the eyewitness testimony of a reliable narrator, that "just and truthful man" whose memory recorded a banquet at Pippin's house where Gertrude angrily repulsed a powerful suitor with an oath. There is no a priori reason to dismiss a literal reading, no clear evidence upon which to assert that the incident is "merely" a literary formula. Yet to assert only the literal value of the report ("what this text means is that a little girl named Gertrude *really* got angry") would displace the question of the significance of her anger away from the text itself onto a putative "emotion-event" that must be imagined to have occurred in the "real" world, a world, moreover, to which the modern reader's access depends chiefly on the text at hand. Conversely, if the tale is deemed to be fabulous, substantially an invention of the narrator's imagination, the question of meaning is all the more compelling: how then do we explain the role of anger in the text? If the narrator had no need to include Gertrude's anger in order to satisfy an audience that knew such a thing to be part of the story, the reader is hard pressed to account for what anger is doing in the text at all. In either case, whether we read the episode as a factual occurrence (however filtered through memory and fashioned to fit the redactors' narrative purposes) or as an imaginative fiction, we are constrained to address the nature of anger itself. And, of course, how we read the anger in the *Life* will depend on the logic of social relations by which we imagine the protagonists of the story to have been governed.

As a small mountain of scholarly literature on the psychological, cultural, and historical study of emotional behavior has surely demonstrated, emotions are feeling-states that have a cognitive component, that is, they involve a mental appraisal of whatever situation prompts their expression.[12] Among the emotions, anger is a feeling-state that is at base antag-

11 Compare the sorts of questions addressed in the context of saga literature by William Ian Miller, *Humiliation* (Ithaca: Cornell University Press, 1993); see esp. chap. 3: "Emotions, Honor, and the Heroic."

12 For the ways in which this seemingly obvious point has in fact been open to contest, see the arguments collected in *The Nature of Emotion: Fundamental Questions*, ed. Paul Ekman and Richard J. Davidson (Oxford: Oxford University Press, 1994), esp. Question 5, "What are the minimal cognitive prerequisites for emotion?" and Question 8, "Can emotions be non-conscious?"

onistic.[13] Many researchers further include in anger's essential definition a prerogative over the moral domain. This framework of understanding attributes to anger an inherent claim about some sense of the "ought," so as to capture the aspect of anger that stems as a response to some sense of what is felt to be "unjustifiable" harm.[14] But beyond these basic and possibly universal qualities of anger, its meaning as an emotion is located in the particular social framework in which it is generated and expressed. Whatever the immediate felt experience or physiological component of emotions, feelings are "cultural acquisitions" intelligible only in the context in which they occur.[15] Cultural anthropologists and historians of emotion alike point to a fundamental variance of patterns in the language and interpretation of emotions: both from place to place and from era to era, words signifying anger reside in different semantic fields, and expressions of anger take place and are received in ways that differ.[16] Manifestly, a reading of Gertrude's anger that depends on "common sense" is of no use in a context with which we have no sensibility in common.

Above all, we must discard interpretations based on broad generalizations or assumptions about what we take to be the essential characteristics of the protagonists. Reading Gertrude's anger as the irrational tantrum of a little girl might be plausible within certain modern premises for understanding children's anger. But as historians have noted, the very word "tantrum" and the complex of associations surrounding it are themselves the product of a dynamic and relatively recent process by which new spheres of emotional control, first for adults in public, then for children within the domestic sphere, were marked out in the course of the

[13] This strategically minimalist and abstract definition of anger is preferred for purposes of historical inquiry by Carol Z. Stearns and Peter N. Stearns, *Anger: The Struggle for Emotional Control in America's History* (Chicago: University of Chicago Press, 1986), pp. 12–17.

[14] For the implication of anger's "ought" in a particular cultural context, see Catherine Lutz, *Unnatural Emotions* (Chicago: University of Chicago Press, 1988), chap. 6: "Morality, Domination, and the Emotion of 'Justifiable Anger'." For more general claims about anger's moral domain, Carol Tavris, *Anger: The Misunderstood Emotion* (New York: Simon and Schuster, 1982), p. 47. For the social logic of anger as a response to unjustifiable harm: Fred R. Myers, "The Logic and Meaning of Anger among Pintupi Aborigines," *Man* (n.s.) 23 (1988): 591.

[15] For a brief and efficient discussion of universalist vs. cultural claims about the nature of emotion, see Robert C. Solomon, "Getting Angry: The Jamesian Theory of Emotion in Anthropology," in *Culture Theory: Essays in Mind, Self, and Emotion*, ed. R. Shweder and R. LeVine (Cambridge: Cambridge University Press, 1984), pp. 238–54; for emotion as "cultural acquisition," see p. 240.

[16] An outline of the concerns of the history of emotion may be found in Peter N. Stearns, "Historical Analysis in the Study of Emotion," *Motivation and Emotion* 10, no. 2 (1986): 185–93. For an introduction to the social constructivist project in exploring emotion, see Rom Harré, "An Outline of the Social Constructivist Viewpoint," in *The Social Construction of Emotions*, ed. Rom Harré (Oxford: Basil Blackwell, 1986), pp. 2–14; for a critique of the strong social constructivist position, see William M. Reddy, "Against Constructionism: The Historical Ethnography of Emotions," *Current Anthropology* (forthcoming).

eighteenth and nineteenth centuries in British and American societies.[17] And just as we can not read Gertrude's anger through our contemporary notions about childhood's "natural" emotions, likewise we can not expect that modern perceptions about whatever we apprehend to be the contemporary rules that guide the expression of women's anger, among other emotions, will inform us about the right, licit, and intelligible deployment of a young aristocratic woman's anger in seventh-century Frankish society.

Given this fact of cultural and temporal variance, it would appear to be the more reasonable path to assume a radical untranslatability between the anger of Gertrude and our own.[18] By this I do not suggest that we are unable to recover some of the force and even some of the particular savor of the behavioral sensibility that informed the *Life* and its audience—and arguably the young Gertrude and her contemporaries as well. I do mean to claim that in acknowledging the insights of the social constructivist approach to anger, we must recognize that "patterns of emotion, like rhetorical phenomena, are culturally indigenous" and accordingly build our interpretation of Gertrude's rage out of evidence derived from the local culture of her time and place.[19]

In seeking to discover something of the salience of this moment of anger in seventh-century Frankish society, we must be attentive to a quality of its communication—or, more precisely, its "evidentiation"—that is not necessarily of concern to the social constructivist project *per se.* Dependent on text as we are, our interpretations must bear within them our attention to the textual construction as well as the social location of an emotion. This of course entails attention to some obvious facts, such as that the author of the *Life* was writing in a particular language (Latin), was working in and for at least the specific cultural milieu of a monastic audience, and was deploying a flexible but not infinite repertory of narrative models and anger idioms to communicate his sense of the event and its meaning in the saint's life. We need also to consider the text not as a passive reflector of cultural data but as an intervention in a dialogue for which we have only one voice: our author's. We cannot assume that the culture that a text depicts is a unified and uncontested field, uniformly determining the actions and responses of its participants, nor can we imagine the text to be an uncritical and unengaged mirror of the material

17 Stearns and Stearns, *Anger,* p. 29.

18 For the "radical intranslatability" view, to which I subscribe, see Solomon, "Getting Angry," p. 240.

19 C. Terry Warner, "Anger and Similar Delusions," in *Social Construction of Emotions,* ed. Harré, p. 135.

it conveys.[20] In reading a text we have to allow for its capacity to participate in the construction of meaning across contested terrains whose boundaries, if unclear to us, may yet determine the manner in which events are represented. I am arguing two related points here: first, that culture informs and frames but does not simply or uniformly determine the expression of human behavior (and so every instantiation or representation of anger requires contextual interpretation to arrive at an understanding of its import) and, second, that texts, far from being transparent and invisible windows onto the events they depict, are in themselves a form of social act and as such shape, refract, and thereby alter the meaning of the data they convey.[21]

There are many ways to narrate anger. When the author of the *VsG* endeavored to record "the example and conduct of the most blessed virgin Gertrude, mother of Christ's family" (*VsG* prologue), he had an array of options through which to tell this story. He began the *Life* conventionally enough, with a general account of Gertrude's meritorious childhood: while in the home of her parents, the holy girl "grew day and night in word and wisdom, dear to God and loved by men beyond her generation" (*VsG*, c. 1). Immediately thereafter, and as we have seen, the narrator places the origin of Gertrude's "election to the service of Christ" in an angry incident during her childhood that took place at a banquet given by her father, an incident that the writer asserts to have been witnessed by an individual whose reliable testimony subtends the *Life*'s account of events. Granting that the basic components of the story were fixed by the constraints of local memory and verisimilitude, we must still inquire into the particular redaction of anger that the episode presents, an anger that is characterized in the text as *furor.* Gertrude exhibits *furor,* or rather, as the text has it, becomes "quasi furore repleta," "as if" or "almost" filled with *furor,* when she is presented with the option of marriage to a richly dressed youth of aristocratic birth. Since every translation is itself a reading of a text, we must attend carefully to how we construe the saint's *furor* in this context. In classical Latin and in the writings of the Latin fathers, *furor* occupies a

[20] Karl Galinsky makes much the same point in his critique of some modern readings of Vergil's intent in depicting Aeneas's anger in the closing scenes of the *Aeneid* in "The Anger of Aeneas," *American Journal of Philology* 109 (1988): 322–23. See also Gabrielle M. Spiegel's now foundational article, "History, Historicism, and the Social Logic of the Text in the Middle Ages," *Speculum* 65 (1990): 59–86.

[21] Contra Miller's thoughtful discussion of interpreting the "emotional life of people long dead" (*Humiliation*, pp. 98–114), which does not seem to me sufficiently to problematize the possibility of contest and change in behavioral meanings within a culture. But see Myers, "Logic and Meaning of Anger," pp. 606–7, who argues that the linguistic representation, "the emotion-word," of a feeling is itself "but a signifier in a system of signifying practices" so that "its meaning is not *given* in reference but produced through its use in social life and its relationship to other signs."

semantic field more violent than that of *ira*, anger. In antiquity, *furor* had the force of raging madness, even insanity; juridically, the person possessed by fury was understood to be "absent from himself."[22] The quality of human *furor* as the straying of the mind that shades into dementia presumably accounts for its transposed use as a marker of heresy in late ancient and medieval Christian discourse.[23] For Bede, *furor*'s close proximity to mania made it an appropriate term to denote an instance of demonic possession whose relief necessitated a miraculous healing.[24] To say simply that the little girl expressed "indignation," or "lost her temper," would hardly seem to convey the disruptive power of Gertrude's wrath. Rather, the saint is explicitly marked as having appeared, to her audience, "furore repleta," "possessed or filled with raging madness."[25] In choosing to cast Gertrude's anger as *furor* the author of her *Life* would seem to have invoked a form of wrath that stood oppositionally to normal human concourse.

The task of endeavoring to enter the imaginative world of the *VsG* is perilously conjectural when we turn from basic, lexicographical levels of meaning to consider where and how the expression of human *furor* was figured as licit and divinely inspired. Fundamental uncertainties about which texts might have been available to the *VsG*'s author vitiate any straightforward survey of possible analogues in contemporary texts. The *VsG* mentions the monastery's acquisition of holy books from Rome and "places overseas" (c.2: transmarinis regionibus—an imprecise reference that might mean Ireland or England or both) and boasts of Gertrude that she had "memorized a whole library of divine law" (c. 3), but more specific information for the author's textual environment is absent.[26] We can,

22 Florence Dupont, *L'acteur-roi, ou, le théâtre dans la Rome antique* (Paris: Belles Lettres, 1985), p. 190, "Pour rendre compte du sens de la loi, les jurisconsultes expliquent que le furieux est considéré comme absent à lui-même"; my thanks to Philippe Buc for this reference. And see the *Thesaurus linguae latinae* (Leipzig: B. G. Teubner, 1900–), s.vv. *furor, furiosus,* where, in legal contexts, the latter term is used to mark those incompetent to transact business on their own account.

23 A. Blaise, *Dictionnaire latin-français des auteurs chrétiens* (Turnhout: Éditions Brepols, 1954), s.v. *furor;* J. F. Niermeyer, *Mediae latinitatis lexicon minus* (Leiden: E. J. Brill, 1993), s.v. *furor.*

24 Bede, *Ecclesiastical History of the English People* 3.2, ed. B. Colgrave and R.A.B. Mynors (Oxford: Clarendon, 1969), p. 248. Historians of medicine Monica Green and Florence Eliza Glaze have suggested to me that *furor* is noted in ancient and early medieval medical literature as a medical (rather than purely emotional) state that sometimes had pathological connotations.

25 For "indignation," see the paraphrase of L. van der Essen, *Étude critique et littéraire sur les vitae des saints mérovingiennes de l'ancienne Belgique* (Louvain: Bureaux de Recueil, 1907), p. 2; McNamara, Halborg, and Whatley render the phrase as "lost her temper" (*Sainted Women of the Dark Ages,* p. 223); both translations/readings seem to me to flatten the force of the text's language and to trivialize the social disruption of Gertrude's actions. But see now the translation in *Late Merovingian France,* ed. Fouracre and Gerberding, p. 320: "But she, as if filled with rage . . . "

26 As Alain Dierkens notes, it is not possible to use the *VsG* to determine even which monastic rule was in use at Nivelles; see his "Prolégomènes à une histoire des relations culturelles entre les îles

however, derive the general sense of *furor* from a few widely read and widely copied texts, intending thereby to get a taste of what might have informed the sensibilities of our author and of the audience for which he wrote, rather than to determine a repertory of exemplary topoi. What follows is an attempt to sort out the rhetorical context in which *furor* is deployed by writers and encountered by readers in seventh-century Frankish society, in the hope of developing a preliminary sense of where and how the term was likely to be used.

No unambiguous models of human *furor* can guide us to the sources with which Gertrude's biographer might have been in dialogue when imagining the moment in question in the saint's life. Even assuming that some close analogue to the Vulgate was among whatever biblical texts were available in the library at Nivelles, the Vulgate itself offers only a single instance of a person *replet[us] furore:* in the book of Daniel, King Nebuchadnezzar is filled with rage in contemplating Shadrach, Meschach, and Abed-Nego (Dan. 3:19).[27] This would hardly appear to be a suitable model for our author's purposes in portraying a saint whose actions are framed as taking place under the direction of God (*VsG,* c. 1). Conversely, divine *furor,* the just rage of God, is so prevalent and so diffuse, particularly in the Psalms, as to be untraceable as a particular stimulant for the author's imagination. Nor should we assume that even the divine *furor* recorded in the Bible was always interpreted positively. So authoritative an exegete as Pope Gregory I could comment on Job's plea to God that he might be hidden until divine *furor* should pass ("ut abscondas me donec pertranseat furor tuus," Job 14:13) with the explanation that God's *furor* is in fact only a temporary precipitate of his relationship with sinful humans. When contemplating divine justice, Gregory tempered Job's *furor* with the Book of Wisdom's *tranquillitas* and held that "it should be known that the term *furor* is not appropriate for the divinity, because no disquiet disturbs the simple nature of God."[28] And if we take divine wrath to be the operative model for Gertrude's rage, we need still to pursue the

britanniques et le continent pendant le haut moyen âge: La diffusion du monachisme dit colombanien ou iro-franc dans quelques monastères de la région parisienne au VIIe siècle et la politique religieuse de la reine Bathilde," in *La Neustrie: Les pays au nord de la Loire de 650 à 850,* ed. Hartmut Atsma (Sigmaringen: J. Thorbecke, 1989), 2:388.

[27] For the *VsG*'s explicit and implicit use of the Bible, see Marc Van Uytfanghe, *Stylisation biblique et condition humaine dans l'hagiographie mérovingienne (600–750)* (Brussels: Paleis der Academiën, 1987).

[28] "Inter haec vero sciendum est quod furoris nomen Divinitati non congruit, quia naturam Dei simplicem perturbatio nulla confundit. Unde ei dicitur: 'Tu autem dominator virtutis cum tranquillitate judicas, et cum magna reverentia disponis nos.'" *Moralia in Job* 10.14, ed. Marc Adriaen, *S. Gregorii Magni Opera,* Corpus Christianorum Series Latina 143A (Turnhout: Brepols, 1979), p. 637; Gregory is quoting Wisdom 12:18.

question of what might warrant the *VsG*'s appropriation of the authority of God's fury by the saint herself for refusal of an earthly husband. As a contrasting example, we might consider an episode recounted in the late fifth-century Legend of Saint Cecilia; there the saint rejects the amorous advances of her husband, Valerian, by invoking the retributive *furor* of her true love, an angel of God.[29] The parallels between Gertrude's rejection of an earthly spouse for a heavenly one and Cecilia's interpellation of an angelic lover between herself and her terrestrial husband serve only to bring into sharper relief the distinction between Gertrude's human *furor,* however divinely sanctioned, and the *furor* of an angelic protector.

It is just conceivable—but to my mind only barely so—that the *VsG* draws its claims for Gertrude's sanctified rage from the hagiographical context that produced Muirchú's *Vita Patricii.*[30] The seventh chapter of the *VsG* makes clear the presence of a Patrician cult at Fosses and intertwines Gertrude's cult with it; it would seem probable that in the communities of Fosses and Nivelles, if anywhere in the Frankish lands, oral or written tradition about Patrick would have received an enthusiastic and proactive audience, primed to incorporate Patrician material and models into the local production of writing about their own holy patrons. However, Muirchú's text appears to have been produced at roughly the same time as the *VsG,* and quite possibly slightly later.[31] An argument for the *VsG*'s direct dialogue with, let alone dependence on, Muirchú's *Vita Patricii* would be tendentious, based more clearly on assumptions about a supposed Irish influence than on textual evidence. However intriguing it is to note that Muirchú's text recounts an episode in which the saint, explicitly named there "holy Patrick," upon growing angry (*irascens*) curses a greedy cattle thief who has made off with the saint's property, this text would appear to illustrate a moment of righteous indignation rather than surging fury. To my ears, the faint and distorted echo between the holy ire of Patrick and the sanctified rage of Gertrude is best understood as no more than that.[32]

[29] "Tunc illa ait [to Valerianus]: Angelum Dei amatorem habeo, qui nimio zelo corpus meum custodit. Hic si vel leviter senserit, quod tu polluto amore contigas me, statim contra te suum furorem exagitat." Quoted in Grégoire, "Matrimonio mistico," pp. 762–63. My thanks to David Ganz for pointing me to this and the previous reference.

[30] *The Patrician Texts in the Book of Armagh,* ed. Ludwig Bieler, (Dublin: Dublin Institute for Advanced Studies, 1979), pp. 62–126; and see Wendy Davies, "Anger and the Celtic Saint," chapter 9 in this volume.

[31] For the dating, see Bieler, *Patrician Texts,* p. 1, and Richard Sharpe, *Medieval Irish Saints' Lives* (Oxford: Clarendon, 1991), pp. 12–14, 16.

[32] For the narrative in which Patrick curses a cattle thief, see Muirchú, *Vita Patricii,* c. 26, in *Patrician Texts,* ed. Bieler, p. 112. And now see the conclusions of Fouracre and Gerberding, *Late Merovingian France,* p. 318, regarding the decided paucity of elements that would mark the *VsG* as being within the Irish hagiographical tradition: it is "very much in the mainstream of the Frankish

Turning to texts produced and circulated in settings roughly similar to that of the monastery at Nivelles, we find that fury would appear not to have been valorized, much less sanctified as God-sent, in the Iro-merovingian and Frankish texts that are earlier contemporaries of the *VsG.* There is a curious resonance between the *VsG* and a sermon by Caesarius of Arles that combines references to a feast at a powerful man's table, a wedding, and the phrase "iracundiae furore repletus." In this passage Caesarius is entreating his brethren to abhor wrath and to come to the altar as to the eternal king's feast: the allusion is to something other than licit, even divinely sanctioned anger.[33] The *Regula ad monachos* and its companion *Regula ad virgines* of Aurelian of Arles both castigate the professed religious (of either sex—the wording is the same for each) who might become "by the instigation of the devil, filled with rage" and cause discord within the monastery.[34] As Lester Little has shown in his judicious survey of monastic rules, in such texts anger within the monastery was seen without exception as inappropriate to the monastic life; for Aurelian, *furor* is indeed imagined to be the result of demonic forces.[35]

Likewise, Jonas of Bobbio's *Vita Columbani* casts Columbanus and his followers as the pacific opponents of discord and wrath. Columbanus's first community in Gaul is lauded by Jonas for the brothers' humility; among the worldly evils they are explicitly said to reject are dissension and anger.[36] Jonas draws marked and repeated contrasts between Col-

---

hagiographic tradition and [is] quite different from the writing about saints by seventh-century Irish authors in Ireland."

[33] "Rogo vos, fratres, diligenter adtendite, si ad mensam cuiuscumque potentis hominis nemo presumit cum vestibus conciscissis et inquinatis accedere, quanto magis a convivio aeterni regis, id est, ab altari domini debet se unusquisque invidiae vel odii veneno percussus, iracundiae furore repletus, cum reverentia et humilitate subtrahere, propter illud quod scriptum est: prius reconciliare fratri tuo, et tunc veniens offer munus tuum; et iterum: amice, quomodo huc intrasti non habens vestem nuptialem?" *Sancti Caesarii Arelatensis sermones,* sermon 227, c. 3, ed. G. Morin, Corpus Christianorum Series Latina 104 (Turnhout: Brepols, 1953), p. 898.

[34] Aurelian of Arles, *Regula ad virgines,* c. 10, PL 68, col. 401: "Quod Deus avertat, si diabolo instigante fuerit aliqua furore repleta, ut ista mandata pertinaci corde contemnat; et una de illis quae discordantes sunt praevenerit aliam, veniam ei petens; si illa cui petet non dimiserit, disciplinam accipiat, ut ad charitatem se corrigat. Et si ambo despexerint, ambae pariter a communione vel a cibo suspendantur; donec invicem sibi reconcilientur." See also and compare his *Regula ad monachos,* c. 12, PL 68, col. 389. Multiple examples of this sort and with much the same flavor can be easily located by reference to J.-M. Clément, *Lexique des anciennes règles monastiques occidentales* (Steenbrugge: Martin Nijhof, 1978), s.v. *furor.*

[35] See Lester Little, "Anger in Monastic Curses," Chaper 1 in this volume.

[36] Of Columbanus and the monks: "modestia atque sobrietas, mansuetudo et lenitas aeque in omnibus redolebat. Execrabatur ab his desidiae atque discordiae vitium, arrogantiae ac elationis supercilium duris castigationum ictibus feriebatur, irae ac livoris noxa sagaci intentione pellebatur." Jonas, *Vita Columbani* 1.5, ed. B. Krusch, in *Ionae Vitae Sanctorum: Columbani, Vedastis, Iohannis* (Hanover: Hahn, 1905), p. 161. Ian Wood argues for the decisive if institutionally delimited influence of the *Vita Columbani* on Merovingian hagiography in "The *Vita Columbani* and Merovingian hagiography," *Peritia* 1 (1982): 63–80.

umbanus and figures of insane and intemperate rage. These are sometimes anonymous evildoers (*Vita Columbani* 1.21) but more often fury is represented by the malefic King Theuderic and Queen Brunhild (1.19, 20, 27, 28), whose conflicts with Columbanus are portrayed with unrelenting hostility by Jonas. Brunhild, especially, is described as being preternaturally savage and implacably wrathful, continuously "furens" to Columbanus's steadfast adherence to godly commands.[37] Predictably, the *Histories* of Gregory of Tours are replete with moments of fury.[38] Like Jonas, Gregory also employs *furor* to portray a violence that is socially destructive in the extreme, and indeed one that is very often depicted as either demonically inspired or employed to demonic ends. The wild bull that ended the life of the martyr Saturninus under the Decian persecutions (*Decem libri historiarum* 1.30), the worker who revenged himself by betraying Vienne during a siege (2.33); the military thug Roccolen, who threatened to burn Tours and its suburbs to the ground (5.4); the overweening pride of Bishops Salonius and Sagittarius that led to "peculation, physical assaults, murders, adulteries, and every crime" (5.20); civil discord in Tours (9.19); the father who attacks his own son with an ax on account of the son's cowardice (9.34); all share in the quality of *furor.* One of Gregory's most vividly rendered portraits of female chaos and destruction is the miscreant nun Clotild, whose *furor* raises to ever higher pitches the violence surrounding the murderous attack on the abbess at Poitiers by participants in the nuns' revolt there (10.15).

So we may well puzzle over the *VsG*'s use of *furor* in the context of a banquet given by Gertrude's father for King Dagobert I, and wonder about the context underlying the narrator's depiction of Gertrude's evident rage as sanctioned by God. What could justify manifest *furor* as an attribute of words spoken *Dei iussione?* The problematic implications of the violent, even potentially sinful excess of angry emotion inherent in the term perhaps explain the author's insertion of the qualifying adverb *quasi:* Gertrude's rage may be real enough to her onlookers at the banquet, but it would seem that her biographer had some reservations about naming her as such for the pious readers of his story. The hagiographer's choice of *quasi* may mark Gertrude's behavior as no more than *evidently* or *almost* filled with *furor,* thus conveying the socially disruptive power of the

[37] For the context of this hostility see Janet Nelson, "Queens as Jezebels: The Careers of Brunhild and Balthild in Merovingian History," in *Medieval Women,* ed. Derek Baker (Oxford: Basil Blackwell, 1978), pp. 31–77.

[38] Gregory of Tours, *Decem Libri Historiarum,* ed. B. Krusch and W. Levison, MGH SSrerMerov 1:1. Although the concordance was designed for use with Arndt's earlier edition, reading for *furor* in this text was made infinitely more efficient by the work of Denise St-Michel, *Concordance de l'* Historia Francorum *de Grégoire de Tours* (Montréal: Université de Montréal, Secteur Antiquité et Études Médiévales, 1982).

saint's rage vis-à-vis her audience even as the text informs its readers that Gertrude was not *wholly* possessed by *furor*'s passion. As a rule, hagiography is not an "epistemologically hesitant" genre; presumably Gertrude's biographer could say whether she was filled with rage or not.[39] The writers of saints' biographies were well accustomed to narrating the inner lives and even the feelings of their subjects; Gertrude's hagiographer relates the saint's internal experience on several occasions in the *VsG*.[40] Moreover, the text depicts the emotional state of her disappointed suitor in simple terms with no hedging: when he left, he left "filled with anger" (iracundia plenus), full stop. This straightforward description of the suitor's wrath indicates that the hagiographer's use of *quasi* to define Gertrude's *furor* cannot be explained simply as a solution to the difficulty intrinsic in the writing of something so internal as feeling. But a reading that concentrates on that *quasi* in an effort to explain away Gertrude's *furor* as an emotion not possible for an exemplary monastic saint is a reading that would substitute a reified notion of monastic culture and its uniform reception of texts about monastic virtues in the place of an account of early medieval monasticism that allows for variety and perhaps contest among visions of the monastic life. Because *furor* is a word with such powerfully negative connotations in early medieval religious discourse, and because its excision from this story would not vitiate the basic narrative of Gertrude's mystical marriage to Christ, we must work to understand why *furor* appears at all in this context. Far from being explained away, the use of *furor* on the part of Gertrude's hagiographer needs to be explained *in*—that is, drawn into our notion of what this text is trying to accomplish.

As recounted in the first chapter of the *VsG*, the precise catalyst for Gertrude's *furor* is Dagobert's question about the young girl's willingness to take as a husband the well-dressed son of a duke of the Austrasians, who has sought her hand frankly "to satisfy earthly ambition as well as for mutual alliance." The text links Gertrude's *furor* with her refusal of that suitor or any other earthly husband and simultaneously interpolates Christ into the marital negotiation as her only proper spouse: "But she, as if filled with *furor*, rejected [the son of a duke of the Austrasians] with an oath, and said that she would have neither him nor any earthly man for

[39] I owe this point, and the felicitous phrase, to William Reddy.

[40] For example, *VsG*, c. 3, in which Gertrude ruminates internally over the heavenly contemplation she hopes to achieve in the monastic life: "infra se cogitabat de celeste contemplatione, quam sibi sine secularium strepitu habere optaverat"; c. 4, where the saint informs the monastery of witnessing a mysterious light while at prayer: she spoke "as if/almost trembling with fear" (ipsa Dei famula quasi pavore perterrita nobis narravit). Here the *quasi* would seem plausibly to have the force of "manifestly" or "evidently"; in any case, as in Gertrude's *furor*, the narrator does not hesitate to name the (internal) emotion.

husband but Christ the lord." The manifest evidence of Gertrude's sole appropriate marriage partner, Christ, is immediately reinforced in the succeeding sentences. First, King Dagobert and his nobles are made to "marvel greatly" and presumably affirmatively over the little girl's words. These are recorded by the *VsG* as having been said under God's command; here the text allows a certain ambiguity about whether that fact was recognized by the young Gertrude's audience at the time or was only subsequently made clear. Second, the suitor leaves "confusus," disturbed and filled with anger, implicitly due to having had his wishes thwarted and possibly in reaction to the slight of having been passed over for a more powerful marriage partner. His anger is figured rhetorically in the text as a response to hers: she is "quasi furore repleta" to his "iracundiae plenus." But his anger is construed with a term, *iracundia,* (irascibility, irritability), that is pitched at a lower heat of passion than is Gertrude's *furor,* and his wrath is denied the explicit status of divine sanction that guides the text's readers in interpreting the saint's rage. He is an incidental player in the drama portrayed in this chapter, insulted and angry, but not in a way that was evidently felt to require further comment on the part of the narrator. Gertrude's wrathful declaration, on the other hand, takes center stage. For through it, according to the text, Gertrude's parents now know "by what manner of king she was loved." The "fact" of the young girl's "marriage" to Christ has thus been effectively accomplished in this narrative sequence, which began by identifying Gertrude's angry rejection as the origin of the saint's election to Christ's service.

Here the text bears certain anxious implications of a *fait* not so easily *accompli.* An unstated but evidently operative understanding shared by all the parties involved in this transaction is that in the early medieval marital economy, where the noble household and the arena of political power are coterminous, Gertrude's matrimonial strategy is a subject of state interest. Gertrude, though described as a little girl and evidently only barely of suitable age for betrothal, will inevitably be married to someone; the suspense of this vignette is not about whether she will be married but to whom.[41] King Dagobert's clear interest in that alliance is made manifest by his role as marriage broker. The positive and negative interests of Gertrude's family in this transaction are not here defined, but the capacity of Gertrude's parents to determine the final identity of her spouse appears

41 Since Gertrude was born in about 625/26, and Dagobert I—present at the feast—died in 639, her age at the time of the banquet may have been anywhere between seven and twelve or thirteen years; Dierkens, "Saint Amand," p. 330. This age fits the marriage pattern of well-born women; see Jean Verdon, "Les femmes laïques en Gaule au temps des Mérovingiens: Les réalités de la vie quotidienne," in *Frauen in Spätantike und Frühmittelalter,* ed. W. Affeldt (Sigmaringen: J. Thorbecke, 1990), p. 243.

rather shaky in the *VsG*'s admittedly retrospective view. The initial request for a marriage between Gertrude and the son of a duke of the Austrasians is portrayed as having been made both to King Dagobert and to Gertrude's parents, but it is Dagobert, depicted as satisfied with the prospect of that alliance, who initiates the marriage negotiations with Gertrude; and it is not Gertrude's parents but rather Gertrude herself, represented in turn as insistent on the supervening commitment of her marriage to Christ, who forestalls the connection. *Pace* the narrator's claim for the aristocratic community's recognition of the saint's new status as one beloved by Christ, we might wonder how strongly the marvel of Gertrude's "true" but in earthly terms indeterminate marriage to Christ had registered on the surrounding society. The next chapter of the *VsG*, which relates events that occur after the death of Pippin, implies that only the monastery founded by the now widowed Itta at Nivelles, and her own and Gertrude's profession at it, afforded the conditions under which Gertrude's marriage to Christ might be accorded the exclusive status of a matrimonial relationship. A further attempt to capture Gertrude's person and wealth in the compact of matrimony evidently occurred; the next chapter of the *Life* relates that in order to prevent some unnamed "violators of souls" (violatores animarum) from tearing her daughter away by force, Itta tonsures Gertrude herself, at which point we are told that "merciful God . . . recalled the adversaries to the concord of peace" (c. 2).

Gertrude's "marriage" to Christ served a dual function in the early history of her monastery. It is the alliance that foreclosed the unwelcome possibility of any other marital relationship with suitors like the duke's son, suitors intent on marriage with the wealthy Gertrude "for reasons of earthly ambition" and whose nuptial plans in chapter 2 of the *VsG* read like an attempted hostile takeover of the family concern.[42] Her "marriage" to Christ was also a foundational compact from which derived both her natal family's and her monastic family's religious authority.[43] Christ is the spouse of highest status in the marital economy in which Gertrude must negotiate, a circumstance that underscores the force of naming Christ's regality in the encomiastic sentence that concludes chapter 1 of the *VsG*. There, following Gertrude's declaration of her pending marriage to Christ, it is Christ's marriage to Gertrude that is foregrounded: "from

[42] For an adumbration drawn from contemporary narrative sources of the pressures and constraints on Frankish noblewomen's marriages, see Verdon, "Femmes laïques," pp. 243–48, and the more extensive treatment in Suzanne Wemple, *Women in Frankish Society: Marriage and the Cloister, 500 to 900* (Philadelphia: University of Pennsylvania Press, 1981), esp. pp. 31–57.

[43] Of course, the two families overlapped to a significant extent; the history of early Nivelles, including the most systematic data about members of the community, is to be found in Hoebanx, *Abbaye de Nivelles*, pp. 45–70.

that day her parents knew by what manner of king she was loved." And of course, Gertrude's status as Christ's beloved spouse in turn subtends the saint's cult and its promise of intercessory potency.

I suggest that it is in this context, defined by the author's pressing need to make definite the potentially precarious terms of Gertrude's marital identity, that we should read the text's portrayal of the saint's *furor.* The degree of Gertrude's evident rage in response to her earthly suitor's proposal signals the nature of the perceived harm to which *furor* is the divinely ordered response. As Gertrude knows (and as others can see only after witnessing her reaction to the prospect of this marriage), she is already promised: what is being proposed to her, then, is not marriage but adultery. Within the frame of reference operating in the *VsG,* the offer of this illicit "second" marriage is at the very least a grave insult to Gertrude, to her family, and to the divine husband by whom she is already beloved. Both in the prescriptive realm of the law codes and the descriptive world revealed by the narratives of Gregory of Tours, adultery figured as a sexual and social crime that stained the honor of a Frankish woman past redemption and exposed her to shameful trial and brutal punishment.[44] In imagining what the imputation of a breach of wifely chastity might mean in Frankish society, perhaps the most telling guide is the matter-of-fact violence with which a woman's family, not only her husband but also her own kin, are recorded as having responded to charges of infidelity. In his *Glory of the Martyrs,* Gregory of Tours tells of "innocent" women condemned, with no further proof than their husband's accusations of infidelity, to submersion in nearby rivers.[45] "Women accused of adultery were weighted with stones and tossed into rivers or burned alive; one husband simply killed his wife and the abbot he found in her bed."[46] The

[44] A woman found guilty of adultery was subject to death in the Burgundian and Lombard laws; see the material collected in Katherine Fischer Drew, "The Law of the Family in the Germanic Barbarian Kingdoms: A synthesis," in *Law and Society in Early Medieval Europe,* ed. K. F. Drew (London: Variorum Reprints, 1988), VIII, pp. 18–19. Both Frankish and Roman law counted adultery as a crime that justified discarding a wife without penalty; see Wemple, *Women in Frankish Society,* p. 42. For an account of Frankish society that emphasizes the particular anxieties of adultery for women, see Michel Rouche, "The Early Middle Ages in the West," in *A History of Private Life,* ed. Philippe Ariès and Georges Duby, vol. 1, *From Pagan Rome to Byzantium,* ed. Paul Veyne, trans. Arthur Goldhammer (Cambridge, Mass.: Belknap Press, 1987), pp. 411–547, at p. 473. For the development of secular and canonical legislation regarding adultery from the Merovingian to Carolingian era, see Régine Le Jan, *Famille et pouvoir dans le monde franc (viie-xe siècle)* (Paris: Publications de la Sorbonne, 1995), pp, 278–81.

[45] Gregory of Tours, *Glory of the Martyrs,* ed. and trans. Raymond Van Dam (Liverpool: Liverpool University Press, 1988), pp. 92–93. Verdon, "Femmes laïques," p. 248, provides a synopsis of the various stories of female adultery recorded by Gregory of Tours.

[46] This is Raymond Van Dam's pithy digest, which to my mind exactly captures the routine quality of the dehumanization that inhered in treatment of a dishonored wife; see Van Dam, *Saints and Their Miracles in Late Antique Gaul* (Princeton: Princeton University Press, 1993), p. 101. For

VsG invites its readers to approve of the saint's rage and to recognize its justice. *Furor,* an emotion appropriately calibrated to the gravity of the harm she has experienced, is the authenticating sign of the saint's marital status. It demonstrates to the onlookers at the banquet Gertrude's transition from an available Pippinid marriage partner to one conjoined to Christ. It translates into the terms of everyday social life the notional, incorporeal relationship that both Gertrude and subsequently her monastic foundation need so much to establish as a manifest truth.

Although the meaning of that moment in which an angry little girl names her true spouse is represented by its narrator as manifestly obvious to everyone present, for modern investigators of the medieval past it nonetheless generates complex and fruitful problems in reading. The problems are arguably most fruitful where interpretive conclusions are least clear, as in the case of Gertrude's rage. Emotion remains a ubiquitous but as yet barely examined category of experience in our texts. Characterizations that place medieval patterns of feeling in that long, *longue durée* of "premodern Western" norms of behavior, where, for example, "anger was freely and publicly expressed as part of a social and familial hierarchy, and also as a function of an emphasis on shame as the chief emotional means of community discipline,"[47] serve effectively to frame medieval life as a backdrop to the implicitly more important narrative of emergent modernity rather than to illuminate the specific and particular conditions in which emotion was expressed in the centuries before the triumph of finance capitalism, the steam engine, and the newspaper. As William Ian Miller has noted in his lapidary summary of some dominant modern images of the emotional life of medieval people, medieval folk are simultaneously cast as "puerile, quick to fly into a rage and then just as quick to swing to almost equally violent and public displays of remorse" and also "benighted, insentient, too brutalized or primitive to have a subtle emotional life."[48]

Medieval affect offers a prime site for methodological consideration because the realm of feeling brings us so close to our own unself-conscious notions of the person: what motivates action, what constitutes perception, what it is to be human. When we write histories of the past in which

violence done by the woman's family, see Gregory of Tours, *Decem Libri Historiarum* 6.36 (p. 307).

[47] Stearns, "Study of Emotion," p. 187, and see Stearns and Stearns, *Anger,* pp. 18–28, for the panoply of mythic stereotypes about "premodern" people's feelings. For a deft consideration of the role that the *longue durée* has come to play in historical writing about early medieval Europe, see the introductory chapter in Guy Halsall, *Settlement and Social Organization: The Merovingian Region of Metz* (Cambridge: Cambridge University Press, 1995).

[48] Miller, *Humiliation,* pp. 93–94. Particularly acute is Miller's attention to the way these same stereotypes are deployed in contemporary middle-class discourse about the poor.

feeling is omitted, we implicitly disregard fundamental aspects of the terms on which people act and interact, and we thus deprive ourselves of important evidence for the framework of understanding in which our subjects conducted the business of their lives. Conversely, even beginning to account for the affective dimensions of medieval life involves us in forms of historicist imagination and attention for which no critical language has as yet been formalized. In a wholly different context, Inga Clendinnen has written that "to offer interpretations without acknowledging their uncertain ground would be less than candid, while to state only what is certainly known would be to leave unexplored what matters most."[49] Explorers of medieval emotion might well consider this a motto.

[49] Inga Clendinnen, preface to *Ambivalent Conquests* (Cambridge: Cambridge University Press, 1987).

PART II

KINGS AND EMPERORS

CHAPTER THREE

Ira Regis: Prolegomena to a History of Royal Anger

GERD ALTHOFF

Whoever reads the penalty clauses of royal diplomas will often find the following or similar provisions: "and if anyone tries to do this, let him know that he will incur our anger, and moreover will have to pay one hundred pounds of gold." The formulaic language of the royal chancellery thus threatens anyone who would dare to defy the king's commands with the royal anger, in addition to a fine.[1] Just as the king had a broad palette of possible ways to display his grace and mercy openly, he could, evidently, also express the exact opposite.[2] Royal anger thus appears as part of his "rulership practice," that is, as part of a personally grounded system of rulership based on a range of unwritten laws. This system has, until now, attracted little attention; in particular, the significance of its forms of demonstrative expression and of their function has not been recognized. It would, however, contribute a great deal to our understanding of public action in the Middle Ages to observe more closely how one staged the just, the mild, and the merciful king, how one

Translated by Warren Brown.

[1] "Quod si facere quis temptaverit, sciat se nostram iram incurrere et insuper auri libras centum compositurum." The quoted example comes from *Die Urkunden Heinrichs III,* no. 315, ed. Harry Bresslau and Paul Kehr, MGH DD 5:431. In addition to *ira,* the terms *indignatio* and *offensa* communicated the same meaning; cf. Rudolf Köstler, *Huldentzug als Strafe: Eine kirchenrechtliche Untersuchung,* Kirchenrechtliche Abhandlungen 62 (Stuttgart: Enke Verlag, 1910), pp. 16–18.

[2] See Gerd Althoff, "Huld: Überlegungen zu einem Zentralbegriff der mittelalterlichen Herrschaftsordnung," *Frühmittelalterlichen Studien* 25 (1991): 260 and n. 6, 263–65; Geoffrey Koziol, *Begging Pardon and Favor: Ritual and Political Order in Early Medieval France* (Ithaca: Cornell University Press, 1992).

displayed royal virtues in concrete situations and acts, and what aims were bound up with such a display. It would be just as interesting to observe how the royal anger threatened in diplomas found expression in specific situations—for anger is in no way a royal virtue.

If one sets out, according to these premises, to observe the indignant and angry king in action, one makes a surprising discovery. Descriptions of a merciless or even angry king and the depiction of his behavior in such situations are rare, at least in the sources most favored by historians, namely, diplomas and historiography. Medieval literature, in contrast, offers a broader spectrum of the possible expressions of anger that stood at the disposal of kings and other people.[3]

This discovery is even more striking when compared to the fact that the historiographical sources never tire of describing royal favor. Every medievalist is familiar with descriptions of how honorably (*honorifice*) or magnificently (*magnifice*) people were received by the king, how wonderfully they were handled and entertained, and how they were loaded down with gifts and finally sent home with all possible honor. Demonstrations of favor belonged fundamentally to royal self-presentation and to the representation of rulership; as such they revealed the character of that rulership.[4] It would not be too far off the mark, therefore, to ask how far it matched the character of that rulership to express ostentatiously the opposite of favor as well. This question has to deal above all with anger. It must not be overlooked that anger had a firm place in the medieval sin catalogs as one of the deadly sins that arose out of the Original Sin.[5]

The much read text *De duodecim abusivis saeculi* (On the twelve abuses of the world), known as Pseudo-Cyprian, was of great importance

[3] See, for example, Martin J. Schubert, *Zur Theorie des Gebarens im Mittelalter: Analyse von nichtsprachlicher Äußerung in mittelhochdeutscher Epik. Rolandslied, Eneasroman, Tristan,* Kölner Germanistische Studien 31 (Köln-Wien: Böhlau, 1991), pp. 130–32, 166; Dietmar Peil, *Die Gebärde bei Chrétien, Hartmann und Wolfram: Erec—Iwein—Parzifal,* Medium Aevum: Philologische Studien 28 (Munich: Wilhelm Fink, 1975), pp. 223–25. The classic discussion of this subject is in Erich Köhler, *Ideal und Wirklichkeit in der höfischen Epik: Studien zur Form der frühen Artus- und Graldichtung,* 2d ed., Beihefte zur Zeitschrift für romanische Philologie 97 (Tübingen: Niemeyer, 1970), pp. 112–13, 133–134.

[4] See on this Thomas Cramer, "Brangend und brogend: Repräsentation, Feste und Literatur in der höfischen Kultur des späten Mittelalters," in *Höfische Repräsentation: Das Zeremoniell und die Zeichen,* ed. H. Ragotsky and H. Wenzel (Tübingen: Niemeyer, 1990), pp. 259–79, esp. pp. 259–61; Thomas Zotz, "Präsenz und Repräsentation: Beobachtungen zur königlichen Herrschaftspraxis im hohen und späten Mittelalter," in *Herrschaft als soziale Praxis,* ed. A. Lüdtke, Veröffentlichungen des Max-Plank-Instituts für Geschichte 91 (Göttingen: Vandenhoeck & Rüprecht, 1991), pp. 168–94, pp. esp. 172–74; Althoff, "Huld."

[5] On sin catalogs: Heinrich Fichtenau, "Askese und Laster in der Anschauung des Mittelalters," in *Beiträge zur Mediävistik: Ausgewählte Aufsätze* 1 (Stuttgart: Hiersemann, 1975), pp. 64–66; see also the article "Zorn," in *Lexikon für Theologie und Kirche,* ed. J. Höfer and K. Rahner, 2d. ed. (Freiburg: Herder, 1965), 10:1403–5; Maria Gothein, "Die Todsünden," in *Archiv für Religionswissenschaft* 10 (1907): 416–18.

for the medieval rulership ethic. The ninth *abusio* of this text treats the subject of the unjust king (*rex iniquus*).[6] In order not to count as such, the medieval king had to fulfill certain requirements, which were grouped under the central heading of "justice" (*iustitia*). At the same time, the king was summoned to self-discipline, which fundamentally meant "to put aside anger, . . . not to elevate the spirit with prosperity, to bear every adversity patiently (iracundiam differre, . . . prosperitatibus animum non elevare, cuncta adversa patienter ferre). Anger and its expressions are diametrically opposed to these postulates. In the Carolingian-era Mirrors of Princes, moreover, piety (*pietas*), clemency (*clementia*), mercy (*misericordia*), and patience (*patientia*) appeared next to *iustitia* as cardinal virtues of rulership.[7] These represent a complete array of virtues that are difficult to reconcile with expressions of royal anger. Theoretically—and it is important to stress this—the ruler was held to mildness, mercy, kindness, and patience; there was no room for expressions of his anger.

Now it would certainly be foolish to represent hastily the theoretical construct presented by the Mirrors of Princes as reality. It was undoubtedly both known and understood in the Middle Ages that rulership had to be respected and feared in order to be effective. Rulership, according to this view, also required *terror,* that is, compulsion and fear, in order to enforce orders and instructions.[8] Such *terror* would have found adequate expression above all in royal anger. The uses of royal anger and its acceptance, therefore, provide evidence for the degree to which the Christian ideal of rulership coincided with the actual behavior of rulers, that is, whether reality approached the ideal or whether—as in other arenas—ideal and reality existed as two separate realms that one did not even try to bring into resonance, "because that assumes perfection."[9]

[6] Siegmund Hellman, *Pseudo-Cyprianus, De duodecim abusivis saeculi,* Texte und Untersuchungen zur Geschichte der altchristlichen Literatur 34 (Leipzig: Hinrichs'sche Buchhandlung, 1910), pp. 51–53; cf. Eugen Ewig, "Zum christlichen Königsgedanken im Frühmittelalter," in *Das Königtum. Seine geistigen und rechtlichen Grundlagen,* Vorträge und Forschungen 3 (Konstanz: Thorbecke, 1956), pp. 37–39; Hans Hubert Anton, *Fürstenspiegel und Herrscherethos in der Karolingerzeit,* Bonner Historische Forschungen 32 (Bonn: Röhrscheid, 1968), pp. 68–70; Matthias Becher, *Eid und Herrschaft: Untersuchungen zum Herrscherethos Karls des Großen,* Vorträge und Untersuchungen 39 (Sigmaringen: Thorbecke, 1993), pp. 167–68.

[7] Cf. Anton, *Fürstenspiegel,* pp. 80–82; see also Rudolf Schieffer, "Der geistliche Einfluß auf den Herrscher," in *Herrschaftsrepräsentationen im ottonischen Sachsen,* ed. G. Althoff and E. Schubert, Vorträge und Forschungen, in press.

[8] Cf. Karl J. Leyser, *Rule and Conflict in an Early Medieval Society. Ottonian Saxony* (London: Edward Arnold, 1979), pp. 35–36; Heinrich Fichtenau, *Arenga: Spätantike und Mittelalter im Spiegel von Urkundenformeln,* MIÖG Erg. Bd. 18 (Graz-Köln: Hermann Böhlaus Nachf., 1957), pp. 38, 45, 62 n. 165, 176–77; Ewig, "Königsgedanken," pp. 31–33 and n. 94, 40.

[9] This represents a judgment by Adam of Bremen concerning the impossibility of following the rule of celibacy. The sentence also appears to provide a key to the medieval understanding of rules, and of adherence to them, in other areas. Cf. Adam of Bremen, *Gesta Hammaburgensis ecclesiae pon-*

The following presents the results of an investigation that took place with the question, How did contemporaries describe the king's anger and how did they judge it? An examination of different time periods should provide clues as to whether or not attitudes toward royal anger underwent any significant changes. It seems almost unnecessary to stress that this investigation can make no claims to completeness; it represents instead a prelude to an as yet unwritten history of anger.

The angry king was well known to late antiquity and the earliest Middle Ages. The ruler openly displayed anger when he decided to go to war. The outbreak of war could be described in the following fashion: "as this decision on the part of the Romans was delivered to Attila, he grew very angry."[10] Such anger also found demonstrative expression in the abuse of one's enemies. Priscus relates elsewhere concerning Attila: "when he was angry, he used to say that his servants were generals [of Theodosius]; he himself, however, had generals of the same rank as the Emperor of the Romans."[11] One of the indispensable skills of an envoy during this period was the ability to react skillfully to the demonstrative anger of his opposite number and defuse it. Thus it was reported of the emperor Justin II that he gave an embassy from the Avars the following lecture: "envoys should be men who understand exactly when they should speak humbly and when proudly, and who look out for that which will still our anger."[12]

The anger of the Merovingian kings, and also queens, is just as omnipresent in the writings of Gregory of Tours. Gregory often characterizes extreme actions by the kings as the result of their anger: "But he, enraged . . . " (At ille ira commotus . . .).[13] Merovingians reacted to deception, treason, insult, or other abuse with fury; this had the consequence that they called out their army or revenged themselves in another fashion on those who had aroused their anger. An outbreak of anger appears more often to have been demonstratively linked to the stripping away of clothes

---

tificum 3.31.76, ed. Bernhard Schmeidler, MGH SSrG 2:173: "Admoneo vos, inquit, et postulans iubeo, ut pestiferis mulierum vinculis absolvamini, aut, si ad hoc non potestis cogi, quod perfectorum est, saltem cum verecundia vinculum matrimonii custodite, secundum illud, quod dicitur: 'Si non caste, tamen caute.'"

10 Cf. Walter Pohl, "Konfliktverlauf und Konfliktbewältigung: Römer und Barbaren im frühen Mittelalter," in *Frühmittelalterliche Studien* 26 (1992): 165–207, esp. p. 179 n. 68.

11 Ibid., p. 187 n. 91.

12 Ibid., p. 196; quotation from Corippus, *In laudem Justini minoris* 3.310–15, ed. K. Halm, MGH AA 3:145.

13 Gregorii episcopi Turonensis, *Decem libri historiarum*, ed. B. Krusch and W. Levison, MGH SSrerMerov 1, for example, 6.11 (p. 281), 6.17 (p. 286), 6.26 (pp. 293–94), or 6.35 (p. 305): "Nuntiatis his reginae, maiore furore succenditur"; 7.14 (p. 336): "Tunc rex his verbis succensus"; 2.41 (p. 91): "Ob hanc causam Chlodovechus indignans, contra eum abiit"; 3.5 (p. 101): "At illa furore succensa"; 3.10 (p. 107): "unde ille maxime commotus, Hispanias appetivit"; 3.31 (p. 126): "Tunc mater eius contra eam frendens, exercitum commovit."

or to other dishonoring acts. Queen Fredegund reacted in this manner when she learned from her former mayor of the palace Leonardus that her daughter had been robbed and dishonored under his escort, while he himself had fled: "When she heard this, she flew into a rage (furore commota), made him take off his own clothes in the church, and ordered him, without clothes and without the weapons-harness that he had received from King Chilperic as a present, to depart from her sight. Even the cooks and bakers, or other persons, whom she heard had returned from this journey, she had lashed, stripped, and mutilated."[14]

Gregory also reports, however, that the Merovingian kings used subtler methods to express their anger. King Theudebald ostensibly told threatening fables when he was angry:

> He was, as they say, mean spirited, and when he grew angry with someone, because he suspected him of enriching themselves on his property, he invented the following fable and told it to him: a snake discovered a bottle full of wine. It crept through the mouth of the bottle and greedily sucked out what was inside. The snake, however, grew so swollen with the wine it had drunk, that it could no longer creep out of the opening through which it had crept in. The owner of the wine appeared, as the snake tried and failed to escape, and said to it: "first give up what you have swallowed; then you can go free." By means of this fable he aroused great anger and hatred against himself.[15]

Royal anger is also implicit in the famous episode of the pitcher, in which King Clovis asked for a pitcher from the booty of his army for himself, in order to return it to the church from which it had been taken. A jealous warrior invoked the drawing of lots in the division of the booty and smashed the pitcher to keep it from the king. "This plunged everyone into confusion, but the king bore the insult with mildness and patience, picked up the pitcher, and gave it to the envoys of the church. He preserved the insult done to him, however, deep within his breast."[16] Clovis could not, apparently, display open anger, because he had to accept the dictates of the drawing of lots. His anger found demonstrative expression a year later, however, as he mustered his army on the Marchfield. As Clovis inspected the weapons of the person who had smashed the pitcher, he declared them to be unkempt and worthless. He took the man's ax and threw it to the

[14] Ibid., 7.15 (pp. 336–37); cf. Siegmund Hellman, "Studien zur mittelalterlichen Geschichtsschreibung I: Gregor von Tours," *Historische Zeitschrift* 107 (1911): 1–43.

[15] Ibid., 4.9 (p. 140).

[16] Ibid., 2.27 (p. 72).

ground; as the man moved to pick it up, Clovis killed him with his own ax. Gregory's only comment: "he frightened everyone a great deal with this act."[17]

Demonstrative anger was, however, in no way an exclusive preserve of the Merovingian kings; they could also be the targets of such anger when they aroused the displeasure of their army (*exercitus*). So it happened to King Chlothar, who refused to begin a war against the Saxons because he thought it unjust. The reaction of his warriors was unmistakable: "Then, enraged (ira commoti), they rose up against King Chlothar, ripped up his tent, pursued him with insults, seized hold of him by force, and wanted to kill him if he delayed any further in marching with them. When Chlothar saw this, he set off unwillingly with them to war."[18]

Royal anger of the kind discussed above also appears in the sources for the early Carolingians, as for example in the Continuation of the Chronicle of Pseudo-Fredegar, written under the supervision of Carolingian followers: "the enraged King Pippin, after the entire army of the Franks had been assembled . . . burned up the greatest part of the land [of the Saxons]."[19] One had already formulated matters thus in the Merovingian period. At the same time, however, a new leitmotif appears in the descriptions of the actions and accompanying emotions of these Carolingians: "The merciful King Pippin, moved by compassion, granted him life and kingdom."[20] Clemency (*clementia),* compassion (*misericordia*), and other Christian rulership virtues now become recognizably more important to the presentation of the fit king (*rex idoneus*) than anger. Let there be no misunderstanding, however: although the kings are represented in this fashion, whether they actually behaved this way is another question.

An investigation of the principal sources for the history of Charlemagne shows that the early Carolingian period in fact marks a caesura in the depiction of royal anger; the Carolingian Royal Annals as well as Einhard's *Life of Charlemagne* have no place for royal anger. Just the opposite: when the Royal Annals characterize Charlemagne with adjectives—which they do frequently—these are clearly fixated on the previously

[17] Ibid., 2.27 (p. 73).
[18] Ibid., 4.14 (p. 146).
[19] *Chronicarum quae dicuntur Fredegarii Scholastici continuationes*, c. 35, ed. Bruno Krusch, MGH SSrerMerov 2:182–83: "Pippinus rex ira commotus, commoto omni exercitu Francorum . . . Saxonia . . . maxime igne concremavit."; similarly c. 42 (pp. 186–87).
[20] Ibid., 37 (pp. 183–84): "Praefatus rex Pippinus clemens ut erat misericordia motus vitam ei et regnum concessit"; in a similar vein c. 38 (p. 185): "rex Pippinus solito more iterum misericordia motus."; also c. 43 (p. 187): "clementiam sue pietatis absolvit"; already in the characterization of the mayor of the palace Grimoald, c. 6 (p. 172): "fuitque vir mitissimus, omni bonitate et mansuetudine repletus, largus in elemosinis et in orationibus promptus."

mentioned Christian rulership virtues: "most gentle" (*mitissimus*), "mildest" (*piisimus*), and "most merciful" (*clementissimus*).[21] Einhard's presentation of Charles follows exactly the same line. Anger is a failing from which Charles is completely free: "Following his father's death, after he had divided the kingdom with his brother [Carloman], he bore [his brother's] enmity and hatred with such patience that it appeared extraordinary to everyone how he did not allow himself even once to be aroused to anger."[22] In addition to the patience stressed here, Einhard describes Charles's kindness and mildness as inborn traits that earned him the love and affection of his subjects: "people conspired against the king both times only because, having given in too much to the cruelty of his wife, he seemed to have departed from his inborn kindness and his accustomed mildness in a frightening manner. In general, he enjoyed throughout his life, both at home and abroad, the highest and most widespread love and affection, so that not even the slightest accusation of unjust severity was ever raised against him by anyone."[23]

Piisimus and *mitissimus* are also adjectives used by Thegan to describe Louis the Pious in his biography, once again in comparison to the antithetical picture of the angry king: "In the same year, the twenty first of his rule, [Louis] granted forgiveness to everyone who had been forced to abandon him. And this was in no way hard or difficult for him, he who is the mildest (*piissimus*) of the emperors, because he had already forgiven his enemies, fulfilling the Word of the Evangelist, where it is said: 'forgive and you will be forgiven.'"[24]

The rejection of the angry king in favor of the patient, mild, and ever forgiving sovereign, conspicuous in every source investigated, directly reflects a growing ecclesiastical influence on the ruler. This is well known for the centuries that follow as a characteristic of the nature of royal rulership.[25] If the Church, on the one hand, offered the ruler the advantage of sacral legitimacy and thereby a stabilization of his rule, it demanded from kings, on the other hand, conduct in line with Christian claims and norms. Claims were not always easy to bring into accord with reality, but behind them stood expectations that the king could not overlook with impunity. It does not appear advisable, therefore, to dismiss the reality of

21 *Annales regni Francorum*, ed. F. Kurze, MGH SSrG 6, a. 772 (*mitissimus*); a. 781; a. 787; a. 788 (*piissimus*); a. 778 (*clementissimus*); in general for a critque of the representation in the Royal Annals see Becher, *Eid und Herrschaft*, pp. 25–26, 36–37, 45–47, 52–53, 59–60, 64–65, 74–76.

22 *Einhardi vita Karoli Magni*, c. 18, ed. G. Waitz, MGH SSrG 25:22.

23 Ibid., 20 (p. 26).

24 *Thegani vita Hludovici imperatoris*, c. 49, ed. G. H. Pertz, MGH SS 2:201; the epithet *mitissimus* is in c. 50 (p. 601).

25 See the detailed treatment in Schieffer, "Der geistliche Einfluß auf den Herrscher."

the quoted descriptions of the *rex piisimus, clementissimus,* and *mitissimus* out of hand. And it is anything but surprising that the kings who were so described were credited with the mastery of their anger.

The Christian rulership ethic that developed under the Carolingians remained binding for the emperors and kings of the following centuries. This was true even though the Mirror of Princes as a literary genre was specific to the Carolingian period, before it bloomed again in the twelfth and following centuries.[26] The fact that no Mirrors of Princes were written in the tenth and eleventh centuries, however, does not mean that attempts to require the obedience of kings and emperors to the dictates of the Christian rulership ethic had faded. The ideological content of the Mirrors of Princes appears in the introductions to diplomas, in liturgical protocols, in pictures, and in historiography. It is certain, therefore, that rulers were continually reminded of their duty to the virtues of *patientia, clementia,* and *misericordia* and to the behaviors that went with them. Expressions of anger stood in opposition to this image of the Christian ruler. Consistent with this, the description of royal anger did not belong to the inventory of ruler representations. It will be enough to present two testimonials to this fact. The first is Widukind of Corvey and his conjuration of royal *clementia,* expressed in the programmatic address to the dedicatee of the work, the imperial daughter and abbess Mathilde, and also presented as a characteristic feature of Otto the Great: "the clemency that always lay near to him" (*vicina sibi semper clementia*).[27] The second is Wipo, the biographer of Conrad II, who wraps the elevation to the kingship of his titular hero in an abundance of admonishments reminiscent of the Mirrors of Princes, at the center of which stands the royal *clementia.*[28] The king's actions, by which he demonstratively proves his willingness and ability to act according to the dictates of *clementia* and *iustitia,* amplify these admonishments. Anger explicitly belongs to those things against which the Archbishop of Mainz warns the king before his entry into office: "When now this almighty King of Kings, author and beginning of all honors, lets the grace of an office flow over the princes of

[26] Cf. Wilhelm Berges, *Die Fürstenspiegel des hohen und späten Mittelalters,* Schriften der MGH 2 (Stuttgart: Hiersemann, 1952), pp. 3–5.

[27] *Widukindi monachi corbeiensis rerum gestarum saxonicarum libri tres* 2.29, ed. P. Hirsch and H.-E. Lohmann, MGH SSrG 60:91; cf. Helmut Beumann, *Widukind von Korvei: Untersuchungen zur Geschichtsschreibung und Ideengeschichte des 10. Jahrhunderts,* Abhandlungen über Corveyer Geschichtsschreibung 3 (Weimar: Walter de Gruyter, 1950), pp. 113–15; in general see Gerd Althoff, "Widukind von Corvey: Kronzeuge und Herausforderung," *Frühmittelalterliche Studien* 27 (1993): 253–73; Karl J. Leyser, *Rule and Conflict,* pp. 35–36, has collected the references to the anger of Otto the Great. None of them, however, imply a positive valuation of anger.

[28] Cf. Wipo, "Gesta Chonradi II. imperatoris," in *Wiponis Opera,* c. 3, ed. H. Bresslau, MGH SSrG 61:20–22; c. 5 (pp. 26–27).

the earth, it will be, according to the nature of its source, pure and clean. If it should fall, however, on people who carry such a dignity unworthily and sully it with pride, envy, desire, greed, anger, impatience, and severity, then they will drink for themselves and their subjects the dangerous drink of injustice."[29]

The thesis of the above sketch—that the postulates of the Christian rulership ethic prevented the depiction of royal anger—can also be tested in the opposite fashion. Anger as a determinant of royal action appears at exactly that moment when the king is to be revealed as unjust (*rex iniquus*). Anger functioned, in other words, as proof that a ruler could not meet the demands of his office. It is no accident that this stands out especially clearly in the judgments of Henry IV by his many opponents. The *Book of the Saxon War* by the Merseburg cleric Bruno provides an excellent example. This book was conceived as a documentation of the crimes of Henry IV in the form of history. It was meant to function as the indictment (*liber accusatorius*) needed for a hearing on the case of Henry IV, held to decide whether or not he should remain the rightful king.[30] In Bruno's presentation, anger fundamentally determines royal actions and decisions. Bruno employs this evaluation both explicitly and implicitly as an accusation of the most serious kind:

> As now the king's anger—ever more strongly inflamed against us with the passage of time—could no longer remain hidden, and as it had already become clear by certain signs what evil he thought to do to us, our princes, singly and together, continually sent embassies to the king, sometimes with and sometimes without letters. They directed only this one urgent request to him, namely, that he summon an assembly of his princes, so that he might, in its presence, either show them their guilt and punish them according to their sentence or allow them to demonstrate their innocence by some test and remain as before in his grace. But they received no gracious response (pietatis responsum) from him, and recognized that he sought their ruin exclusively and in every way; therefore they directed em-

[29] Ibid., 3, p. 21: "Is omnipotens rex regum, totius honoris auctor et principium, quando in principes terrae alicuius dignitatis gratiam transfundit, quantum ad naturam principii pura est et munda. Cum autem pervenerit ad eos, qui hanc dignitatem indigne tractaverint et eam cum superbia, invidia, libidine, avaritia, ira, impatientia, crudelitate polluerint, sibi et omnibus subiectis, nisi poenitendo se purgaverint, periculosum potum iniquitatis propinabunt."

[30] Cf. Gerd Althoff, "Pragmatische Geschichtsschreibung und Krisen I: Zur Funktion von Brunos Buch vom Sachsenkrieg," in *Pragmatische Schriftlichkeit im Mittlelalter: Erscheinungsformen und Entwicklungsstufen*, ed. H. Keller, K. Grubmüller, and N. Staubach, Münstersche Mittelalter-schriften 65 (Munich: Wilhelm Fink, 1992), esp. pp. 97–99; see also Monika Suchan, *Die Causa Heinrichs IV.*, Monographien zur Geschichte des Mittelalters, in press.

> bassies to the nearby princes and asked them humbly to calm the anger of the king.[31]

Bruno then inserted into his presentation a letter about this situation, which the archbishop of Magdeburg had sent to his colleague in Mainz. The letter ends with an urgent appeal:

> Present this to our lord [Henry IV] and advise him, by the fear of God, to consider that we are also men, so that he does not, to the danger of his soul, drive us to ruin though we be innocent. If your Highness should turn out to be unscrupulous and of little conscience in this matter, God's strict justice will demand our souls from you. If, however, the king does not want to listen to your just advice, then we ask and charge you, that you and yours will at least not permit yourselves to be used as the tools of his anger, and endanger life and soul by serving his rage.[32]

Both Bruno's representation and the archbishop's letter contrast with the Saxons' attempts to reach an amicable compromise, according to the customs governing the handling of conflict, with the anger-driven behavior of the king, support of which would endanger the salvation of one's soul. This argumentation effectively uses the postulates and prohibitions of the Christian rulership ethic in order to characterize and to condemn Henry. Bruno ends his "statement for the prosecution" with exactly this accent:

> they barely managed in the end to extract from the king, who was more worn down by our persistence than moved by pity (pietas), the answer that they could only recover his goodwill when they unconditionally handed over themselves, their freedom and everything that they possessed into the king's power. This, however, they refused to do, because they had often found in the past that he was totally without compassion (pietas).[33]

Henry's actions are, according to this evaluation, determined by anger instead of *pietas.* One can hardly characterize the *rex iniquus* more appropriately.

Anger also dictated, in Bruno's opinion, Henry's reaction to the destruction of the Harzburg:

[31] Bruno, *Brunos Buch vom Sachsenkrieg,* c. 41, ed. H.-E. Lohmann, MGH Deutsches Mittelalter 2:40–41.
[32] Ibid., 42 (p. 43).
[33] Ibid., 43 (p. 43).

> In the meantime, he revenged himself for the destruction of his fortress, not exactly as he wanted, but as well as he could at that moment, and ordered all castles and fortifications in this land to be torn down, with the exception of the old strongholds that had been built for the honor of the kingdom. That this order came not from the quiet strength of righteousness, however, but rather from the passionate agitation of an angry heart, was especially visible in the fact that he ordered many castles destroyed against which nothing evil had been said; on the other hand, he permitted many that were infamous for robberies and plunderings to stand, when money was offered him.[34]

Once more, a Christian rulership virtue—*iustitia*—is cleverly juxtaposed against the anger that determines Henry's actions, and a clear judgment is thereby delivered about those actions.[35]

According to Bruno, the princes of the Empire had already referred to the obligations of the Christian ruler when they gave Henry this advice: "If he had already, by his own fault, lost a land blessed with every good thing because he had naively followed foolish advice, then they would counsel him, if he wanted to listen to them, to let go of his anger (furor), to demonstrate himself to the peoples under him to be just and mild (iustus et pius) as was fit for a king, and to listen no more to those whose bad advice had led him into error."[36]

In all of the cases cited, allusions to royal anger have the function of highlighting Henry's failings as a ruler and of outlining the counterimage of the Christian king. That serious accusations were leveled thereby can be demonstrated once more by counterevidence. The sources that defend Henry and adjudge his actions as justified—specifically the *Carmen de bello saxonico* (Song on the Saxon War) and the *Vita henrici quarti imperatoris* (Life of the Emperor Henry the Fourth)—have no place for anger. Instead, they stress the king's *pietas* and *clementia* entirely according to the tradition discussed above.[37] In contrast, anger dictates the actions of

[34] Ibid., 34 (p. 36).

[35] See, similarly, Lampert von Hersfeld, "Annales," in *Lamperti monachi Hersfeldensis opera,* ed. O. Holder-Egger, MGH SSrG 38, a. 1075 (p. 277), a. 1075 (p. 319), a. 1076 (p. 363), with the accusations raised by the Saxons against Henry IV, in which his anger is used as an argument; this argument also appears in the characterization of Anno of Cologne and of the citizenry of Cologne: a. 1074 (pp. 238–39).

[36] Bruno, *Sachsenkrieg* 30 (p. 33).

[37] *Carmen de bello saxonico* 1.5.8, ed. O. Holder-Egger, MGH SSrG 17:1: "nulli pietate secundum"; 2.5.204 (p. 13): "Supplicibus mitis, contrarius atque superbis"; 3.5.253 (p. 22): "Quis vel nunc veniam clementia regia donat"; 3.5.278 (p. 22): "Subdere clementi, supplex substernere miti". The *Vita Henrici quarti imperatoris,* ed. W. Wattenbach, MGH SSrG 58, stresses Henry's mildness in, for

Henry's enemies.[38] The *Carmen de bello saxonico* ends programmatically: "now show those who now beseech you, or who will do so in the future, what they have to hope from you when they give themselves up to you, mild King."[39] The emphatic praise of the ruler in the first chapter of the *Vita Henrici* also follows this motif: "O praise the outstanding man of piety and humility!"[40] Only once does the *Carmen* present Henry as inflamed by anger. The cause was the desecration of churches and graves by the Saxons: "As soon as the king, who is extraordinarily mild and brave in battle, heard of this crime, his heart burned, inflamed with the desire for justice, and anger against such presumption gripped him. Wild rage burned in his just heart; it was not that his rights but that those of God had been infringed which pained him."[41] Here the extremity of the crime permitted anger in a just cause, which concerned not the king's own interests but rather the rights of God. Only because of this did Henry, according to this picture, depart from his accustomed mildness.

Later developments show that a new motif appears here, one that will later grow more pronounced. Just anger, anger in a just cause, anger in the battle for justice and right, all find themselves in the twelfth century more frequently included in the praise of the ruler. *Iustitia* as a maxim for the deeds of the ruler assumes greater importance than *clementia,* a shift that makes possible once again praise for the ruler who employs anger as a weapon in the fight for *iustitia.* Otto of Freising and Rahewin, the biographers of Frederick Barbarossa, provide important evidence for this transformation.[42] Otto presents the new motif right away in his description of Barbarossa's elevation to the kingship: the king, even on this joyous occasion, refused to honor a minister's request for forgiveness, although it was made prostrate at the king's feet. Strict justice (*rigor iustitiae*) took precedence for Barbarossa. Interestingly, it took precedence not over *clementia* but rather over the crime of absolution (*vitium remissionis*). Forgiveness

---

example, c. 2 (p. 14): "mitius tamen quam culpa exigeret, correxit"; c. 4 (p. 18): "sed sciens in ultione freno uti, longe infra metam culpae cohibebat habenas vindictae."

[38] *Carmen* 1.5.28 (p. 2): "Furor hinc evenerat omnis"; 1.5.63 (p. 3): "Aeque maiores, aeque furuere minores"; 3.5.3 (p. 14): "Concipit immanem diro sub corde furorem"; the *Vita Henrici* contrasts Henry IV with his son of the same name in the context of conflict in c. 9 (p. 31): "hinc pater, inde filius, hinc pietas, inde furor consedit."

[39] *Carmen* 3.5.293–94 (p. 23): "Nunc tibi supplicibus propone quibusque futuris, Quid de te sperent, dum se tibi, rex pie, dedent."

[40] *Vita Henrici* 1 (p. 11): "O virum pietatis et humilitatis laude insignem!"

[41] *Carmen* 3.5.44–49 (p. 15): "Nec mora, percepto rex magnus crimine tanto, Egregia pietate nitens, fortissimus armis, Zelo iusticiae flammato pectore fervet, Adversum tantos praesumptus colligit iras; Ignescunt animi iusto sub corde feroces; Non sua iam, sed iura Dei violata dolebat."

[42] Bishop Otto of Freising and Rahewin, *Die Taten Friedrichs oder richtiger Cronica,* ed. F.-J. Schmale, trans. A. Schmidt, Ausgewählte Quellen zur deutschen Geschichte des Mittelalters: Freiherr vom Stein—Gedächtnisausgabe 17 (Darmstadt: Wissenschaftliche Buchgesellschaft, 1965).

is judged pejoratively just as clearly as anger or lack of pity was earlier.[43] Not only royal strictness, however, but also royal anger governs Barbarossa's actions in the picture painted by his biographers. The admittedly most drastic example will be quoted first, in order to give an impression of the consequences that Barbarossa's anger could have:

> As the emperor on his return learned of the stiff-necked stubbornness of his enemies, indignation and also anger gripped him over the fact that they, who in their nearly extreme distress should have humbly asked for mercy, still attacked, and did not shy away from harassing their conquerors, although they were shut in by an oppressive siege. Several times already they had tried in their sorties to set fire to the siege machines, or to destroy towers, or to fatally wound several of our people, and no opportunity for boldness or brawling presented itself that they, ignorant of their approaching fate, let slip by; and whereas one assumed that their bravado was already broken, they arrogantly celebrated what they had done. It was a terrifying sight, when those who were outside the walls cut off the heads of the dead and played with them like balls, and threw them from the right into the left hand, and thereby horribly swaggered and made fun; the people in the city, however, considering it to be dishonorable if they dared any less, maimed without mercy, limb by limb on the walls, prisoners from our army, and thereby offered a woeful theater. Frederick was, for a while, sad and justifiably indignant about these failures. Since he could not dam up the fighting spirit of these lunatics, and the awe of the Emperor could not restrain their grim frenzy, he decided to inflict a strict punishment on those headstrong people, in order at least to tame, by the unmistakable finality of the death penalty, those whom patient gentleness had not brought to the right path. He ordered, therefore, that revenge be taken on their prisoners and that these be hanged on gibbets before the gates. But that stubborn people, who all too gladly paid things back in the same coin, dragged several of our people, who lay in chains, in the same manner to their execution and hanged them on a cross. Then Frederick spoke: "Has our humanity itself called out even those committed to destruction against us? Have you nourished your insolence on our gentleness? Up until now, we have spared you despite the battle, have taken mercy on your prisoners, have held faith with our hostages, have unwillingly brought siege engines against your walls, and have

[43] See Otto of Freising, *Cronica* 2.3 (pp. 286–88); cf. Gerd Althoff, "Konfliktverhalten und Rechtsbewußtsein: Die Welfen in der Mitte des 12. Jahrhunderts," *Frühmittelalterliche Studien* 26 (1992): 331–52, 338 n. 25.

> always held our warriors, who are hungry for your blood, in check. You hold all this for naught, and provoke us to your destruction, to the extermination of your sons and grandsons. So will I apply the laws of war, so will I fight with your obstinacy and no longer spare you, who have not wanted to spare yourselves." Thus he spoke, and, enraged that those who found themselves in the condition of prisoners had placed themselves on the same level with the victors, he announced by means of a herald that they would not be permitted any longer to seek refuge with him and to hope for mercy; for no one would be spared. They should instead fight with all their strength and look to their own salvation as best they could, for he would from now on let himself be guided in everything by the laws of war. Then he ordered their hostages, forty in number, to be brought out and executed. In the meantime, several prisoners, namely six distinguished knights from Milan who had been seized while holding treasonous conversations with the Piacentini, were brought forth. For Piacenza, as reported above, remained at that time faithful to the emperor only with feigned devotion and false obedience. One of the prisoners brought forward was, however, a nephew of the bishop of Milan, a rich man, whose counsel all of the Ligurians trusted to an extraordinary degree. These men he ordered to be led to execution, disregarding their promises of rich ransoms, and so the end of their lives was the same as that of those mentioned previously.[44]

Indignation (*indignatio*) and anger (*ira*) are repeatedly mentioned here as the motives for Barbarossa's actions. These actions not only repaid injuries in kind but also, via the declaration that no one would be spared, fundamentally renounced royal clemency, at least in this case. No hint of criticism of Barbarossa's behavior, it must be stressed, appears in Rahewin's presentation.

Royal anger is similarly presented in a neutral or a positive light in several other places. "Enraged" (indignatione motus), Barbarossa turned his army against Milan after he and his army had been led astray into infertile regions by the Milanese consuls. According to Otto's version of events, it made Barbarossa's anger worse that because of their hunger and the bad weather everyone was inciting him against Milan. A further ground for his bitterness lay in the fact that the Milanese wanted to divert him from his legal position with money.[45] Chroniclers had not represented royal behavior in this fashion in previous centuries. "Inflamed by

[44] Otto of Freising, *Cronica* 4.55–56 (pp. 612–14).
[45] Ibid., 2.18 (p. 314).

righteous indignation" (iusta indignatione inflammatus), Barbarossa interrupted a speech by Roman envoys.[46] Repeatedly increased *indignatio* was also his reason for personally, and "not without the greatest danger" (non sine maximo periculo), overcoming a steep rise at the siege of Spoleto and penetrating into the city.[47] The account follows the same lines when Otto introduces a report of a campaign against Milan with the comment "and he turned his anger to vanquishing the obstinacy of the Milanese"[48] and when Veronese envoys urged Barbarossa to direct the "thorns of his indignation" (indignationis sue aculeos) against the Milanese and the Romans.[49] The emperor's anger could also turn on his own people, however: "The returning knights heard only threatening words from the princes, and the emperor flayed them with the following words."[50] More examples follow. The angry ruler was once more respectable.

Despite this novel evaluation of royal anger, both biographers and their contemporaries remained aware that "divine as well as human laws require that the greatest mildness must constantly reside in the ruler," as Frederick himself announced in a letter after his victory over Cremona.[51] The Bishop of Piacenza had also admonished Barbarossa in the same vein: "Even if they [the Milanese] are by rights to be put in their place with an extraordinarily heavy penalty, the imperial clemency (clementia) will fittingly exercise such restraint that you will punish their wrong not as they have earned but rather as befits you. The crime of the Milanese must not stand higher for you than your dignity, so that it does not appear as if you were more concerned with stilling your anger than with your good reputation and with justice."[52]

As one might expect, the new conception of the ruler's obligations and behavior did not replace the old but rather accompanied it. Nonetheless, this represents a serious change. The possibility that the ruler might let his actions be dictated by a just anger, and that he might grow angry in his zeal for justice, broadened once again the range of his options and lifted the all too obligatory duty to leniency and forbearance. That this change occurred not just on a theoretical level, but also had serious practical consequences, is demonstrated by the escalation of atrocities during Barbarossa's Italian campaigns, acts that were justified under the catchword *iustitia.* This conclusion is justified even more by subsequent develop-

[46] Ibid., 2.32 (p. 346).
[47] Ibid., 2.37 (pp. 358–60).
[48] Ibid., 2.52 (p. 384): "et ad compescendam Mediolanensium contumaciam iram convertit."
[49] Ibid., 2.47 (p. 376).
[50] Ibid., 3.37 (p. 472).
[51] Ibid., 4.73 (p. 660).
[52] Ibid., 4.26 (p. 576).

ments up to the time of Frederick II, for whom righteous anger was so important that he considered himself the Hammer of the World.[53] Expressions as well as descriptions of royal anger are thus important indicators of a structural change that rulership in general went through beginning in the eleventh century.

The observations sketched here have to be seen against a certain background, namely, the customs governing communication in the time period discussed.[54] Communication in medieval public life was decisively determined by demonstrative acts and behaviors. People revealed their ranks and positions in a multifaceted manner, using signs and firm rules of behavior to express their relationship to one another. Rituals of greeting and of gift exchange belong in this context. All of these signs, sometimes bundled together in rituals and stage performances, had the goal of transmitting a clear and unmistakable message. These customs bestowed a certain security on public interactions. Signals made clear one's intentions for better or for worse; demonstrative behavior created obligations for the future. Friendship was shown by common feasting, hostility by cursing or throwing filth. Similarly, the king demonstrated his determination to go to war with raging anger, his mildness with a flood of tears. Many of the mannerisms of medieval communication, which may appear to us as overemotionalized, were bound up with this demonstrative function—especially the demonstration of anger. It is even more remarkable, however, that after the eighth century anger took a back seat to the gentler emotions in the symbolic repertoire of the king. These observations testify to the effectiveness of the Christian rulership ethic, even though we cannot completely dismiss the possibility that the descriptions of royal anger bear the stamp of this ethic more strongly than behavior in real life. Both the renaissance of royal anger in the twelfth century and the concomitant reappearance of demonstrative anger in the repertoire of royal behaviors strongly suggest that the descriptive and the behavioral planes, even in the centuries previous to the twelfth, did not lie that far apart.

[53] See Klaus J. Heinisch, *Kaiser Friederich II.* in *Briefen und Berichten seiner Zeit* (Darmstadt, Wissenschaftlicher Buchgesellschaft, 1968), p. 471; Frederick II's imperial self-representations and political propaganda, as revealed in the excerpts offered by Heinisch, easily permit the conclusion that royal anger was now freed from the restrictions of the Christian rulership ethic and that it had become a much-used tool of royal self-representation.

[54] See the reflections in Gerd Althoff, "Demonstration und Inszenierung: Spielregeln der Kommunikation in mittelalterlicher Öffentlichkeit," *Frühmittelalterliche Studien* 27 (1993): 27–50; see also Gerd Althoff, *Spielregeln und Kommunikation in mittelalterlichen Herrschaftsordnungen* (Darmstadt: Wissenschaftliche Buchgesellschaft, 1997).

CHAPTER FOUR

"Just Anger" or "Vengeful Anger"? The Punishment of Blinding in the Early Medieval West

GENEVIÈVE BÜHRER-THIERRY

Men in power were not to allow themselves to be carried away by anger—on that both the classical tradition and the Church Fathers were in accord. Such behavior was contrary to the good use of reason and numbered among the principal vices that had to be combated. Alcuin was echoing this tradition when he defined anger as the eighth vice, capable of provoking all sorts of evils and responsible in particular for iniquitous judgments: "Anger is one of the eight principal vices. If it is not controlled by reason, it is turned into raging fury, such that a man has no power over his own soul and does unseemly things. For this vice so occupies the heart that it banishes from it every precaution in acting and in seeking right judgment."[1]

If anger was reprehensible for all mankind, it was still more so for kings, who were supposed to know how to control the movements of their flesh and how not to allow themselves to get carried away, since the essential function of kings was to do justice. Following Gregory the Great, almost all the Mirrors of Princes of the Carolingian period took it upon themselves to remind the sovereign of this task.[2] In particular, Smaragdus of

I thank Jean-Claude Schmitt and Barbara Rosenwein for their useful suggestions.

[1] Alcuin, *Liber de virtutibus et vitiis* 31, PL 101, col. 634: "Ira una est de octo vitiis principalibus, quae si ratione non regitur, in furorem vertitur: ita ut homo sui animi impotens erit, faciens quae non convenit. Haec enim si cordi insidit, omnem eximit ab eo providentiam facti, nec judicium rectae directionis inquirere." For more on this view, see Richard E. Barton's chapter in this volume.

[2] Gregory the Great, *Moralia in Job* 26.28, PL 76, col. 381: "Bene autem sancti viri Scripturae sacrae

Saint-Miheil devoted an entire chapter to this issue in his *Via regia.*[3] Like Alcuin, Smaragdus saw in the anger of the king a major danger: that he would not render justice but rather give himself over to vengeance.[4]

But this conception is not only Christian; it appeared already in the classical Roman period, particularly in the writings of Seneca, where anger was responsible for iniquitous and irreversible judgments.[5] Thus Seneca told of a governor of Syria, carried away by anger (*furens*), who condemned three innocent men to death.[6] During Rome's transformation into an empire, this idea was accentuated in the writings of historians clinging to Senatorial traditions. They stigmatized abuses of power by "evil" emperors and in this way succeeded in defining the tyrant: the ruler who allowed himself to be governed by his impulses and who, in particular, overturned justice through totally arbitrary and enormously cruel sentences.[7]

Only with the first century A.D. and the beginning of the persecution of the Christians did a new sort of judicial penalty appear in the Roman world: different kinds of mutilation, which could be substituted for or added to capital punishment.[8] But if there now existed legislation, which progressively became better established and resulted in a system of afflictive penalties quite precisely codified in the late Empire, there was nowhere mention of blinding. Yet that punishment seems to have been widely practiced against the first Christians, as is demonstrated by numerous passages in the writings of Lactantius; and later it became an archetype of martyrdom.[9] Blinding was even more rarely attested to in Roman law than it was in the barbarian law codes, where it sometimes was the punishment for sacrilegious acts such as setting fire to a church.[10]

---

testimonio reges vocantur, quia praelati cunctis motibus carnis, . . . modo ignem furoris exstinguunt." On this conception of royalty in the Carolingian Mirrors, see Michel Senellart, *Les arts de gouverner. Du regimen médiéval au concept de gouvernement* (Paris: Seuil, 1995), 93–97.

3 Smaragdus of Saint-Mihiel, *Via regia* 24, PL 102, cols. 963–64, a chapter entitled "De reprimenda ira."

4 Ibid.: "Depone ergo, mitissime rex, auxiliante Domino, iram, et noli per iram rederre vindictam."

5 This condemnation of anger should be ranked with the condemnation of all the passions by the Epicurean and Stoic schools in the pursuit of ataraxia. See Pierre de Labriolle, "Apatheia," in *Mélanges Alfred Ernoud* (Paris: Klincksieck, 1940), pp. 215–23.

6 Seneca, *Dialogues* 1: *De ira*, ed. A. Bourgery (Paris: Belles-Lettres, 1922), c. 1–18.

7 Lucien Jerphagnon, "Que le tyran est contre-nature: Sur quelques clichés de l'historiographie romaine," *Cahiers de philosophie politique et juridique* 6 (1984): 41–50.

8 Ramsay Macmullen, "Judicial Savagery in the Roman Empire," in *Changes in the Roman Empire: Essays in the Ordinary* (Princeton: Princeton University Press, 1990), pp. 204–17.

9 Lactantius *De mortibus persecutorum* 36, PL 7, col. 252. For the codification of mutilations in the late Empire, see Clèmence Dupont, *Le droit criminel dans les Constitutions de Constantin*, vol. 2, *Les peines* (Lille: Morelet Corduant, 1955), pp. 18–20. On blinding as martyrdom, see Gudrun Schleusener-Eichholz, *Das Auge im Mittelalter* (Munich: Finck, 1985), pp. 360–62.

10 *Lex Baiwariorum* 1.6, MGH LL 2:274. However, this provision concerns only slaves.

Nevertheless, those in power continued to blind those who dared to oppose them—one reason why this punishment often appeared as the fruit of arbitrary decision, or an abuse of power by the "judge" who had allowed himself to be carried away by anger or by hatred.

Cases of punishment by blinding were, however, rare in the West.[11] Although the practice is sometimes mentioned in the writings of Gregory of Tours, it is always described as the result of the abuse of power by the "bad king" Chilperic: in book 4 of his *Histories,* which is entirely focused on this king, Gregory not only speaks of the cruelty of Chilperic, who behaved as a bad judge—pronouncing unheard-of sentences such as the gouging out of eyes, unknown in Frankish legislation—but also presented him explicitly as a new embodiment of Nero.[12] Indeed, for Gregory, Nero was the very type of the persecutor of Christians.[13] Thus the punishment of blinding was always, in the sixth century, presented in relation to martyrdom on the one hand and to the abuse of power signifying "tyrannical" practices on the other.[14]

By the same token, the gouging out of eyes was certainly part of the authentic martyrdom inflicted in 676 on bishop Leodegar of Autun by his political adversaries, under the direction of the mayor of the palace, Ebroin. Leodegar's *Vita* was composed c. 692 at Saint-Symphorien d'Autun at the request of his successor. The author, a monk who had probably been alive at the time of the events (if he had not in fact been an eyewitness), spoke in chapter 23 of the siege of the city of Autun by an army impelled by "fury" and allied to the "tyrant" Ebroin.[15] Abbot Meroald, who tried to deflect the leader of the expedition by reminding him of the words of the Gospel, "For with what judgment you judge, you shall be judged" (Mat. 7:2), found himself confronting a man as hard-hearted as Pharaoh, who refused to raise the siege until he had satisfied his "fury" by

[11] A nearly exhaustive list of cases of blinding has been made by Meinrad Schaab, "Die Blendung als politische Massnahme im abendländischen Früh-und Hochmittelalter" (dissertation, University of Heidelberg, 1955).

[12] Gregory of Tours, *Decem libri historiarum* 6.46, MGH SSrerMerov 1:320.

[13] Ibid., 1.25 (p. 20): "primus contra Christi cultum persecutionem excitat."

[14] On the figure of Chilperic as the "bad king" and the parallel with Nero in the work of Gregory of Tours, see Martin Heinzelmann, *Gregor von Tours "Zehn Bücher Geschichte": Historiographie und Gesellschaftskonzept im 6. Jahrhundert* (Darmstadt: Wissenschaftliche Buchgesellschaft, 1994), esp. pp. 47–49, 158–65.

[15] *Gesta et passio sancti Leudegarii episcopi et martyris* 18, MGH SSrerMerov 5:299: "Ebroinus tyrrannus." On this *Vita prima,* see Bruno Krusch, "Die älteste Vita Leudegarii," *Neues Archiv* 16 (1891): 563–93; and Joseph-Claude Poulin, "Saint Léger d'Autun et ses premiers biographes (fin VIIe–milieu IXe siècle)," *Bulletin de la Société des Antiquaires de l'Ouest* 14 (1977): 167–200. It is translated into English in *Late Merovingian France: History and Hagiography, 640–720,* ed. and trans. Paul Fouracre and Richard A. Gerberding (Manchester: Manchester University Press, 1996), pp. 193–253.

taking Leodegar prisoner.[16] The bishop therefore decided to give himself up, to save his city from massacre. In their wickedness, his jailers immediately thought of subjecting him to a punishment both inhuman and unnatural by gouging out his eyes: "like wolves they received [him] as booty, contriving the most iniquitous invention as punishment, for they tore from his head the light of his eyes. In this blinding, he was seen to bear the cut of the iron with superhuman strength."[17]

The elements of this narrative were once again taken directly from Roman literature: the iniquitous judge, persecutor of the just (e.g., Nero or Pharaoh); the arbitrary cruelty that resulted in unnatural punishment (blinding); the fury and madness characteristic of a tyranny, that is, of a government either illegitimate (Ebroin) or arbitrary (Chilperic); the victim ranked among the martyrs. The attitude of Chilperic or Ebroin was not dictated by reason but rather, according to authors who were clearly antagonistic to them, by a vengeful anger. The punishment of blinding served here as a motif to stigmatize the intolerable character of authority exercised by unjust men; it entered neither into the framework of well-established law nor into a system of sanctions of symbolic significance.

Such a system, nevertheless, began to emerge in the kingdom of the Visigoths beginning in the early seventh century, when blinding constituted an alternative to the punishment of death in several cases. Indeed, a new article in the law of the Visigoths drawn up under Chindaswinth (642–53) stipulated that those who revolted against the king were subject to capital punishment unless the king granted them their life—in which case they were to lose their eyes and their goods were to be confiscated. But the interest of this text lies above all in the justification that it sets forth: "But if perhaps out of the promptings of piety his life should be spared by the prince, let this not happen unless his gouged-out eyes are taken in place of his life, so that he may not see the damage by which he had wickedly been lured."[18]

Thus the guilty man could not rejoice in the death of the king whom he had wanted to eliminate, because he could not see him. If the punishment of blinding here took on a clearly political character, we should note that it

[16] *Gesta et passio sancti Leudegarii,* c. 23 (p. 305): "sed quia iam tamquam lapides duritiam, sicut quondam rex Aegyptius obduraverat corda, ad verba divina nullatenus potuit emollire, comminans, non se ab inpugnatione civitatis discedere, quodadusque Leudegarium valeat comprehendere et *suae furores vesanum desiderium* satisfacere" (emphasis added).

[17] Ibid., 24 (p. 306): "tanquam lupi suscoeperunt eam in predam, iniquissimum poene excogitantes comentum, nam ab eius capite lumen evellerunt oculorum, in qua evulsione ultra humana natura incisionem ferri visus est tollerare."

[18] *Lex Wisigothorum* 2.1.8, MGH LL 1:55: "Quod si fortasse pietatis intuitu a principe fuerit illi vita concessa non aliter, quam effosi oculis relinquatur ad vitam, quatenus nec excidium videat, quo fuerat nequiter delectatus."

was directly tied to the person of the king. Only the king might commute the punishment; and blinding was no longer a result of his fury but, on the contrary, an effect of his piety. Above all, he was punishing a serious attack on the royal person: attempted regicide.

Despite its tormented history, toward the middle of the seventh century the Visigothic royalty attained the height of its power, and this was matched by the exterior *éclat* that marked the reigns of Chindaswinth and his son, Recceswinth. The sovereign, instituted and inspired by God, was to be represented by a special luster, in large part based on Byzantine traditions rich with possibilities in the Iberian peninsula.[19] A good example of this "luster" emanating from the royal person is furnished by the dedication that Bishop Eugenius of Toledo (d. 657) wrote for the preface to his commentary on the *Hexameron* of Dracontius, which he prepared at the request of Chindaswinth: "O little book, [you who are] about to see the distinguished face of the prince . . . when you begin to approach the entrance of the royal hall and to see the throne, radiant with shining gold."[20]

Thus blinding became a "political" punishment that tended to deprive the person who attacked the royal majesty from the capacity to contemplate this majesty in its very radiance. Historians have carefully studied the development of this punishment of blinding—applied sometimes to the emperors themselves, sometimes to their opponents—in eighth-century Byzantium.[21] But we must also realize that this relatively new practice also affected the Carolingian West at the same time. In these various contexts, in the East as in the West, blinding was no longer interpreted as a sign of the "fury" that animated the evil prince; rather, it was the manifestation of a legitimate power, of the prince "in majesty," who thus defended the *éclat* of his person and of his reign.

In fact, it is clear that the number of blindings carried out for political reasons grew visibly beginning with the reign of Charlemagne. Here this penalty was primarily applied against those who revolted against the king, in commutation of the death penalty, and hence in a context identical

19 Hans-Joachim Diesner, *Politik und Ideologie im Westgotenreich von Toledo: Chindaswind,* Sitzungsberichte der sächsichen Akademie der Wissenschaften zu Leipzig, Philologisch-historische Klasse 121/2 (Berlin: Akademie-Verlag, 1979), p. 22.

20 Eugenius of Toledo, *Dracontii de laudibus Dei,* MGH AA 14:27: "Principis insignem faciem visure libelle, . . . coeperis ut limen aulae regalis adire atque auro rutilo radiantem cernere sedem." The same use of this vocabulary of light is found in the epitaph for Chindaswinth by the same author; see ibid., p. 250.

21 Schaab, "Blendung als politische Massnahme," pp. 21–33; Evelyne Patlagean, "Byzance et le blason pénal du corps," in *Du châtiment dans la cité: supplices corporels et peine de mort dans le monde antique. Table ronde de l'Ecole Française de Rome, 9–11 November 1982* (Rome: Ecole Française de Rome, 1984), pp. 405–26.

with the law of Chindaswinth. Nevertheless, it is difficult to establish a connection between the Visigothic law and the application of this particular punishment in the Carolingian world, even though we know that many churchmen from the Iberian peninsula were refugees in the Frankish Kingdom after the Muslim invasions and that they brought their books and their traditions with them.[22] We know, too, the influence of the "Goths"—Agobard of Lyon, Theodulf of Orléans and, of course, Benedict of Aniane—at the Frankish court through the reign of Louis the Pious. Though there is no hard proof for the reception and use of that precise article of Visigothic law, it is nonetheless clear that the Frankish conception of royalty—redefined by the anointments of 751 and 754—and (above all) their conception of the imperial dignity—"renewed" for Charlemagne in 800—were evolving toward some of the forms of affirmation of power that drew their inspiration from the Roman heritage, as much Western as Eastern.

This evolution was marked in particular by the reappearance of the notion of lèse-majesté, that is, crime against the state or king, a juridical category that had almost disappeared during the Merovingian period but had been preserved by imperial law, particularly by the law *Quisquis* in the Theodosian Code.[23] References to lèse-majesté became more and more frequent in the course of the ninth century, and ultimately the term came to include every form of rebellion against the king or emperor.[24] But if that crime was normally to be punished by pain of death, as the Roman law stipulated, nevertheless quite often it was replaced by the penalty of blinding.[25] Thus at the judicial hearing (*placitum*) of Worms, called by Charlemagne, the conspirators of the Thuringian revolt of 786 were con-

22 Pierre Riché, "Les réfugiés wisigoths dans le monde carolingien," in *L'Europe, héritière de l'Espagne wisigothique,* ed. Jacques Fontaine and Christine Pellistrandi (Madrid: Casa de Velasquez, 1992), pp. 177–83.

23 *Codex Theodosianus* 9.14.3, cited in Lothar Kolmer, "Christus als beleidigte Majestät. Von der *Lex Quisquis* (397) bis zur Dekretale *Vergentis* (1199)," in *Papsttum, Kirche und Recht im Mittelalter: Festschrift für Horst Fuhrmann zum 65. Geburtstag,* ed. Hubert Mordek (Tübingen: Niemeyer, 1991), pp. 1–13. On the general history of the idea of lèse-majesté, see Jacques Chiffoleau, "Sur le crime de Majesté médiéval," in *Genèse de l'Etat moderne en Méditerranée: Approches historique et anthropologique des pratiques et des représentations,* Colloquium de l'École Française de Rome 168 (Rome: École Française de Rome, 1993), pp. 183–213. For the disappearance of the idea of lèse-majesté in the Merovingian period, see Marcel Lemosse, "La lèse majesté dans la monarchie franque," *Revue du Moyen Age Latin* 2 (1946): 5–24.

24 Oskar Hageneder, "Das *crimen maiestatis,* der Prozess gegen die Attentäter Papst Leos III. und die Kaiserkrönung Karls des Grossen," in *Aus Kirche und Reich. Studien zu Theologie, Politik und Recht im Mittelalter, Festschrift für Friedrich Kempf,* ed. Hubert Mordek (Sigmaringen: Thorbecke Verlag, 1983), pp. 55–79.

25 See the reference to Roman law in *Annales regni Francorum,* ed. Friedrich Kurze, MGH SSrG, p. 114, referring to those who wanted to depose Pope Leo III: "Post paucos autem dies iussit eos, qui pontificem anno superiore deposuerunt, exhiberi; et habita de eis questione secundum legem Romanam ut maiestatis rei capitis dampnati sunt."

demned to be blinded, deprived of their honors, and divested of their property.[26] Those who followed the revolt of Pippin the Hunchback in 792 suffered a similar fate.[27] In both cases, the writer of the annals reporting these events brought to the fore the regularity of the procedure and the kindness of King Charles, who could have condemned the conspirators to death.[28] Blinding, now a legal sanction, was here the act of princely clemency and no longer the outcome of his fury. By availing himself of this punishment, the emperor manifested the legitimacy of his power, following perhaps the Byzantine model, but developed also around a conception proper to imperial power centering on the theme of light. This conception attained its apogee during the reign of Louis the Pious (see Genealogical Table).

The age of Louis the Pious was punctuated by multiple seditions and great violence, perpetrated as often against the emperor as against his entourage. This explains the frequent recourse to the theory of lèse-majesté, even though this theory had already been present in Carolingian legislation since the imperial coronation of Charlemagne.[29] One of the most well-known cases of punishment by blinding in the early Western Middle Ages is that of Bernard of Italy, the nephew of Emperor Louis, in 819; but it is far from being alone. Indeed, it seems that these punishments of blinding were not the fruit of arbitrary decisions by an all-powerful sovereign, but rather corresponded to a judicial system that permitted the emperor to manifest fully the character of his power.

In the first place, it is well attested that these punishments of blinding were pronounced in the context of a crime of lèse-majesté, even if sometimes the circumstances are not very clear. At the beginning of the reign of Louis, a political housecleaning at the court at Aachen ended in the condemnation to death, as *reus maiestatis* (guilty of high treason), of several magnates who saw their penalty commuted into blinding, though we do not know exactly for what crime.[30] More clear is the case of Bernard of

[26] *Annals of Lorsch,* a.786, MGH SS 1:32: "ubi decernens, quod hii qui potissime in hac coniuratione devicti sunt, honore simul ac luminibus privarentur."

[27] Einhard, *Annales Fuldenses,* a. 792, ed. Friedrich Kurze, MGH SSrG, p. 12: "Coniuratio Pippini contra patrem facta in Baioaria cito detecta et compressa est, auctoribus factionis partim mortem, partim exilio et caecitate damnatis."

[28] This attitude of the sovereign towards the rebels in his power was characteristic of the Carolingian period, as Gerd Althoff has well demonstrated in "Königsherrschaft und Konfliktbewältigung im 10. und 11. Jahrhundert," *Frühmittelalterliche Studien* 23 (1989): 265–90.

[29] Hageneder, "Das *crimen maiestatis,*" pp. 77–79. On the reign of Louis the Pious, see Karl-Ferdinand Werner, "*Hludovicus Augustus:* Gouverner l'empire chrétien—idées et réalités," in *Charlemagne's Heir. New Perspectives on the Reign of Louis the Pious (814–840),* ed. Peter Godman and Roger Collins (Oxford: Clarendon, 1990), pp. 3–123.

[30] Astronomer, *Vita Hludowici,* c. 21, MGH SS 2:618. On this point, see Werner, "Gouverner l'empire," p. 30.

Genealogical Table. Carolingians Mentioned in the Text

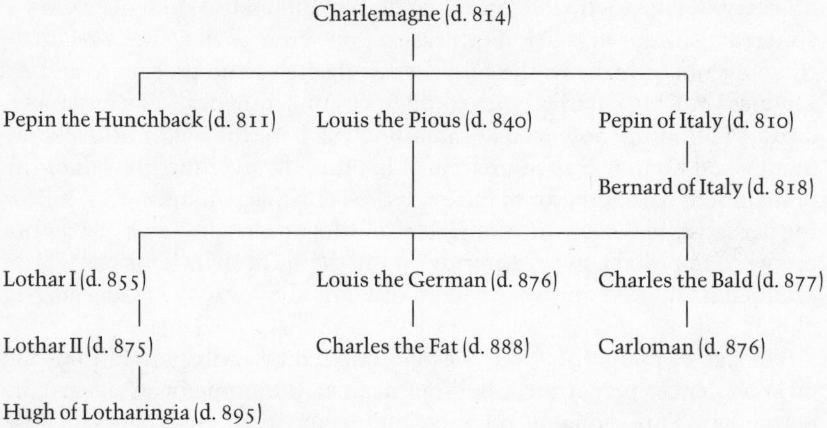

Italy, who (according to the chronicle of Moissac) contemplated usurping the imperial dignity or (according to the Royal Annals) wanted to institute a "tyrannical regime" and (according to Thegan, the emperor's biographer) to foment an abominable conspiracy.[31] For these writers, all of whom were favorable to Louis the Pious, it was essential to establish a distinction between legitimate power—the emperor's—and the power of the usurper, the potential tyrant.[32]

But in this same milieu of clerics active at the court of the emperor, the imperial function was also defined as a source of light.[33] The biography of Louis the Pious, written a short time after his death by an anonymous cleric called the Astronomer, best reflects the tendency to define the imperial function as a kind of splendor.[34] Following the traditions of antiquity and of the Orient that considered eclipses of the sun to presage the death of emperors, the Astronomer announced the imminent passing of

[31] Thegan, *Vita Hludowici imperatoris,* c. 22, MGH SS 2:596: "Inde revertens venit ad sedem suam Aquisgrani et post pascha habuit conventum magnum populum et omnes investigavit infidelium nequissimos conspirationes huius rei." For the chronicle, *Chronicon Moissiacense,* a. 817, MGH SS 1:312: "Audiens autem Bernhardus, rex Italiae, quod factum erat, cogitavit consilium pessimum, voluitque in imperatorem et filios eius insurgere et per tyrannidem imperium usurpare." For the Royal Annals, *Annales regni Francorum,* a. 817 (p. 147): "Nuntiatum est ei [imperatori] Bernhardum nepotem suum, Italiae regem, quorundam pravorum hominum consilio tyrannidem meditatum iam omnes aditus."

[32] On the bias of the sources, see Jörg Jarnut, "Kaiser Ludwig der Fromme und König Bernhard von Italien. Der Versuch einer Rehabilitierung," *Studi Medievali* 30 (1989): 637–48.

[33] For the corpus of texts, see Helene Siemes, "Beiträge zum literarischen Bild Kaiser Ludwigs des Frommen in der Karolingerzeit" (dissertation, University of Freiburg, 1966); and above all Peter Godman, "Louis the Pious and his Poets," *Frühmittelalterliche Studien* 19 (1985): 239–89.

[34] Herwig Wolfram, *Splendor imperii. Die Epiphanie von Tugend und Heil in Herrschaft und Reich,* Mitteilungen des Instituts für österreichische Geschichtsforschung, Ergänzungsband 20, no. 3 (Graz: Hermann Böhlau, 1963).

Louis by a total eclipse of the sun, which recalled as well the death of Christ: "[There was] an unusual eclipse of the sun, for when the light disappeared, the darkness so prevailed that it seemed no different than true night. For this was a portent that the greatest mortal light set upon the candlestick that was shining over all in the house of God (I speak of the emperor of most pious memory) would very soon be taken from [human] affairs, and the world would be left in the sorrow of darkness by his absence."[35] This text was very likely inspired by the words that Christ addressed to the apostles in the Gospel of Matthew: "Neither do men light a candle and put it under a bushel, but upon a candlestick, that it may shine to all that are in the house. So let your light shine before men, that they may see your good works and glorify your Father who is in heaven" (Mat. 5:15, Douai translation).

The house of God, the *domus Dei* mentioned in both texts, represented the church, *ecclesia,* the community of Christians that the emperor illuminated by his presence. If the parallel between the two texts suggested above all a conception of the Christian prince as the promoter of the faith—which Louis in fact did see as his role and his function—the Astronomer no less presented the emperor as the source of light that guided and illuminated his people, thus making clear that his death hurled the Christian world into the darkness of civil war.[36]

Nevertheless, this theme of light was not new, for one may see its traces at the end of Charlemagne's reign and the beginning of Louis's. Thus in 814 bishop Theodulf of Orléans composed a liturgical poem in sixteen strophes to celebrate the entry (*adventus*) of the emperor and his family into the city of Orléans. This poem, with its vocabulary of light quite usual in Theodulf's work (perhaps inherited from the traditions of the Visigothic royalty),[37] begins thus:

35 Astronomer, *Vita Hludowici* 62, (p. 376): "delinquium solis insolitum: in tantem enim lucis recessu tenebrae praevaluerunt ut nihil a noctis veritate differre videretur. Portendebatur enim per hoc, maximum illud lumen mortalium quod in domo Dei super candelabrum positum omnibus lucebat, piissimae recordationis imperatorem dico, maturrime rebus substrahendum, mundumque eius abscessu in tenebris tribulationem relinquendum." On astrological interpretations in the Middle Ages, see Karl-Ferdinand Werner, "Gott, Herrscher und Historiograph: Der Geschichtsschreiber als Interpret des Wirken Gottes in der Welt und Ratgeber der Könige, 4–12 Jahrhundert," in *Deus qui mutat tempora: Menschen und Institutionen im Wandel des Mittelalters. Festschrift für Alfons Becker,* ed. Ernst-Dieter Hehl (Sigmaringen: Thorbecke, 1987), pp. 1–31.

36 On this passage, see Siemes, "Beiträge zum literarischen Bild," p. 103; on Louis's conception of his role and, in particular, on his missions to convert the nordic peoples, see most recently Karl Hauck, "Der Missionsauftrag Christi und das Kaisertum Ludwigs des Frommen," in *Charlemagne's Heir,* ed. Godman and Collins, pp. 275–96; and Olivier Guillot, "L'exhortation au partage des responsabilités entre l'empereur, l'épiscopat et les autres sujets vers le milieu du règne de Louis le Pieux," in *Prédication et propagande au moyen âge,* ed. George Makdisi and Dominique Sourdel, Penn-Paris-Dumbarton Oaks Colloquia, vol. 3 (Paris: PUF, 1983), pp. 95–97.

37 Ann Freeman, "Theodulf of Orleans: A Visigoth at Charlemagne's Court," in *L'Europe, héritière de l'Espagne wisigothique,* ed. Fontaine and Pellistrandi pp. 185–94.

Behold! Caesar, pious and kind, is here,
Who brilliantly shines over the whole world,
And reigns over all with goodness by the grace of Christ.[38]

and ends by this characteristic strophe, which connects the emperor with the type of Christ in majesty:

Let there be for the father and son, for you, and for the [Holy] Spirit
Splendor and honor, eternal and perpetual,
As now in the present, so also forever in future ages.[39]

We know that Theodulf, who fell into disgrace in 818 and was probably involved in the revolt of Bernard of Italy, was a representative of the first generation of Carolingian intellectuals, those who began their career at the court of Charlemagne during the years 770–780 and who were particularly active in the theological quarrels centered on the adoptionists on the one hand and the Byzantines on the other.[40] The reuse of architectural themes emphasizing light, themes inherited as much from Visigothic Spain as from the Christian East, is attested to at Aachen as well as at Germiny-des-Prés, where the oratory was constructed on Theodulf's orders.[41] It is in this context that the famous words of Notker the Stammerer describing the radiant appearance of Charlemagne on the second floor of the chapel at Aachen must be understood: "The most glorious of kings, Charles, was standing next to the brightest window, shining like the rising sun and conspicuous in gems and gold. He leaned upon Heito (for that was the name of the bishop previously sent to Constantinople)."[42]

Heito, bishop of Basel (803–23) and abbot of Reichenau (806–23), who appeared here at the side of the emperor, had been part of the ambassadorial party sent by Charles to Constantinople in 811; he must be counted, like Theodulf, among Charlemagne's most loyal supporters: those who, for example, undersigned his "testament," as reported by

[38] Theodulf of Orléans, *De adventu Hludowici Augusti Aurelianos,* carmen 37, strophe 1, ed. Ernst Dummler, MGH Poet 1:529.

[39] Ibid., strophe 16.

[40] Godman, "Louis the Pious and His Poets," p. 248, expresses some doubt about Theodulf's role in Bernard's revolt.

[41] Jean Hubert, "Germiny-des-Prés," *Congrès archéologique* 93 (1931): 534–68; R. Krautheimer, "The Carolingian Revival of Early Christian Architecture," *Art Bulletin* 24 (1942): 1–38. For Aachen see Heinrich Fichtenau, "Byzanz und die Pfalz zu Aachen," *Mitteilungen des Instituts für österreichische Geschichtsforschung* 59 (1951): 1–54; and Günther Bandmann, "Die Vorbilder der Aachener Pfalzkapelle," in *Karl der Grosse. Lebenswerk und Nachleben,* ed. Wolfgang Braunfels, vol. 3, *Karolingische Kunst* (Düsseldorf: Schwann, 1965), pp. 424–62.

[42] Notker Balbulus *Gesta Karoli Magni* 2.6, ed. Hans Haefele, MGH SSrG 12:56.

Einhard in the *Vita Karoli.*[43] When Heito renounced all his offices in 823, it was after having actively collaborated in the reform of the church, a reform set into motion by Benedict of Aniane and Louis the Pious. We know that he took part in the great council of 816 and that he was probably the author of the famous "plan of Saint Gall."[44] Nevertheless, it is not impossible that he, like Theodulf, repudiated the emperor over the blinding of Bernard of Italy. One of the most famous texts rehabilitating Bernard, the *Visio cuiusdam pauperculae mulieris,* was probably written by Heito or at least by a member of his immediate entourage.[45] This text described the merits of Bernard and the emperor in terms of light: on the wall of Paradise, where the names of the elect were inscribed, the name of Bernard shone in letters of gold, while that of Louis, which cast only a feeble light, was nearly effaced:

> She [the poor woman] reads it and finds the name of former King Bernard written in letters brighter than those of anyone else there. Afterwards she reads the name of King Louis, so obscure and obliterated that she could hardly recognize it. "What does it mean," she said, "that this name is so obliterated?" "Before he committed homicide against Bernard," [the angel] replied, "no one's name was clearer. The death of the one was the obliteration of the other."[46]

In rendering bad justice, the emperor lost the splendor that normally characterized him, since previously his name had been more brilliant than all the others. The good king, the one who judged in the fear of God, without committing any abuse of power and without letting himself be carried away by the desire for vengeance, shone, by contrast, like the sun upon rising:

> The just ruler of men,
> the ruler in fear of God

[43] Einhard, *Vita Karoli,* c. 33, ed. Louis Halphen (Paris: Belles Lettres, 1967), p. 100. On this group of aristocrats, see Karl Brunner, *Oppositionnelle Gruppen im Karolingerreich* (Vienna: Hermann Böhlau, 1979), p. 71.

[44] On Heito of Basel as the author of the plan of St. Gall, see Walter Horn and Ernest Born, *The Plan of St. Gall: A Study of the Architecture and Life in a Paradigmatic Carolingian Monastery* (Berkeley: University of California Press, 1979), 1:11–12.

[45] Hubert Houben, "*Visio cuiusdam pauperculae mulieris.* Überlieferung und Herkunft eines frühmittelalterlichen Visionstextes (mit Neuedition)," *Zeitschrift für die Geschichte des Oberrheins* 124 (1976): 31–42.

[46] Ibid., p. 42: "Legit namque illa et invenit nomen Bernharti quondam regis tam luculentis litteris exaratum sicut nullius ibidem fuit, postea Hlodouuici regis tam obscurum et oblitteratum, ut tam agnosci potuisset. Quid est, inquid, quod istud nomen tam oblitteratum est? Antequam, ait, in Bernhartum homicidium perpetrasset, nullius ibi nomen clarius erat. Illius interfectio istius oblitteratio fuit."

is like the light of dawn, the sun in the east
in a morning without clouds.

(2 Sam. 23:3)

Those were the last words of David, which all the intellectuals at the court of Charlemagne, Heito as well as Theodulf, must have known. The characteristic quality of Charles, the "new David," which Louis had inherited, was that of the just king, the *rex iustus,* who illumines and guides his people and thus might be described in terms of light.

If the critics of imperial policy condemned Louis at the beginning of the 820s, the idea of an office, a *ministerium,* defined in terms of light persisted far longer and even became a "commonplace" in Carolingian poetry. The *Poem of Louis the Pious,* composed during the years 828–30 by Ermold the Black, who was inspired more or less directly by Theodulf of Orléans, compared, at the end of his dedication, the glory of the emperor to the light of the sun: "the prince who, from the height of his throne, raises up the abject, pardons the sinners, and, equally with the sun, shines his rays into the vastness."[47]

At the same time, about 829, Walahfrid Strabo, pupil of Heito of Basel, tutor of Charles the Bald and loyal *fidelis* of Louis the Pious, composed a panegyric in two parts on the latter king's glory.[48] In it the figure of the *rex iustus,* who, like Moses, led his people toward the light of salvation, was opposed to the figure of the tyrant (*rex iniquus*), personified by Theodoric the Ostrogoth, who dragged Christians toward the darkness of heresy.[49] This long poem, just like the one that follows, which celebrates the arrival of Louis and his entourage at the palace, overflows with terms pertaining to a vocabulary of light, borrowed from both the Old Testament and classical authors, especially Vergil and Venatius Fortunatus.[50] Here the sacred and messianic function of the emperor was marked by a visible sign: the emanation of divine splendor, which Walahfrid expressed by using his vocabulary of light.[51]

We must consider that beginning with the years 820–30, at the apogee of the reign of Louis, the great lay and ecclesiastical magnates were ex-

[47] Ermold the Black, *Poème sur Louis le Pieux,* ed. Edmond Faral (Paris: Belles Lettres, 1964), p. 4. On Ermold, see Godman, "Louis the Pious and His Poets," pp. 280–87.

[48] Walahfrid Strabo *De imagine Tetrici,* carmen 23, MGH Poet 2:370–78.

[49] On all of these texts, see Siemes, "Beiträge zum literarischen Bild," pp. 132–55; Godman, "Louis the Pious and His Poets," pp. 274–78; and F. Thürleman, "Die Bedeutung der Aachener Theodorich-Statue für Karl den Grossen und bei Walahfrid Strabo: Materialen zu einer Semiotik visueller Objekte im frühen Mittelalter," *Archiv für Kulturgeschichte* 59 (1977): 25–65.

[50] For the poem that follows, see Walahfrid Strabo, *De imagine tetrici,* carmen 24 (p. 279).

[51] For example, ibid., carmen 23, vv. 155–57 (p. 378): "Ora sacri cornuta patris splendore corusco;/ Hunc cui fulgorem divi consortia verbi / Eddiderant, qui in terrigenis mitissimus extat." See also Wolfram, *Splendor imperii,* p. 133.

horted to participate in the *ministerium* (functions, duties, and dignities) of the king:[52] in effect, he shared a part of his splendor with those whom he associated with his *ministerium;* and henceforth they became trustees answerable for the brilliance of Louis's reign. Here surely is a key to understanding the symbolic meaning of the blinding of political opponents, such as Bernard of Italy: by revolting against the king or trying to usurp his functions, these men lost the capacity to participate in his *ministerium;* and the punishment that deprived them of their sight, which only the legitimate emperor had the right to pronounce, demonstrated that they had been cast forever into the world of darkness, incapable at one and the same time of seeing the king who radiated splendor and of reflecting the portion of brightness that had once been confided to them.

If this is correct, the penalty of deprivation of sight was the fruit of serious thought, begun during the reign of Charlemagne, on the quality of the imperial function; it was no "medieval cruelty" signifying some arbitrary act of power. Rather, it was understood as a special manifestation of imperial power, based on Byzantine practices. We may clearly see this from examples taken from the period following the reign of Louis the Pious, particularly from the reign of Charles the Bald.[53]

The punishment of blinding pronounced in 873 by Charles the Bald against his own son Carloman—who was guilty of rebellion—is another famous case. We should note that on the surface it was comparable to that of Bernard of Italy: a close member of the royal family had entered into open rebellion with the goal of usurping the royal office. Thus the authors favorable to Charles the Bald, especially Regino of Prüm and Hincmar of Reims, presented Carloman as a person extremely dangerous to the peace of the kingdom and the Church, his behavior rendered still more wicked by the fact that he had renounced his clerical estate. Thus Regino did not hesitate to accuse Carloman of apostasy and to compare him to Emperor Julian: "Afterward, withdrawing from the religion of the church through apostasy, unthinkingly casting off and scorning the grace that had been given to him by the laying on of hands, he became another Julian. He collected together a not insignificant mob of plunderers and began to lay waste the churches of God, to attack those institutions of peace, to plunder them all and to perpetrate unheard of evils."[54]

[52] Olivier Guillot, "Une *ordinatio* méconnue: le capitulaire de 823–825" in *Charlemagne's Heir,* ed. Godman and Collins, pp. 455–86, and idem, "L'exhortation au partage des responsibilités," in *Prédication et propagande,* pp. 87–110.

[53] It seems that at Byzantium only the emperor had the privilege of condemning a person to blinding. See Schaab, "*Blendung als politische Massnahme,*" chap. 2, esp. pp. 30–32.

[54] Regino, *Chronicon,* a. 870, ed. Friedrich Kurze, MGH SSrG, p. 100: "Post haec per apostasiam recedens ab ecclesiastica religione, abiciens ac spernens neglegenter gratiam, quae ei data erat per

For his own part, Hincmar accused Carloman of having made common cause with the Normans, who were devastating the kingdom—a particularly serious form of treason because it resulted in enfeebling the Christian realm and aiding the pagans: "by acclamation of all present [he was sentenced] to be deprived of his eyes so that the pernicious hope of the haters of peace might be disappointed in him, and the church of God and Christianity in [Charles's] realm might not be disturbed by sedition in addition to the attacks of the pagans."[55]

Apostasy, tyranny, high treason, lèse-majesté: we find here all the chief accusations that might lead to a death sentence. The same sources insisted in other ways on the absolutely normal nature of the proceedings instituted against Carloman, who was first stripped of his deaconry before being judged and condemned. As in the case of Bernard, the sentence of blinding pronounced against Carloman was not the act of an abuse of power, of royal aggravation brought on by anger. Rather, it was understood as the manifestation of a sovereign and legitimate power. Here the sufferers were those who had been accused of wanting to establish a tyranny.

We ought perhaps to connect the condemnation to blinding with the notions of a properly imperial power to which Charles the Bald adhered beginning in 869. Although he had been vested officially by the pope with the imperial dignity only in 875, his coronation in 869 as king of Lotharingia at the church of St. Stephen at Metz had enhanced his royal power because, from that time forth, he ruled more than one kingdom.[56] To appropriate the right to condemn someone to blinding—was that not trying to act as an emperor after the Lotharingian coronation of 869 but before the imperial coronation of 875?

The same reasoning may be applied to other cases of blinding, as for example that of Louis of Provence by Berengar of Italy in 905. The competition between the two men turned precisely on the imperial dignity as conceived within the Byzantine tradition.[57] This is suggested on the one hand by the marriage of Louis to the daughter of the *basileus* Leo VI around the year 900 and on the other hand by the Greek garb that Berengar

---

impositionem manus, alter Iulianus efficitur. Collecta quippe predonum non modica turba ecclesias Dei cepit devastare, ea, quae pacis sunt, inpugnare, cuncta diripere et inaudita mala perpetrare."

[55] *Annales de Saint-Bertin* a. 873, ed. C. Dehaisnes (repr., Champion, Paris: 1980), p. 232: "luminibus, acclamatione cunctorum qui adfuerunt, orbari, quatenus perniciosa spes pacem odientium de illo frustrata foret, et ecclesia Dei ac christianas in regno ejus cum infestatione paganorum seditione exitiabili perturbari non posset."

[56] Janet L. Nelson, *Charles the Bald* (London: Longman, 1992), pp. 219–20.

[57] Rudolf Hiestand, *Byzanz und das Regnum Italicum im 10. Jahrhundert* (Zurich: Fretz und Wasmuth, 1964), p. 134.

assumed after 915, which recalled to some extent that worn by Charles the Bald.[58]

To condemn to blinding is to demonstrate the essential quality of a ruler's authority, to make the gesture of the legitimate sovereign who has attained the full majesty of his office. Only under these conditions was blinding considered by contemporaries a truly just decision. By the same token, it is not surprising to see this practice condemned by the detractors of a royal or imperial power when they considered it illegitimate. This was particularly true for Lothar I in the conflict that saw him oppose his father and his brothers, as recounted by Nithard. During the revolt that Lothar waged in 830 against Louis the Pious and his counselors, he managed to seize the brother of Bernard of Septimania, one Herebert, blind him, and then lead him under strong guard to Italy.[59] It is very probable that Lothar intended by this gesture to show the imperial quality of the power with which he thought himself invested, a point that Nithard did not neglect to make in the preceding chapter.[60] Nevertheless, the author did not recognize Lothar's power as legitimate: in Nithard's view, Lothar usurped the place of Louis and, while claiming to restore the res publica, in fact handed it over to his greedy friends.[61] This first "usurpation" was followed by many other misdeeds, for Lothar, according to Nithard, did not carry out his promises, sowed discord in the kingdom, and went so far as to treat with the pagans in order to injure his brother Louis the German.[62] His condemnation to blinding of Herebert, a magnate of the kingdom, must be placed in this context; it might well have appeared as the first "tyrannical" gesture of Lothar in the eyes of contemporary partisans of Charles.

The same disapproval is found, even more explicitly, in the *Annals of Fulda* on the subject of Carloman's blinding at the command of his father. The redactor of the third part of these annals, which were in fact written at Mainz by someone who did not much like Charles the Bald, deemed the manifestations of his royal power abusive and tyrannical, and the annalist

[58] On Berengar, see Carlrichard Brühl, *Deutschland-Frankreich. Die Geburt Zweier Völker* (Cologne: Böhlau, 1990), pp. 516–18.

[59] Nithard, *Historiarum libri IV* 1.3, ed. Ernst Müller, MGH SSrG, p. 3: "Bernardus quoque fuga lapsus in Septimaniam se recepit; Eribertus frater eius captus ac luminibus privatus in Italia custodiendus traditur."

[60] Ibid., 1.2 (p. 3): "Lodharius vero post discessum eius universum imperium haberet, cui et unam secum imperatoris nomen habere concessit."

[61] Ibid., 1.3 (p. 4): "Res autem publica quoniam quisque cupiditate illectus sua querebat, cotidie deterius ibat." On this point, see Yves Sassier, "L'utilisation d'un concept romain aux temps carolingiens. La *res publica* aux IXe et Xe siècles," *Médiévales* 15 (1988): 17–29; and Philippe Depreux, "Nithard et la *Res publica:* un regard critique sur le règne de Louis le Pieux," *Médiévales* 22–23 (1992): 149–61.

[62] Nithard, *Historiarum* 4.2 (p. 42).

linked this to the king's blinding of his son:[63] "Charles, tyrant of Gaul, put aside fatherly compassion and ordered his son Carloman, who held the office of deacon, to be blinded."[64]

Let us note the limitations created by the annalist, who was combating Charles's pretensions to be called *imperator* and *augustus* since 869, as reported earlier in the *Annals:* he reduced Charles's territorial power in a most significant way: in 873 Charles was not yet a legitimate emperor; he was only the king of one of the Frankish kingdoms, Gallia, the westernmost part; and he abused his power by blinding an important person who should have been protected by his office as deacon and by the filial ties that united him to the king. This was not far from the "unnatural" tyrant of the Roman world, who forgot the sacred bonds of the *familia.*[65]

By way of comparison, it is necessary to mention what the same annalist of Mainz said about the blinding of Hugh of Lotharingia, the son of Lothar II and of Waldrada, at the command of his uncle, Emperor Charles the Fat, in 885: "Hugh, son of King Lothar, whose sister was wed by Gottfried, was accused before the emperor [Charles the Fat] of being a promoter of Gottfried's conspiracy against the emperor's kingdom. Wherefore, called before the emperor and convicted of the crime, he, together with his brother-in-law, was deprived of the light of his eyes; and, thrust into the monastery of St. Boniface at Fulda, he experienced the [just] end of a tyrant.[66]

Here the sentence against Hugh appeared fully justified to the author: Hugh was guilty of "conspiracy" against the legitimate power of his uncle, the emperor; and what is more, he acted with the help of his brother-in-law Gottfried, a newly converted Dane who had not really renounced his pillaging ways.[67] Thus it was he who was guilty of "tyranny"—which he had pretty well proven by an entire life of rebellion[68]—and not his uncle,

[63] On the political position of the author, see Martin Lintzel, "Zur Stellung der ostfränkischen Aristokratie beim Sturz Karls III," *Historische Zeitschrift* 166 (1942): 457–72; and Hagen Keller, "Zum Sturz Karls III," *Deutsches Archiv* 22 (1966): 333–84.

[64] *Annales Fuldenses,* a. 873 (p. 78). Earlier the same annalist had suggested that Charles had taken the title of emperor after being crowned king of Lotharingia: "Karolus vero rex . . . in urbe Mettensi diadema capiti suo ab illius civitatis episcopo imponi et se imperatorem et augustum quasi due regna possessurus appellare praecepit." (a. 869, p. 69.)

[65] Jerphagnon, "Que le tyran est contre-nature," pp. 41–42. The tyrant was described as someone who systematically violated all taboos and who was guilty, in particular, of "impiety" toward his *familia.*

[66] *Annales Fuldenses,* a. 885 (p. 103.)

[67] On the story of Gottfried, see Ludwig Buisson, "Formen normannischer Staatsbildung," in *Studien zum mittelalterlichen Lehenswesen,* Vorträge und Forschungen 5 (Lindau: Thorbecke, 1960), pp. 122–24.

[68] On Hugh of Lotharingia, see Eduard Hlawitschka, *Lotharingien und das Reich an der Schwelle der deutschen Geschichte,* Schriften der MGH 21 (Stuttgart: Anton Hiersemann, 1968), pp. 17–19; and Keller, "Zum Sturz Karls III," pp. 346–47.

who, on the contrary, exercised the imperial power legitimately. The familial tie, explicitly mentioned, was nevertheless apparently not enough for the annalist to reproach Charles the Fat for the lack of mercy (*miseratio*) with which the same annalist had charged Charles the Bald. It was not blinding as such, nor family ties, that was decisive for the annalist of Mainz when he condemned the act of Charles the Bald; it was his lack of legitimacy as emperor that disqualified him from marking his power in this way.

Thus the penalty of blinding was intimately bound up with ideas about legitimate power and tyranny. Indeed it served, in some ways, as a line of demarcation. When the emperor blinded someone who had attacked his *ministerium* in hopes of usurping or tarnishing it, he did not abuse his power nor commit an arbitrary act inspired by uncontrollable anger. He acted within a clearly determined framework: if not a law code, at least a system of references and ideas that recognized his monopoly on this particular form of violence. As were most forms of judicial penalties in the early Middle Ages, blinding was the exact opposite of the barbaric use of arbitrary and unnatural power. For it was acceptable to contemporaries only within the context of the highest justice: that rendered by someone who, though on earth, was clothed in the splendor of the divine.

CHAPTER FIVE

What Did Henry III of England Think in Bed and in French about Kingship and Anger?

PAUL HYAMS

In Westminster Palace, at that time arguably the most important royal residence in the country, Henry III (1216–72) possessed an impressive state bedroom, the Painted Chamber, so named from the succession of mural decorative schemes it once held. Late in an eventful reign, a dominant feature of the interior decoration was the series of eight splendid depictions of francophone Virtues, each caught triumphant in the act of trampling her corresponding Vice underfoot. Over each picture flew crowned angels; around were scattered relevant heraldic devices. The pictures were grouped in pairs. The whole was brightly colored in proper regal style, yet with "a certain refined meekness" appropriate for a state bedroom.[1] One of the four couplings juxtaposed Largesse and Debonereté. Largesse was defeating without apparent difficulty Covoitise, generous open-handedness being the obvious counter to covetous greed. That made sense. But what was the French maiden Debonereté doing as the victorious opponent of the Latin lady Ira?

That these questions occurred to me at all I owe to the creative scholarship and energy of an art historian, Paul Binski, whose excellent monograph *The Painted Chamber at Westminster* furnished both my starting point and much continued inspiration, for nothing now survives of the paintings or their former location. This chapter thus takes off promisingly

[1] Paul Binski, *The Painted Chamber at Westminster*, Society of Antiquaries, Occasional Papers, n.s. 9 (London: Society of Antiquaries, 1986), p. 42.

from a lost painting in a lost room of a palace largely destroyed long ago. My intention is not to attempt to compete with the art experts, a task out of the question for one as challenged as I in both visual perception and observational skills. Rather, I seek merely to trace from basically documentary materials the understanding needed to decode this one picture and receive its message.[2]

Mise-en-scène

So we must first look at the room itself and then examine our image more fully. Until its destruction in the fire of 1834 the Painted Chamber was perhaps the third most important public location (after the two great halls) in the series of rambling structures known as Westminster Palace.[3] It measured nearly twenty-five by eight meters and its ceiling was nearly ten meters from the floor. The enclosed space was rather well lit by five sizable windows, including those on the east wall that looked out onto the river Thames.[4]

It was very much a State Room, used for serious public purposes on formal occasions. It provided a solemn, public space suitable for ceremony and the display of public images. Here the king faced tax delegations and some of the very early parliaments. Here he had six thousand beggars fed in 1243. And here in 1279, his son, Edward, accepted the homage of Alexander II, king of Scots.[5] Most of the time, though, it must have been available for less public purposes as a royal "with-drawing" room. Chambers were places of some privacy for their king or lord. Others, intimates and *familiares* included, entered on special invitation only. It was into a chamber of his, for example, that King John had in 1207 ushered his kitchen cabinet, as we might say—drawn from men that Magna Carta called his "evil brood"—to discuss Irish politics and prepare a coup against the administration of William de Briouze.[6] Thus we may expect

[2] I dedicate this chapter with its Westminster associations to Barbara Harvey to enjoy alongside her *Cloister and the World: Essays in Medieval History in Honour of Barbara Harvey*, ed. John Blair and Brian Golding (Oxford: University Press, 1996). There are others to thank. I have received specific help from my friends and colleagues Robert Calkins, Alice Colby-Hall, Art Groos, Lauren Helm Jared, Carol Kaske, and Henry Mayr-Harting, and also from the editor (especially) and other contributors to this book.

[3] See Binski, *Painted Chamber*, p. 10, for a plan of the relevant southern end.

[4] Ibid., p. 37, offers a conjectural reconstruction sketch plan, here Fig. 11. See ibid., plates 26–32 for some idea of the room's dimensions and character.

[5] Ibid., pp. 34–35.

[6] *L'histoire de Guillaume le Maréchal*, ed. Paul Meyer, 3 vols. (Paris: Renouard, 1891–1901), lines 588–94. The author does not place the incident in any specific chamber, but John E. A. Jolliffe, *Angevin Kingship* (London: Black, 1955), pp. 185–86, suggests Gloucester in November 1207.

the Painted Chamber to be used both for public formal purposes and, on occasion, for ones more personal to the king and those whom he cared to invite.

Patently the architectural focus of the room lay on a bed. It must have been of impressive dimensions, one of those state beds that have been described as "a chamber within the chamber."[7] We know from Joinville that Henry's royal brother-in-law, St. Louis, had sat on the end of just such a bed to mete out justice in celebrated style. These beds must be part of the prehistory of that notorious institution of the ancien régime, the "lit de justice," by which selected solemn functions of royal rule were performed from a special throne shaped somewhat like a bed and accordingly named a *lict.* One perhaps characteristic use of our bed was for a new king's stylized repose after his ritual bath and while awaiting the formal summons to his coronation at nearby Westminster Abbey.[8]

And yet this bed was for more than state use. It was curtained off in Henry's pet Solomonic color scheme of green with gold stars. It was therefore possible to gain some privacy within it and even to sleep. Doubtless this was not what would today be called real privacy. Great men never slept without attendants and often had company in bed.[9] The comfort such a bed afforded cannot have compared to that of a decent modern motel. Repairs to the decorations confirm one's feeling that the Westminster Chamber, so close to the river Thames, must have been a damp room. Hence the insertion of a fireplace in 1259, and hence also the fire that started there in the bleak February of 1263, which earns an important place in the present story by destroying the Chamber's previous furnishings and decorative scheme.

We can therefore reasonably imagine King Henry there on occasion preparing himself for sleep. What might he have seen before he nodded off? We know in fact a great deal of the now lost program into which the room was launched after the fire, at some time in the mid- to late 1260s (Fig. 11). There had been little refurbishment here in the Painted Chamber during

[7] Sarah Hanley, *The Lit de Justice of the Kings of France* (Princeton: Princeton University Press, 1983), pp. 15–17.

[8] Richard A. Jackson, *Vive le roi: A History of the French Coronation from Charles V to Charles X* (Chapel Hill: University of North Carolina Press, 1984), pp. 131–38. I have benefited here, thanks to the kindness of Peggy Brown, from a draft of the prefatory chapter to Elizabeth A. R. Brown and Richard C. Famiglietti, *The Lit de Justice: Semantics, Ceremonial, and the Parlement of Paris, 1300–1600* (Sigmaringen: J. Thorbecke, 1994).

[9] It ought no longer to be necessary to add that this practice carries no necessary sexual innuendos. See for example John Gillingham, *Richard the Lionheart* (New York: Times Books, 1978), and C. Stephen Jaeger, "L'amour des rois: Structure sociale d'une forme de sensibilité aristocratique," *Annales ESC* (1989): 547–71, for the cohabitation in such a bed of Kings Richard I and Philip Augustus of France.

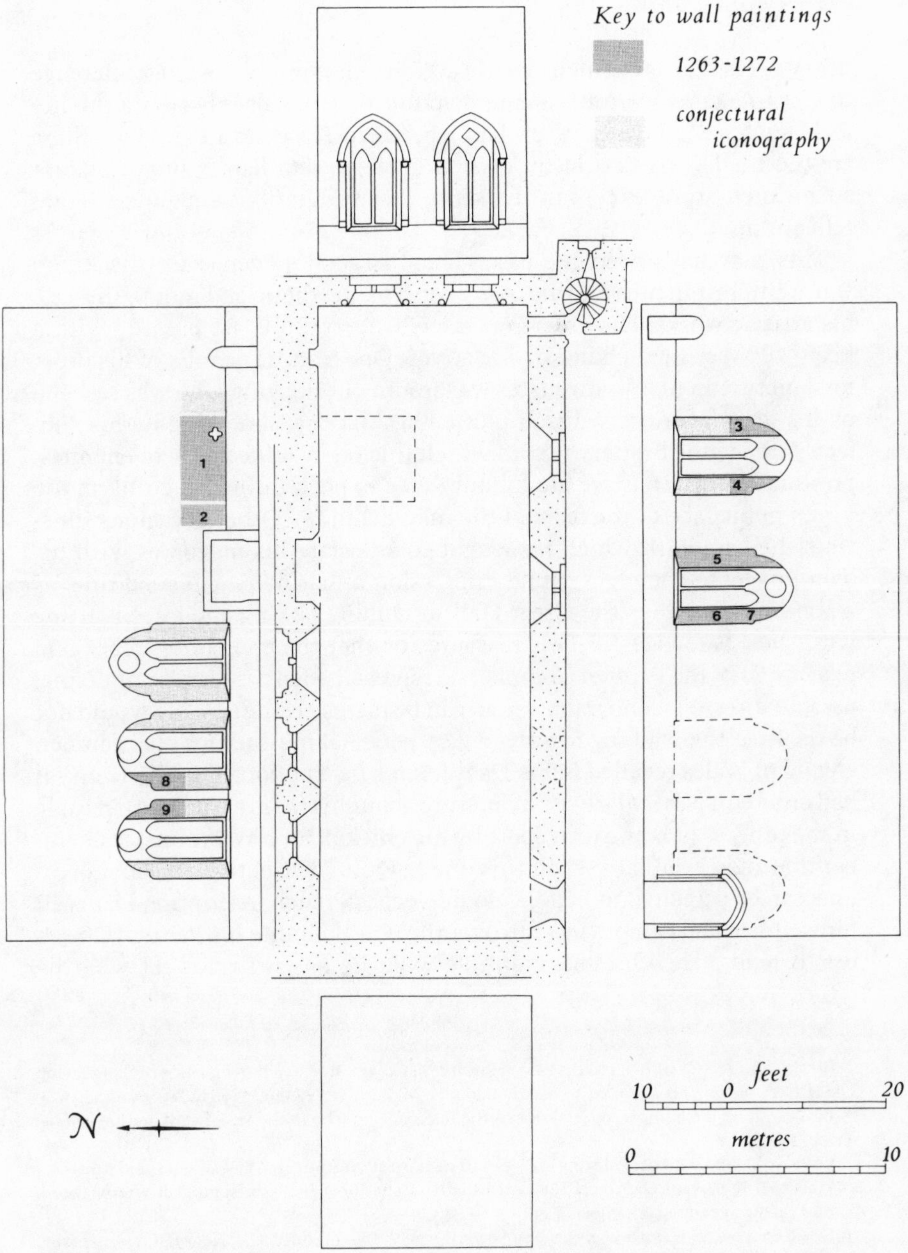

Figure 11. The Painted Chamber: Conjectural plan of bed (broken line) and murals, after Binski, *Painted Chamber,* Fig. 3, reproduced here courtesy of the Society of Antiquaries, London.

thirty years that saw much artistic activity elsewhere.[10] A 1267 reference to *picturae circa lectum*[11] seems to point toward a date between the fire and Henry's death in 1272, probably between 1263 and 1267. Since these are the final years of a bitter civil war, they seem hardly propitious for such expenditure, except in the sense that tribulations encourage moral reflection.

This may have been the case. There is good evidence for the king's warm interest in pressing his own concerns, aesthetic and moral, through his artistic works. His orders on the Chancery Rolls are phrased with a keen, very personal choice of adjectives. One from 1256 tells of his order for a picture in his Westminster washroom of "the king who was rescued by his dogs from the sedition plotted against the same king by his subjects." Since the bestiary text to which this refers talked only of enemies, presumably external, we are for once able to peek through a chink in the king's pubic face to the fears of the man behind.[12] Other occasions illustrate the care with which he sought to associate his magnates with his own image, to convey a public impression of harmony and good rule, as when he ordered for the Great Hall in Dublin "a king and queen sitting with their baronage."[13] This reassures us that the choices of image and placement of the Painted Chamber do represent Henry's own "moralizing, parable-directed iconography" and can bear close reading.[14] He would not be the first English king to order a very personal message for his chamber. Gerald of Wales recalled in his *De principis instructione* the way Henry II had ordered a particularly nasty picture about his family troubles (an eagle in the process of being torn apart by his chicks!) for a Westminster chamber that may even have been this one.[15] Quite distinctive personal opinions can be detected, too, in the double-edged French inscription Henry III himself had had painted in 1236 over the new door into his Painted Chamber. It read, "He who does not give what he has, will not get what he

[10] Binski, *Painted Chamber,* pp. 4, 22–23; Howard M. Colvin, R. Allen Brown, and Arnold J. Taylor, *The History of the King's Works,* 5 vols. (London: H. M. Stationery Office, 1963–82), vol. 1, chap. 4.

[11] Binski, *Painted Chamber,* pp. 17–18, 42; the reference may be to the St. Edward pictures alone; see pp. 38–40.

[12] David J. A. Ross, "A Lost Painting in Henry III's Palace at Westminster," *JWCI* 16 (1953): 160–61. I imagine that the "wardrobe where the king usually washes his head" was signficantly rather more private than the Painted Chamber.

[13] David Carpenter, "King, Magnates, and Society: the Personal Rule of King Henry III, 1234–1258," *Speculum* 60 (1985): 60–61, gives among other examples his placement of the shields of the earls of England alongside his own in his new choir at Westminster.

[14] Binski, *Painted Chamber,* pp. 43–46, collects many examples in support of this view of Henry's attention to the details of image placement and message.

[15] Gerald of Wales, *De principis instructione,* 3.26, in Giraldus Cambrensis, *Opera,* ed. J. S. Brewer, J. F. Dimock, and G. F. Warner (London: Rolls Series, 1861–91), 8:285–86; hereafter *DPI.*

wants."[16] Parliamentary commoners exiting from some tough negotiation session in the Chamber may have read this less as a commentary on the courtly virtue of Largesse, celebrated elsewhere in the room, than as an inducement for them to be forthcoming with their *plena potestas* and grant the king his taxation!

There is nothing second-rate about this painting; it is fine art fit for a king. Experts have noted stylistic and other links with other court art from the second half of Henry's reign. In particular they adduce half a dozen splendid manuscripts, panel paintings, and *objets* as rich in material substance as in sophistication of paintwork. These spotlight the court as a "focus for international ideas," and their "strong sense of actuality and detail of information" reinforces our willingness to subject them to close readings.[17] I shall return in due course to the finely illustrated manuscript *Estoire le seint Ædward le rei,* connected with but perhaps not quite part of this group.

One immediately apparent concern of our pictures is to guard the king from the terrors of the night. Straight behind the bed was the *Coronation of St. Edward.*[18] This was almost life-size, as befits the subject of Henry's lifelong and rather obsessive interest in this his saintly protector. I shall have more to say about St. Edward. Henry also had in mind another holy model. In imitation of the sixty *fortes* who stood guard around king Solomon's bed in the Song of Songs (Cant. 3:7–8), he ordered a representative knight-guardian on each side of the bed.[19]

The rest of the scheme aims to provide edifying role models for visual consideration. Directly across from the bed were two more stories from St. Edward's life as recounted in the *Estoire le seint Ædward le rei,* his encounter with St. John in pilgrim's garb and his recovery of a fabled ring. The remainder of the available walls was probably covered with the Virtues and Vices, each pair of contending values beside a tall lancet window. Almost opposite the bed and slightly to a sleeper's right were Largesse and Covoitise, then Deboneretè in triumph over Ira. These were as visible as they could be from the bed, though their heads are turned leftward to the main door at the western end, which had recently been made for ordinary visitors.[20]

16 Binski, *Painted Chamber,* p. 13: "Ke ne dune ke ne tine ne prent ke desire."
17 Ibid., pp. 51, 64; and generally on stylistic comparisons, pp. 45–61.
18 Ibid., color plate 1.
19 Ibid., plate 3. It seems telling that the Glossa Ordinaria ad *en lectulum* (both interlinear and marginal) interprets the guardians as preachers engaged in securing the sleeper's hopes for eternal rest in due course. For the truly peaceful, one night's sleep thus symbolized future salvation. I have used *Biblia Latina cum Glossa Ordinaria,* with introductions by Karlfried Froehlich and Margaret T. Gibson (Turnhout: Brepols, 1992).
20 Binski, *Painted Chamber,* pp. 36–42.

Debonereté and Ira

Our picture (Fig. 12) shows the virtuous Debonereté, crowned in gold, holding a shield slung from a richly ornamented belt and embellished with a differenced version of the arms of England.[21] She is framed by a thin, decorated gold arch-rib culminating in a sharply pointed trefoil. To her left, on the outside of the grouping, runs a band of heraldic shields in which those of England (undifferenced) and of Saints Edmund and Edward alternate. Debonereté gazes down on her own shield, sad but determined. She is dressed in blues (contrasting nicely with the bright red of her sister, Largesse), the over-dress edged with gold-thread embroidery and cut away at the shoulders pinafore-style to reveal a mail shirt worn over the tunic. To emphasize that she is there on business, she carries in her right hand a large switch of twigs neatly bound together at three points for ease of use; this is the switch of justice.[22] She hovers over the tiny figure of Ira, kneeling on the light-colored ground with her body so contorted as almost to face the viewer, and apparently just at the point of total prostration as in acknowledgment of defeat. Ira's auburn hair hangs to the ground; she clutches it in both hands and is apparently trying to tear it out. The evident contrast between our two ladies is heightened by differences both in scale and color; Ira, like the other vices, is depicted in pastel shades; she is both punier and less positive than her opponent. These points apply to the whole group of ladies. Virtues are larger, so brightly colored as to command the viewer's eye and dominate their drabber, vicious sisters. Each pairing privileges the positive, the virtuous, patently in order to make a point.[23]

Remedies for Anger

Why Debonereté and what was her point? The question is not trivial. Much may hang on how virtues were paired with their opposing vices (or

[21] The image reproduced here is not the original, which was destroyed with the rest of the room and its decoration in the fire of 1834. By very good fortune, two excellent artists had copied the wall paintings in the previous generation. I have focused here on the version by Charles Stothard (1786–1821). It may be checked against an independent copy by Edward Crocker (ca. 1757–1836), of which Binski, *Painted Chamber,* plate 6 (b) is a monochrome reproduction. Binski, pp. 24–30, rehearses the scholarly ground rules for studying a lost painting through copies.

[22] Binski, *Painted Chamber,* p. 42. Robert Jacob, *Images de la justice: Essai sur l'iconographie judiciaire au moyen âge à l'âge classique* (Paris: Léopard d'or, 1994), pp. 110–14, 224–29, shows judges and (more often) sergeants bearing *bâtons* or *baguettes de justice;* yet he sees the sword and scales as more usual attributes of Justice herself.

[23] My Cornell colleague Alice Isen has brought to my attention modern studies indicating that people tend to cope primarily with negative affect, so that in (normal) people negative feelings dissipate relatively quickly. This would certainly fit the visual rhetoric here.

Figure 12. The Deboneretè mural as copied by Stothard, 1819. Reproduced courtesy of the Society of Antiquaries, London.

sins) during the Middle Ages. For Anger (Ira), by far the most common opposition was with Patientia. The initial context is monastic. Anger destroyed the conditions for the monk's all-important participation in the *opus Dei.* Patience was the best means to defeat this danger. Never among monks was there call for aggression. Left to itself, anger will self-destruct in time. So artists depict Ira in the process of suicide, sometimes running herself through with her own sword, or at the least tearing her hair in despair. Her opponent need do little more than await the inevitable end.[24] Patently, there is some psychological aptness. One can easily illustrate the self-destructive nature of anger from personal experience. Patientia conveys, also, satisfying overtones of Christ's Passion and suffering.

But what has this to do with kings? Carolingian and later churchmen certainly pressed their monastic virtues onto their royal masters for entirely comprehensible motives.[25] They exhorted their kings to be *mitis* or *mansuetus,* gentle, much in the sense of the admonition of the Sermon on the Mount: "Blessed are the *mites*" as the Vulgate Latin has it.[26] The resulting scenario may have been much less appealing to the kings themselves and their secular attendants. Patientia, a prime virtue for monks, was much less obviously commendable in a king, deputed by God to perform a very different *opus* in the dirty world of secular politics. Even in the thirteenth century, the patience to suffer evil was not what secular magnates and barons wanted of their king. They knew that their realm needed effective leadership and abhorred the notion of a *rex inutilis* quite as much as their ecclesiastical cousins did, albeit with a rather different ideal of utility. The prime functions of a good king for them inevitably include such *im*patient actions as the defense of the realm from enemies without, maintenance of the peace within, and the doing of good, strong justice on wrongdoers. One can see this from coronation oaths exacted from kings both before and long after Henry III.[27] It was the good king's duty to lead his *bellatores* at the Church's nod onto the battlefield with secular sword unsheathed against enemies of all kinds, the unbelieving

[24] In Chapter 1 of this book Lester Little discusses the tradition of spectacular images in manuscripts of Prudentius's *Psychomachia* (Figs. 1–4). Little gives some others scarcely less spectacular (Figs. 5–6). Herrad of Landsberg, *Hortus Deliciarum,* ed. Rosalie Green, 2 vols., Studies of the Warburg Institute 36 (London: Warburg Institute, 1979), p. 191, pl. 112, nos. 264–66, is an extraordinary example that is not to be missed. The iconographic range is both wide and lasting. Robert E. Kaske, "*Piers Plowman* and Local Iconography: The Font at Eardisley, Herefordshire," *JWCI* 31 (1968): 84–86, notes two examples in schemes of virtues and vices from twelfth-century English church fonts and nicely connects the details with the depiction of Wrath in *Piers Plowman.*

[25] Gerd Althoff documents some of these motives in Chapter 3 above.

[26] Clerical writers nevertheless continued to press for Patience as a royal virtue into and beyond the thirteenth century, as appears below.

[27] John W. Legg, *Three Coronation Orders,* Henry Bradshaw Society 19 (London: Henry Bradshaw Society, 1903), pp. 41–43.

enemies of Christ abroad[28] and heretics, Jews, and others at home. Reflective churchmen recognized their own interest to channel royal anger into approved directions rather than to prohibit it absolutely.

Ira regis had on occasion received a highly positive characterization in the early Middle Ages. Throughout the period, clerical treatments of anger generally note at least in passing that there was good as well as bad anger. Every scholar and preacher knew plenty of Bible authorities for God's anger, even that of Jesus himself, and certainly of the righteous indignation of believers confronted with evil. Who better to exercise a distant reflection of *ira Dei* against sin than kings, long considered to be God's earthly representatives in the business of correction? Scholars have demonstrated the emergence especially under the Carolingians of a persuasive ecclesiastical plea for a kingly ideology of clemency and restraint. The critique implies as target an existing secular ideology of *ira regis*, less easily documented perhaps, but just as real.[29]

To explain the full resonance of our picture, I need next to sketch the process by which, in England as elsewhere in Europe, bridle and bit were imposed on royal anger. The sometimes idiosyncratic language of English historiography must not be allowed to mask the way Norman, Angevin, and Plantagenet kings accord with the general European developmental pattern. J. E. A. Jolliffe makes in his own way a classic case for the autumnal survival of *ira regis* into Angevin England.[30] All good lordship, he argued, centered on "discriminatory protection." It was the lord's duty to arrange matters in the interests of his friends, to ride against and destroy their enemies, who were his enemies too. The challenge for his man, his baron, was to ensure (by the way he pleaded his case) that he gained inclusion in the desired category, as friend not foe, and thus to persuade his lord, more or less in the terms of the oath he swore at the time of the homage ceremony, that his enemies were indeed the lord's too, that he would love those his lord loved, and that those whom he shunned his lord should also shun.[31] The prudent man must take serious account of his

[28] Or even at home: Robert C. Stacey, "Crusades, Crusaders, and the Baronial *Gravamina* of 1263–64," *Thirteenth Century England* 3 (1991): 137–50, describes thought about events very close in time to our paintings.

[29] I have in mind something along the lines of the secular model of marriage expounded by Georges Duby, *The Knight, the Lady, and the Priest,* trans. Barbara Bray (New York: Random House, 1983). By its nature, this model could hardly be documented from texts as clear as those adduced by Prof. Althoff in Chapter 3 above. In the light of such considerations, my own unlettered inclination would be to view the motif of Just Anger deployed around Frederick Barbarossa (see Althoff above) as remodeled and made explicit rather than new. But clearly different views are possible, as I suggest below.

[30] Jolliffe, *Angevin Kingship.*

[31] For this form of words, which I do not care to label a "fealty," see conveniently William Stubbs, *Select Charters*, ed. Henry W. C. Davis, 9th ed. (Oxford: Clarendon Press, 1913), pp. 73–74. I argue in

lord's anger. He sought to unleash it in his own interest and feared greatly its being turned against himself.

From the time of Henry II onward, rule changes progressively squeezed out the more extreme forms of this private lordship, as the Angevin legal reforms brought relations between lord and man increasingly under the cold outsider scrutiny of royal law.[32] Royal justices liberated by their minimal investment in the politics of a particular lordship easily dismissed seignorial anger as an irrelevancy, certainly no excuse for violence, now simply proscribed as unjust and illegal and as contravening a view of noble custom that the king would if necessary enforce even against the lords themselves.[33]

One lord stood out for a time against these changes, the king himself. As lord over lords, he was able to retain the benefits of the older patterns of behavior for a while.[34] The Angevins, burdened by their coronations with special duties qua king and thus the beneficiary of equally special rights, were happy to expunge anger from the souls of their subjects (as they were now beginning to call them) while retaining for themselves the power to indulge in *ira regis* as required.[35] Henry II and his sons ruled the realm quite largely through their passions, allowing at times very full play to their personal hates, the royal fear and favor. For them "discriminatory protection" remained "an admitted aspect of royalty with a positive constitutional effect."[36] The king's *ira* continued to set the men who were its objects at the very edge of the king's peace; it publicized the removal of protection to allow one's enemies to sue at law or even attack in physical force, confident of impunity. The victims knew and understood its force. A bishop of Lincoln, totally nonplussed when informed of his loss of Henry I's royal grace, at once fell off his horse with a stroke.[37] His successor, St. Hugh, knew much better how to ride out the storm, if necessary

---

Rancor and Reconciliation in Medieval England (forthcoming), chap. 6 that plaints along these lines to lords constitute a prehistory to the common-law action of trespass.

32 The subtle general account of Stroud F. C. Milsom, *The Legal Framework of English Feudalism* (Cambridge: Cambridge University Press, 1976), represents a received view under current revision. This marvelous work is so deeply engrained in a tradition of lawyers' common-law history that outsiders need guidance on the details of its argument. There are a number of good reviews; my own effort is to be found in *English Historical Review* 93 (1978): 853–61.

33 For the exemplary illustration of the abbot of Bury's comeuppance in the Cockfield case, see Sir James Holt, "Notions of Patrimony," *TRHS*, 5th ser., 33 (1983): 193–98, 218; and my own "The Charter as a Source for the Early Common Law," *Journal of Legal History* 12 (1991): 80–81.

34 The situation was naturally different on the occasions when the English king was forced to acknowledge the lordship of another, such as the king of France.

35 Jolliffe, *Angevin Kingship*, pt. 1, esp. chap. 4: "Ira et Malevolentia."

36 Ibid., p. 90 n. 1. This is pretty much Milsom's "disciplinary jurisdiction" with teeth.

37 Richard W. Southern, *Medieval Humanism and Other Studies* (Oxford: Blackwell, 1970), pp. 224–25.

by sailing closer to the wind than lesser men dared. His monastic hagiographer made his *Magna Vita* into a virtual casebook of spectacular political anger and the spiritual counters to it.[38] Men continued to proffer for royal *benevolentia* or the remission of the king's *ira* or *malevolentia* in the late twelfth century and on into the thirteenth, much as they undoubtedly had for ages before. There is nothing special about this. Germany and other medieval kingdoms can furnish similar cases if one looks for them. Angevin England is unusual only in its dangerous habit of routinely registering such matters in writing (on the royal Pipe Rolls), one reason for the calamitous events of 1215 leading to the extraction of Magna Carta.

One question raised by this formal evidence is the reality or otherwise of the king's anger. Not all the anger of kings constitutes *ira regis,* which was reserved for political show and public consumption and in no sense for private catharsis. Yet to convince its recipients, the formal anger must threaten violence and resemble the real thing. The existence of genuine anger among actual kings, to the point where it is sometimes scarcely controllable, seems to me a necessary precondition for any wide acceptance of formal *ira regis,* in much the way that forged coins will not pass unless they bear some close resemblance to the genuine coin of the realm. To distinguish the occasional public temper tantrums in which some kings indulged (illustrations below) from the assumption of anger for political ends is a challenge which it is not necessary to take up here. But there is no reason why a formal declaration of *ira regis* should always involve, for example, those physiological reactions that ordinarily accompany anger.[39] Adept kings vested themselves in political anger as required, much as politicians have always assumed diplomatic illness, for public effect. The reader is compelled to consider, accept, or reject anecdotes presented by the sources on the unsatisfactory basis of their look and feel.

Angevin royal tempers were apparently on the short side. Henry II was notorious for his rages. One of Becket's friends noted an early example of the king's *solitus furor* in 1166, long before that most famous outburst which propelled the four knights to ride off and elevate St. Thomas to martyrdom. The way the letter-writer told the story, this was no piece of controlled political drama for public consumption. Henry "flung his cap

[38] *Magna Vita Sancti Hugonis,* ed. Decima L. Douie and Hugh Farmer, 2 vols. (London: Nelson, 1961–62; repr., Oxford: Oxford University Press, 1985), 1:115–17, is the anecdote referred to concerning Henry II's "cousins of Falaise"! See also pp. 1:71, 114, 115–17; 2:6, 95–105, 114–15, 155, 188–89, 203–4. Karl J. Leyser, "The Angevin Kings and the Holy Man," in *Saint Hugh of Lincoln,* ed. Henry M. R. E. Mayr-Harting (Oxford: Clarendon Press, 1987), pp. 49–73, is the best commentary. Leyser's comments on the anecdote are on pp. 58–59; his remark on "the ruthless logic of [kings'] own *ira,*" p. 53, is especially noteworthy in the present context.

[39] Carol Tavris, *Anger: The Misunderstood Emotion,* rev. ed. (New York: Simon and Schuster, 1989), chap. 3.

from his head, pulled off his belt, and sitting as it might be on a dung heap started chewing pieces of straw."[40] A royal temper beyond control can hardly be the whole story, or Henry II's success at his zenith would be hard to understand. One may indeed suspect that self-discipline contributed substantially to his achievements. Certainly, commentators as widely different as Richard FitzNeal, an admiring servant who knew his king well, and Gerald of Wales, a bitter critic, agreed on this. They each (in virtually the same order and with a shared biblical citation) remarked on his concern for peace, his genuine efforts at self-restraint (he was hampered especially by the fact that his children usually started shouting matches), and his clemency, which some felt he overdid.[41] Their measure of agreement shows that the Church required different things of its kings according to circumstance as well as whom you asked.

It is quite possible even as "late" as Henry III's own reign to find churchmen in sympathy with *ira regis,* providing it was directed away from them at proper targets. They expected their kings to unleash their anger on crusade, or as the Church's secular arm to justice heretics and even to enforce duly laid excommunications on a routine basis.[42] Even during the twelfth-century golden age of Gregorian ideology, however, there was a growing number of clerical critics. Voices in the schools tightened the conditions for the exercise of royal power and cast doubt on its unfettered validity.[43] For this sentiment—that kings also ought to follow the custom that they and their royal law enforced on others—the Angevin Magna Carta of 1215 and its subsequent reissues provide excellent illustration.[44]

[40] The letter is found in *Materials for the History of Thomas Becket,* ed. James C. Robertson and J. Brigstocke Sheppard, 8 vols. (London: Rolls Series, 1875–85), 6:72; but it is not included as a genuine product in *The Letters of John of Salisbury,* ed. W. J. Millor, S. J. and Christopher N. L. Brooke, vol. 2 (Oxford: Clarendon Press, 1979). Frank Barlow, *Thomas Becket* (London: Weidenfeld and Nicholson, 1986), chap. 11, gives a clear account of Becket's murder, and Wilfred L. Warren, *Henry II* (London: Eyre, Methuen, 1973), pp. 183, 210–11, discusses these and other examples. See also Raoul C. van Caenegem, *English Lawsuits from William I to Richard I,* 2 vols., Selden Society 106–7 (London, 1990–91), 1:372–73, for an *indignatio* which the abbot of St. Albans had to placate in time.

[41] Richard FitzNigel [FitzNeal], *Dialogus de Scaccario,* ed. and trans. Charles Johnson, rev. ed. (Oxford: Clarendon Press, 1983), pp. 75–77; Gerald of Wales, *Expugnatio Hibernica* 1.46, in Giraldus Cambrensis, *Opera,* ed. Brewer, Dimock, and Warner, 5:303–4; *DPI* 2.4 (p. 165).

[42] Jolliffe, *Angevin Kingship,* p. 96 cites Roger of Wendover on the king as the instrument at least of God's anger, as "flagellum Dei" or "virga furoris Dei."

[43] Philippe Buc, *L'ambiguité du livre: Prince, pouvoir, et peuple dans les commentaires de la bible au moyen âge* (Paris: Beauchesne, 1994), surveys *sacra pagina;* cf. Kenneth Pennington, *The Prince and the Law, 1200–1600* (Berkeley: University of California, 1993), chap. 1 for the law schools. Jolliffe, *Angevin Kingship,* pp. 97, 100, was aware of the move for a new ideal of *Rex mansuetus.*

[44] This theme shines through the various reissues of the 1215 Magna Carta into its final form of 1225. James C. Holt, *Magna Carta,* 2d ed. (Cambridge: Cambridge University Press, 1992), is the best general guide, esp. chaps. 4, 9. Magna Carta as a document thus current under Henry III should be read along with such contemporary documents as the "Bractonian" *Addicio de Cartis* (*Bracton on the Laws and Customs of England,* ed. George E. Woodbine, rev. ed. [Cambridge: Harvard University,

One can plot the progress of this more critical attitude from the chroniclers' clerical eulogies of princes in the century or so after 1066. Norman chroniclers still often took the older line of praise for the capacity to inspire fear among the realm's enemies.[45] But Jean de Marmoutiers, writing in the 1170s, recalled Count Geoffrey of Anjou in gentler terms. "Gentle, agreeable and extremely kind by nature, he was merciful toward citizens and indulgent to offenses and wrongs committed against him. He patiently ignored the insults he heard brought against him by many, was agreeable and pleasing to absolutely everyone, especially the knights, and was so good and kind that those whom he had subdued by force, he really overcame by his clemency."[46] Here, in a characterization of Henry III's great-grandfather, are already most of the elements for an updated paradigm. The ruler should be gentle. He should suffer wrongs patiently and exercise clemency. In a word, kings should inspire love rather than fear.

The change, though long prepared, did not take place overnight. William of Poitiers, loudly though he praised the Conqueror's martial qualities, makes his *clementia* a virtual leitmotif of the panegyric.[47] Henry II, on the other hand, like his contemporary Frederick Barbarossa, was still praised in the old way,[48] and even admirers feared that he conceded too much to his enemies.[49] Doubtless in this as in so much else, the Capetians set the fashion for the Angevins to follow. The treatment by William le Breton, biographer to Philip Augustus (d. 1223), of an occasion of some consider-

1968–77), 2:110). Note that there has been no full reexamination of this interpolation since the revelation (by Samuel E. Thorne, translator's introduction to ibid., vol. 3), that the "Summa de legibus" was not by Henry de Bracton but a complex production of the 1220s and 1230s. See Brian Tierney, "Bracton on Government," *Speculum* 38 (1963): 295–317 and more specifically Michael Prestwich, *English Politics in the Thirteenth Century* (London: Macmillan, 1990), p. 21, and Michael T. Clanchy, "Did Henry III Have a Policy?" *History* 53 (1968): 208.

45 C. Stephen Jaeger, *The Origins of Courtliness: Civilizing Trends and the Formation of Courtly Ideals, 939–1210* (Philadelphia: University of Pennsylvania, 1985), pp. 200–5 cites a whole group of eulogy texts with shrewd comment. His citation of Robert of Torigny on Henry I (from PL 149, col. 886) is now printed in *The Gesta Normannorum Ducum of William of Jumièges, Orderic Vitalis, and Robert of Torigni*, ed. Elizabeth M. C. van Houts (Oxford: Clarendon Press, 1992–95), 2:216.

46 *Chroniques des comtes d'Anjou et des seigneurs d'Amboise*, ed. Louis Halphen and René Poupardin (Paris: Picard, 1913), p. 177: "Fuit igitur mitis, gratus, benignissimi animi; in cives clemens, offensarum et injuriarum indultor fuit. Convicia sibi a multis illata audiens, patienter dissimulavit; tante etiam bonitatis et benignitatis fuit ut, quos armis subegerat, clementia magis vicerit." Cf. also Southern, *Medieval Humanism*, p. 231, on Henry I.

47 Jaeger, *Origins*, p. 200, singled out for citation Guillaume de Poitiers, *Histoire de Guillaume le conquérant*, ed. Raymonde Foreville (Paris: Belles Lettres, 1952), pp. 12–14; but see pp. 20, 58, 62, 96, etc.

48 Jolliffe, *Angevin Kingship*, p. 109, cites one such text. Althoff's discussion of praise of the newer kind for Henry II's contemporary Frederick Barbarossa, in Chapter 3 above, makes a helpful comparison. *Jordan Fantosme's Chronicle*, ed. Ronald C. Johnston (Oxford: Clarendon Press, 1981), lines 45–53, 125–26, 129, 243, and esp. 508–15, nicely shows the range of responses to anger in various situations in a vernacular epic on Henry II's suppression of the 1173–74 revolt.

49 It is all too sadly apt to be writing this on the day of Yitzchak Rabin's Jerusalem funeral.

able importance to Henry III, the French victory at Bouvines over his father's Continental allies in 1214, is a case in point. He praised Philip's amazing clemency (*mira principis clementia*) afterwards. Philip had made a fine haul of counts and other nobles, now liable, William says, by both Roman law and good French custom to the death penalty for their rebellion and lèse-majesté. Philip's demonstration of meekness and mercy constituted an unheard-of pious novelty in the biographer's inaccurate but pardonable view.[50]

The Rise of Self-Restraint on the Secular Scene

The challenge for the historian is first to find a context for this apparent shift in sensibility and then to place kings and other powers within the process. Here I follow the lead given by Stephen Jaeger in his original if idiosyncratic *The Origins of Courtliness.* In search of the "civilizing process," which he sensed had to precede and create the demand for that flowering of courtly literature which is one of the great creative triumphs of the Western Middle Ages, he turned to the massive study of Norbert Elias.[51] Elias, blissfully unversed in the Middle Ages, had sought to explain the court cultures of a much later period in terms of their more proximate causes. His insights into the implied changes induced Jaeger to transfer his questions and some of his lines of argument to the high Middle Ages.

Jaeger proceeded to seek a prehistory for courtliness earlier than had been conventional among literary specialists of the period. One can see elsewhere in this volume that he nevertheless overrated the originality of his tenth- and eleventh-century sources. He emphasized the courts within which, he suggested, the courtly vocabulary was born. He argued for the birth of an ethics of restraint in the milieu of episcopal as much as royal courts in tenth-century Germany. He showed how successful Ottonian and Salian bishops responded to the challenge of reconciling their episcopal duties and roles with those of life at the royal court. The result was the gradual, sometimes faltering generation of a court strategy appropriate for devout churchmen. This strategy's major roots were arguably less Christian than antique. Once developed, it was ripe for dissemination beyond the ranks of churchmen. It served in time to assist the taming of rough, secular nobles into acceptable courtiers, capable of doing whatever was

[50] Henri-François Delaborde, ed., *Oeuvres de Rigord et de Guillaume le Breton* (Paris, 1882), 1:290–91, using the Virgil commonplace "parcere subiectis et debellare superbos" to summarize Philip's overall policy.

[51] Norbert Elias, *The Civilizing Process*, trans. Edmund Jephcott, 2 vols. (Oxford: Blackwell, 1978).

necessary to succeed in the sharp competition to win first the prince's attention and then his favor and benevolence. In this game, there were inevitably more losers than winners. The well-trained player had to learn to mask his true feelings often, to hide his hatreds behind an affable front, to lie and dissemble, in a word, to act the courtier. This new ethic of public life generated, and was perhaps in turn deeply affected by, a whole new vocabulary of courtliness, which Jaeger traces with elegant precision. By the twelfth century, the new secular ethic was widely available in the Christian West for study by the young and ambitious jostling for position at the gates and in the halls and the courts of the rich and powerful.[52]

Predictably, much of the vocabulary was borrowed from the Church. The term *Disciplina,* representing possibly the most central concept of all, came obviously enough from the monastic novice-house. It points to the need not just for obedience but for the self-discipline, as we might say, that must precede and accompany it. The processes by which this newly uncovered secular virtue was inculcated into noble youths are patently important and well worth detailed study of a kind that does not yet exist. Jaeger has little concrete to offer. What he does contribute is an understanding of the manner in which notions such as discipline were introduced into vernacular entertainment literature and romances almost as soon as they were set into the written form that alone makes them available to our eyes.[53] Jaeger goes so far as to contend mischievously yet plausibly that the courtliness in "courtly love" preceded the love! However that may be, he seems to establish firmly the more widely welcome point that these romances were major transmitters and transformers of courtly values including, among other things, his ethics of self-restraint.

One can easily prove this from any study of *mesure,* that preeminent courtly virtue, whose high valuation is almost ubiquitous in the romances, which frequently highlight the tendency of its contrary, *desmesure,* to upset the courtly applecart, to destroy the happy surface atmosphere of court life. All this is highly pertinent to much of the anger discussed elsewhere in this book, though naturally enough few people were prepared to describe their own actions in terms of *desmesure!*[54]

[52] Jaeger, *Origins,* chaps. 1, 7, 8, and 11, present the gist of his argument.

[53] He has, I think, the twelfth century in mind. I worry about the odd, contrary texts visible from rather earlier which hint that we may date the absurdly overstated shift from epic to romance much too late. There are, for example, a number of late-Roman romances that survived the early Middle Ages in Latin and vernacular versions. My pet illustration is the Old English "Apollonius of Tyre," which is more or less coeval with the very different "Battle of Maldon"; but see generally Elizabeth Archibald, *Apollonius of Tyre: Medieval and Renaissance Themes and Variations* (Rochester, N.Y.: Boydell and Brewer, 1991). Then there is the intriguing *The Ruodlieb,* ed. and trans. C. W. Grocock (Chicago: Bolchazy-Carducci, 1985), which Jaeger, *Origins,* pp. 130–32, 169–70, 269, patently knows well.

[54] I have in mind more particularly the articles by Richard E. Barton (Chapter 7) and Stephen D.

While the jury is still out on major portions of both Jaeger's specific argument and the schemata of Elias whence it sprang, it is already clear enough that we have a major secular civilizing process to juxtapose and integrate with the Twelfth-Century Renaissance of the clerical schools. But the objector may reasonably inquire what direct impact can literary themes like *mesure* make on "real" life in a tough, secular world.

Over the last few years, John Gillingham, in a series of remarkable papers firmly based on an unfashionably intensive reading of narrative sources, has offered his own answer to this and connected questions as far as they concern England.[55] He first detected a marked change from an old to a newer view in the attitude of the chroniclers William of Malmesbury and Orderic Vitalis as they were writing their works during the second quarter of the twelfth century. Previously, accepted dogma had held that it was both prudent and legitimate to deal with defeated enemies by killing them, *tout simple.* The newer view preferred to spare noble lives in return for payment of a fat ransom. This was in part a declaration of knightly labor union rules. It was comforting to know as one rode off to battle that you and your genteel peers were not expected to go so far as killing each other, that you merely competed for the twin prizes of knightly valor and earthly swag. Victory now brought applause and enrichment without too direct a risk of death. This new dispensation applied to those who merited it, men of high birth, or to put it another way, the French speakers of England. It did not apply to the low-born or to the non-English from the "Celtic Fringe." These meddled in noble affairs at their own risk; for them failure still meant death, just as in the good old days. To define those excluded, our two chroniclers forged from antique materials a new definition of the barbarian.

Although these developments obviously participated in the much wider shifts of sensibility studied by Jaeger and others, Gillingham understandably describes them as the "birth of English Imperialism." But the wider context prompted him to go further. He now points to a strong behavioral contrast between the temperature of politics in England before and after the Norman Conquest, a genuine sea change. Where Anglo-Saxon royal successions and court politics had been notably savage, William I was

---

White (Chapter 6) below. We might perhaps have made more of the fact that *desmesure,* like beauty, lies mostly in the eye of the beholder, that is, those on the receiving end. The judgments are by their nature usually both instrumental and political.

[55] John Gillingham, "Conquering the Barbarian: War and Chivalry in Twelfth-Century Britain," *Journal of the Haskins Society* 4 (1992): 67–84; idem, "The Beginnings of English Imperialism," *Journal of Historical Sociology* 5 (1992): 392–409; idem, "1066 and the Introduction of Chivalry into England," in *Law and Government in Medieval England and Normandy: Essays in Honour of Sir James Holt,* ed. George Garnett and John Hudson (Cambridge: Cambridge University Press, 1994), pp. 31–55. The forthrightness with which Gillingham restricts his claims to England is noteworthy.

"the first chivalrous ruler in English history."[56] Chivalry for Gillingham is "a secular code of values . . . in which a key element was the attempt to avoid brutality of conflict by treating prisoners in a relatively humane fashion." He presents a powerful case in support of the contention that this new chivalrous pattern of politics was widely accepted in England by the reign of Stephen, thus providing a context both for a new humanity in war and politics and also for the imposition of the new standards of judgment on kings that we have already seen emerging during the twelfth century.

The point is not that all cruelty was suddenly outlawed. It is that the new line of criticism revised the definition of the licit and placed restraints on the rest. Doubtless this preference originated and remained strongest among the monks and clerics who wrote chronicles, but it patently did not end with the clergy. It implied, among much else, the extension of the spreading secular ethics of noble restraint to the anger of kings; and it seems that well before 1215 it was so widely accepted that a king could ignore it, as perhaps John did, only at his grave risk.

The Influences on a King

By the time Henry III was born in 1207, then, the well-educated English nobleman could expect to be exposed to an ethics of restraint during the normal course of his upbringing. Kings' sons were no exceptions, but they were obviously a special case. It is worth pausing for a moment to ask in what manner and form this new ethics might have reached the young Henry. In the absence of any single work composed specifically for the young king's instruction,[57] information on these matters is not easy to come by.

We have few details concerning Henry's doubtless crucial early education. His personal tutors until age fourteen worked harder on his political and knightly formation than on book-learning.[58] There must have been more that we do not know. He showed as an adult, for example, a rather

[56] Gillingham, "1066," pp. 38–40.

[57] Such as the *Somme le Roi,* written ca. 1279–80 for the future Philip the Fair but later much read and translated in England. In the absence of a modern edition, Charles-Victor Langlois, *La vie en France au moyen âge* (Paris: Hachette, 1928), 4:123–98, conveys the gist. On "ire" (pp. 155–56), the author recommends compromise to avoid the disasters that follow from the anger of high personages. "Débonaireté" appears as a virtue (p. 175) among the goods of nature.

[58] Nicholas Orme, *English Schools in the Middle Ages* (London: Methuen, 1973), pp. 22–23 sketches the general pattern into which he should be fitted. David Carpenter, *The Minority of Henry III* (Berkeley: University of California, 1990), pp. 241–42, 258, gives the little that is known of the tutors.

shaky understanding of the Roman Law notions of kingship.[59] His books, far fewer in number than his father's and including a perhaps significant number of romances, were otherwise mainly liturgical and designed apparently more for admiration or show than private study.[60] Human teachers and intimates, actual people around him at courts, are the most likely vehicles of influence. Prominent among these, doubtless, were the king's confessors, in the years of his personal rule mostly friars like John of Darlington in the 1250s.[61]

Many contemporary writings enable us to sense the kinds of message these human influences will have brought to bear on our king. Although the schema of our painting firmly directs our inquiry toward the literature on virtues and vices, three other kinds of literature can also be expected to have had some impact on Henry's mind-set. The first is perhaps the least immediate: learned discussions in the schools about anger as one of the passions. Henry's life virtually spans the period in which the new Aristotelian insights were deployed to bring order to philosophical and theological understanding of anger. Thomas Aquinas's *Quaestiones Disputatae de Malo* appeared just about the same time that our paintings did. His treatment of anger there contains much that was irrelevant to kings along with a certain amount that a confessor might consider relevant enough to press on a royal penitent.[62]

The morals of vernacular literature were probably much more important. French romances directly illuminate the courtly context within which English noble political players viewed their king and his actions. Their major value here is that they brought ethical ideas out of their clerical context into the court world. Henry owned some of these romances and likely heard or read others. The splendor of the painting argues for at the very least public lip-service to the chivalric imperatives they broadcast.

But the strongest contender for attention is nevertheless very clerical in character. The traditional schemes of cardinal (or deadly, in the sense that they were considered "mortal") sins and virtues has been termed "as real as the parish church itself."[63] The tradition of the Seven Deadly Sins can

[59] Clanchy, "Did Henry III Have a Policy?" pp. 203–16.

[60] Michael T. Clanchy, *From Memory to Written Record,* 2d ed. (Oxford: Blackwell, 1993), pp. 161–62.

[61] The absence, to my knowledge, of any study of these royal confessors does seem an extraordinary gap. For France, see note 116 below.

[62] The *Quaestiones* are edited as vol. 23 of the Dominican *Opera Omnia* (Rome: Commissio Leonina, 1982), question 12, "De Ira," is on pp. 233–45. Compare, for example, the discussion in art. 1 on good anger against sin as legitimate in the execution of judgments "ex zelo justicie" (pp. 236–37).

[63] Morton Bloomfield, *The Seven Deadly Sins: An Introduction to the History of a Religious Con-*

claim to be the single most successful monastic bequest to western culture. It remains in current popular use in our own day.[64] In the thirteenth century, prelates, preachers, and confessors all vigorously promoted it as a means to reform the secular world around them. Texts expounding the schema belonged in the basic kit that diocesan statutes expected local priests to possess for their pastoral work, and figure among the plethora of pastoral aids flooding out in Henry's day. Though aimed for the most part at believers far below the royal court level, they nevertheless reveal concerns that applied to the king, whose case for his own salvation was surely affected by his public acts. The reforming bishops who promoted this movement were just the men to bring their moral positions to the king's attention. These included such points as the existence of *bona ira* (good anger) against one's own or one's neighbor's sin, and the need—quite as important for the king as any bishop or ecclesiastical judge—to correct wrongs not *per iram* but as meekly as Jesus had.[65] Henry can hardly have been untouched by the basic teachings on anger in this pastoral literature.

Yet when all is said and done, we seek here another tradition that opposed virtues not to sins as such but to vices. The opposition of virtues and vices is less obviously clerical or pastoral and more up-market with its antique antecedents. Yet books devoted explicitly to it form, it is said, "a characteristically Christian genre of literature."[66] Its products included more than one tradition of illustration.[67] More to the point, books composed for the elementary education and moral instruction of princes seem to have drawn upon this genre and habitually used the language of "vice."[68] This Mirror of Princes literature was substantially remodeled after the middle of the thirteenth century into an almost new genre radiat-

---

cept (1952; repr., [East Lansing]: Michigan State University, 1967) remains the standard treatment today. Richard Newhauser, *The Treatise on Vices and Virtues in Latin and the Vernacular,* Typologie des sources du moyen âge occidental, fasc. 68 (Turnhout: Brepols, 1993), pp. 181–93, usefully summarizes the development into our period.

64 Thomas Pynchon et al., *Deadly Sins* (New York: Morrow, 1993), a series of essays first published in the Book Review section of the Sunday *New York Times,* shows that the tradition retains its allure to the present day.

65 *Councils and Synods . . . Relating to the English Church,* ed. Frederick M. Powicke and Christopher R. Cheney, 2 vols. (Oxford: Clarendon, 1964), 1:216–7, 307; 2:905, 1067, may serve as illustrations from the 1240s and later.

66 Newhauser, *Treatise,* p. 14, finds nothing comparable among Jews or Muslims.

67 Adolf Katzenellenbogen, *Allegories of the Virtues and Vices in Medieval Art,* Studies of the Warburg Institute 10 (London: Warburg Institute, 1939; repr., Toronto: Medieval Academy, 1989), the classic account, is especially strong on the tradition stemming from illustrated MSS of Prudentius's *Psychomachia;* see Chapter 1, Figs. 1–4, above.

68 The elementary pre-schools nature of the instruction is important as showing a genuine will to influence the malleable young; it is shared by the kind of nonroyal works discussed by James Powell, *Albertanus of Brescia: the Pursuit of Happiness in the Early Thirteenth Century* (Philadelphia: University of Pennsylvania, 1992).

ing from the Capetian court and the milieu of the friars.[69] Exemplars of this literature participate in the mendicants' efforts to bring moral reform to the laity in a form that it might easily internalize; but they also emphasize the king's special duty to provide an example to his people.[70] While they remain distinct from specifically pastoral works on sin (preachers' aids, confessors' manuals, bishops' statutes and the like), there are signs of convergence both in language (an equation of vice and sin) and content. It is therefore possible to indicate with at least some confidence the kinds of thought on anger likely to have influenced our king's plans for the walls of his chamber.

I take my examples from two works of about the right time and place.[71] In about 1217 Gerald of Wales stopped writing his *De principis instructione*, book 1 of which is a conventional Mirror of Princes. Though it was aimed at the infant Henry III himself, there is no reason to believe that it ever came to his notice. This may have been lucky for its author who had devoted books 2 and 3 to a sustained attack on Henry II.[72] Guillaume Peyraut (Peraldus) wrote first a "Summa de vitiis" (ca. 1236) and then later (1248) a "Summa de virtutibus," each at exhaustive length.[73] The two summae were circulating together by the 1250s and soon became massively influential in England as well as France.

Gerald and Peraldus appear to a casual reader to hold rather conventional views. While closer study may adjust this preliminary judgment, their conventionality may actually enhance their value to us. What we need to know is how much of the restraint ethic outlined above they might have conveyed to a royal recipient, and to what degree they further valorized this ethic with the host of classical and Christian authorities they summoned to its support. Patience remains for both writers a royal virtue, though less prominently perhaps than in an earlier age. The imita-

[69] Jean-Philippe Genet, *Four English Political Tracts of the Later Middle Ages*, Camden Society, 4th ser., no. 18 (London: Camden Society, 1977), pp. ix-xii; Jenny Swanson, *John of Wales: A Study of the Works and Ideas of a Thirteenth-Century Friar* (Cambridge: Cambridge University Press, 1989), p. 56.

[70] *DPI*, pp. 5, 9, 47, etc., already emphasizes this among the reasons to demand special self-discipline of princes.

[71] I was unable to consult the "Breviloquium" of John of Wales, written even closer to the right date in the mid-1260s; see Swanson, *John of Wales*, chap. 3.

[72] Robert Bartlett, *Gerald of Wales, 1146–1223* (Oxford: Clarendon Press, 1982), pp. 69–72.

[73] I have used *Reverendissimi Domini Guilielmi Peraldi . . . summae virtutum ac vitiorum*, 2 vols. (Cologne: Boerztzter, 1629). "Clementia" is treated within the virtue of Temperance in *Summa virtutum* 3.3.6 (ibid., 1:183–87; see p. 7 for "Modestia"), and "Ira" is tractatus 8 of the *Summa vitiorum* (2:283–300). A historical study—those I know of are almost all by literary scholars—could throw immense light on the moral thought of the period. It should take account of other works such as Peraldus, *Virtutum vitiorumque exempla* (Lyons: Jean-Baptiste de Ville, 1680), which I know through R. E. Kaske's copy, thanks to the kindness of Carol Kaske.

tion of Jesus is the best reason to detest anger.[74] The prince must face the dilemma of whether to seek love or to elicit fear from his people. Gerald leaned toward love; Peraldus more positively took his stand on the Gospel admonition to love one's enemies.[75] Both argue for clemency. Gerald would have his prince remit offenses, soften penalties, and lean toward pardon even for the guilty. Each writer cites Seneca on the subject with relish. Too many punishments were as bad an advertisement for a prince as too many funerals for a doctor. The ideal role model was the stingless King Bee![76] Yet justice remains of necessity the prime virtue for a prince, justice exercised without cruelty (save as a last resort), not from anger but zealously for its own sake.[77] Readers of Gerald, and probably of Peraldus must certainly have carried away with them the recognition that the prince's main task was to strike a just balance between on the one hand, the duty imposed by his royal office to emulate God the Father and mete out justice and, on the other, the requirement that he perform that office in a manner compassionate enough for the Son Jesus himself. The effort to strike this balance was already in Gerald's day an exercise that cried out for the application of Aristotelian notions of the mean, a fact worth recalling when we return to the examination of our picture.

From Latin to Vernacular Culture

I have focused my discussion to this point on clerical ideas expressed in more or less good Latin. It is time to return to the vernacular. Many of the most significant Latin terms singled out for analysis by Jaeger gained entry into the mother tongues of the laity in due course, not always in the order we might have predicted. There is no sign, for example, that English

[74] *DPI*, pp. 15–18; Peraldus, *Summa vitiorum* 8.1.5.6 (2:291).

[75] *DPI*, pp. 11, 43, 142–43; Peraldus, *Summa vitiorum* 8.1.4; 8.2 (2:291–92); cf. Jean de Marmoutiers at note 46 above.

[76] *DPI*, pp. 21–27; Peraldus, *Summa virtutum* 3.3.6 (1:186) retells the myth of the King Bee, also to be found, for example, in Thomas of Chobham, *Summa confessorum*, ed. F. Broomfield, Analecta Medievalia Namurcensia 25 (Louvain: Éditions Nauwelaerts, 1968), pp. 418, 421; and Thomas of Chobham *Summa de arte praedicandi*, ed. Franco Morenzoni, CCCM 82 (Turnhout: Brepols, 1988), p. 257. This Thomas, sub-dean of Salisbury (d. ca. 1235), writing in the decades around 1215, is another likely candidate to have been among those who transmitted to the king clerical insights and commonplaces from the cardinal sins tradition. For anger, see *Summa confessorum*, pp. 38, 319–20, 327, 474, 534, and esp. pp. 414–20. The very number of his pastoral writings with much overlapping of material (Morenzoni, introduction to *Summa de arte praedicandi*, pp. xiv–xxx, discusses in addition to those already mentioned both his *Sermones*, ed. Franco Morenzoni, CCCM 82A [Turnhout: Brepols, 1993]) and the still unedited "Summa de commendatione virtutum et extirpatione vitiorum") strengthen his claims to attention.

[77] *DPI*, pp. 25, 34–39; Peraldus, *Summa vitiorum* 8.2; 8.4.3 (2:284–86).

speakers applied the key term "discipline" outside ecclesiastical contexts in Henry III's day.[78]

It had, however, in *Zuht* a German equivalent whose story is worth a minor digression. In Middle High German literature, the opposition of *Zuht* to *Zorn* (anger) was a literary commonplace; individual works preferred one or the other at the author's choice. Predictably enough, the *Niebelungenlied* rather favored *Zorn.* Its authors many times over declared their approval of the old order of legitimate anger and vengeance in an epic that turned a sour, skeptical eye on its romance overlay.[79] The more obviously *cultivé* Wolfram of Eschenbach was markedly pro-*Zuht* in his masterpiece, *Parzifal,* one incident from which cannot be denied a hearing. Young Parzifal had met the Fisher King who sent him on ahead to stay over that night in a castle of his, a fine, impressive structure standing "as though turned on a lathe." The castle's denizens treated Parzifal in noble fashion, once he had announced himself the owner's guest. They relieved him of his arms and travel-stained clothes and brought him hot water in which to bathe. He received, in short, the whole courtly treatment, including a gift of a fine new silk robe. Soon it was time to dine. The knight who approached Parzifal to summon him to hall was unfortunately something of a wag. He pretended to be angry with Parzifal and assumed a humiliatingly arrogant tone. The hypersensitive young knight was crushed and so furious that, as the poet notes, it was lucky for that knight that they had taken away Parzifal's sword. Since there was nothing immediate to do, Parzifal "clenched his fist so tightly that the blood gushed out from beneath his nails and wet the sleeve of his cloak." So it often is that when one tries hardest to suppress and conceal anger, one succeeds only in making it even more obvious. The knights around certainly noticed it. One of them undertook to calm the youth and explain the joke, giving the young man excellent advice: "Show yourself courteous (*zuht*) toward him. . . . Go in . . . you are the honored guest . . . and cast off the burden of your wrath (*Zorn*)."[80]

Perhaps, in a reversal of the usual procedure, this Middle High German opposition may assist us to comprehend the French juxtaposition of our image. Old French *debonaire* and its derivatives originate in an adjectival phrase deriving from the substantive *aire,* which in turn stems from Latin

[78] *Middle English Dictionary,* ed. Hans Kurath et al. (Ann Arbor: University of Michigan Press, 1952-), s.v. "discipline," esp. sense 4, suggests a complex semantic trajectory for the word.

[79] The point is clear enough from the English version of *The Nibelungenlied,* trans. Arthur T. Hatto (Harmondsworth, England: Penguin, 1965).

[80] Wolfram von Eschenbach, *Parzival* 5.229, ed. Edvard Hartl (Bern: Franke, 1951), p. 115. See the translation by Helen M. Mustard and Charles E. Passage (New York: Vintage Books, 1961), pp. 125–26. My colleague Arthur Groos led me to this text and helped me to read and understand its thrust.

area, a word with a range of spatial connotations from a region or other geographical area down to a single room or some such smaller area.[81] By extension the term then came to refer to the people or race who sprang from a region and to their qualities, which could be good, bad or worse. The connecting link between birthplace and noble blood seems to be an equation of OFr *aire* and nest, as in the eyrie of an eagle.[82] Roland serves as the classic exemplar. After Ganelon had nominated him to the dangerous rear guard, he barked angrily back at the "malvais hom de put aire." Much later in the poem, he addressed Archbishop Turpin's noble corpse as that of a "gentilz hom, chevaler de bon aire." Similar usage is found in other twelfth-century works from the Anglo-Norman kingdom, such as Beroul's *Tristan* and Wace's *Roman de rou.*[83]

The complimentary *debonaire* seems to have taken deeper root than the insults; *de bon aire* soon merges into an integrated adjective, where the others remain as phrases into the thirteenth century and later.[84] Good knights are called debonair, alongside the attribution of other characteristically noble and courtly qualities as *cortoisie, franchise, largece,* and physical beauty. Their speeches and the good sense with which they avoid stupidity may all be termed debonair.[85] The virtue is no male monopoly; noble ladies and especially queens can be debonair too.[86] This perhaps helps explain the prominence of the capacity for showing pity and mercy among the word's further connotations.

The depiction by William Marshall's biographer in the 1220s of an emotive episode from 1194 makes an excellent illustration. Count John, the future king of Runnymede, had led a rebellion against his elder brother Richard I, absent on crusade. It had failed, of course. Now he feared his

[81] In *L'histoire de Guillaume le Maréchal,* ed. Meyer, line 6832, the reference is to the space among his companions into which William threw a (stolen) purse. I base my collection of texts on those cited in *Altfranzösisches Worterbuch,* ed. Adolf Tobler and Ernest Lommatzsch (Berlin: Weidmann, 1925–95), s.vv. "aire," "debonaire," etc., and on the *Anglo-Norman Dictionary,* ed. Louise W. Stone and Willliam Rothwell (London: Modern Humanities Research Association, 1977–92), s. vv. "aire," "boneire," "deboneire," etc.

[82] To illustrate this sense of the word, see *Le roman de rou de Wace,* ed. A. J. Holden, 3 vols. (Paris: Picard, 1970–73), vol. 2, lines 247, 270.

[83] Beroul, *Le roman de Tristan,* ed. Edouard Muret (Paris: Firmin Didot, 1903), lines 3096, 3918, 4108, 4152; *Roman de rou,* ed. Holden, vol. 1, line 24; vol. 2, lines 386, 1836; vol. 3, lines 241, 5457. Cf. *The Romance of Horn, by Thomas,* ed. Mildred K. Pope, vol. 1, Anglo Norman Text Society, vols. 9–10 (Oxford, 1955), lines 1239–40.

[84] For example, *Duremart le galois,* ed. Joseph Gildea (Villanova, Penn.: Villanova Press, 1966), lines 120, 256, 2106, 5714 (the unusual "demalaire"), 10728 ("de trop mal aire"), 10752.

[85] Chrétien de Troyes, *Le chevalier au lion ou le roman d'Yvain,* ed. David F. Hall (Paris: Livre de Poche, 1994), lines 1305–8; *Histoire de Guillaume le Maréchal,* ed. Meyer, lines 2553, 3067.

[86] For example, Beroul, *Roman de Tristan,* line 4152; *Roman de rou,* ed. Holden, vol. 1, line 24; vol. 3, line 241.

brother's vengeance and would not willingly enter the royal presence. Richard sent him a message of reassurance,

> Li reis est simples et pitos
> E plus deboneire vers vos.
>
> (The king is straightforward and merciful
> And more debonair toward you.)

to promote a reconciliation at the expense of his false counselors. The poet concludes the scene as follows:

> Totes veies est dreit que pére
> Debonaireté e franchise
> Kant ele est en cuer d'ome mise
> Mais itant vos di, c'est la some,
> Que de nul cuer de malveis homme
> Ne puet issir nul bonté.[87]
>
> (In any case it is right
> That debonairness and generosity of heart appear
> When each is placed in a man's heart;
> But I can tell you this much, here is the nub,
> That from the heart of a wicked man
> No goodness can emerge.)

In this semantic climate, debonair is sometimes equated with *clemens.*[88] In similar fashion Jesus is sometimes called debonair, and the phrase from the Sermon on the Mount already quoted becomes in thirteenth century French: "Blessed are the debonair, for they shall inherit the earth."[89] When chansons de geste call their King Louis "the Debonair"

[87] *Histoire de Guillaume le Maréchal,* ed. Meyer, lines 10398; 10420–25. Reconciliation required a dangerous physical approach to the angry party. Actual events show how the greatest men could fear to come before an angry king (see below).

[88] Cf. *Roman de rou,* ed. Holden, vol. 2, lines 1835–36.

[89] George F. Jones, *The Ethos of the Song of Roland* (Baltimore: Johns Hopkins University Press, 1963), pp. 20, 59. *Middle English Dictionary,* ed. Kurath et al., s.v. "debonaire" and derivatives; these usages attest to a blending of gentleness in Jesus' image and the courtesy of Arthur; note especially the *Wooing Lord* (ca. 1225) where "debonairshipe" by not taking vengeance gains love. In the Glossa Ordinaria ad Mt. 5:4, *beati mites,* the "mitis" man is one "unaffected by asperity or bitterness of mind and instructed by the simplicity of faith to bear with patience every wrong" and "unaffected by either rancor or anger, so bearing everything with equanimity." The remarks on the "mansuetus" are also relevant.

(where Latin chroniclers and modern authors say "the Pious"), they are perhaps not being entirely complimentary; the implication may be that he has too little legitimate anger and is unwilling to pursue vengeance against the common enemy.[90] The same notion, when put in a more positive mode, recalls the argument about royal clemency above. The debonair man, knight, or king is he who possesses the courtly self-confidence to seek renown by sparing his enemies. Thus the 1274 French translation of William le Breton's Latin panegyric of the victor of Bouvines has Philip Augustus acting "from the great *debonaireté* and pity of his heart," whereas the original had said that the king was "mitis et misericors."[91]

Notions of this kind are certainly relevant to our inquiry. Henry III's brother-in-law was this Philip's grandson, Louis IX of France. Westminster eyes were frequently directed across the Channel. St. Louis seems to me to have been not merely Henry's main rival but also the standard against which he constantly measured himself. The results, visible in the design of Henry's abbey,[92] could undoubtedly be discerned also in the style and behavior of his court.

St. Edward the Confessor: Royal Role Model

It is, however, surely time to turn our attention back once more to Westminster and to Henry III's own royal circle. The clinching arguments about the basic meaning of our Lady Deboneretė center on St. Edward the Confessor, Henry's own beloved protector. The image of Edward as a particularly debonair role model must already have been traditional. A substantial body of writing about him surfaced during the twelfth and early thirteenth centuries, much of it centered upon his and Henry's Westminster Abbey. Wace in his *Roman de rou* had, for example, written of him for Henry II in the 1170s:

Li reis Ewart fu de bon aire
Ne volt a home nule tort faire,
Sainz orgoil e sainz covoitise,

[90] See the attempt to flatter Louis in *Le couronnement de Louis,* ed. Edouard Langlois (Paris: Classiques françaises du moyen âge, 1968), line 661.
[91] *Receuil des historiens des Gaules et de la France* (Paris: Palmé, 1738–1904), 17:412.
[92] See Paul Binski, *Westminster Abbey and the Plantagenets* (New Haven: Yale University Press, 1995).

Volt faire a toz dreit justise.[93]

(King Edward was of noble birth
And willed wrong to no man;
Lacking pride and greed,
He wished to do good justice to all.)

A generation later Gerald of Wales, and quite unsolicited, also tried to present this same king to the infant Henry III as a model of pious kingship in the public eye and chose to illustrate his point with a tale of royal clemency in a royal chamber.[94]

Whether any of this reached Henry is impossible to know. In compensation, we possess a superb, contemporary witness to St. Edward's resonance for his successor in the *Estoire le seint Ædward le rei.* This pious life comes from so very close to the king and his familiar circle that it is a judgment call whether it better represents the view of the king himself or those trying to influence him. The experts now confer authorship of the French text with a fair degree of finality upon that great chronicler and all-rounder, Matthew Paris. The date when Matthew composed it and the provenance of the surviving and very finely illuminated manuscript remain under debate.[95] Matthew wrote the book for a small circle of very great ladies with close connections to the royal court; one, indeed, was the queen's sister, married to the king's brother, Earl Richard of Cornwall. The target audience, secular and female, helps to explain both the fine illuminations (distantly related to our wall paintings) and the choice of French, appropriate since laypeople lack *lettrure,* full (i.e., Latin) literacy.[96] Our manuscript, however, is not Matthew's own. It is rather a Westminster Abbey product, from "a professional, probably metropolitan establishment with connections to the royal works at Westminster and Windsor." Opinions as to date of composition converge on the two critical decades of personal rule before the revolt of 1258 and probably cannot plausibly be narrowed down further. Were we nevertheless to persist in seeking an occasion for publication, candidates might be 1245, when

[93] *Roman de rou,* ed. Holden, vol. 3, lines 5457–60. Wace may have been following the nun of Barking's *La vie d'Edouard le confesseur,* ed. Osten Sodergard (Uppsala: Almqvist and Wiksells, 1948), on which see M. Dominica Legge, *Anglo-Norman Literature and Its Background* (Oxford: Clarendon Press, 1963), pp. 60–61.

[94] *DPI,* pp. 129–31.

[95] The modern edition by Kathryn Y. Wallace, *La estoire le seint Ædward le rei,* Anglo-Norman Text Society 41 (London: Anglo-Norman Text Society, 1983) uses the same line numbering as the earlier one in Henry R. Luard, *Lives of Edward the Confessor* (London: Rolls Series, 1858), pp. 27–157. Montague R. James, *La estoire le seint Ædward le rei* (Oxford: Roxburghe Club, 1920) is a facsimile edition of the manuscript.

[96] *La estoire,* ed. Wallace, lines 3355–64.

Henry rededicated his and St. Edward's abbey church at Westminster, and 1254, when Lord Edward, the saint's namesake, married Eleanor of Castile.[97]

Unlike our wall paintings, then, neither Matthew's text nor the Westminster illuminations were actually made for the king. Yet everything points to their creators' close knowledge of the court and its ways. The personal critical interest in Henry's deeds on the part of the exceptionally well informed Matthew is evident to any reader of his chronicles. His fellow monks at Westminster and their illustrators can also hardly have failed to know the royal court at first hand.[98] It is therefore very much possible that the *Estoire* represents an outside, even critical view of Henry in the shadow of his saintly predecessor. In reconsidering the *Estoire* recently, Paul Binski, having first leaned in this direction, judiciously recalls that "such admonitory thinking" fits just as well into the atmosphere of the royal court itself.[99] Whichever view one takes—and Matthew's baronial sympathies are well attested—there can be little doubt that Henry would hear and take to heart the message of the *Estoire.*

This message was not one to inspire a king to brilliant worldly success. Matthew began by distinguishing two kinds of saintly models of English king. First came an idiosyncratic selection of English warrior-kings, such as Arthur (*sic!*), Cnut (*sic!*) and Edmund Ironside, but not for example Alfred. Only then does Matthew find for St. Edward the just peer group of mostly martyr-saints. The point seems to be to excuse Edward (and possibly Henry too) from the need to compete on the basis of martial achievement.[100] What follows is perhaps more clerical *vita* than romance, for all its French phrasing. Binski characterizes it as a portrayal of Edward as "a skilled capitulator" to the baronial will.[101] This is possibly an overstatement. The *Estoire* is something more than a paean to political passivity. We should perhaps read it less as an expression of how Henry himself may have seen his royal functions than an indication of how he and his beloved saint appeared to hostile eyes. Henry himself may have read it so.

Suggestively, the work seems to present a paradigm of ideal Christian kingship together with its opposite: a presentation of the usurper Harold, the size and interest of which is significantly augmented beyond what

[97] On all these questions, the most recent examination is that of Paul Binski, "Reflections on *La estoire le seint Ædward le rei:* Hagiography and Kingship in Thirteenth-Century England," *Journal of Medieval History* 16 (1990): 333–50; see esp. pp. 334–35, 337–38.

[98] Richard Vaughan, *Matthew Paris* (Cambridge: Cambridge University Press, 1958) is a convenient guide to Matthew's various writings; cf. pp. 168–81 for the *Estoire.* On Westminster at this time, see Gervase Rosser, *Medieval Westminster, 1200–1540* (Oxford: Clarendon Press, 1989).

[99] Binski, "Reflections," pp. 340–31, 348.

[100] *Estoire,* ed. Wallace, lines 1–18.

[101] Binski, "Reflections," pp. 346–47.

Matthew found in his source, the twelfth-century Latin life by Ailred of Rielvaux. Matthew's six uses of our word *debonaire* or its derivatives suggest a design to present St. Edward as the debonair king par excellence. No saint in Paradise showed more "simplicité debonaire" with the single exception of Jesus when he pardoned the thief hanged alongside Him during His own Passion.[102] When everyone was pressing the king to break earl Godwin, against whom he had every reason to feel just anger, Edward, because he was debonair and did not wish to cause discord demurred; he preferred to leave matters to God, who did in due course take "grant vengance" on his behalf by bringing the earl sudden death "a hunte, dolur e a peine."[103] In general,

> Cruel a ses enemis
> Debonaire ert a ses amis.[104]
>
> (He was cruel to his enemies
> But debonair to his friends.)

He was a lamb to his own people and their immediate neighbors, with a special preference for advancing his own barons while courteously (curtoisement) avoiding flatterers and aliens of uncertain loyalty, but he was a harsh lion to the barbarians (barbarin).[105] Above all, he was "duz e debonaire" in supporting or curing the wretched and the poor.[106] It is no wonder that those who traveled to court to see the king went away more "*curteis*" than before, having learned *mesure*, good sense and equally good manners from St. Edward and his court of courtesy.[107]

The whole work deserves much fuller commentary. My brief exposition has of necessity restricted itself to its direct bearing on Deboneretė. It should be clear enough even so that the word, and the concepts behind it, were flexible enough to convey a variety of messages. The good Christian king came in different shapes and sizes. He might be expected to combine courtliness and mercy with justice as in the firm peacemaking of Henry's royal father, John.[108] Beyond question, the *Estoire* contained a great deal

[102] *Estoire*, ed. Wallace, lines 1050–57.
[103] Ibid., lines 3253–76, esp. 3257–58, 3271–72.
[104] Ibid., lines 910–11.
[105] Ibid., line 912.
[106] Ibid., lines 1915–16, 2660, 4009.
[107] Ibid., lines 896–99.
[108] The reference here is not to the kind of defense case made by Doris M. Stenton, *English Justice between the Norman Conquest and the Great Charter, 1066–1215* (London: American Philosophical Society, 1963), chap. 4 but effectively refuted by Ralph V. Turner, *The King and His Courts: The Role of John and Henry III in the Administration of Justice, 1199–1240* (Ithaca: Cornell University

to provoke a pious and sensitive king to reflection about the performance of his royal duties.

Twilight Meditations?

Let us take this as a cue to return to Henry, as he awaits sleep perhaps, on the state bed in the Painted Chamber. What might he have been thinking about Anger? We are certainly now in a position to make some informed guesses. I imagine him lying on the great bed, hopeful of the protection of his guardian saint and the surrounding guardian knights. While his eyes remain open and alert, he directs them through the squint to the cross on the altar of his chapel or across the room to the regal depictions of Virtues and Vices, including ours. He perhaps meditates upon St. Edward and his own fallible efforts at emulation. Or perhaps he muses over the day's reading. One kind of fine, richly illustrated book he certainly has seen, and may very well have held and enjoyed, is a Bestiary. Its author regards anger as tending to lead to oppression of the innocent, and thus licit only against those who had actually wounded someone. The law of Christ, he adds, calls for even the guilty to go free.[109] Might a sleepy king, one wonders, have been reminded of such thoughts by Deboneretè's royal shield or the many other heraldic lions in the Chamber?

Anger was certainly a candidate for bedtime meditations. That Henry had an anger problem is well known; his most sympathetic modern biographer concedes his "impatient nature."[110] Matthew Paris conveys the impression that the reign, and more particularly the years of personal rule from 1234 to 1258, were marked by frequent flare-ups of personal anger. Matthew went to some pains to trace the evil consequences for the realm and people of the king's lack of self-restraint in angry confrontations with such politically significant figures as Earls Roger Bigod and Simon de Montfort.[111] For all of Matthew's known hostility to the king and his

Press, 1968). John and his Chief Justiciar can be seen from the plea and other rolls hard at work negotiating peace settlements in a number of politically sensitive and feudlike disputes. I document and explicate this utterly neglected function of good government at the top in my *Rancor and Reconciliation*, chap. 7.

109 Terence H. White, *The Bestiary: A Book of Beasts* (New York: Capricorn, 1960), p. 9. This text entered the tradition through the so-called Second Family attributed to England and Northern France in the early twelfth century. I am not suggesting that Henry read in bed. Not even kings enjoyed that pleasure in the ill-lit thirteenth century.

110 Frederick M. Powicke, *Henry III and the Lord Edward* (Oxford: Clarendon Press, 1960), 1:71, 342. Clanchy, "Did Henry III Have a Policy?" pp. 207–19, reviews the narrative evidence for Henry's personal attitudes and character; cf. idem, *England and Its Rulers, 1066–1272* (London: Fontana, 1983), pp. 222–30.

111 For these examples, see Matthew Paris, *Chronica Majora*, ed. Henry R. Luard (London: Rolls Series, 1872–84), 5:32, 234.

policies, his testimony must be taken seriously. As a good monk, Matthew saw anger as an offense against God, who might take vengeance and may indeed have done so in the case of Henry's royal peer, Alexander II of Scotland. It was no more than his duty to point out the dangers as he saw them.[112]

Less hostile witnesses than Matthew Paris recount anecdotes of Henry's vulnerability to the pressure of the political moment. This is sometimes evident from the official rolls of his own government. Two instructive illustrations claim retelling. The first comes from the great political crisis that ushered in his period of personal rule in 1234.[113] Among the previously powerful officials to be removed in disgrace was the Poitevin Treasurer, Peter des Rivaux. Henry summoned him to a special audit of affairs from his time in office. Peter was highly suspicious and feared for his skin. His messengers announced to the king that he was unwilling to come without a safe-conduct, and they used undiplomatic *verba dura* in saying this. The king was at first furious and, as he was later to recall, burst out into *aspera verba per iram;* to seek a safe-conduct from the king in time of proclaimed peace (which it now was) was superfluous, a bad precedent and, surely, a calculated insult. Henry regained his self-control with a struggle and made a reasoned answer *benigne.* It still took much shuttle diplomacy and some mediation from the saintly archbishop of Canterbury before des Rivaux could be induced to appear. Since our sources for the episode are the *coram rege* rolls in Latin, we cannot expect to find mention of Deboneretė.[114] Yet they describe a classic instance of Henry in his prime, first failing and then succeeding in self-control, an excellent exemplification of the Deboneretė approach.

A second *exemplum* comes from the end of the reign, in 1270. A land dispute had led to bitter enmity between Earl John de Warenne and Alan de la Zouche.[115] A suit between two such august royal intimates necessarily came before King's Bench justices to be heard in Westminster Hall. The parties appeared in person, and flying insults, *verba contumeliosa* more shameless than was proper, turned proceedings into a furious *debaccatio.* Alan was unaware that the earl's servants had come armed, against all the rules. They eventually set aside the reverence due to court and king

112 Ibid., pp. 88–89. Clanchy, "Did Henry III Have a Policy?" p. 204 ("patently the least reliable part of his chronicle"), takes a different view.

113 Powicke, *Henry III and the Lord Edward,* 1:136–38, 152.

114 *Curia Regis Rolls* (London: H. M. Stationery Office, 1922–), 15:1031, 1064, 1091, 1126, 1225, 1289.

115 I mostly follow the revealing account of Thomas Wykes, *Annales Monastici,* ed. Henry R. Luard (London: Rolls Series, 1869), 4:233–35. The details of the settlement can be found in *Calendar of Patent Rolls, 1266–1272* (London: H. M. Stationery Office, 1913), p. 280, and elsewhere on royal records. Powicke, *Henry III and the Lord Edward,* 2:584–85, gives some account of the incident.

(who, though not actually in the hall was in the palace close by), and attacked Alan, who fled for his life toward the royal Chamber (!) with the servants in hot pursuit. His own men rescued him with difficulty and rowed him seriously wounded, away up the Thames. When a formal complaint on his behalf reached the king and his heir, they burned with a strong *ira* at the enormity of so public an offense. It could not be allowed to go unpunished. Earl John was at once summoned into their presence to answer the allegations and do justice, as the law and custom of the realm required. Now the earl's life and limb were at risk. He was advised not to go. The Lord Edward and other magnates were confidently approaching with a strong force of soldiers when two other earls were able to mediate and secure him temporarily until he placed himself at the king's mercy and was granted terms. These included a public oath, to be sworn by him and fifty fellow knights, that the deed was not premeditated but done in the heat of anger (non ex precogitata malitia . . . sed ex motu iracundie nimis accensu). The storm abated, even though de la Zouche died soon after. It would seem that *Deboneretė* did not yet entirely exclude all expression of justifiable *ira regis*.

It follows that royal advisers including, certainly, his confessors needed to distinguish proper from improper expressions of royal anger, even if the king refused to do so.[116] Our mural represents in its way one attempt to persuade or remind the king to eschew violent anger and respond to provocation and frustration in courtly but firm style. No loyal servant close to the king would have advocated that he suffer humiliation willingly. *Patientia* was not what they wanted of their king. He must perform zealously his prime royal duty of meting out justice without a trace of lust for revenge even when he felt wounded by events. This was a noble, perhaps faintly highfalutin ideal in a time that saw much political upheaval, including open civil war and all kinds of humiliation for Henry, from constitutional restraints to arrest and actual physical constraints. The restoration of peace in 1267 would have hardly diminished the attractions of Deboneretė. The civil war had been very bitter, much more so than the earlier one with which Henry's reign had begun after Magna Carta. Loyalists clamored for their reward, implying the disherison of former rebels. Plenty of voices called for the aged king and his son to unleash *ira regis* in some sense against the enemies of the realm. It was

[116] As noted, there seems to be no modern study of royal confessors, mostly Dominican friars, in this period. For France, we now have Georges Minois, *Le confesseur du roi: Les directeurs de conscience sous la monarchie française* (Paris: Fayard, 1988), which I consulted too late to incorporate in this paper; also Lester K. Little, "Saint Louis' Involvement with the Friars," *Church History* 33 (1964): 1–24.

against such a background, and somewhat prematurely, that the pope wrote to Henry in October 1265, urging him to exercise clemency.[117]

The papal letter began with three invocations. God was feeder of the hungry; he was "Father of mercies and God of all consolation;" and he was "a just judge . . . and God of vengeances, who doles out to each the wages he has earned, punishment to those who perform wicked persecution, but by deserved dispensation joy and salvation to innocence, so that the just may rejoice to see vengeance upon the impious, and delight in the justice of the Lord." The clear message was that of Deut. 32:35: that vengeance was for God not the king to take.[118] The pope went on to implore the king to exercise clemency and *benignitas* on the grounds that they imitated Jesus on the cross and would strengthen his rule. This would provide a good example for the Lord Edward, too, "for *humanitas remissionis* will entice more of your men back to love than harsh punishment would, since the lust for revenge sates the hatred of a few but irritates that of the many."

Henry or his advisers may have heeded the appeal. The 1267 Dictum of Kenilworth diverted any quest for physical vengeance against former rebels onto fiscal lines. The demand was for heavy redemptions, measured in years of revenues. This did, it is true, ruin some families, but rarely and rather slowly. Much turned on the protracted litigation and negotiations between the disinherited and those who now held their lands. Attention and enmities were diverted from the king and his son. Many ex-rebels still felt bound to seek from the king remission of his rancor after they had gained readmission to his peace. Plea and chancery rolls reveal the whole complex process in detail to those with the patience to follow the traces.[119] The classic study of all this describes Henry's treatment of the Montfortians as displaying "noble restraint"; it might even better be understood as a public expression of Debonereté in action.[120]

The suggested date of 1262/67 for our painting of crowned virtues and their vices in the Painted Chamber begins to look very plausible in the

[117] *Foedera* (1816) 1.1.463, cited by Clive H. Knowles, "The Disinherited, 1265–1280: A Political Study of the Supporters of Simon de Montfort and the Resettlement after the Barons' War" (Ph.D. dissertation, University of Wales, 1959), p. 69; the majority of this dissertation has never been published. There is partial compensation in Knowles's articles noted below.

[118] Against Deut. 32:35 one should of course place Rom. 12:19 and Heb. 10:30, which draw appropriately meek counters to the Old Testament view.

[119] Knowles, "Disinherited," p. 61, gives some of the references.

[120] Clive H. Knowles, "Provision for the Families of the Montfortians Disinherited after the Battle of Evesham," *Thirteenth Century England* 1 (1986): 124–27. See also idem, "The Resettlement of England after the Barons' War, 1264–7," *TRHS*, 5th ser., 32 (1982): 25–41; and John R. Maddicott, "Edward I and the Lessons of Baronial Reform: Local Government, 1258–80," *Thirteenth Century England* 1 (1986): 1–30.

light of the foregoing. Our picture of Debonereté pressed home in the nicest possible way essential bedtime lessons. Anger was a sin for all, not least for kings. No one proposed to indulge Henry III in *ira et malevolentia* as their fathers once had his grandfather and uncles. He must find the kind of courtly remedies appropriate to a king, and make good his commitment to his saintly predecessor, confessor, and saint to pursue the oath toward the regal virtues of Largesse, Truth, Fortitude, and Debonereté. If he himself could not do so, since he was by this time an old man, then surely this was the duty of his son, who bore the saint's name. But the Lord Edward had other, sometimes less pleasant thoughts that would in due course lead to further decoration of the Chamber perhaps equally visible from its bed.[121]

[121] Historians have yet to take note of the Old Testament and especially Maccabean paintings ordered by Edward I in the context of the 1290 Expulsion of the Jews. See Binski, *Painted Chamber*, chap. 3, for details.

PART III

LORDS AND PEASANTS

CHAPTER SIX

The Politics of Anger

STEPHEN D. WHITE

Just king, in this dire distress of your native land, get angry for a purpose.
—Orderic Vitalis

Oh God, our true Father . . . what shall I do, now that I have lost my ear even though I am in the right? If I don't avenge myself, I'll never be happy again!
—Raoul de Cambrai

I hate you so much that I should not favor you with my hatred.
—William of Malmesbury

When Marc Bloch wrote more than fifty years ago about "modes of feeling and thought" in feudal society, he treated "emotional instability" (l'instabilité des sentiments) as a primary characteristic of medieval people, who manifested this trait so often, he thought, as to complicate the problem of explaining medieval politics.[1] According to Bloch, "The despairs, the rages (fureurs), the impulsive acts, the sudden revulsions of feeling present great difficulties to historians, who are instinctively disposed to reconstruct the past in terms of the rational. But the irrational is an important element in all history and only a sort of false

For criticisms and bibliographical references I thank, along with the editor and the other contributors, my audiences at the University of Saint Andrews and at Edinburgh University; I also thank Caroline Walker Bynum, Robert Bartlett, Fredric L. Cheyette, Kate Gilbert, John Hudson, C. Stephen Jaeger, Donald Maddox, Jeff Rider, and Sharon Strocchia. I owe more than I can acknowledge to William Ian Miller.

[1] The epigraphs are from *The Ecclesiastical History of Orderic Vitalis* 11.11, edited by Marjorie Chibnall (Oxford: Clarendon, 1969–80), 6:63; *Raoul de Cambrai,* ed. and trans. Sarah Kay (Oxford: Clarendon, 1992), lines 4832–34; and William of Malmesbury, *De gestis regum Anglorum,* c. 439, Rolls Series (London, 1889), p. 511.

shame could allow its effects on the course of political events in feudal Europe to be passed over in silence."[2]

To explain the emotionalism of medieval society and the resulting irrationality of medieval politics, Bloch looked first at "the vicissitudes of the human organism" and proposed that poor diet and a "low standard of hygiene" had produced an unusually "nervous sensibility." Examining the material environment as well, Bloch argued that the sensibility of medieval people was rendered all the more nervous by their subjection to "ungovernable forces." Living "close to nature," they had only minimal means of controlling it, so that "behind all social life, there was a background of the primitive, of submission to uncontrollable forces, of unrelieved physical contrasts," as epidemics, famines, and "constant acts of violence" endowed medieval life with "a quality of perpetual insecurity." Here, Bloch's argument resembled that of Huizinga, who had previously alluded to "that perpetual oscillation between despair and distracted joy, between cruelty and pious tenderness which characterize life in the Middle Ages."[3]

To explain the emotional instability of medieval people more fully, Bloch finally turned to their culture, treating it mainly as a force that failed to control their emotions, much less soften their uncouthness (*rudesse*). After citing the "astonishing" sensitivity of medieval people to what they understood as "supernatural manifestations," he attributes "the emotionalism" of medieval civilization to an absence of "moral or social" conventions that would later require even "well-bred people to repress their tears and their raptures." Here, Bloch's argument is congruent with that of Norbert Elias, whose 1939 study of "how the behavior and affective life of Western people slowly changed after the Middle Ages" focused on "the psychical process" of civilization and repression.[4] In its

[2] Marc Bloch, *Feudal Society,* trans. L. A. Manyon (Chicago: University of Chicago Press, 1961), p. 73. See idem, *La societé féodale: La formation des liens de dépendance* (1939; repr., Paris: Editions Albin Michel, 1949) 1:116–20, discussed in Jean-Claude Schmitt, "'Façons de sentir et de penser': Un tableau de la civilisation ou un histoire-problème," in *Marc Bloch aujourd'hui: Histoire comparée et sciences sociales,* ed. Hartmut Atsma and André Burguière (Paris: Éditions de l'Ecole des Hautes Etudes en Sciences Sociales, 1990), pp. 407–19.

[3] J. Huizinga, *The Waning of the Middle Ages: A Study of the Forms of Life, Thought, and Art in France and the Netherlands in the Fourteenth and Fifteenth Centuries,* trans. F. Hopman (1924; repr., London: Penguin, 1990), p. 10. In a new translation the passage refers to "the vacillating moods of unrefined exuberance, sudden cruelty, and tender emotions" (Johan Huizinga, *The Autumn of the Middle Ages,* trans. Rodney J. Payton and Ulrich Mammitzch [Chicago: University of Chicago Press, 1996], p. 2). Lucien Febvre criticized Huizinga on just this point: "Sensibility and History: How to Reconstitute the Emotional Life of the Past," trans. K. Folca, in *A New Kind of History: From the Writings of Febvre,* ed. Peter Burke (New York: Harper and Row, 1973), pp. 12–26 esp. pp. 16–19.

[4] Norbert Elias, *The Civilizing Process: The History of Manners and State Formation and Civilization,* trans. Edmund Jephcott (Oxford: Blackwell, 1978), p. xii. Henry Osborn Taylor had previously treated Christianity as the source of emotional progress: *The Medieval Mind: A History of the*

emphasis on the absence of cultural controls on the expression of emotion, Bloch's thesis also resembles the position of J. E. A. Jolliffe, who asserts that the Angevin king "rules by his passions more than by his kingship"; that Henry II "served his purposes of state" by freely expressing his natural "impulses"; that John sometimes ruled through "uncontrolled emotion"; and that "the ruler's personal hates and fears were released as efficient forces to play about the political world." In the Angevin world, according to Jolliffe, "Tears and prostrations, violence and contrition, the kiss of peace and the stab in the back, were recurrent moods of statecraft when nerves lay closer to the surface than they do to-day and conventions of restraint were weaker."[5]

Although Bloch did not document his argument about medieval modes of feeling, he presumably based it on the histories, chronicles, charters, letters, chansons de geste, and other sources that he often cited as evidence in *Feudal Society* and that do, in fact, refer to the tears, raptures, and rages of medieval people. Underlying his interpretation of such passages one can detect a version of the view that "emotions are psychobiological processes that respond to cross-cultural environmental differences but retain a robust essence untouched by the social or cultural."[6] According to this orthodoxy, as represented by one of its critics, "emotion contrasts sharply with cognition. . . . Emotions are feelings which have little to do with what one thinks. Feelings include localized physical sensations like hunger and pain, as well as unlocalized sensations like anger and joy. . . . One can direct one's thoughts but one cannot control one's feelings, which are a natural consequence of events. And feelings can be so strong they prevent clear thinking and lead to irrational action."[7]

This way of understanding emotions implicitly shaped Bloch's discussion in several ways. Above all, it led him to interpret displays of emotion as unambiguous signs of feelings that medieval people had not learned to

---

Development of Thought and Emotion in the Middle Ages (London: Macmillan, 1911), 1:330–50. While arguing that a "civilizing process" took place in earlier European societies, C. Stephen Jaeger transforms Elias's position by locating its beginnings in the tenth century and its main cause, not in competition for royal or lordly favor, but in "the allying of the apparatus of government with a system of education" (*The Origins of Courtliness: Civilizing Trends and the Formation of Courtly Ideals, 939–1210* [Philadelphia: University of Pennsylvania Press, 1985], p. 9). See also Jaeger, *The Envy of Angels: Cathedral Schools and Social Ideals in Medieval Europe, 950–1200* (Philadelphia: University of Pennsylvania Press, 1994).

[5] John E. A. Jolliffe, *Angevin Kingship*, 2d ed. (New York: Barnes and Noble, 1963), pp. 87, 101, 102, 95, 102.

[6] Lila Abu-Lughod and Catherine A. Lutz, "Introduction: Emotion, Discourse, and the Politics of Everyday Life," in *Language and the Politics of Emotion*, ed. Abu-Lughod and Lutz (Cambridge: Cambridge University Press, 1990), p. 2.

[7] Roy d'Andrade, *The Development of Cognitive Anthropology* (Cambridge: Cambridge University Press, 1995), p. 218.

repress and that sometimes constituted irrational motives for political behavior.[8] Bloch's concern with the precultural dimension of emotion is also evident in his emphasis on so-called core emotions such as rage and sorrow rather than emotions such as pity or awe and in his assumption that religious belief heightened emotionalism instead of constituting specific emotions.[9] Bloch, moreover, never explored the relationship between emotions and their linguistic representations. Whereas he studied the semantic fields of words such as "serf" or "vassal," which he treated as cultural constructs whose meanings were ambiguous and changeable, he did not examine the meanings of Latin or vernacular terms for "anger" or "sorrow." Nor he did he consider the possibility that emotion terms, like status terms, figure in different kinds of texts, each of which may represent emotion differently and pose distinct interpretive problems. Furthermore, although Bloch himself distinguished irrational from rational political acts, he never asked how or whether medieval people distinguished appropriate from inappropriate expressions of emotion. Finally, because he tried to identify and explain the emotional style of feudal society *generally* without regard to such variables as class, status, gender, or regional identity, he neither located medieval emotions in particular political settings nor studied the emotional setting of political actions.[10]

[8] See Catherine A. Lutz, *Unnatural Emotions: Everyday Sentiments on a Micronesian Atoll and their Challenge to Western Theory* (Chicago: University of Chicago Press, 1988), p. 5. For other work treating emotion from this perspective, see, in addition to works cited in the two previous notes, *Human Motives and Cultural Models*, ed. Roy d'Andrade and Claudia Strauss (Cambridge: Cambridge University Press, 1992); Catherine Lutz and Geoffrey M. White, "The Anthropology of Emotions," *Annual Review of Anthropology* 15 (1986): 405–36; Geoffrey M. White, "Emotions Inside Out: The Anthropology of Affect," in *Handbook of Emotions*, ed. Michael Lewis and Jeannette M. Haviland (New York: Guildford, 1993), pp. 29–40; Keith Oatley, "Social Construction in Emotions," in *Handbook of Emotions*, pp. 341–52. See also *Explaining Emotions*, ed. Amélie Oksenberg Rorty (Berkeley: University of California Press, 1980); *Emotion*, ed. Margaret S. Clark, *Review of Personality and Social Psychology* 13 (London: Sage Publications, 1992); and *The Social Construction of Emotions*, ed. Rom Harré (Oxford: Blackwell, 1986). See also the extensive literature cited in William Ian Miller, *Humiliation and Other Essays on Honor, Social Discomfort, and Violence* (Ithaca: Cornell University Press, 1993), chap. 3; and work cited in this volume by Catherine Peyroux and Richard E. Barton. Peter N. Stearns recently lamented that "the constructivist theory of emotion" had been "largely ignored by professional historians" ("History of Emotions: The Issue of Change," in *Handbook of Emotions*, p. 17).

[9] On the concept of core emotions, see d'Andrade, *Development of Cognitive Anthropology*, pp. 218–27; and Geoffrey White, "Anthropology of Affect," pp. 31–33. For a different view of "basic emotions" see Robert Plutchik, "Emotions and Their Vicissitudes: Emotions and Psychopathology," in *Handbook of Emotions*, p. 59.

[10] See Miller, *Humiliation*, p. 98. Robert Bartlett locates "certain patterns of emotions" and "psychological characteristics" (e.g., "energy, brutality and appetite for domination"), not in medieval society generally, but in the Norman military aristocracy during one phase of its history, see Bartlett, *The Making of Europe: Conquest, Colonization and Cultural Change, 950–1350* (London: Penguin, 1993), pp. 85, 88. Bloch's discussion of emotions in *Feudal Society* did not incorporate ideas he later treated in a section on anger, feuding, and violence (p. 130).

Whereas Bloch historicized the emotions of medieval people by equating them with feelings, which, when inadequately repressed or channeled, generated irrational political behavior, this chapter explores the possibility that by rereading sources similar to Bloch's one can reach different conclusions about the anger of nobles during the central Middle Ages. Influenced by recent work on medieval emotions, notably William Ian Miller's ideas about "the affective life of the heroic" in medieval Iceland, I start from the assumption that "emotional meaning is fundamentally structured by particular cultural systems and particular social and material environments" and that "emotion concepts . . . presuppose concepts of social relationships and institutions, and concepts belonging to systems of judgements, moral, aesthetic and legal."[11] Against this background I briefly consider two issues that Bloch either ignored or failed to problematize, namely the display of anger by nobles in particular political settings and the linguistic representation of such displays. Without undertaking a systematic study of language or regional variation and without directly addressing questions about changes over time in lordly anger, I try to identify a few broad patterns that closer studies would doubtless modify. The main problem is how to interpret the displays of aristocratic anger and associated emotions such as grief that are described in eleventh-, twelfth- and early-thirteenth-century political narratives, including vernacular accounts of imaginary politics. Should we follow Bloch in seeing these displays as signs of emotional instability and political irrationality? Or can we interpret the anger of lords differently by locating it within a distinctive political culture or discourse?

A provisional survey of representations of anger in both historical sources and imaginative literature leads to several conclusions about vocabulary and discourse. To begin with, because there is considerable cross-

[11] Lutz, *Unnatural Emotions*, p. 5; Errol Bedford, "Emotions," *Aristotelian Society Proceedings* 57 (1957): 304, cited in Shula Sommers, "Understanding Emotions: Some Interdisciplinary Considerations," in *Emotion and Social Change: Toward a New Psychohistory*, ed. Carol Z. Stearns and Peter N. Stearns (New York: Holmes and Meier, 1988), pp. 25–26. Within medieval history, this view of emotions has been developed most fully in Miller, *Humiliation.* See also Paul R. Hyams, "Feud in Medieval England," *Haskins Society Journal* 3 (1992): 1–21; C. Stephen Jaeger, "L'amour des rois: Structure sociale d'une forme de sensibilité aristocratique," *Annales ESC* 46 (1991): 547–71. On emotions in Old French literature, see Georges Lavis, *L'expression de l'affectivité dans la poésie lyrique française du moyen âge (XIIe-XIIIe siècles)* (Paris: Belles Lettres, 1972); André Burger, "Le rire de Roland," *Cahiers de civilisation médiévale* 2 (1960): 2–11; Jean Frappier, "La douleur et la mort dans la littérature françaises des XIIe et XIIIe siècles," in *Histoire, mythes et symboles* (Geneva: Droz, 1976), pp. 85–109; Paul Rousset, "Recherches sur l'émotivité à l'époque romane," *Cahiers de civilisation médiévale* 2 (1959): 53–67; George Fenwick Jones, *The Ethos of the Song of Roland* (Baltimore: Johns Hopkins University Press, 1963), esp. pp. 83–88, 178–80; and Peter Haidu, *The Subject of Violence: The Song of Roland and the Birth of the State* (Bloomington: Indiana University Press, 1993), esp. pp. 69–83.

cultural variation with respect to how emotions are displayed, verbalized, and represented in texts and with what frequency, it is worth noting that during the central Middle Ages, anger and other emotions such as grief were clearly and routinely marked and dramatized in many kinds of texts written both in France and in Anglo-Norman and Angevin England. Although the differences between Latin and Old French texts need to be investigated more closely, as do differences between histories of lay politics and imaginary narratives of noble deeds and adventures, it is worth exploring the hypothesis that, for certain purposes, these different kinds of texts have much in common and can be provisionally treated as forming a single discourse.[12] Whereas "saga authors and saga characters," according to William Ian Miller, "do not especially like to indulge themselves in emotion talk" so that emotions must often be inferred from literary context, Old French storytellers and their characters show no such aversion to the representation and verbalization of emotion in general or anger in particular.[13] The concordance to *Roland* confirms any reader's sense that the poem represents emotions very frequently, giving anger and grief special prominence.[14] From early in the story, when Ganelon feels so much distress (*doel*) that "he almost bursts with anger (ire)," to the end, when Charlemagne appeases "his great anger (grant ire)," both Franks and Saracens repeatedly display and verbalize anger and grief.[15] Emotion talk is also pervasive in epics such as *Le charroi de Nîmes* and *Raoul de Cambrai* and in *romans d'antiquité* such as *Le roman d'Alexandre* and *Le roman de Thèbes.*[16] Jordan Fantosme's historical poem about the wars of Henry II in 1173–74 is a treasure trove of emotion talk, most of it angry.[17] Whether or not emotions and emotion talk take on new meanings in

[12] On the use of literary sources for social and legal history, see William Ian Miller, *Bloodtaking and Peacemaking: Feud, Law, and Society in Saga Iceland* (Chicago: University of Chicago Press, 1990), p. 45 and n. 1.

[13] Miller, *Humiliation,* p. 108.

[14] See Joseph J. Duggan, *A Concordance of the Chanson de Roland* ([Columbus]: Ohio State University Press, 1969), *svv. curucus* (3), *curuciez* (1); *doel* (31), *doels* (1), *dolor* (2), and *dolur* (1); *ire* (11), *ireement* (3), *irur* (6); *maltalant* (2), *maltalentifs* (1); *mortel rage* (2), *esrages* (1), *rage* (2). In references to concordances, I give, in parentheses, the number of references for each word cited. Because I retain the Old French case-endings and variable spellings used in the texts I cite, certain Old French words in the text and notes appear in several different forms.

[15] *La chanson de Roland,* ed. Gérard Moignet, 3d ed. (Paris: Bordas, 1969), lines 304, 3989.

[16] *Le charroi de Nîmes,* ed. J.-L. Perrier (Paris: Librairie Honoré Champion, 1982); *Raoul de Cambrai,* ed. Kay; Alexandre de Paris, *Le roman d'Alexandre,* ed. E. C. Armstrong et al. and translated into modern French by Laurrence Harf-Lancner (Paris: Livre de Poche, 1994); *Le roman de Thèbes,* ed. and trans. Francine Mora-Lebrun (Paris: Livre de Poche, 1995).

[17] *Jordan Fantosme's Chronicle,* ed. and trans. R. C. Johnston (Oxford: Clarendon, 1981), lines 34 (*esrage*), 45 (*rage*), 54 (*ire*), 125 (*irez*), 129 (*rage*), 238 (*dolenz et irez*), 243 (*irur*), 346 (*curesçus et dolent*), 366 (*rage*), 508 (*ire*), 736 (*iré*), 785 (*irer*), 817 (*iriez*), 823 (*rage*), 861 (*curucier*), 969 (*enragier*), 1026 (*aïr*), 1114 (*irascuz*), 1235 (*curusceit*), 1252 (*rage*), 1317 (*grant ire*), 1420 (*irur*), 1707 (*iré*), 1859 (*enragié*), 1900 (*marri*), 2029 (*irascu*), 2053 (*irié*).

Arthurian stories, anger and grief are still frequently mentioned, displayed, and verbalized in such works as Béroul's *Roman de Tristan,* Marie de France's "Laïs de Lanval," the romances of Chrétien de Troyes, *The Didot Perceval,* and *La mort le roi Artu.*[18]

Emotion talk is easy to find, not just in vernacular literature, but also in several kinds of eleventh- and twelfth-century Latin texts, where, for example, the terms *ira, malevolentia,* and *dolor* seem to replace their cognates *ire, mattalent,* and *dol.* The frequent use of such words makes it easy to track anger through the *Histories* of Rodulfus Glaber, the early eleventh-century *Conventum* between Hugh of Lusignan and William of Aquitaine, and the letters of Fulbert of Chartres and Lanfranc.[19] Anger is also on display in a Latin narrative poem on the battle of Hastings by Guy of Amiens and in writings by William of Poitiers, William of Malmesbury, and Galbert of Bruges.[20] Although Suger and Orderic Vitalis each employs

[18] Béroul, *The Romance of Tristan,* ed. and trans. Norris J. Lacy, Garland Library of Medieval Literature, ser. A, vol. 36 (New York: Garland, 1989): *aïr(e)* (271, 1896); *coroços* (3160); *dolent* (983), *doloit* (718), *dolor* (1366, 1497), *dolors* (844), *duel* (338, 1069, 1079, 1129, 1562); *engrés* (862, 2124, 2891); *enrage* (1468, 1488), *enragiez* (1480); *ire* (203, 542, 772, 888, 990, 1070, 1126, 1888, 2012, 2582), *iriez* (1029, 2080, 2814); *mautalent* (182, 332, 539, 553, 1068, 2226, 2363, 2660, 3219, 3533). See also Marie-Louise Ollier, *Lexique et concordance de Chrétien de Troyes* (Montréal: Institut d'Etudes Médiévales, Université de Montréal, 1986), *svv. corroz* (18), *dolent* (69), *doler* (2), *doloir* (46), *dolor* (40), *doloros* (4), *dolorosement* (2); *ire* (57), *irié* (29), *irieement* (1); *mautalent* (14), *mautalentif* (1); *triste* (6), *tristece* (1); and Pierre Kunstman and Martin Dubé, *Concordance analytique de La Mort le Roi Artu,* 2 vols. (Ottawa: Editions de l'Université de Ottawa, 1982), *svv. corouz* (11), *corrocier* (51); *doel* (86), *dolant* (60), *dolerex* (10), *dolerousement* (2), *doleur* (22), *doloser* (2); *ire* (2), *ireement* (1), *iriez* (3); *mautalent* (5). See also, for example, *The Didot Perceval,* ed. William Roach (Philadelphia: University of Pennsylvania Press, 1941), pp. 268–75. The preferences of authors for one word for anger rather than another would be worth investigating. Among those who suggest that emotions play a new role in romances is Jaeger, who argues, for example, that Chrétien's romances "put forward a model of behavior to the laity" (*Origins of Courtliness,* p. 242).

[19] For *ira,* see, for example, Rodulfus Glaber, *The Five Books of the Histories,* ed. and trans. John France (Oxford: Clarendon, 1989), 2.4 (p. 58), 3.3 (p. 98), 3.4 (p. 100), 3.36 (p. 158); for *furor,* 2.16 (p. 80), 3.14 (p. 116); for *odium,* 2.6 (p. 106); for *feritas,* see 2.5 (p. 60), 2.6 (p. 62). See also *Le Conventum (vers 1030): Un précurseur aquitain des premières épopées,* ed. George Beech, Yves Chauvin, and Georges Pon (Geneva: Droz, 1995), "Index du *Conventum*" (pp. 171–81), *svv. contristare* (3), *dolens* (1), *ira* (3), *irascere* (3), *letare* (1), *tristis* (2). For *ira* and *furor* see *The Letters and Poems of Fulbert of Chartres,* ed. and trans. Frederick Behrends (Oxford: Clarendon Press, 1976); nos. 1, 16, 44, 59; on *furor* as a corrupt form of anger, no. 71. For *ira* see also *The Letters of Lanfranc Archbishop of Canterbury,* ed. and trans. Helen Clover and Margaret Gibson (Oxford: Clarendon, 1979), nos. 22, 33b; for *rancor* nos. 16, 33a.

[20] Usually with the word *ira. The Carmen de Hastingae Proelio of Guy of Amiens,* ed. Catherine Morton and Hope Muntz (Oxford: Clarendon, 1972), line 448; Guillaume de Poitiers, *Histoire de Guillaume le Conquérant,* ed. and trans. Raymonde Foreville (Paris: Belles Lettres, 1952), *iratus* (1.25; 2.22), *furiosus* (1.44, 2.14); *furiosus* (2.25); William of Malmesbury, *De gestis regum Anglorum,* c. 306 (p. 362), c. 321 (p. 374), c. 392 (p. 469), c. 394 (p. 133), c. 398 (p. 475), c. 419 (p. 498), c. 438 (p. 511); Galbert of Bruges, *De Multro, traditione, et occisione gloriosi Karoli comitis Flandriarum,* ed. Jeff Rider, Corpus Christianorum, Continuatio Mediaevalis 131 (Turnhout: Brepols, 1994); and Galbert of Bruges, *De Multro, traditione, et occisione gloriosi Karoli comitis Flandriarum,* Instrumenta Lexicologica Latina (Turnhout: Brepols, 1995), under the forms of *furor, furibundus,* and *ira.*

a distinctive repertoire of emotion terms, both authors frequently allude to their main characters' anger and grief.[21] Many references to anger can be found in accounts of Anglo-Norman and Angevin lawsuits and in the royal records and narrative sources cited in Jolliffe's discussion of Angevin royal anger. As Richard Barton shows in this volume, eleventh- and early-twelfth-century Western French charters represent *ira* not only in the anathema clauses that Lester Little has studied, but also in accounts of gifts and disputes.[22]

Although emotion talk is far more common in Northern French and English sources than it is in sagas, a preliminary survey suggests that its scope is relatively narrow, particularly if we focus on the emotions that are repeatedly mentioned and dramatized rather than on emotions that are simply mentioned.[23] In the absence of any systematic survey of emotion words in Old French, Anglo-Norman, or Latin of this period, it is impossible to determine whether the total emotional vocabularies of these languages (in their written forms) were closer in size to those of Taiwanese Chinese (750 terms) or English (400 terms) or to the eight-word vocabulary of a group in central Malaysia (the Chewong).[24] But the emotional vocabulary that is actively and repeatedly used to represent and dramatize emotions in narratives of aristocratic politics, historical or imaginary, seems to be largely limited to anger, grief, shame, love, hatred or enmity, fear, and joy. Even though Latin has a couple of words for anger (*malevolentia, ira*) and Old French has a few more (*coroz* and *rage,* as well as *ire* and *mautalent*), these different terms do not necessarily mark more

21 *Ecclesiastical History of Orderic;* Suger, *Vie de Louis VI le Gros,* ed. Henri Waquet (Paris: Belles Lettres, 1964); Suger, *The Deeds of Louis the Fat,* trans. Richard Cusimano and John Moorhead (Washington, D.C.: Catholic University of America Press, 1992). For passages from Suger see below at notes 31 and 61; for passages from Orderic see below at notes 30, 40, 45, 52, 53, 55.

22 See, e.g., the following cases, drawn from various kinds of sources, in *English Lawsuits from William I to Richard I,* ed. Raoul C. Van Caenegem, vol. 1, *William I to Stephen (Nos. 1–346),* Publications of the Selden Society 106 (London, 1990), nos. 1, 7, 8, 9, 10A, 134, 139, 143, 147, 183, 190, 204A, 204B, 223, 239D, 276B; and vol. 2, *Henry II and Richard I (Nos. 347–665),* Publications of the Selden Society 107 (London, 1991), nos. 360, 405, 406. On the "passions that must lie behind many of the dry-sounding Domesday entries recording *clamores* and *invasiones*" see Hyams, "Feud," p. 5. On royal anger, see Jolliffe, *Angevin Kingship,* pp. 87–109; Hilda Grassotti, "La ira regia en Leon y Castilla," in *Miscelanea de Estudios sobre instituciones Castellano-Leonesas* (Bilbao: Editorial Najera, 1978), pp. 3–132; and the chapters by Gerd Althoff and Hyams in this volume. For references to *ira* in charters see Barton's chapter in this volume; see also *Cartulaire de l'abbaye de Saint-Aubin d'Angers,* ed. Bertrand de Broussillon (Angers: Germain et Grassin, 1896–1903), nos. 112, 135, 270, 303, 372, 750, 780, 826, 860; *Cartulaire de l'abbaye de Noyers,* ed. C. Chevalier, Mémoires de la Société archéologique de Touraine 22 (Tours, 1872), no. 24; *Cartulaire de l'abbaye cardinale de la Trinité de Vendôme,* ed. Charles Métais (Vannes: Lafolye, 1893–1904), vol. 1, nos. 16–17, 340; *Cartulaire de l'abbaye de Saint-Vincent du Mans,* ed. R. Charles and Menjot d'Elbenne (Mamers: Fleury et Dangin, 1886–1913), no. 132. For hatred or enmity, see *Saint-Aubin,* no. 750; *La Trinité,* no. 204; *Saint-Vincent,* no. 686; for weeping, *La Trinité,* no. 168.

23 A study of religious texts would surely generate a different picture of twelfth-century emotion talk.

24 Paul Heelas, "Emotion Talk across Culture," in Harré, *Social Construction of Emotion,* p. 238.

than one clearly identifiable form of anger.[25] Moreover, the scope of emotion talk is even narrower in cases where, in both Old French and Latin, anger and grief merge to form a single emotion—a kind of sad anger, angry sadness, or grief.[26] If medieval political narratives privileged relatively few emotions, then the changes in affect that Bloch took as evidence of emotionalism, emotional instability, and political irrationality of medieval people generally were presumably few in number as well. In texts of this kind, at least, political actors are mainly represented as drawing on only a tiny repertoire of emotional shifts as they get angry, move from sadness to joy or joy to sadness, or put away their anger. No one seems to move—as characters in modern European or American fiction might—from ennui to disgust, from pity to horror, or from awe to hilarity.

Surges of anger can be tracked very easily in political narratives, which not only describe people as angry but also represent characters who display anger physically and sometimes declare it verbally. In *Roland,* Ganelon's eyes flash; and after Roland laughs at him, he is so distressed that he almost bursts with rage and nearly loses his senses.[27] When "maddened with rage" two conspirators against Count Charles the Good of Flanders were "furious and ferocious in countenance," according to Galbert of Bruges, "tall and savage in stature, inspiring terror in everyone who saw them."[28] King Eteocles reddens with anger (*maltalent*).[29] In Orderic Vitalis's *History,* the angry Turks (*stomachati*) show "their ferocity with their burning eyes and stern gestures"; Henry I trembles with anger.[30] In Suger's life of Louis the Fat, the angry prince groans and sighs; "mad" Germans gnash their teeth in fury, as do the raging murderers of

[25] See Georges Matoré, *Le vocabulaire et la société médiévale* (Paris: Presses Universitaires de France, 1985), p. 107. See also Georges Kleiber, *Le mot "ire" en ancien Français (xie-xiiie siècles): essai d'analyse sémantique,* Bibliothèque Française et Romane, Ser. A: Manuels et Études Linguistiques 41 (Paris: C. Klincksieck, 1978). *Marer* and *aïrer* are also worth tracking. Grassotti treated royal *indignatio* along with royal *ira* ("La ira regia," p. 3).

[26] See Robert Francis Cook, *The Sense of the 'Song of Roland'* (Ithaca: Cornell University Press, 1987), p. 51 n. 69: "*dolur* and *ire* are closely associated, and either could express the combination of anger and sorrow." In *Roland,* according to Jones, "*doel* is often used . . . to denote the dismay or chagrin felt by the victim of an insult or injury" (*Ethos of the Song of Roland,* p. 83). See also Gerald J. Brault, *The Song of Roland: An Analytical Edition,* vol. 1, *Introduction and Commentary,* (University Park: Pennsylvania State University Press, 1978), p. 166 and p. 406 n. 10, citing bibliography on weeping.

[27] *Roland,* lines 303–5.

[28] Galbert, *De Multro* c. 17, ed. Rider, lines 42–43 (p. 43); and Galbert of Bruges, *The Murder of Charles the Good, Count of Flanders,* trans. James Bruce Ross (1959; repr., New York: Harper & Row, 1967), p. 126. One enemy of Sainte Foy "ranted and raved irrationally with furious passion"; another "gnashed his teeth, roared with savage fury, and spewed out . . . blasphemous poison" (*The Book of Sainte Foy* 1.5, trans. Pamela Sheingorn [Philadelphia: University of Pennsylvania Press, 1995], p. 44; *Liber miraculorum sancte Fidis* 1.5, ed. Auguste Bouillet, Collection de textes pour servir à l'étude et à l'enseignement de l'histoire, 21 [Paris: Alphonse Picard, 1897], p. 25).

[29] *Roman de Thèbes,* lines 1478–79; see also lines 1409–10, 8662, 8786–87.

[30] *Ecclesiastical History of Orderic,* 10.24 (5:368–69), 8.15 (4:226–27).

Guy, lord of La Roche-Guyon. Hugh of Le Puiset was so "enraged by his lengthy captivity [that] he was like a dog chained for a long time; it becomes mad and remains so, as a result of the drawn-out interval spent in chains. When set free, it rages beyond all bounds; unchained, it bites and tears things to pieces."[31] A late-eleventh-century scribe at Saint-Aubin d'Angers describes a litigant whose argument inspires angry abuse from onlookers.[32] In *Jordan Fantosme's Chronicle,* one lord's heart "is full of anger and his blood boils with rage"; the king of Scotland is enraged; Humphrey de Bohun is "angry in his heart"; King William "almost . . . swoons away for the wrath that lies at his heart"; William de Mortimer fights like "an angry boar."[33] Although romances sometimes thematize or ironize uncertainty about what emotions a character feels, should feel or conceals, these texts, too, describe displays of emotions that do not have to be inferred from context.[34] In *La mort le roi Artu,* Lancelot gets very angry ("molt durement corrouciez"); Hector jumps up angrily ("toz corrouciez et pleins de mautalent").[35] In Béroul's *Tristan,* Frocin "flushes and bristles with rage (mautalent)": "the dwarf's face darkened, then turned pale." Later, "[King Mark's] face darkened with rage; he could hardly contain his anguish (duel). He angrily (par ire) commanded that Iseut be brought to him."[36] A collection of such passages could presumably serve as the basis for conclusions similar to those of George Lakoff and Zoltan Kövecses, whose study of American English showed, inter alia, that "expressions that indicate anger . . . are structured in terms of an elaborate cognitive model that is implicit in the semantics of the language." Like the cultural model of anger implicit in American English, the medieval French model of anger, one may assume, was far from being arbitrary and was instead linked to medieval people's perceptive experience of their own physiology.[37]

[31] Suger, *Vie,* c. 10 (pp. 54–55), c. 17 (pp. 116–17), c. 21 (pp. 152–53); Suger, *Deeds,* pp. 52, 78, 95. On analogies between angry men and mad dogs, see Edward Muir, *Mad Blood Stirring: Vendetta and Factions in Friuli during the Renaissance* (Baltimore: Johns Hopkins University Press, 1993), esp. pp. 222–38. On anger in early modern Europe, see also Kristen B. Neuschel, *Word of Honor: Interpreting Noble Culture in Sixteenth-Century France* (Ithaca: Cornell University Press, 1989), pp. 22–23.

[32] *Saint-Aubin,* ed. de Broussillon, no. 387; discussed in Stephen D. White, "Proposing the Ordeal and Avoiding It: Strategy and Power in Western French Litigation, 1050–1110," in *Cultures of Power: Lordship, Status, and Process in Twelfth-Century Europe,* ed. Thomas N. Bisson (Philadelphia: University of Pennsylvania Press, 1995), p. 118.

[33] *Jordan Fantosme's Chronicle,* lines 243, 736, 817, 1310, 1859.

[34] Examples of both ways of treating emotions can be found in Chrétien de Troyes, *Yvain (Le Chevalier au Lion),* ed. David F. Hult (Paris: Livre de Poche, 1994).

[35] *La mort le roi Artu: Roman du 13eme siècle,* ed. Jean Frappier, 3d ed. (Geneva: Droz, 1964), c. 19, lines 1–3; c. 24, lines 36–37.

[36] Béroul, *Romance of Tristan,* lines 332, 335, 1068–70.

[37] George Lakoff and Zoltan Kövecses, "The Cognitive Model of Anger Inherent in American English," in *Cultural Models in Language and Thought,* ed. Dorothy Holland and Naomi Quinn

Whether or not lay nobles were the only medieval people to be represented as manifesting anger in the specific ways just noted,[38] several words used regularly to represent their anger were also used to designate the anger of ecclesiastical magnates, saints, and God. In biblical texts, God displayed his *ira* as frequently as King John displayed his in Angevin records. In prayers and other texts, Anselm freely ascribes *ira* to saints and to god.[39] Orderic uses *ira* for divine anger as well as royal.[40] Miracle stories mention not only the anger of Saint Foy's enemies but also "the anger of the Highest Creator" and "the holy virgin's avenging displeasure."[41] Lanfranc writes to Baldwin abbot of Bury St. Edmunds on behalf of a man who had incurred the abbot's ire.[42] Besides showing that displays of anger did not in themselves carry pejorative connotations, were not practiced only by unrestrained, violence-prone laypeople, and need not be read as signs or symptoms of either high emotionalism or political irrationality, texts imputing *ira* to God and God's saints support two other conclusions about the representation of anger. First, there must have been well-understood conventions about when it was appropriate for an author to impute anger to people about whose emotions he had no definitive knowledge. Otherwise how could the author have known, for example, whether to represent God or a dead saint as angry? Second, there must also have been well-understood conventions about when it was appropriate to display anger. Otherwise, monastic, saintly, or divine anger could have been read by contemporaries as a sign of animalistic fury, emotionalism, or political irrationality and could now be used as evidence of a demented religiosity, not just the severe faith that R. W. Southern attributes to Anselm.[43]

Difficult as it is to discern and decode conventions about either the display of anger or its representation, medieval emotion talk was often used in such a way as to suggest that when writers imputed anger to specific people, they did so, not because they had direct knowledge of their feelings (if there is such a thing), but rather because they considered this emotion to be appropriate to a particular situation. In other cases, writers represented emotions whose inappropriateness was supposed to be evident to all. On the one hand, the association between anger and plunder-

(Cambridge: Cambridge University Press, 1987), pp. 220, 219.

[38] Compare other discussions of the representation of anger in this volume.

[39] See *A Concordance to the Works of St. Anselm*, ed. G. R. Evans, (Millwood, N.Y., 1984), 2:764–65.

[40] *Ecclesiastical History of Orderic* 10.15 (5:286–87).

[41] *Book of Sainte Foy* 1.4 (pp. 57–58), 1.1 (pp. 46, 50); *Liber miraculorum sancte Fidis* 1.4 (p. 23), 1.1 (pp. 11, 14).

[42] *Letters of Lanfranc*, no. 22 (pp. 104–5).

[43] R. W. Southern, *Saint Anselm: A Portrait in a Landscape* (Cambridge: Cambridge University Press), p. 215.

ing or evildoing was so well established in eleventh-century sources that in writing to Robert the Pious, Fulbert of Chartres reflexively represents the plundering of crops in the vicinity of his church as an expression of the plunderers' anger; later the author of the *Gesta Stephani* imputes anger to those responsible for outbreaks of violence in England after the death of Henry I.[44] Orderic Vitalis and many other authors routinely impute anger to people attacking their enemies.[45] Just as grief is sometimes so intimately associated with doing penance, petitioning, seeking mercy, or prayer that anyone who performs these acts may be depicted as weeping, anger can be imputed to any human or supernatural being who takes revenge.[46] On the other hand, conventions about displaying anger were so clear that nobles could be implicitly or explicitly criticized for showing excessive or totally inappropriate anger. The author of the *Conventum* criticizes count William of Poitou by representing him as being aggrieved when he should have been delighted.[47] In *Roland,* Charlemagne criticizes Ganelon for displaying too much anger.[48] In *Le roman de Tristan* King Mark's rages are among the clearest signs of his inability to take good counsel and rule his kingdom properly.[49] In *Raoul de Cambrai,* the unjustifiable fury in which Raoul burns Origny is clearly distinguishable from the justifiable anger he shows when claiming his rightful inheritance.[50] Suger portrays several of Louis VI's adversaries unfavorably by showing them displaying excessive anger.[51] Orderic uses a similar rhetorical strategy in representing the fury of the Danishmend emir Malik-Ghazi and that of Count Waleran, who crippled peasants by cutting off their feet.[52] In a lengthier passage, Orderic represents Duke Robert's fury as

44 *Letters of Fulbert,* no. 59 (p. 103); *Gesta Stephani* 1.1, ed. and trans. K. R. Potter, rev. ed. (Oxford: Clarendon, 1976), p. 5.

45 *Ecclesiastical History of Orderic,* 10.6 (5:218–19).

46 For an example of weeping and petitioning, see *Letters of Fulbert,* no. 4 (pp. 12–13); on the entire subject see Geoffrey Koziol, *Begging Pardon and Favor: Ritual and Political Order in Early Medieval France* (Ithaca: Cornell University Press, 1992). On weeping and repentance, see Jean-Charles Payen, *Le motif du repentir dans la littérature française médiévale (des origines à 1230)* (Geneva: Droz, 1968). According to Ailred of Rievaulx, "tears . . . are the signs of perfect prayers" (Walter Daniel, *The Life of Ailred of Rievaulx,* ed. and trans. F. M. Powicke [New York: Oxford University Press, 1951], p. 20).

47 Beech, *Le Conventum,* p. 126, lines 68–69: "Ut autem audivit comes, letus esset debuisset, fuitque tristis." In miracle stories, pejorative meanings are attached to the anger of a saint's enemies, though not to the saint's anger.

48 *Roland,* line 327: "trop avez maltalant." On this scene see, for example, Burger, "Le rire de Roland."

49 See, for example, Béroul, *Tristan,* lines 862–65, 888, 3110; Iseut thinks that God has wrought a miracle when Mark gets angry at her enemies (lines 3203–5).

50 "Count Raoul was heartily angry (irié) with the townspeople" (*Raoul de Cambrai,* line 1284); "in a towering rage (grant maltalant), Raoul addresses [the king]" (line 505).

51 See note 31 above.

52 *Ecclesiastical History of Orderic,* 10.24 (5:362–67), 12.39 (6:349).

follows: "Robert crossed to Normandy, bursting with rage and grief (ira et dolore), and savagely attacked those of his compatriots who had attempted to help their weak lord, leaving a trail of fire and slaughter behind him. Like the dragon of whom John the apostle writes in the Apocalypse, who was cast out of heaven and vented his bestial fury by warring on the dwellers of the earth, the fierce disturber of the peace, driven from Britain, fell in wrath (furibundus) upon the Normans."[53]

Whether or not these sources ever provide accurate information about the emotions actually experienced or expressed by medieval people, they encode well-understood conventions about displaying anger in political settings. Otherwise, many passages representing anger would have seemed as bizarre, comic, worrisome, or unfathomable to contemporaries as they sometimes do to modern readers.

Because all these texts presuppose cultural competence in emotion talk and expression on the part of characters, authors, and audience and because they also presuppose an ability to evaluate displays of anger, references to displays of anger cannot be competently interpreted out of relation to the political contexts in which the displays occur. One important issue to consider is where and when people display anger or other emotions. Emotions are often performed *publicly* instead of being shared among intimates or experienced in isolation.[54] Those who show grief by weeping weep openly. Those who are angry sooner or later broadcast their anger to others, enacting their enmity before audiences. Anger is displayed not only in battle but also in court. Public displays of anger are almost always made by kings or other males whose noble status entitles them to express anger; the displays occur in a limited number of predictable settings.[55] The settings are predictable because displays of anger can usually be read as conventionalized responses to certain kinds of past political acts, as political acts in themselves, and as motives for future political acts of certain kinds. Contrary to what Bloch implied, rage is hardly ever represented in such a way as to suggest that it was uncaused; through various narrative devices, it is clearly linked to an antecedent act to which anger is

53 Ibid., 11.3 (6:30–31).

54 See Jaeger, "L'amour des rois."

55 For peasant *ira*, see, in addition to Paul Freedman's chapter in this volume, Guillaume de Poitiers, *Histoire de Guillaume le Conquérant* 25 (p. 59); *Ecclesiastical History of Orderic* 11.19 (6:83). According to Pierre Bourdieu, "the use of language, the manner as much as the substance of discourse, depends on the social position of the speaker, which governs the access he can have to the language of the institution, that is, to the official, orthodox and legitimate speech. It is the access to the legitimate instruments of expression that makes *all* the difference ("Authorized Language: The Social Conditions for the Effectiveness of Ritual Discourse," in *Language and Symbolic Power* [Cambridge: Harvard University Press, 1991], p. 109).

a response, frequently a justifiable one. In the *Charroi de Nîmes,* William's anger (*maltalent*) is a response to his lord's failure to reward him for past service.[56] On one occasion in *Roland,* Charlemagne responds with anger (*mautalent*) when Turpin disobeys him.[57] In Hugh the Chantor's *History of the Church of York,* King William gets angry because the archbishop-elect of York refuses to make his profession to the archbishop of Canterbury.[58] In *La mort le roi Artu,* Lancelot gets very angry when his host is brought down at a tournament; Hector jumps up angrily thinking that Arthur has spoken maliciously about Bors; Arthur feels grief and anger because Lancelot left a tournament wounded; Gawain gets angry when the girl of Escalot rejects him.[59] In Orderic's *History* the emperor Henry V is *iratus* because the Pope disobeys his order to sing mass; William II is tormented by anger and grief (*ira* and *dolor*) because a siege of his is getting nowhere; William of Roumare is angry because Henry I responds offensively to his request for his mother's land; Richer of Laigle is angry when he fails to secure his father's English lands; Henry I's angry attack on Conan is a response to the latter's pleas for mercy; the same king gets angry when his army deserts him.[60] The young Louis VI gets angry when his tents are burned.[61]

More than an emotional response to a past political act, a display of anger also involves a quasi-juridical appraisal of the act and of the person or persons deemed responsible for it.[62] To display anger about an action publicly is to construe the action as an injury, as a wrongful act causing harm, damage, or loss, as an offense against a person's honor. So one has a right to get angry and to do what angry people can and should do. As Barton notes in chapter 7, the display initiates a political process that is

[56] *Charroi de Nîmes,* ed. Perrier, lines 105, 119.

[57] *Roland,* line 271.

[58] Hugh the Chantor, *The History of the Church of York, 1066–1127,* trans. Charles Johnson (London: Nelson, 1961), p. 3.

[59] *La mort le roi Artu,* c. 19, lines 1–3; c. 24, lines 36–37, line 41; c. 26, line 50.

[60] *Ecclesiastical History of Orderic,* 10.1 (5:196–97), 10.10 (5:259); 12.34 (6:333), 12.4 (6:197), 8.15 (4:226–27), 13.30 (6:487).

[61] Suger, *Vie,* c. 4 (pp. 20–25).

[62] "Emotions glossed as anger frequently encode judgments about violations of person and moral order . . . [T]alk about anger becomes an idiom for moral argumentation" (Geoffrey M. White," Emotion Talk and Social Inference: Disentangling in Santa Isabel, Solomon Islands," in *Disentangling: Conflict Discourse in Pacific Society,* ed. Karen Ann Watson-Gegeo and Geoffrey M. White [Stanford: Stanford University Press, 1990], p. 71). "Even for 'simple' emotions like sadness, or anger, or fear, some appraisal seems to be a part of the definition of the emotion . . . anger implies an appraisal that something frustrating or unfair has happened and that the responsible agent should be attacked" (d'Andrade, *Development of Cognitive Anthropology,* p. 220). "Emotions may be defined as *socially constituted syndromes (transitory social roles)* which include an individual's *appraisal of the situation* and which are *interpreted as passions, rather than as actions*" (James R. Averill, *Anger and Aggression: An Essay on Emotion* [New York: Springer-Verlag, 1982], p. 6).

supposed to satisfy the anger. If the anger is unjustified or expressed excessively, it can be contested, as it is when Darius formally tells Eteocles, "Lord, . . . by my faith, you are getting angry at me wrongfully (a tort)."[63] Anger may be construed as animalistic fury or be pejoratively represented in some other way.[64] But it can also be justified explicitly:

> Then began earl Robert to be strongly affected
> When he saw his wife taken, he had good reason to be angry,
> And saw his companions slain by hundreds and by thousands:
> The colour began to change in his face.[65]

Before angrily killing Conan, Henry I responds to the duke's plea for mercy in an extended passage justifying noble anger:

> "By my mother's soul, there shall be no ransom for a traitor, only more rapid infliction of the death he deserves." Then Conan, groaning aloud, cried in a loud voice, "For the love of God, allow me to confess my sins." But Henry, stern avenger of his brother's injury (injuriae), trembled with rage (ira) and, scorning the wretch's prayers, thrust him violently with both hands, hurling him down from the window of the tower. Shattered by this frightful fall, he was dead before he reached the ground. His body was then tied to a horse's tail and dragged shamefully through all the streets of Rouen as a warning to traitors.[66]

Taking revenge on an enemy is thus associated with emotional transformations on both sides:

> Polynice faints and weeps.
> But the king [Adraste] runs to him.
> "Stop weeping," he says.
> "If you have grief from his death,
> Avenge it. Watch over those who killed him
> and who gained joy from it.
> Make sure that their joy and happiness
> You turn into grief."[67]

[63] *Roman de Thèbes*, lines 8761–62.

[64] In addition to the fury of the slayers of Count Charles the Good (note 28 above) and that of three brothers who would not settle with their brother's slayer (Hyams, "Feud," pp. 2–3), see also *Gesta Stephani*, ed. Potter, pp. 2, 5.

[65] *Jordan Fantosme's Chronicle*, lines 1077–81. Barton cites a similar phrase from *Raoul de Cambrai*.

[66] *Ecclesiastical History of Orderic*, 8.15 (4:225–27).

[67] *Roman de Thèbes*, lines 7453–58.

Anger and other emotions are thus located routinely in similar narrative sequences. These scripts proceed from perceived injury to shame/anger/grief to enmity/loathing/hostility and finally to angry revenge; meanwhile, the emotions of people on the other side of the dispute follow a different but related trajectory. In *Jordan Fantosme's Chronicle,* Walter FitzRobert angrily (*aïreement*) seeks revenge (*vengement*) on the battlefield and makes his enemies grieve (*dolent*).[68] In Orderic Vitalis's *History,* for example, the fusion of anger into a retaliatory political process is repeatedly illustrated: "The proud, quick-tempered (iracundus) king [William Rufus] had a tenacious memory, and did not forget an injury unless he he had avenged it"; "[William II] could do nothing to weaken his enemies but, fuming with vexation (stomachatus), grew all the more bitterly hostile to them"; "[the King] vented his wrath on the people of the province who resisted him and punished them by cruelly ravaging their lands. With a great force of soldiers he tore up their vines, trampled down their corn, and laid waste the whole province"; angry at "those who tried to withhold the sceptre of the realm from his son," Louis VI "planned to take deadly vengeance."[69]

When public displays of anger are located in eleventh- and twelfth-century political narratives, they do not provide evidence of emotional instability; instead, they reveal the position occupied by displays of anger in a relatively stable, enduring discourse of disputing, feuding, and political competition. Anger, in other words, has a well-defined place in political scripts in which other emotions figure as well.[70] In these scripts, which have many variants and are merely sketched out here, displays of anger and other emotions are correlated with the stage that a conflict has reached; they are often signs of a disputant's honor or shame and thus have a normative dimension.[71] Although the scripts have many variants, are subject to change over time, and can be ironic or humorous as well as dramatic or tragic, many of them include these elements:

1. When a noble is successful in the competition for honor, he should have joy and show it; like grief, joy has a propensity to circulate among friends, who should share it.[72] At the beginning of *Roland,* Charlemagne's

[68] *Jordan Fantosme's Chronicle,* lines 1032–39.

[69] *Ecclesiastical History of Orderic,* 10.4 (5:209), 10.8 (5:235), 10.8 (5:243), 13.12 (6:434).

[70] Arguing that the American model of anger "has a temporal dimension," Lakoff and Kövecses outline a multistaged "prototype scenario" that proceeds from "offending event" to "anger" to "attempt at control" to "loss of control" to "act of retribution" ("Cognitive Model of Anger," pp. 210, 211).

[71] Miller's *Humiliation* contributes to the large, expanding literature on honor and shame. For a recent discussion, see Frank Henderson Stewart, *Honor* (Chicago: University of Chicago Press, 1994).

[72] "The opposite of *doel* is *joie.* Just as *doel* most often resulted from defeat or failure, *joie* most often resulted from victory or success" (Jones, *Ethos of the Song of Roland,* p. 87).

joy is clearly the by-product of the honor he gains when his army takes Cordoba, shatters its walls, takes booty, and either slaughters or converts the pagans. This joy contrasts with the anger that colors the rest of the poem. In *Le roman de Thèbes,* Atys's knights were full of joy because he gave them fine gifts. Before Erec undergoes the Joy of the Court, King Evrain tells him:

> "If you succeed with joy in this,
> you will have conquered a greater honor
> than any man has ever conquered;
> and God grant, as I desire,
> that you may come out of this with joy."[73]

In this discourse, joy is not a strong core emotion that medieval people were too uncouth to repress; it is a public marker of honor for *sires.* It has to be. Chrétien's repeated references to it would be utterly idiotic if it were simply a matter of feeling very good. Joy, associated with a gain in honor, is also treated as the polar opposite of anger as well as sorrow, both of which are linked to shame:

> "We shall soon hear [Yder] say something
> that will cause us either joy or anger (ire):
> either Erec is sending him to you here
> as your prisoner, to be at your mercy,
> or else he is coming out of audacity,
> to brag among us madly
> that he has vanquished Erec or killed him."[74]

2. When nobles lose honor by losing land, friends, or battles, by enduring damage or loss, by suffering insults and injuries that they have yet to avenge, their joy should turn to shame, which they display as grief or anger. This is the emotion displayed by William of Orange when his lord refuses to give him a fief in return for his long service; by count Geoffrey Martel after a cousin of his is killed by one of his castellans; and by a late eleventh-century magnate named Warnerius, who is so enraged by the shaming experience of being bound by his enemy's squire and then shut up

[73] *Roland,* lines 96–102; *Roman de Thèbes,* line 6905; Chrétien de Troyes, *Erec and Enide,* ed. and trans. Caroleton W. Carroll (New York, Garland, 1987), lines 5618–22

[74] Chrétien, *Erec,* lines 1161–67. In *La mort le roi Artu,* c. 74, lines 29–30, anger and joy are contrasted in the same way.

in a box that he threatens to tear the squire apart.[75] With the loss of honor, which can be experienced vicariously, joy turns to anger and/or grief:

> When [the king and queen] saw [Erec's] wounds
> their joy turned to anger.[76]

Those who fail to show anger when they have been shamed are open to criticism and are liable to being shamed by their friends and goaded into anger.

3. If the shamed, grieving, angry victim needs help from a superior in taking vengeance against his enemies, he should approach him dolefully, tearfully, and deferentially and, in these ways, try to make him angry. This is the emotional posture represented in Suger's descriptions of lords who petitioned Louis VI for help against their political rivals.[77] Political and emotional purposes are neatly fused in these acts, which are meant to inspire pity for the alleged victim and provoke anger at the victimizers; they should also engage the honor of the victim's lord and inspire or shame him into directing his anger at the victim's enemies.[78]

4. The people shamed and angered should then unleash their anger at the enemies who shamed them and for whom they display hatred and loathing. The anger is expressed in different ways and in varying degrees of intensity. In eleventh-century Western France, the anger of lay litigants against their enemies takes such forms as plundering livestock, verbal abuse, assaulting peasants, destroying mills, arson, and other aggressive acts that are often subsumed under that mystifying, overused rubric "violence."[79] Anger is so closely associated with all these acts that a scribe at Noyers described the outbreak of a *guerre* between the count of Anjou and the lord of L'Isle-Bouchard with the phrase, "anger arose."[80]

5. A disputant's anger should abate either when he avenges his shame by overcoming his enemies or when he makes peace with them, in which case anger and enmity should turn into love. At the end of *Roland,* Charlemagne's anger is appeased when his vengeance is done.[81] In *Raoul de Cambrai,* after Bernier seeks a settlement with Gauthier by asking him to "forgive your anger (maltalent) against us," the two men embrace "con

[75] Stephen D. White, "Feuding and Peace-Making in the Touraine around the Year 1100," *Traditio* 42 (1986): 241–46.

[76] Chrétien, *Erec,* lines 4168–69. For a shift from joy to grief (*doel*) see *Roman de Thèbes,* line 6984.

[77] See, for example, Suger, *Deeds,* c. 3 (p. 31), c. 5 (p. 34), c. 18 (pp. 83, 86).

[78] Seeking help from equals or inferiors probably involves processes very different from the one in which the litigant tries to incorporate others into his own feelings of anger and shame.

[79] See Stephen D. White, "Debate: The 'Feudal Revolution,' II," *Past and Present,* no. 152 (1996): 205–23.

[80] Stephen White, "Feuding," p. 241.

[81] *Roland,* lines 3989, 3975.

ami et parent." A similar ceremony of reconciliation was used in around 1100 to end a feud in which the death of Philip Savaricus at the hands of Geoffrey of Montbazon had first given rise to great lamentation among Philip's kin and had then impelled them to unleash great enmity against Geoffrey and his kin.[82] How long these accords would last was uncertain.[83]

The political interpretation of lordly anger offered here has several implications that cannot be reconciled with Bloch's ideas about medieval modes of feeling, with Jolliffe's view of Angevin statecraft, or with the view that a clerically inspired movement "from violence to restraint" transformed aristocratic culture during the twelfth century.[84] Like public grief and mortal enmity, lordly anger was not an unrestrained, unrepressed force that stimulated political irrationality and generated rampant violence. It was an important element in a secular feuding culture that resembled the religious feuding culture of what Little calls Romanesque Christianity.[85] Both displays of anger and the representation of such displays had political and normative force. Instead of simply describing the feelings of medieval people, passages representing anger often figured in rhetorical strategies designed, for example, to present an irate character in a favorable or unfavorable light by indicating whether or not he conformed to established conventions about displaying anger. Instead of directly expressing one's uncontrolled emotional response to political events, a display of anger or grief was often the product of emotional engineering by others, acting for political purposes. Rather than assuming that a lord's anger and expressions of hatred automatically produced irrational acts of political violence, we should posit a much more complicated relationship between displays of lordly anger and the many different political acts that angry lords instigated. In spite of their cultural significance and ideological force during the twelfth and thirteenth centuries, the writings of clerics and others about the need to restrain lordly anger, repress aristocratic violence, or civilize the nobility should not be taken as accurate representations of lay political practices or lay culture.

The rage of medieval nobles was not a physiologically generated response to external stimuli that medieval culture did not adequately repress; in most of its forms, it is also distinguishable from the battle rage

[82] *Raoul de Cambrai,* lines 5174–81; Stephen White, "Feuding," pp. 236–37.

[83] The argument that litigants sometimes preferred concords to judgments is not meant to imply anything in particular about whether, in fact, the former worked better than the latter.

[84] C. Stephen Jaeger, "Courtliness and Social Change," in *Cultures of Power,* ed. Bisson, p. 301.

[85] Lester K. Little, "Romanesque Christianity in Germanic Europe," *Journal of Interdisciplinary History* 23 (1993): 453–74.

that Wendy Davies cites in this volume. Anger was incorporated into political postures and processes; it was part of an entire discourse of feuding or retaliatory disputing, which provided scripts or schemas for representing, interpreting, and experiencing competition for honor and other kinds of conflict.[86] Although Jolliffe, unlike Bloch, amply documented his assertions about the role of passion, natural impulses, nerves, and uncontrolled emotion in medieval politics, his evidence generally represents royal *ira et malevolentia* not as an expression of an individual's impulses, passions, or emotions, but as a process in which royal anger was not only politicized but also collectivized, officialized, and bureaucratized.[87] Are we then dealing, as Jolliffe said we were, with evidence of "the more violent passions"?[88] Are we dealing with passion or emotion at all, as we commonly understand them? Along with the problem, discussed by Catherine Peyroux, of determining whether the experience of lordly anger resembles our own experience of anger, there is the additional problem of understanding anger as a political practice that involved more than individual experience.

Whether or not displays of lordly anger express what we would recognize as anger, they were gestures of a feuding culture.[89] The same is true of other emotional displays. The hatreds expressed by lords were not simply passions or uncontrolled, unrepressed emotions. Bloch himself acknowledged that the phrase "mortal hatred" had "an *almost* technical meaning," which Robert Bartlett has now explicated.[90] A specialized, political meaning can also be given to mortal rage, outrage, and rage itself, which, in the form of royal *ira* or *indignatio,* Grassotti considered a "political institution," without, however, reducing it to its political or legal meaning.[91] Both anger and hatred could be collectivized and politicized, as they were when Aimery of Aver, after killing Ralph of Furnols, "became hateful (odiosus) to [Ralph's lord] Aimery of Faye-la-Vineuse and to all the men of the latter's castle."[92] Grief, too, had political significance in feuds. Whether or not those whom medieval sources represented as weeping felt what we would understand as grief or sorrow, their displays of grief often

[86] The same point could be illustrated by a discussion of hatred or sorrow.

[87] See Jolliffe, *Angevin Kingship,* pp. 87, 101, 102, 95, 102. His evidence included not only narratives by such authors as William of Newburgh but also pipe rolls, letters patent, fine rolls, close rolls, and royal charters.

[88] Ibid., p. 100.

[89] On forms of feud see Hyams, "Feud," esp. pp. 6–7. On the relation between feelings and gestures, see Miller, *Humiliation,* p. 100. On the problem of knowing how to compare our anger and theirs, see also Peyroux in this volume.

[90] Bloch, *Feudal Society,* p. 128; Robert Bartlett, "'Mortal Enmities': The Legal Aspect of Hostility in the Middle Ages" (photocopy).

[91] Grassotti, "La ira regia," p. 3.

[92] Stephen White, "Feuding," p. 230.

constituted political acts inextricably associated with the process of making a legitimated political claim. As Hyams explains, for "the man wronged by someone stronger than himself" and seeking revenge, the best way of getting help from a superior was to tell him a story that would move him to pity, identification, and then action: "You might humble yourself before him with tears, gestures, even the tearing of garments and prostration on the ground. You sought to shame the great man into taking up your cause for fear that by his inaction shame would redound on him. You would strive to represent the wrong you had suffered as an injury to his honor as well as yours. Where the appeal was to a lord, this task was relatively easy. You had suffered the injury while in his service, for example, or in contempt of his protection or peace. What was he going to do about it?"[93] As Hyams glosses this scene, emotional display, physical posture, and political act are all neatly fused together.

This entire procedure is neatly parodied in branch 1 of the *Roman de Renart* when, at King Lion's court, Pinte, supported by Chantecler and three companions, complains that Renard has killed her sister. After laying out her complaint,

> Pinte collapsed in a swoon on a paved floor and the others followed suit. . . . Then, when they came round from their swoon . . . they all went to where they saw the king seated and fell at his feet, whilst Chantecler knelt and wet those feet with his tears. When the king saw Chantecler, he took pity on the noble youth. Nothing in the world would have restrained him from heaving a deep sigh. He raised his head in wrath (mautalant). There was never a beast . . . so bold as not to feel fear when their lord sighed and roared. . . . Couard the hare was so terrified that for two days he had a fever. The whole court trembled together, and the most courageous shook with fear. In his rage (mautalant) the king raised his tail and thrashed about in such distress that the entire building resounded. Then he spoke his mind.

Assuring Pinte that "your distress grieves me," the king—who had previously been bored by complaints against Renard—promises to take "dire vengeance" on the fox.[94]

Since, in such cases, a person's display of grief had the political purpose of encouraging another person to show mercy to him and anger at his enemy, it is clear that some of the emotional shifts that Bloch took as

[93] Hyams, "Feud," p. 12.

[94] *The Romance of Reynard the Fox,* trans. D. D. R. Owen (Oxford: Oxford University Press, 1994), p. 10; *Le roman de Renart,* ed. Jean Dufournet and Andrée Méline (Paris: Flammarion, 1985), branch 1, lines 338–77.

evidence of an individual's emotional instability were orchestrated by others; other shifts were self-orchestrated. In either case, the display of emotion is mediated by an appraisal of the appropriateness of an emotion to a given political situation. The process of generating emotions such as anger took different forms, depending not just on the emotion that had to be produced but also on the total political context. One way of making a man angry was to force him to take notice of the shameful injuries that he or his friends had suffered. Whether or not this kind of goading occurs publicly, it instigates both an emotional and a political transformation. Angered by King Louis's refusal to give the Cambrésis to Raoul de Cambrai, Guerri successfully goads his nephew Raoul into getting angry:

> He went quickly out of the [king's] room and entered the ancient hall in anger (maltalant). Raoul is playing chess like a man who meant no harm: Guerri sees him and seizes him by the arm, tearing his fur mantle. "Son of a whore," he called him—quite without foundation—"cowardly brute, why are you here playing games? I tell you truly, you haven't enough land to rub down an old nag on!" Raoul heard him; leaping to his feet, he speaks so loudly that the great hall shakes and many noble men all down the hall could heard him: "Who is taking it from me? I think him very foolhardy!" Guerri replies: "I'll tell you now: it's the king himself—how he must regard you as disgraced (honi)!—who should be upholding and warranting (tensé et garanti) us." Hearing this, Raoul's blood boiled. . . . In a great rage (grant maltalant), Raoul addresses [the king].[95]

In Suger's *Vie de Louis VI le Gros,* a display of anger is stimulated by tearful petitioning: "A hundred complaints against this forceful and criminal man [Ebles of Roucy] had been tearfully lodged with the lord King Philip, but the son [Louis] heard only two or three before he angrily assembled a medium-sized host of about seven hundred knights . . . and hurried to Reims. . . . He ravaged the lands of the tyrant and his accomplices . . . to avenge the wrongs done by him."[96] On another occasion Louis whipped up his own anger after someone "treacherously" set fire to his tents: "[He

[95] *Raoul de Cambrai,* lines 480–505. On goading, see Miller, "Choosing the Avenger: Some Aspects of the Bloodfeud in Medieval Iceland and England," *Law and History Review* 1 (1984): 159–204; and Stephen D. White, "Clotild's Revenge: Politics, Kinship, and Ideology in the Merovingian Bloodfeud," in *Portraits of Medieval and Renaissance Living: Essays in Memory of David Herlihy,* ed. Samuel K. Cohn, Jr., and Steven A. Epstein (Ann Arbor: University of Michigan Press, 1996), pp. 107–30. On warranty, see Paul R. Hyams, "Warranty and Good Lordship in Twelfth-Century England," *Law and History Review* 5 (1987): 437–503. On an election dispute in which an abbot of Saint-Père inflamed the anger of his patron, Count Odo of Chartres, see *Letters of Fulbert,* no. 1 (p. 5).

[96] Suger, *Deeds,* c. 5 (pp. 34–35); Suger, *Vie,* c. 5 (pp. 26–27).

took] this affront very badly, for he had never experienced or known this sort of setback before . . . he did the customary thing for one his age who seeks to do worthy deeds. He stirred up his anger; and it stirred him into action. His desire to get swift revenge for the insult consumed him as he shrewdly and cautiously summoned men from all sides and tripled the size of his host. He frequently groaned and sighed that it would be better to die than suffer such shame."[97]

If an outburst of anger was a political act involving more than the onset of a physiological condition, the cooling of anger had a political dimension as well. After the young Louis VI had deliberately worked himself into a rage, others had to appease his wrath. The task was accomplished partly by his adversary, who applied "a great deal of charm and flattery" to "settle the young man down," and partly by the prince's friends, as "the pleas of many men, the advice of intimate counsellors, and the repeated . . . request of his father calmed [the young man's] fighting spirit."[98] The appeasement of anger is a common motif in histories, biographies, charters, and chansons de geste, where changes in emotional affect are socially generated by conventionalized arguments that friends, enemies, or third parties use to appeal to a man's sense of honor.[99]

Whether lay nobles were simply conforming to religious models when they displayed righteous anger or whether, as seems more likely, the relationship between secular and religious anger assumed a dialectical form, displays of lordly anger certainly had their parallels in religious practices and ideology. Given the interpenetration of lay and religious cultures, it is not surprising to find similarities between the anger and enmity of secular lords, on the one hand, and the anger of god, saints, and monks, on the other. Within Benedictine communities, as Little notes, the most influential biblical passages on anger were taken from the Psalms and Deuteronomy. In clamors and charter malediction clauses from the ninth, tenth, and eleventh centuries, these passages, along with others about divine vengeance, are used in such a way as to treat anger as a political force directed against the Lord's enemies.[100] Whether or not monks justified this form of verbal aggression by citing Gregory the Great's distinction between "a curse that is prohibited, because it proceeds from hatred and a desire for revenge, and a legitimate curse, which is pronounced out of love

97 Suger, *Deeds,* c. 4 (p. 33); Suger, *Vie,* c. 4 (pp. 22–23).

98 Suger, *Deeds,* c. 4 (p. 34); Suger, *Vie,* c. 5 (pp. 24–25).

99 See *Ecclesiastical History of Orderic* 7.10 (4:49, 51), 7.14 (4:75), 11.36 (6:176), 12.4 (6:195–197), 12.5 (6:201), 12.8 (6:207), 12.12–15 (6:217–27). On the relationship between appeasing anger and ending a dispute, see Fredric L. Cheyette, "Suum cuique tribuere," *French Historical Studies* 6 (1970): 287–99.

100 Lester K. Little, *Benedictine Maledictions: Liturgical Cursing in Romanesque France* (Ithaca: Cornell University Press, 1993), pp. 65, 68.

of justice," monastic curses, according to Little, were meant to express "corporate, never individual indignation."[101] This collective anger, moreover, could be appeased in the reconciliation ceremonies that were meant to terminate disputes in which monks had previously exchanged angry, hostile gestures with lay enemies. However one explains the striking similarities between the feuding culture of Benedictine monks and that of the noble kin groups from which the monks were recruited, the emotional shifts that Bloch read as evidence of "emotionalism" seem to have been encoded as deeply in the former as they were in the latter.

Because displays of anger are associated with political acts that can be favorably or unfavorably represented, it is not surprising to find authors using descriptions of such displays to evaluate the person who displays anger. Representing another person's anger is never a neutrally descriptive or politically neutral act. To condemn a local count for his role in an election dispute, Fulbert of Chartres shows him displaying a kind of fury or mad anger attributed several centuries later to King John.[102] Whether or not all writers viewed anger in the same way, they took it for granted there were conventions about what forms it could take and how and when it should be displayed.

If displays of emotion were both highly conventionalized and socially generated, if they were associated with collective political processes, and if representing them unfavorably was often part of a political strategy, then the relationship between medieval anger and emotionalism, on the one hand, and violence or political irrationality, on the other, becomes problematic. There are certainly examples of furious nobles acting in what later French law knew as "hot anger" and personally committing what are conventionally known as acts of violence.[103] But between displays of anger and uses of force against others there is often a gap that must be filled with more than the violent personality of the eleventh-century knight. The gap usually includes a lot of time, a lot of planning, additional people to commit the acts of violence, and people, material objects, or animals who are all held vicariously liable for the anger and shame that someone has suffered. In other words, anger and acts that we would probably classify as violent are mediated by political processes that are marked

[101] Ibid., pp, 99, 25. On ecclesiastical support for "retributive justice," as well as reconciliation and compromise, see Hyams, "Feud," p. 17.

[102] *Letters of Fulbert,* no. 1 (pp. 2–9).

[103] On hot anger, see, for example, Natalie Zemon Davis, "Angry Men and Self-Defense," in *Fiction in the Archives: Pardon Tales and Their Tellers in Sixteenth-Century France,* (Stanford: Stanford University Press, 1987); see, more generally, the remarkable discussion of honor, violence, crime, punishment, and pardon in Claude Gauvard, *"De grace especial": Crime, état et société en France à la fin du moyen âge* (Paris: Publications de la Sorbonne, 1991), 2:703–952.

by displays of emotion and colored by emotion talk but are not reducible to emotions or expressions of emotional impulses.

The final and most general implication of this argument about interpreting displays of anger by lay nobles can be put in the form of a question: Does the argument reduce emotional displays to signs of political dispositions or to communicative devices that also served an evaluative function? Does it thereby transform the history of medieval emotions—which Bloch, like Huizinga and others, treated as an interesting story of impulsive, emotionally intense people—into nothing more than an arid, semiotic analysis of politics and political culture? Does it necessarily reduce lordly anger to a mere political institution or to a simple political message?[104] Not really. This chapter argues that displays of anger are essential elements in a "technology of power" that each lord must have used in a slightly different way and that cannot be reduced to the usual categories of political history and cannot be neatly classified as either overt or symbolic violence.[105] Rejecting the idea that medieval nobles were emotionally unstable or caught in a primitive stage of arrested cognitive development, I see the changes in the emotions they publicly displayed as correlated with the instabilities of medieval politics. But in discussing the strategic use of emotions by individuals and groups to attain short- or long-term political goals, I have tried not to trivialize medieval emotions by politicizing them or by explaining them in functional terms but rather to emphasize the emotional dimensions of both medieval politics and medieval law.[106] In doing so, I have abandoned the model of emotions that is implicit in Bloch's discussion. But I certainly acknowledge the importance of links between medieval displays of anger and the psychology of the male nobles who did the displaying. Links of this kind are posited by various discussions of honor, by Bourdieu's analyses of habitus and bodily

[104] F. G. Bailey, *Strategems and Spoils: A Social Anthropology of Politics* (1969; repr., Oxford: Blackwell, 1985), p. 29: "A competitor confronts his opponent by making statements (either in words or actions) about his own command over resources (both human and material) in order to intimidate an opponent. . . . The messages can be subtle and elaborate, involving bluff and counter bluff."

[105] On technologies of power, see Michel Foucault, *Discipline and Punish: The Birth of the Prison,* trans. Alan Sheridan (New York: Random House, 1979), chap. 1. On Pierre Bourdieu's distinction between symbolic and overt violence, see, for example, John B. Thompson, introduction to Bourdieu, *Language and Symbolic Power,* pp. 23–25.

[106] Hyams has used a similar strategy by focusing on "motives," "emotions," "feelings," "emotional context," "passions," and "modes of thought" associated with both strong and weak feud and, perhaps, with litigation generally ("Feud," pp. 5, 6, 13, 16); among the emotions he cites are fury, anger, chagrin, grief, and pity (pp. 12, 14). For sound criticisms of functionalist approaches to anger and revenge, see Edward Muir, "The Double Binds of Manly Revenge in Renaissance Italy," in *Gender Rhetorics: Postures of Dominance and Submission in History,* ed. Richard Trexler (Binghamton, N.Y., 1994).

hexis, by Miller's account of the "affective life of the heroic," and by work on the construction of masculinity.[107] One important step to take in explaining lordly anger during the central Middle Ages would be to treat "the sense of honor" as something that mediates between the inner emotional worlds of upper-class males and the outer world of politics, where, at critical junctures, anger and other emotions have the potential to become powerful political forces. A related project would involve showing how medieval society produced a class of people who could give expression to a kind of anger in which political and legal meanings were always embodied.

[107] See also Robert Bartlett's discussion of the "image of the conqueror" (*Making of Europe*, pp. 89–90). Muir makes good use of "double-bind theory" ("Double Binds of Manly Revenge"). On habitus and bodily hexis see, for example, Bourdieu, *Language and Symbolic Power.*

CHAPTER SEVEN

"Zealous Anger" and the Renegotiation of Aristocratic Relationships in Eleventh- and Twelfth-Century France

RICHARD E. BARTON

In 1120 Juhel, lord of Mayenne, wished to found a priory of the abbey of Marmoutier. After giving a number of his own properties to this priory, Juhel asked two of his men, Rainaldus Droolinus and Guarinus Probus, to contribute to his project.[1] While Rainaldus agreed, Guarinus refused. Juhel did not take this refusal lightly. As he recounts: "having become greatly angered with him, I said he was my serf (colibertus) and I was able to sell him or burn his land, or give it to whomever I might want as befit the land of my serf; and rising against him, I would have laid violent hands on him had not Clementia, my wife, and Bishop Hildebert of Le Mans, Abbot William of Marmoutier, and many other honest men forcefully ushered me into the inner chamber."[2]

Earlier versions of this essay were presented in January 1995 at the annual meeting of the American Historical Association and in February 1996 at the University of California Medieval Seminar. Various aspects of it have benefited from the comments and criticism of Sharon Farmer, Anne Barton, Christine McCann, Fiona Harris Stoertz, Lauren Helm Jared, Warren Hollister, Patrick Geary, Paul Hyams, Stephen White, Lester Little, Paul Freedman, Barbara Rosenwein, and John LeRoy.

[1] *Cartulaire Manceau de Marmoutier,* ed. Ernest Laurain (Laval: Goupil, 1945), 2:15–17. I suggest a date of 1120–28 for the charter in Richard Barton, "Lordship in Maine: Transformation, Service, and Anger," *Anglo-Norman Studies* 17 (1995): 58 n. 84.

[2] "Rainaldus Droolini libentissime sua gratia annuit et in perpetuam eleemosynam ecclesie dedit. Guarinus vero Probus dixit quod nec daret nec venderet, et cum nec prece nec precio possem aliquid impetrare, iratus graviter contra eum, dixi ei quod meus colibertus erat et poteram eum vendere vel ardere, et terram suam cuicumque vellem dare tamquam terram coliberti mei, et insurgens in eum violentas manus injecissem in eum nisi Clementia, uxor mea, et Ildebertus, Cenomanensis epi-

Juhel's description of his anger in this incident is of great interest. He had been seized by what theologians would call a *turbatio mentis,* a troubling of the mind. One might think that Juhel's anger, which very nearly led to violence, would have been condemned as sinful and antisocial, especially given the theological identification of anger as a deadly sin. Yet not all anger was considered sinful. Indeed, anger was frequently justified as necessary and righteous, especially when exercised by those with rightful authority. Such justified lordly anger could and did serve as a warning sign to society, announcing to all that the current situation was unacceptable and that social relationships would have to be restructured. In fact, contrary to the predictions of the theologians, many incidents involving an angry lord ended not in violence but in compromise and mediation.

The resolution of the dispute between Juhel and Guarinus, moreover, clarifies this process of restructuring and mediation. After Juhel's outburst, the two men retired from the chamber. Juhel reports:

> On the next day many honest men came to me, saying to me that I had acted unjustly against Guarinus Probus, because my father had enfranchised him and on account of this Guarinus built my father a prison located next to the gate of my castle. I responded that by then I lived, rode, and held the age of intelligence, but I had neither consented to the enfranchisement nor desired it, and thus it ought to be made invalid. At last Clementia, my wife, and Chotardus of Mayenne, a man prudent and intimate to me, came and mentioned to me a means of peace in the following manner.[3]

This passage reveals the true cause of the quarrel and of Juhel's anger. The incident is not merely the result of intemperance, but has its roots in a clear issue of power, authority, and lord-vassal conflict. The issue concerns Juhel's rights as a lord, and the extent to which he can exercise them over his onetime serf (*colibertus*), Guarinus. In this case, then, anger is a reflection of Juhel's conception of himself as a lord and acts as a doorway through which Juhel can address the true problem: the precise nature of his lordship over Guarinus Probus.

---

scopus, et Guillelmus abbas Majoris monasterii, et multi alii probi viri me vi introduxissent in cameram interiorem" (*Cartulaire Manceau de Marmoutier,* ed. Laurain, 2:16).

[3] "Illa die recessimus ab invicem. In crastinum vero venerunt ad me multi probi viri dicentes mihi me injuste egisse contra Guarinum Probum, quia pater meus franchiverat eum et ob hoc fecit sibi carcerem lapideum juxta portam castri mei situm; quibus ego respondi quod ego jam vivebam et equitabam et intelligibilem etatem habebam, nec consensi nec volui, unde irritum debet fieri. Tandem venerunt Clementia, uxor mea, et Chotardus de Meduana, vir prudens et mihi privatus; taxaverunt modum pacis in hanc formam" (ibid., 16–17).

The dispute ended with a compromise. Chotardus of Mayenne arranged a complicated series of gift exchanges, involving items of symbolic importance, between Juhel, Guarinus, and Chotardus. In the end Juhel agreed to enfranchise Guarinus and all his progeny, and Guarinus agreed to contribute to Juhel's foundation. Everyone left with what he wanted. What had started in anger and the threat of violence ended in peaceful compromise.

This example neatly encompasses several critical points about the uses of anger in aristocratic society. First, it reflects the twofold definition of anger created by medieval theologians. This definition saw anger normally as a deadly sin but acknowledged that in certain situations it could be legitimate, righteous, and necessary. Second, it suggests a connection between the theological notion of zealous, righteous anger and the aristocratic exercise of lordship. Third, it makes a strong connection between the performance of lordly anger and processes of dispute resolution, especially by compromise and mediation. Indeed, properly zealous anger could serve as a sign that social relationships would have to be renegotiated, preferably by peaceful means.

Medieval writers, unlike modern historians, were extremely interested in anger and its application in society.[4] Theologians, for instance, usually saw anger as a vice and thus included it among the deadly sins from at least the sixth century.[5] Indeed, by the twelfth century, a Victorine scholastic could consider anger one of the three vices most offensive to God: "These vices, that is pride, envy and anger, are the most noticed by God, for pride denies God, envy blames God, and anger drives God away."[6] To consider but a handful of representative examples is to demonstrate that anger was universally seen as a dangerous sin. Alcuin, for instance, saw anger as a sin because it clouded judgment, bred intemperance, and caused a variety of social ills, including vengeance and fighting.[7] For Hincmar of

[4] Several works provide information on anger in the context of the seven vices; see Morton Bloomfield, *The Seven Deadly Sins: An Introduction to the History of a Religious Concept* (East Lansing: Michigan State College Press, 1952); Richard Newhauser, *The Treatise on Vices and Virtues in Latin and the Vernacular,* Typologie des sources du moyen âge occidental 68 (Turnhout: Brepols, 1993); and Adolf Katzenellenbogen, *Allegories of the Virtues and Vices in Mediaeval Art* (London, 1939; repr., Toronto: University of Toronto Press, 1989). None of these, however, focuses on the social meaning of anger in the way that Lester K. Little has done for pride and avarice in "Pride Goes before Avarice: Social Change and the Vices in Latin Christendom," *American Historical Review* 76 (1971): 16–49.

[5] Bloomfield, *Seven Deadly Sins,* pp. 69, 72.

[6] Pseudo-Hugh, *Allegoriae in Novum Testamentum* 2.4, PL 175, col. 775: "Haec igitur vitia, id est superbia, invidia, ira maxime Deo adversantur. Superbia namque Deum negat, invidia accusat, ira fugat." The text is a product of the mid-twelfth century Victorine school.

[7] Alcuin, *De virtutibus et vitiis liber ad Widonem comitem,* PL 101, cols. 613–38. For an example of these ideas: "illa ira mala est, quae mentem turbat, ut rectum consilium perdat" (col. 631). For the ill

Rheims, writing in the ninth century, anger became a huge weight upon the soul and the mind, one that caused internal agitation and an inflammation of thought. As such it led to a host of social evils.[8] In the twelfth century, Hugh of Saint Victor and other Victorines wrote about the soteriological and social dangers of anger,[9] and in the early thirteenth century Thomas of Chobham devoted an entire *quaestio* of his *Summa confessorum* to a discussion of the ill effects of anger.[10] All four believed that anger led to greater evils, both within the individual and in society. For the individual, it caused a loss of the tranquillity and placidity of mind necessary for rational action and thought; this agitation led one to lose sight of God, and therefore to doom one's soul to perdition. Within society, anger led to insults, fights, murder, vengeance, and other violence. In a word, then, the angry man was indeed a sinner.

Except, as it turned out, when he was not. All four of these theologians qualified their discussions of the inherent sinfulness of anger. Alcuin considered the anger that a man directs at his own sins and his own mistakes to be "just and necessary."[11] Hincmar, moreover, set forth a more formal dichotomy between anger motivated by zeal and anger motivated by vice; anger through zeal was generated from virtue, whereas anger from vice was obviously motivated by vice. In describing this "good" anger, Hincmar quoted the Psalmist (Ps. 4:5, "Be angry and do not sin") and pointed out that anger against one's own vices and errors was good and just.[12]

---

effects deriving from anger: "de qua, id est ira, pullulat tumor mentis, rixae et contumeliae, clamor, indignatio, praesumptio, blasphemiae, sanguinis effusio, homicidia, ulciscendi cupiditatis, injuriarum memoria" (col. 634). In chapter 4 above Geneviève Bührer-Thierry cites the same text in demonstrating that anger was considered one of the principal sins.

[8] Hincmar of Rheims, *De cavendis vitiis et virtutibus exercendis ad Carolum Calvum regem,* PL 125, col. 857 ff., but esp. cols. 877–78. Hincmar argued that through anger one lost wisdom, relinquished justice, abandoned the pleasures of life, broke or ruptured concord, cast away the light of truth, and excluded the splendor of the Holy Spirit from the soul.

[9] For the views of Hugh of Saint Victor and his school on anger, see Hugh of Saint Victor, *De quinque septenis,* in Hugh of Saint Victor, *Six Opuscules Spirituels,* ed. Roger Baron, Sources Chrétiennes 155 (Paris: Éditions du Cerf, 1969), pp. 100–119; Pseudo-Hugh, *Allegoriae in Novum Testamentum,* PL 175, cols. 774–82; and Hugh of Saint Victor, *De fructibus carnis et spiritus,* PL 176, cols. 997–1006. For but one example of this school's opinions on anger, *Allegoriae in Novum Testamentum,* col. 774: "Ira est irrationabilis perturbatio mentis."

[10] Thomas of Chobham, *Summa confessorum,* ed. F. Broomfield, Analecta Medievalia Namurcensia 25 (Louvain: Éditions Nauwelaerts, 1968). For his definitions of anger, see p. 414.

[11] Alcuin, *De virtutibus et vitiis,* c. 34, PL 101, col. 631: "Illa ira est justa et necessaria, quando homo contra propria irascitur peccata, et contra seipsum indignatur, dum male agit. Dicit enim propheta: 'Irascimini, et nolite peccare' [Ps. 4:5]."

[12] Hincmar, *De cavendis vitiis et virtutibus exercendis,* c. 2, PL 125, col. 880: "Sed inter haec solerter sciendum est, quod alia est ira quam impatientia excitat, alia quam zelus format. Illa ex vitio, haec ex virtute generatur. Si enim nulla ira ex virtute surgeret, divinae animadversionis impetum Phinees per gladium non placasset. . . . De hac ira per Psalmistam dicitur: 'Irascimini et nolite peccare' [Ps. 4:5]."

Hugh of Saint Victor echoed Hincmar's distinction. Anger is good, he said, when because of it you refuse to do evil; it is bad, when because of it you refuse to suffer evil.[13] Thomas of Chobham, like Hincmar, carefully distinguished good anger from bad anger. In fact, he used the same dichotomy of *ira per zelum* and *ira per vitium.*[14] Anger through zeal occurred when one grew angry against vices and those who committed vices, and thus this type of anger was virtuous.[15] Here it may be significant that Thomas, unlike Hincmar, saw righteous or zealous anger in more social terms; zealous anger was usefully directed against others who committed sins, not just against oneself and one's personal sins.[16] Although Thomas also cautioned against giving full reign to zealous anger, since it could easily grow too hot and blind reason, he remained hopeful about its abilities to counter and extirpate evils: indeed, he could look to Christ's expulsion of the moneylenders from the temple as an excellent example of this sort of righteous anger.[17]

Why did these authors, after making strong statements about the sinfulness of anger, provide seeming exceptions to their rules? The most obvious answer is that they needed to account for the presence of anger in the Bible, especially in the Old Testament.[18] Stories of the wrath of God, the wrath of Old Testament kings, and even of Jesus Christ would have been familiar to both laymen and clerics.[19] Indeed, some may even have known

[13] Pseudo-Hugh, *Allegoriae in Novum Testamentum,* col. 775: "Est autem bona ira, qua dedignaris malum facere; mala vero, qua dedignaris malum pati."

[14] Thomas begins his *distinctio* on anger with two *questiones,* one entitled *De ira per zelum,* the other *De ira per vitium: Summa confessorum,* p. 414.

[15] "Ira autem per zelum est quando irascimur contra vitia et contra vitiosos, et possumus optare quod talis ira crescat, quia virtus est" (ibid.).

[16] This tendency to find acceptable social uses of anger may be a product of the genre in which Thomas was writing. As a manual for confessors, his work was supposed to distinguish acceptable from unacceptable actions. It is nevertheless interesting for our purposes that Thomas went further than any of the other three theologians in discussing specific examples of acceptable zealous anger. For instance, in discussing blows ("De percussione"), he made sure that his reader understood that "blows and murder followed from anger," yet argued nevertheless that blows (and homicide, which stems from blows) can be both licit and illicit. See ibid., pp. 420–21.

[17] Ibid., p. 414. Thomas warns of the dangers of too much zealous anger but then goes on to cite the episode of Christ and the moneylenders, concluding with the same metaphor that Hincmar used (see Hincmar, PL 125, col. 880). There are so many similarities between Hincmar's and Thomas's approaches to anger that one wonders whether Thomas may not have seen Hincmar's work, but this is mere speculation.

[18] Indeed, it is not surprising that three of the four authors mentioned the passage from Psalms that proclaims, "Grow angry, and do not sin" (Ps. 4:5).

[19] An interesting contradiction about the ability of Christ to grow angry exists in Thomas of Chobham's treatment of anger (*Summa confessorum,* p. 414). Thomas announces that anger is a perturbation of the mind, and that Christ never experienced such agitation because he never had a perturbed mind (*perturbatam rationem*). Only in humans, because the flesh is weak, does the mind become disturbed thus. In the next paragraph, however, Thomas uses the example of Christ driving the merchants from the temple as an example of the "good" application of zealous anger (*ira per*

of Lactantius's reading of divine anger as righteous and correcting.[20] These stories would thus have demanded explanation in the light of the traditional understanding of anger as a sin. But beyond accounting for biblical anger, it seems probable that certain "agitations of the mind" found in everyday human interaction would have been seen as virtuous, or at least acceptable.[21] While perhaps not representative of a strict *turbatio mentis*, ecclesiastical expressions of ritual anger, or *clamor*, such as those found in monastic maledictions and the curse clauses of tenth- and eleventh-century charters, come to mind in this context.[22] In these ritual expressions of anger, anger was portrayed as a positive social force for bringing peace and for punishing the sinful. Royal wrath, too, was considered an acceptable form of anger. This does not mean that medieval society expected kings to be angry all the time or that all royal rage was considered acceptable, merely that royal wrath was one of the many potential components of kingship.[23] Indeed, kings such as Henry II of England and his sons were often expected to grow angry.[24] And, given the topos of royal wrath,

---

zelum). Although none of the biblical versions of this story (Matt. 21:12–13; Mark 11:15–17; Luke 19:45–46; or John 2:14–17) explicitly describes Christ as "angry," Thomas clearly perceived this to be evidence of acceptable anger.

[20] Lactantius, *De ira Dei liber*, ed. Christiane Ingremeau, Sources Chrétiennes 289 (Paris: Éditions du Cerf, 1982). Lactantius challenged the Roman Stoic tradition (as exemplified in Seneca, *De ira*, vol. 1 of *Dialogues*, ed. Abel Bourgery, [Paris: Belles Lettres, 1961]) of anger as detrimental to the well-being of the properly tranquil soul. Although the ideas embodied in Lactantius's text seem to be the root of medieval ideas of *ira per zelum*, the fact that only seven manuscripts of *De ira Dei liber* are now extant (according to Christiane Ingremeau, in Lactantius, *De ira*, pp. 57–59) suggests that Lactantius's ideas were not transmitted directly to the medieval authors (such as Hincmar and Thomas of Chobham) who adopted the doctrine of zealous anger. In chapter 1, Lester Little notes the influence of Augustine and Gregory the Great upon notions of zealous anger, so perhaps Lactantius's ideas had been mediated by these standard medieval *auctoritates*.

[21] In Chapter 6, Stephen White echoes the point that medieval authors often found anger to be appropriate behavior.

[22] See Chapter 1 above and Lester K. Little, *Benedictine Maledictions: Liturgical Cursing in Romanesque France* (Ithaca: Cornell University Press, 1993). For a curse clause from the same region as the case of Juhel and Guarinus, see *Chartularium insignis ecclesia cenomannensis quod dicitur liber albus capituli*, no. 184, ed. René Lottin (Le Mans: E. Monnoyer, 1869), dated ca. 936–37: "sit maledictus in civitate, maledictus in agro, maledictus ante et retro, maledictus viscera ejus, et omnia interiora ventris illius. Dei quoque iram omnimodis incurrat, atque sanctos quorum extitit insultator, in cunctis suis actibus contrarios sentiat. Penis eciam infernalibus tradatur, cum diabolo perpetuo cruciandus."

[23] The chapters on royal anger in this volume all emphasize the restraints placed upon the exercise of kingly anger. Hyams, for example, suggests that the paintings in the royal bedchamber in Westminster were designed to urge King Henry III to take up *deboneretė* and put aside anger (*ira*). While it is clear that emotional restraint was also expected of medieval kings, the chronology of this "civilizing" tendency is still problematic (as Hyams himself demonstrates). We only need think of Premier Kruschev's performance of righteous anger in the General Assembly of the United Nations to recognize that anger remains to this day a component (albeit a less frequently used one) of the exercise of power.

[24] See John E. A. Jolliffe, *Angevin Kingship*, 2d ed. (London: A. and C. Black, 1963), pp. 87–109; and

we might logically expect an *imitatio regis* on the part of all persons in positions of power and authority. Like God and kings, lords too might grow righteously angry when evil threatened their position or the areas under their protection.[25]

The linkage between notions of divine anger and righteous royal and lordly anger is worth emphasizing. For if God, the ultimate source of authority in the universe, was known to have become righteously angry when his will was flouted, then kings and lords, also representing legitimate authority in the world, should have been able to grow righteously angry with those who flouted their will.[26] Moreover, if theology and social reality tended to equate possession of authority with the legitimate expression of anger, it would not be long before the persons who resisted such authority would come to be seen as sinful, as deserving recipients of zealous rage.[27] It was a neat circular argument, for it depended upon a self-perception of legitimacy on the part of the lord exercising righteous rage; in other words, legitimacy was to be found in the eyes of the beholder. Those who grew angry at subordinates would have seen it as legitimate regardless of the perceptions of their contemporaries.[28] Despite these

---

Wilfrid L. Warren, *Henry II* (Berkeley: University of California Press, 1973), pp. 183, 210–11, 387–88, 630.

[25] White, Chapter 6 above, identifies the performance of anger with a secular political and feuding culture.

[26] For a recent treatment of a political *imitatio Dei* by secular rulers, see Geoffrey Koziol's *Begging Pardon and Favor: Ritual and Political Order in Early Medieval France* (Ithaca: Cornell University Press, 1992).

[27] In one such instance the recipient of righteous rage was considered to be like the devil or a demon. Viscount Berengar of Narbonne had grown angry at a former dependent who had flouted his will and authority. In his anger, Berengar described his enemy's actions to be "like the devil" (*quasi diabolus*): see *Querimonia Berengarii adversus Guifredum archiepiscopum Narbonensem . . .*, PL 143, col. 840. Though the precise translation of this phrase is not at all clear (Paul Hyams is right to remind me in a private communication that we do not know whether Berengar meant "like the devil," "like a demon," or "a kind of demon/devil"), it seems likely that the inference Berengar expected to be drawn from the phrase "quasi diabolus" was that of treason and the rejection of legitimate authority. Such an interpretation of the actions of his subordinate—as treacherous and specifically diabolical—might help explain some of the lordly violence against all underlings, including peasants (see chapter 8 by Paul Freedman).

[28] Not all lordly behavior was considered legitimate. In Chapter 4, Geneviève Bührer-Thierry notes the existence of potentially tyrannical royal and lordly behavior, suggesting a connection between fury and madness on the one hand and tyranny, or illegitimate authority, on the other. While this is an important point, we must not be too quick to equate anger (*ira*) with fury (*furor*), as it was often only the latter term that connoted true loss of rational self-control. Alcuin, for instance, observed that if not ruled by reason, anger would be transformed into fury; see *De virtutibus et vitiis*, c. 31, PL 101, col. 634 ("Ira una est de octo vitiis principalibus, quae si ratione non regitur, in furorem vertitur.") Indeed, in Chapter 2 Catherine Peyroux emphasizes the dangerous dementia implied by the use of the word *furor*. For Peyroux, *furor* carried "disruptive power" and was opposed to "normal human concourse"; it was more extreme and more dangerous than *ira* or *iracundia*. For Western French narrative texts, such a distinction between *ira* and *furor* seems to hold: *ira* usually allows for a potentially positive outcome (perhaps normal human concourse?), while *furor* describes irrational,

problems of perception, the connection between righteous anger and legitimate authority held great importance for the construction of personal bonds in aristocratic society. For the prince or the lord could, by this reasoning, view resistance to his will as resistance to the divinely ordained sociopolitical hierarchy. Thus not only did the distinction between good and bad anger have theological and soteriological importance, it had wide-ranging implications for the nature of social and hierarchical bonds among the lay aristocracy.

The lay understanding of the social role of anger is perhaps best exemplified in an important treatise written by Peter of Blois in the 1180s.[29] In it Peter, speaking through an unnamed abbot of Bonneval, attempts to persuade King Henry II and the reader to abandon vengeance, pride, and anger and to embrace more "Christian" virtues. Not surprisingly, Peter has the abbot win the disputation, and he has Henry reluctantly agree that meekness, temperance, and humility are preferable. But in the course of the dialogue, Peter puts into Henry's mouth arguments that seem very close to what actual laymen might have thought about anger and vengeance. Peter's Henry argues that anger and cursing are satisfying ways of appeasing vengeance that cannot be carried out physically.[30] He also expresses outrage over his betrayal by his sons and vassals, and suggests that the appropriate reaction to such betrayal is anger directed at the traitors. Indeed, Henry conveys a strong sense of righteous indignation and repeatedly asserts that it cannot be bad for him to grow angry and smite those who unjustly persecute him. Peter's Henry even uses the Bible as justification for his rage, remarking that if it was acceptable for Old Testament kings to grow angry, it must be acceptable for him to grow angry.[31] And, in what was surely his trump, Peter's Henry observes that "God himself grows angry."[32] These analogies—between Henry and God and Henry and the Biblical kings—only serve to underline the implicit connection between righteous anger and legitimate authority.[33] Finally, the king sug-

---

bestial anger. Further research into the various Latin terms for "anger" and their meanings is clearly necessary.

[29] Peter of Blois, *Dialogus inter regem Henricum secundum et abbatem Bonevallis*, ed. R. B. C. Huygens, *Revue Bénédictine* 68 (1958): 87–112, under the title "Un écrit de Pierre de Blois réédité."

[30] "Si isti missi sunt ad malefaciendum michi, quare non sum ego missus ad malefaciendum vel maledicendum malefactoribus meis? Si non possum eis malefacere quantum volo, maledicam tamen quantum potero, nam maledictio ipsa quodammodo species ultionis michi est et grata consolatio in adversis" (ibid., p. 98).

[31] Ibid., pp. 98–99.

[32] Ibid., pp. 99–100. Among other telling comments, Peter has Henry say, "Deus ipse irascitur. . . . Quomodo ergo stabiliam cor meum, ut non irascar, maxime contra illos, quorum contra me sunt omnia opera, omnia verba, omnesque cogitaciones in malum?"

[33] It is significant that the actual Henry II echoed the literary Henry's equation of royal and divine anger. In the conclusion to one charter, Henry warned, "If anyone should attempt to infringe or annul my above-mentioned donation, or presume in any way to threaten it, let him incur the malevolence,

gests that it is especially appropriate for him to show zealous anger when confronted by unjust attacks and tribulations from his enemies.[34] The sense of betrayed lordship, since it was his own sons and his longtime vassals who betrayed him, is particularly strong here.

We have now seen that clerics and theologians were willing to concede the existence of justified or zealous anger, even if they were doubtful that it could be exercised without falling into sin. Yet can their arguments be reconciled with the actual performance of anger in lay society? Here the dispute between Juhel of Mayenne and Guarinus Probus is again illustrative. As was outlined above, Juhel had grown enraged when Guarinus refused to help him found a priory of Marmoutier, physical violence was narrowly averted, and the bonds between the two men were renegotiated through a complicated process of mediation, gift exchange, and compromise. This incident embodies both constructions of anger. That anger, as a *turbatio mentis,* could be bad was clearly shown by the reaction of the witnesses to Juhel's outburst. Nevertheless the positive social realignment that came about through Juhel's anger, and Juhel's belief that his rightful authority had been unjustly challenged, tie it also to the concept of zealous anger.

The key to understanding Juhel's anger lies in his relationship with Guarinus Probus. The extant record of the dispute notes that Guarinus had been enfranchised by Juhel's father at a time when Juhel "lived, rode, and held the age of intelligence," but the record further adds that Juhel claimed to have neither consented to nor desired the enfranchisement.[35] His exclusion from the earlier agreement was obviously a sore point with Juhel, for it implied that he possessed little prestige and no authority. When Guarinus later refused to contribute to Juhel's foundation, it served as a further slight to Juhel's status. By questioning the fundamental bonds linking Juhel to his vassal (Guarinus) and to his property (the land his father had granted to Guarinus), Guarinus effectively challenged both Juhel's personal honor and, since honor was an essential component of lordship, his competence as lord.[36]

---

indignation, and anger of Almighty God *and me*" (emphasis added). For this text, see *Recueil des actes de Henri II, roi d'Angleterre et duc de Normandie concernant les provinces françaises et les affaires de France,* ed. Léopold Delisle and Élie Berger (Paris: Imp. Nationale, 1906–27), 2:244 ("Si quis vero hanc prescriptam donationem meam infringere vel cassare attemptaverit, vel aliquo modo imminuere presumpserit, omnipotentis Dei malivolentiam, iram et indignationem incurrat et meam"). Warren, *Henry II,* p. 388, also cites this text.

[34] "Inimici mei cotidie contra me invalescunt et 'superbia eorum qui me oderunt ascendit semper' [Ps. 73:23]. Quomodo ergo possem humiliare cor meum ad misericordiam, qui video inimicos meos contra me exaltari in iracondiam?" (Peter of Blois, *Dialogus,* p. 102).

[35] *Cartulaire Manceau de Marmoutier,* ed. Laurain, 2:15–17.

[36] For the crucial connection between lordship, honor, and property, see Aron Gurevich, "Représentations et attitudes à l'égard de la propriété pendant le haut moyen âge," *Annales ESC* 27 (1972): 523–

Furthermore, the specific circumstances of Juhel's position added to the threat of Guarinus's challenge. At the time of the dispute Juhel was young and had but recently assumed the lordship of Mayenne.[37] Moreover, he was almost certainly a second son, who was not expected to inherit Mayenne and whose lordship was thus potentially less legitimate and less secure than if he had been the elder brother.[38] Thus not only was Guarinus challenging Juhel's honor and competence as a lord, he was challenging a weak young lord who had yet to demonstrate fully the legitimacy of his lordship. Given the seriousness of this challenge and the cultural links existing between anger and rightful authority, it was entirely appropriate that Juhel respond to Guarinus by resorting to a performance of righteous, lordly anger. Such a performance served to defend his honor, to inform Guarinus and the other bystanders that Juhel recognized the seriousness of the challenge, and to let them know that he was willing to renegotiate the bonds existing between himself and Guarinus. Indeed, given the cultural connections between zealous anger and lordship, it seems likely that Guarinus himself anticipated an angry response to his actions and that he hoped that anger would herald a process of negotiation and compromise.[39]

Indeed I would suggest that the performance of lordly anger was frequently linked to compromise and negotiation. This connection is logical, if a bit indirect. If anger signaled the initiation of a process of restructuring social relationships, and if, as Fredric Cheyette, Stephen White, and Patrick Geary have forcefully argued,[40] disputes during this period were often

---

47; and Stephen D. White, "The Discourse of Inheritance in Twelfth-Century France: Alternative Models of the Fief in *Raoul of Cambrai*," in *Law and Government in Medieval England and Normandy: Essays in Honour of Sir James Holt*, ed. George Garnett and John Hudson (Cambridge: Cambridge University Press, 1994), pp. 173–97. See also White's Chapter 6 above. For more on the meaning of aristocratic property, see Stephen D. White, *Custom, Kinship, and Gifts to Saints: The* Laudatio Parentum *in Western France, 1050–1150* (Chapel Hill: University of North Carolina Press, 1988); and Barbara H. Rosenwein, *To Be the Neighbor of Saint Peter: The Social Meaning of Cluny's Property, 909–1049* (Ithaca: Cornell University Press, 1989).

[37] Juhel's father, Walter of Mayenne, was dead by 1116. *Cartulaire de Saint-Michel de l'Abbayette, prieuré de l'abbaye de Mont-Saint-Michel (997–1421)*, ed. Arthur Bertrand de Broussillon (Paris: A. Picard et fils, 1894), no. 9, indicates that Walter's other son, Hamelin, was lord of Mayenne in 1116. Hamelin, probably the older brother of Juhel, attests several charters from 1116 to about 1118 as lord of Mayenne, but disappears sometime between 1118 and 1120. Juhel's first datable appearance as lord of Mayenne comes in 1120 in the first of the string of charters detailing the founding of the priory of Marmoutier at Mayenne, of which this case is one. See note 1 above for the dating of this charter.

[38] It is likely that the lords of Mayenne were starting to favor primogeniture at this time. Evidence for this may be seen in *Cartulaire de l'Abbayette*, no. 9. For the thesis that primogeniture began to predominate in France around 1100, see Georges Duby, *The Chivalrous Society*, trans. Cynthia Postan (Berkeley: University of California Press, 1977), chaps. 3, 7, 9, and 10, and, for example, p. 147.

[39] In Chapter 6 White suggests that displays of anger were often the product of other people's efforts at "emotional engineering"; here Guarinus is clearly trying to engineer a more satisfactory relationship with his lord.

[40] Fredric L. Cheyette, "Suum cuique tribuere," *French Historical Studies* 6 (1970): 287–99; Stephen

settled by compromise and mediation, then a link between anger and compromise seems not merely possible but probable.[41] Indeed, what is most interesting in the Juhel case is that violence did not follow anger, despite dominant ecclesiastical assertions that it would. Rather, Juhel's anger forced a situation whereby both sides could express the real issues underlying the dispute (Juhel's competence as lord and Guarinus's freedom) and whereby both could expect to have their fears and concerns addressed. That such a complex compromise occurred within one day of Juhel's rage shows that compromise was not unfamiliar in this society and that in expressing his rage Juhel was probably aware that he was initiating a process whose conclusion would satisfy both sides.[42]

Many of the features exhibited in Juhel's story are also found in William of Malmesbury's description of the rebellion of Geoffrey Martel against his father, Count Fulk Nerra of Anjou. Fulk had ceded practical control of the county to his son when

> He [Geoffrey], having acted savagely and harshly against the inhabitants of the county, and having acted haughtily toward the very source of his power [i.e., his father], and having been commanded to lay aside the magistracy and his symbols of power, arrogated much to himself so that he took up arms against his father. Then the already

---

D. White, "Pactum . . . legem vincit et amor judicium: The Settlement of Disputes by Compromise in Eleventh-Century Western France," *American Journal of Legal History* 22 (1978): 281–308; and Patrick J. Geary, "Living with Conflicts in Stateless France: A Typology of Conflict Management Mechanisms, 1050–1200," in *Living with the Dead in the Middle Ages* (Ithaca: Cornell University Press, 1994), pp. 125–62. For other treatments of the resolution of disputes, see Barbara H. Rosenwein, Thomas Head, and Sharon Farmer, "Monks and Their Enemies: A Comparative Approach," *Speculum* 66 (1991): 764–96; Stephen D. White, "Feuding and Peacemaking in the Touraine around the Year 1000," *Traditio* 42 (1986): 195–263; *The Settlement of Disputes in Early Medieval Europe,* ed. Wendy Davies and Paul Fouracre (Cambridge: Cambridge University Press, 1986); and *Disputes and Settlements: Law and Human Relations in the West,* ed. John Bossy (Cambridge: Past and Present, 1983).

41 Cheyette, "Suum cuique tribuere," was the first to emphasize the degree to which disputes in the twelfth and thirteenth centuries were settled not by formal, official decree, but rather by an informal process involving compromise and arbitration. White, "*Pactum . . . legem vincit,*" extends and strengthens Cheyette's argument. Geary, "Living with Conflicts," has also adopted this framework.

42 For instances of compromise in the charters of Western France, see White, "*Pactum . . . legem vincit.*" Another useful example is found in *Cartulaire de l'abbaye de Saint-Vincent du Mans (premier cartulaire, 572–1188),* ed. Robert Charles and Samuel Menjot d'Elbenne (Le Mans: A. de Saint-Denis, 1886–1913), nos. 303–11 (dated 1050–1100). This series of charters, while more laconic in language than that of Juhel and Guarinus, outlines a nearly identical dispute between a certain Raherius and the abbot of Saint Vincent. While nowhere is anger mentioned per se, the situation is so close that one imagines the emotion to have been present even if the word is not. In this dispute Raherius and the abbot come to several *concordiae* through the assistance of mediation. Issues of power and servitude are also concerned here (with Raherius accused of being a serf [*colibertus*]), and the end result is a similar compromise, with each side gaining most of what it desired.

cold and exhausted blood of the old man grew hot with anger, and he broke his youthfully insulting son in a few days with much counsel from more mature men, so that carrying a saddle on his back for several miles, Geoffrey displayed himself prostrate at the feet of his father. He, whose old animosity still throbbed, rose up, and kicking Geoffrey as he lay, repeated three and four times "You are conquered, conquered at last." His spirit survived being conquered, and indeed was so distinguished, that he responded "By you alone father, because you are my father, am I conquered; by all others I am unconquered." With his swollen soul mollified by this speech, Fulk comforted the shame of his child with paternal compassion and restored him to his principality.[43]

Many elements of this story resemble those of Juhel's case. Fulk's anger was a clear sign of his displeasure with his son. The incident was also one of honor, power, and lordship, for again Fulk became angry when Geoffrey began to disobey him, thus threatening Fulk's honor and authority as count. Again, the anger is a sign that this relationship needed to be restructured. What differs in this case is the outcome of the story, for Fulk got almost everything he wanted: submission from his son, respect, and maintenance of his own position of authority. Geoffrey was forced to perform a humiliating ritual of submission.[44] In this case Fulk's anger was appeased by conciliatory gestures from his son. If this is not quite the same degree of compromise as that exhibited in the dispute between Juhel and Guarinus, it nevertheless does represent an alternative to violence and bloodshed. Moreover, Geoffrey did remain in nominal control of the county, despite his humiliation. Thus both father and son salvaged some-

[43] William of Malmesbury, *De Gestis Regum Anglorum, Libri Quinque,* ed. William Stubbs, Rolls Series 90 (London: H.M.S.O., 1889; repr., Kraus, 1964), 2:292. William writes:

> Ille in provinciales immane quam dure, in ipsum collatorem honoris quam superbe actitans, jussusque magistratum et fasces deponere, adeo sibi arrogavit ut contra patrem arma sumeret. Tunc senis frigidus jam et effoetus sanguis ira incaluit, filiumque juveniliter insultantem paucis diebus maturiori consilio adeo infregit, ut, per aliquot miliaria sellam dorso vehens, pronum se cum sarcina ante pedes patris exponeret. Ille, cui vetus animositas adhuc palpitaret, assurgens, et pede jacentem pulsans, "Victus es, tandem victus," ter quaterque ingeminat: superfuit victo spiritus, et quidem egregius, ut responderet, "Tibi pater soli, quia pater es, victus; ceteris omnibus invictus sum." Hoc relatu tumentis animus emollitus, patriaque pietate verecundiam prolis consolatus, principatui restituit.

[44] This ritual—carrying a saddle on one's shoulders—is also found in the epic *Raoul de Cambrai.* In it, Raoul attempted to atone for his actions against Bernier, and offered to carry Bernier's saddle on his back. Moreover, Raoul promised to tell everyone he met—from men at arms to young girls—that it was Bernier's saddle he was carrying. All of the knights were impressed by this generous attempt at reconciliation. See *Raoul de Cambrai,* ed. Sarah Kay (Oxford: Oxford University Press, 1992), lines 1580–1601.

thing positive out of the incident: Fulk his honor and dignity, and Geoffrey his position as heir.

Two other eleventh-century documents contain incidents of anger that reflect these themes of legitimate authority and the need to restructure lord-vassal relationships. The first is the famous *Conventum* forged between Count William of Aquitaine and Hugh, lord of Lusignan, during the 1020s, in which Hugh outlines the abuses he allegedly incurred in the service of the count.[45] In one incident, Count William is said to have grown exceedingly angry when he learned that Hugh had made a contract to marry the daughter of Count William's enemy, Ralph, viscount of Thouars. The count rushed to Hugh and humbly said, "Do not accept the daughter of Ralph as your wife. I will give you whatever you ask of me, and you will be my friend over all others save my son." Hugh did what the count commanded, and on account of his love and fealty to the count, sent the woman away.[46] Here Count William's anger, like Juhel's, was sparked when his subordinate flouted his honor, position, and authority; just as Guarinus had defied Juhel by refusing to contribute to an endowment, so Hugh defied the count by arranging a marriage alliance with the count's enemy. As in the case of Juhel and Guarinus, anger served here as a sign that something was sour in the relationship of Hugh and William; it informed Hugh that William wished to restructure their relationship. Again, anger is seen to be the proper possession of those in authority. Compromise, too, is evident in this case: William received Hugh's promise to break his engagement, while Hugh in return received a promise of *amicitia* from William. Geary has argued convincingly that the entire text of the *Conventum* should be seen as an attention-grabbing device on Hugh's part to force the count to grant respect and honor to Hugh, and this particular episode fits well with such a hypothesis.[47] Much as Guarinus's intransigence forced Juhel into anger and eventual reconciliation, Hugh's actions represent part of a strategy designed to force a renegotiation of his relationship with Count William.[48]

Sentiments similar to those expressed in the previous examples also

[45] *Le Conventum (vers 1030): Un précurseur aquitain des premières épopées,* ed. George Beech, Yves Chauvin, and Georges Pon, Publications romanes et françaises 212 (Geneva: Droz, 1995). This work replaces the earlier edition by Jane Martindale in *English Historical Review* 84 (1969): 528–48.

[46] "Ut audivit comes iratus est valde, properavitque ad Hugonem cum humilitate et dixit ei: 'Noli accipere Radulfi filiam in uxorem, ego dabo tibi quocumque petieris mihi, meusque eris amicus super omnes preter filio meo.' Fecitque Ugo quod precepit ei comes, et propter ejus amorem fidelitatemque mulierem in occulto dimisit" (*Conventum,* p. 123, lines 13–18). Stephen White, Chapter 6 above, also notices the prevalence of anger in this text.

[47] Geary, "Living with Conflicts," p. 146 and n. 54.

[48] Other evidence of anger appears in similar contexts in the *Conventum:* p. 128, lines 94–108; p. 133, lines 220–35.

appear in the complaint issued by Viscount Berengar of Narbonne against Archbishop Guifred of Narbonne.[49] The context of this dispute was a long-term struggle for control over the archbishopric of Narbonne, and the text represents Viscount Berengar as the blameless victim of Guifred's persecutions. The language of the document is illustrative, especially at one point. Berengar relates how he had brought up the young archbishop (who received this benefice at the age of ten) in his household, and how he had subsequently trusted Guifred to be his spiritual guide and to remember their ties of blood.[50] But Guifred did not treat him with the honor he deserved as lord, guardian, and foster father. "Rising up, like the Devil," Berengar complained, "he [Guifred] haughtily and unexpectedly exasperated me and provoked me to anger; he built castles against me and made cruel war against me, in which nearly a thousand men were killed from both sides."[51] The two men patched up their quarrel with a declaration of the Truce of God, but once again, according to Berengar, Archbishop Guifred and his men broke the truce.[52] Although the element of compromise is certainly not present here (indeed, if we believe Berengar, Guifred seems never to have kept his word), Berengar's anger seems related to the situations described above. He grew angry because the current state of his relationship with Guifred had become unacceptable and especially because Guifred, who was his dependent and the former subject of his paternal authority, was rejecting what Berengar saw as his rightful position as *senior.* His anger should be seen again as a warning sign that Berengar wished to renegotiate their relationship. Although mediation was impossible in this case, the cause of Berengar's anger and its clear connection to issues of power and authority allow a clear parallel to be drawn between Berengar's situation and those of Juhel, Fulk, and Count William.

Thus far I have attempted to provide a typology of the meaning of anger to the aristocracy of France during the high Middle Ages. I have suggested that anger was an acceptable and viable method by which aristocrats signaled their displeasure with existing social and hierarchical relation-

[49] Viscount Berengar of Narbonne, *Querimonia Berengarii adversus Guifredum archiepiscopum Narbonensem . . .*, PL 143, cols. 837–44. This source is discussed by Elisabeth Magnou-Nortier, *La société laïque et l'église dans la province ecclésiastique de Narbonne (zone cispyrénéenne) de la fin du VIIIe à la fin du XIe siècle* (Toulouse: Association des Publications de l'Université de Toulouse–Le Mirail, 1974), pp. 463–68.
[50] Berengar, *Querimonia,* col. 840.
[51] "Tunc surgens, quasi diabolus, superbe atque repente exacerbavit me, et provocavit ad iracundiam et aedificavit super me castra, venitque cum ingenti exercitu super me, et fecit mihi guerram crudelem, et fuere interempti pro ea ex ultraque parte fere millia hominibus" (ibid., col. 840). See note 27 above for the possible meanings of "quasi diabolus."
[52] Ibid., cols. 841–42.

ships, that expressions of anger by lords who felt their authority to be challenged should be connected to the theological concept of zealous anger, and that such anger usually commenced a process by which these relationships were reconceived.

With this in mind, there is one last source to consider in analyzing the social meaning of aristocratic anger: the epic poem *Raoul de Cambrai.*[53] This complicated and bloody narrative relates the ongoing struggle between the faction of Raoul of Cambrai and his kinsmen (Guerri the Red and Gautier) and that of the four sons of Herbert of Vermandois and their kin (especially Bernier) over possession of the Vermandois.[54] This protracted conflict allows the anonymous author of the poem to explore the potential incompatibility of ties of kinship and vassalage and the emotional motivations for aristocratic behavior. Given these general themes and the violence with which they are played out, the epic serves as an exceptionally useful source of information about the practice of aristocratic anger.

Notwithstanding the prevalence of anger in the text, the resolution of the characters' anger and the significance that anger thereby acquires might initially seem to run counter to many of the arguments I have made up to this point. Indeed, the epic is one of chronic violence and warfare, frequent incidents of betrayal and revenge, and repeated warnings about the dangers of intemperance.[55] The first third of the story, for instance, in which Bernier wrestles with the conflicting emotions of loyalty toward Raoul (his lord) and loyalty toward the members of his family (whom Raoul is attacking), does not seem to suggest that anger could play a role in resolving disputes peacefully. First Raoul refuses to moderate his anger, thereby losing the fidelity of Bernier; later it is Bernier who refuses to allow his anger to be soothed, thereby preventing an amicable settlement of their dispute. Thus, despite frequent attempts at negotiation and mediation, the inability of both Bernier and Raoul to moderate their anger leads inexorably to the epic battle in which Bernier slays Raoul, his former lord.[56]

[53] *Raoul de Cambrai,* ed. Kay. Kay, pp. ix–lxxiii, discusses the complicated manuscript tradition and dating of the text. Although a written form of *Raoul* existed by the middle of the twelfth century (pp. lxii–lxv, lxxii–lxxiii), the extant version of the poem appears to have been redacted in the early thirteenth century.

[54] For a brief summary of the plot, see *Raoul de Cambrai,* pp. li–lv.

[55] The author of *Raoul de Cambrai* announces the last theme quite early in the poem. Commenting on Raoul's immoderate streak, he noticed that "an unbridled man has great difficulty surviving" (line 323).

[56] *Raoul de Cambrai,* lines 1–3541. Hearing Raoul's abuse of his family and his mother (lines 1451–86), Bernier resorts to righteous anger (lines 1470–71), at which point Raoul strikes Bernier and Bernier forsakes his vassalage and flees the court (lines 1517–49). Raoul then tries to make amends

Yet even though all the characters fail to possess the temperance so praised by the theologians, the evidence of anger in *Raoul de Cambrai* does conform to the typology set forth above. In every instance, a character reacts to a slight to his honor, power, or authority as lord.[57] The anger that results is clearly the extreme response of an attempt to redress these slights,[58] and although the anger never succeeds in accomplishing what I see as its main purpose—the successful renegotiation of social bonds—this failure may be explained by the nature of the epic itself. *Raoul de Cambrai,* I think, was meant to be read or heard not as "fact" but rather as a didactic tragedy. The continual violence and the lack of any solution to the violence was meant as a cautionary lesson: anger was seen as a just and essential part of medieval society,[59] but taken without temperance it could go too far. In this sense, the epic echoes the theologians' dilemma about zealous (good) and sinful (bad) anger. Indeed, what is most striking about *Raoul de Cambrai* is not the prevalence of anger and violence, which were always associated with disputes, but rather the constant failure of attempts at mediation and compromise.[60] The story is a tragedy, then, because the intemperance of a few condemns the characters' best efforts at mediation to failure and leads to the ruin of all.

---

with conciliatory words and gestures (lines 1550–1604), but Bernier categorically rejects the offer (lines 1605–19). Later on Bernier tries to mend the breach, but despite all counsel from his kin, Raoul refuses to put away his anger (lines 1976–2024), and the fateful battle erupts in which Raoul himself is killed. The feud does not end, however, with the death of Raoul; Raoul's kinsmen Guerri the Red and Gautier continue the struggle against Bernier and his family. By the end of the poem, Gautier and Bernier are also dead.

[57] For slights to honor, see ibid., lines 2142–58: Raoul's anger is directly connected to the dishonor he felt when Bernier criticized him publicly. The crucial significance of honor to this story and to medieval society at large has been underlined by Stephen D. White in "Discourse of Inheritance in Twelfth-Century France" and in Chapter 6 above. Wendy Davies, chapter 9 below, emphasizes the importance of slights to honor in provoking curses.

[58] See, for instance, Guerri's anger at King Louis's decision to disinherit Raoul: Guerri "contested" this "shameful treatment" of his nephew, and left the room in anger (*Raoul de Cambrai,* lines 475–82).

[59] When Bernier abandons the army of Raoul for that of his relatives, Raoul asks why Bernier is leaving "in anger"; his men reply that "he has good cause for grievance, he has served you with his steel blade and you have rewarded him terribly. . . . May God our judge confound whoever blames him for wanting revenge" (*Raoul de Cambrai,* lines 1556–63). Bernier's ally Ernaut, having lost his hand in battle, also believes that he has good reason for anger (lines 2960–69).

[60] For examples of attempts at mediation, see the occasion on which an abbot mediates peace between the faction of Bernier and that of Guerri and Gautier (*Raoul de Cambrai,* lines 5120–63); this peace lasts for many years before it is broken. Raoul, too, offered to purchase peace and reconciliation with Bernier by performing a humiliating public ritual (lines 1578–1601). The best example, however, comes in the series of speeches made by both sides before the great battle in which Raoul is killed. The uncles of Bernier repeatedly counsel that compromise and reconciliation are better than war and violence (lines 1916–55, 2025–45, 2081–2106, 2869–2909); underscoring Geary's point about choosing arbiters who are known to both sides, the uncles even send Bernier himself to negotiate a compromise. That these attempts continually fail is the real tragedy of the story.

Raoul de Cambrai provides a fitting summation for this discussion of anger. While the outcome of the poem—death to all the main characters—is clearly not the outcome desired in the other cases presented above, the text reminded the medieval audience of several things. First, it affirmed that anger was justifiable ("I have good reason to be angry," said Bernier)[61] and that it was good to act on that anger to restructure the bonds of society. At one point, for instance, Raoul, brought to his senses by Bernier's anger, realizes the errors of his actions and offers generous compensation to Bernier; to a degree, then, Bernier's anger had achieved its goal in bringing about a rearrangement of their relationship.[62] That it failed should not blur the importance of the role of anger in leading to the resolution of disputes. In this sense, then, the anger found in *Raoul de Cambrai* serves to exemplify the theological concept of zealous or righteous anger. Second, the poem reminded the aristocratic audience that temperance, too, was a virtue. It demonstrated that anger, if unappeased through mediation and negotiation, brings tragedy to all. In a society where honor was paramount, where anger could be used to defend one's honor, the epic argued that honor should not outweigh temperance and the moderate use of zealous anger. Indeed, failure to realize that the process of renegotiation and mediation had been successful led to the widespread death, misery, and warfare with which *Raoul de Cambrai* concludes.

Thus it is that in *Raoul de Cambrai* we can find a microcosm of this chapter's thesis. I have argued that medieval people conceived of the role and place of anger in lay society in two separate, yet interrelated and mutually compatible ways. One saw anger as a dangerous, even evil, emotion, leading to sin and damnation. This conception is easily seen in the works of the theologians, in the tragic message of *Raoul de Cambrai,* and in the assumption underlying the aristocratic need to resolve anger by mediation and negotiation before it led to violence and greater sin. The other understanding of anger was formed by the practical exigencies of everyday life in a society without a strong centralized government, and it acknowledged the existence of a justifiable, "good," anger. "Good" anger came about through the righteous zeal that flowed out of the exercise of

[61] *Raoul de Cambrai,* line 2909.

[62] Given my point about the tendency for righteous anger to be connected to the holding of power and authority, it might seem odd that it is Bernier who becomes angry at what his lord has done to him. Yet power and authority must be legitimate to be righteous, and here the author of *Raoul de Cambrai* raises serious questions about the hierarchical relationship between the two men. Bernier continually proves himself the equal of Raoul in wealth, generosity, nobility, and prowess. Who, then, was really deserving of authority and honor—Raoul or Bernier? Who was supposed to show the zealous anger? Given this purposeful ambiguity on the part of the author, we should not be surprised that both Raoul and Bernier exhibit righteous anger.

legitimate authority, and while it was also articulated by the theologians and by the author of *Raoul de Cambrai,* it is best illustrated by the renegotiation of social bonds initiated by the righteous anger of Juhel of Mayenne.

CHAPTER EIGHT

Peasant Anger in the Late Middle Ages

PAUL FREEDMAN

The vast majority of writers from the thirteenth to early sixteenth centuries imagined the anger of peasants in two fundamental ways: peasant anger was ludicrous with respect to individuals, and it was capable of instigating terrifying mass violence. In Germany, where satires against peasants formed a popular literary genre, peasants attempting to imitate the valor of knights are shown maiming and killing one another in their foolish rage. In chroniclers' accounts of insurrections, from the Jacquerie to the German Peasants' War of 1525, peasants are depicted as raping, pillaging, and slaughtering, their actions are likened to those of ravening beasts.[1] Comic or murderous, peasant anger was quintessentially irrational.

We should not assume that medieval authors had a uniformly hostile view of the peasants whose suffering could, in fact, be portrayed with sympathy. Rustics were sometimes credited with a simple piety that earned them God's favor. Nevertheless, their anger could only exceptionally be represented as dignified, not only because that would be more socially subversive than acknowledging in general terms the injustice of society, but because anger was an essentially noble prerogative.

Although numbered among the deadly sins, anger was not in itself

[1] The implications of these images were described in the widely noted article of Stephen Greenblatt, "Murdering Peasants: Status, Genre, and the Representation of Rebellion," *Representations* 1 (1983): 1–29.

necessarily always wicked. As pointed out elsewhere in this book (particularly by Gerd Althoff, Richard Barton, and Lester Little), the Bible often accepts or praises righteous ire. The Psalms are infused with anger against those who defy God (e.g., Ps. 139:21–22). Divine wrath figures in both Old and New Testaments to avenge oppression on the Day of Judgment (Is. 13:9; Rom. 2:5, Rev. 6:17).

For classical culture as well, a measured anger was regarded as high minded and praiseworthy. In Plato's *Laws* (73b-d) and Aristotle's *Nichomachean Ethics* (4.5, 1125b26 ff.) thoughtful anger is appropriately mobilized against evil actions or to defend one's dignity. Achilles exemplified destructive immoderate anger, but a just and restrained indignation was the basis for courage. A modicum of anger, "the mind's sinews," was required in order to distinguish oneself in battle.[2]

In the secular world of the Middle Ages, anger accompanied the defense of honor. As demonstrated throughout this volume, nobles, kings, and saints acted to avenge feints and trespasses against their reputation and charisma. This does not mean that medieval great men were childishly undisciplined or irrationally violent. Violence was the result not of blinding rage but of a calibrated response to defend affronted honor.[3] Even seemingly impulsive acts of aristocratic violence, such as those ubiquitous in the Icelandic sagas, resulted from a well-understood code of self-regard and response to offense.[4] Yet, for all its calculation, noble anger was, after all, a rather immediate, vivid form of negotiation. Undertaken with a deliberation that belies its literary rendition as purely spontaneous, chivalric rage was nevertheless real anger, a necessary stiffening of resolve to excel at war or to avenge dishonor.

Ludicrous and Cataclysmic Peasant Rage

In the eyes of literate observers, peasants and other subordinate groups might get enraged, but under normal circumstances they were helpless to

[2] Plato, *Republic* 411b. The Stoics and Epicureans disputed this, regarding all anger as excessive impulse, as passion.

[3] Stephen D. White, "Feuding and Peacemaking in the Touraine around the Year 1000," *Traditio* 42 (1986): 195–263; Patrick J. Geary, "Living with Conflicts in Stateless France: A Typology of Conflict Management Mechanisms, 1050–1200," in Geary, *Living with the Dead in the Middle Ages* (Ithaca: Cornell University Press, 1994), pp. 125–62, originally published as "Vivre en conflit dans une France sans état: Typologies des mécanismes de règlement des conflits (1050–1200)," *Annales ESC* 42 (1986): 1107–33.

[4] William Ian Miller, *Humiliation and Other Essays on Honor, Social Discomfort and Violence* (Ithaca: Cornell University Press, 1993), pp. 15–25, 116–24.

do anything much about it except, perhaps, by trickery. They might be credited with a certain sagacity to avenge (or more likely evade) mistreatment by their betters, but that very adroitness was rendered necessary because open confrontation, required for the maintenance of honor, was out of the question.[5] Elite observers regarded the peasant as lacking honor, as a creature of appetite and immediate needs, not as one endowed with a reputation to be challenged or defended.

Lacking military power, medieval peasants (again under normal circumstances) were not considered threatening. In the French romances they are presented as frighteningly hideous, large, dark, and misshapen, but they are armed only with the most primitive weapons (usually clubs) and tend to be docile. There is no question of their offering any effective opposition to the knight.[6] In a notorious poem, Bertran de Born rejoiced at the return of spring, the season for war and profitable attacks on a hapless rural rabble.[7]

The rustic was by definition unwarlike. In the scheme of the Three Orders he labors in return for a protection (sacred and secular) that he cannot provide for himself. Peasants were supposed to make poor soldiers for the same reason that they were unfit for love: they were rooted to the soil, incapable of feeling the passion necessary for courage or love. In *Seifried Helbling,* a cycle of German didactic poems of the thirteenth century, a peasant begs his lord to release him from military service to return to his farm and plow where he belongs.[8] Writing in the first years of the fourteenth century, Ottokar of Styria mocked the foolishness of the abbot of Admont for summoning peasants to his army, as they are fit only for ignoble (if useful) agricultural activities.[9]

Similarly, peasants (or at least male peasants) make inept and unsatisfactory lovers. Toil with the plow, not love, is what they are best at, according to the comic theorist of love Andreas Capellanus.[10] As with righteous indignation, so love was an aristocratic trait. The Latin translation and commentaries to the Arabic *Viaticum* identify lovesickness as a

[5] James C. Scott, *Domination and the Arts of Resistance: Hidden Transcripts* (New Haven: Yale University Press, 1990), pp. 40–41, 162–66.

[6] For example, the rustic herdsman that Calogrenant encounters is frightening in appearance, but he is armed only with a club and is quite docile in his behavior. Chrétien de Troyes, *Yvain,* ed. Mario Roques, *Le chevalier au lion (Yvain)* (Paris: Honoré Champion, 1963), vv. 286–409, pp. 9–13.

[7] Bertran, "Be.m plai lo gais temps de pascor," ed. William Paden, Jr., et al., *The Poems of the Troubadour Bertran de Born* (Berkeley: University of California Press, 1986), no. 30 (p. 339).

[8] Cited in *Quellen zur Geschichte des deutschen Bauernstandes im Mittelalter,* ed. Günther Franz (Darmstadt: Wissenschaftliche Buchgesellschaft, 1974), no. 146, pp. 374–79.

[9] Ottokar von Steiermark, *Österreichische Reimchronik,* MGH Dt Chron 5, pt. 1, lines 26176–98 (p. 346).

[10] Andreas Capellanus, *On Love* 1.11, ed. and trans. P. G. Walsh (London: Duckworth, 1982), p. 222.

nobles' disease. Love (*eros*) resembles valor (*heros*) and nobility (*herus*); thus high birth, bravery, and love go together.[11]

In German literature, peasants *could* be violent and stir themselves to bloodthirsty deeds by an immoderate and inappropriate rage. Their ridiculous anger is an inept aping of chivalric ways. It was particularly the peasant who attempted to become a knight that provided a standard object of ridicule. Germany had a large number of professional fighters of modest origin as well as a substantial population of impoverished knights. The question whether or not members of lower classes could be knights did not arise in most other countries, or if it did (as in Spain, where there were low-born knights in frontier towns), it did not provoke the same obsessive concern with defending the boundaries of chivalric status.

Perhaps the best known account of the fatal consequences of peasants seeking to become knights is the poem *Helmbrecht*, written around 1280.[12] The young peasant Helmbrecht becomes a robber knight, leaving his farm despite his father's exhortation to remain beside the plow. Helmbrecht does not lack physical ability to fight, but he is completely wanting in the discretion, judgment, and morality that chivalry requires. He and his cronies terrorize the countryside, killing indiscriminately. They are successful for a time, but their behavior is an incompetent pastiche of courtesy, from affecting nonsensical figures of speech to parading around in ridiculously elaborate clothes. Among their false chivalric affectations is a proclivity to pick fights by fancying slights to their honor. Their anger may be deliberate but it is absurd. Helmbrecht boasts that he will be avenged on a certain rich man who let out his belt and blew the foam off his beer in Helmbrecht's presence. He would be lacking in courage and unworthy of love, Helmbrecht claims, if he were to leave these slights unavenged. Love, honor, and anger—the emotional nexus of chivalry—are here ludicrously conjoined.

Helmbrecht comes to a bad end—arrested, maimed, and finally killed—his downfall the product not of inability to fight but of a peasant character utterly at odds with chivalry. He and his companions are ignorant of what constitutes honor and are incapable of the anger appropriate to defend it, so that they are savagely violent and foolish at the same time.

In the 150 song-poems attributed to the south-German poet Neidhart

[11] Mary Frances Wack, *Lovesickness in the Middle Ages: The Viaticum and Its Commentaries* (Philadelphia: University of Pennsylvania Press, 1990), pp. 51–73; idem, "The *Liber de heros morbo* of Johannes Afflacius and Its Implications for Medieval Love Conventions," *Speculum* 62 (1987): 324–44.

[12] Wernher de Gartenaere, *Helmbrecht*, ed. Ulrich Seelbach and trans. Linda B. Parshall (New York: Garland, 1987) vv. 1145–76 (pp. 76–79).

(who died sometime between 1237 and 1245), the first-person narrator (Neidhart's poetic persona) is an impoverished knight who lives in a peasant village.[13] He cuts an amusing figure as he attempts to seduce the rustic girls, often employing an inappropriately delicate language of yearning. Even when successful, the contrast between courtly sentiments and the reality of his inferior surroundings is comical. Neidhart's peasant rivals, especially the boorish Engelmâr, are easily infuriated and stupidly violent, often inflicting bloody mayhem in the course of their drunken brawls.

The rustic males of Neidhart's village are overdressed and sport swords and other knightly weapons. They are dangerous only to themselves, notably at dances where they habitually start fights as anger and festivity are joined. The peasants' innate lack of control is brought out at the fête when Engelmâr steals a mirror belonging to Vriderûn, the object of Neidhart's desires. In one poem this theft results in a fight in which one peasant is killed, while in another poem Engelmâr loses one of his legs. Neidhart himself is an amused if ineffectual spectator. In one version of the incident he rejoices (while hiding in a wine vat) at the self-destructive fury of the peasants.[14] In a third song-poem the theft of the mirror provokes a mêlee that leaves thirty dead and most of the rest without feet.[15] The peasants use their weapons murderously but almost randomly in absurd imitation of their social superiors, demonstrating a characteristic lack of control in how they avenge slights. The villagers are "full of rage," so much so that Neidhart says, with comic delicacy, that he could not bear the sight of an altercation in which five villagers were killed.[16]

At the end of the Middle Ages and well into the sixteenth century, the figure of Neidhart would be transformed from hapless, lovelorn knight to Neidhart Fuchs ("the Fox"), a trickster who sets himself up as the enemy

[13] The standard edition, *Die Lieder Neidharts,* ed. Edmund Weissner, 2nd ed., Altdeutsche Textbibliothek 44 (Tübingen: Max Niemeyer Verlag, 1984), is based on definitions of the genuine Neidhart corpus established by Moriz Haupt in the mid-nineteenth century. Haupt rejected as spurious poems that were obscene, coarse, or violent. No doubt some of the poems are by later imitators, but there is now no consensus on how to determine the difference. For the purpose of examining the overall popularity of peasant violence as a literary theme, whether individual poems date from Neidhart's time or a century later is not of crucial significance. I have benefited greatly from Elizabeth Traverse, "Peasants, Seasons and *Werltsüeze:* Cyclicity in Neidhart's Songs Reexamined" (Ph.D. dissertation, Pennsylvania State University, 1995).

[14] *Die Berliner Neidhart-Handschrift c (mgf 779): Transkription der Texte und Melodien,* ed. Ingrid Bennewitz-Behr, Göppinger Arbeiten zur Germanistik 356 (Göppingen: Kümmerle Verlag, 1981), no. 19 (18) (p. 64), no. 11 (pp. 33–34).

[15] Ibid., no. 33 (32) (p. 91).

[16] Ibid., no. 117 (p. 295).

of the peasants.[17] In this cycle of verse stories, Neidhart performs sadistic pranks on the villagers, and the frenzied, cartoonish anger with which they respond is part of the comedy. Here, however, they do not fight among themselves. Rather than violence, they display a persistent gullibility more in keeping with French stereotypes (such as are found in the *fabliaux*).

The lack of restraint, reverse chivalry, and bestial savagery became common iconographic elements in depicting German peasants. Heinrich Wittenwiler, author of *Der Ring* (ca. 1400), refers to the peasant brawl as customary, so predictable that at one point he tells the reader it is not quite time for the fight to begin.[18] A peasant wedding celebration turns into chaos when Schindennak ("Cutthroat") gets angry with Eisengrein (the name of the wolf from the Renard poems) for scratching the hand of the former's niece. The resulting war between two villages ends in mass slaughter.

Brawling brought on by foolish anger would be associated with peasants in Germany and the Low Countries until the eighteenth century. Festivities such as weddings or village holidays were frequent subjects for painting and woodcut illustrations signifying lack of mental and bodily control. Among the almost mandatory activities were clumsy dancing, gluttony, vomiting, and fighting.[19]

Contemporary observers of peasant revolts also described the anger of peasants as irrational, but now dangerous and terrifying rather than amusing. The rustics were presented as reverting to a violent animal rage during their insurrections. In 1233 Pope Gregory IX proclaimed a crusade against the Stedinger peasant rebels in the ecclesiastical province of Bremen, likening them to wild beasts who spill blood like water, sparing no one regardless of age or sex.[20] Chroniclers of the French Jacquerie of 1358 dwelt with horrific fascination on images of peasant fury. Jean le Bel describes the peasants as "enraged" like animals, an inchoate mob, a swarm, perpetrators of rape, murder, and fiendish torments. His account was followed by

[17] *Die Historien des Neithart Fuchs nach dem Frankfurter Druck von 1566*, ed. Erhard Jöst (Göppingen: Kümmerle Verlag, 1980).

[18] Heinrich Wittenwiler, *Der Ring*, ed. Bernhard Sowinski (Stuttgart: Helfand Edition, 1988) vv. 6245–46 (p. 267): "es was nicht zeit, / daz sich derheben scholt ein streit" (it was not yet time for a fight to begin); vv. 6456–57 (p. 276): Dar umb so cham der gpauren schimph / Nach ir gewon ze ungeluimph (Thus the peasants, as is their custom, turned their festivities into misfortune).

[19] Keith Moxey, "Festive Peasants and the Social Order," in *Peasants, Warriors, and Wives: Popular Imagery in the Reformation* (Chicago: University of Chicago Press, 1989), pp. 35–66; Paul Vandenbroeck, "Verbeeck's Peasant Weddings: A Study of Iconography and Social Function," *Simiolus* 14 (1984): 79–124.

[20] *Quellen Bauernstandes*, no. 117 (p. 312): "et ferino more, feris bestiis crudelius sevientes, nulli parcunt sexui vel etati, effundendo sanguinem sicut aquam."

Froissart, who added a few touches, such as making the peasants "mad dogs" rather than unspecified beasts.[21] Even the chronicler Jean de Venette, who described the peasants as capable of articulating grievances and electing leaders, presents a carnivalesque atmosphere of rape, pillage, and murder (especially of children).[22] The same lack of forethought and feral rage that produced internecine strife in the Neidhart brawls is here deployed against the nobility. This seems to contradict the French literary convention that peasants are not threatening. What is different is that whereas they are cowardly or merely ineptly violent as individuals, the peasants become murderous when formed into a mob, like a stampede of normally tractable animals. In formal military terms they remain unimpressive, at least according to historians' depictions. Froissart could, on the one hand, describe peasant atrocities committed against helpless noble women and children but at the same time derisively characterize the Jacquerie's fighting forces as comprised of serfs who were "black, small, and badly armed."[23]

The English Rebellion of 1381 was described in lurid terms similar to those employed for the Jacquerie. Neithard Bulst has argued that fourteenth-century chroniclers attributed more rational (or at least understandable) motives to the English rebels than to their French counterparts.[24] Yet probably the single most hysterical account of a peasant insurrection (albeit literary rather than historical) is the dream vision of the English Rising presented in John Gower's *Vox clamantis.*[25] In Gower's nightmare the peasants undergo horrifying transformations: "They who had been men of reason before took on the appearance of unreasoning brutes."[26] Anger is not so much a primary motivation as the product of a collective malady, a mass epidemic. The fundamental nature of the peasants (despite the expression "men of reason") is that of domestic animals. Gower writes of the rebels "refusing the halter" and, when they are finally tamed, lying "patiently under our foot," the oxen returned to their yoke.[27] The rabble are likened to farm animals that have gone wild with absurd

[21] Marie-Thérèse de Medeiros, *Jacques et chroniqueurs: Une étude comparée de récits contemporains relatant la Jacquerie de 1358* (Paris: Honoré Champion, 1979), pp. 30–33, 50.

[22] Ibid., pp. 76–77.

[23] Ibid., pp. 52–53.

[24] Neithard Bulst, "'Jacquerie' und 'Peasants' Revolt' in der französischen und englischen Chronistik," *Vorträge und Forschungen* 31 (1987): 791–817.

[25] John Gower, *Vox clamantis* 1, in *The Complete Works of John Gower,* ed. G. C. Macaulay (Oxford: Clarendon Press, 1902), 4:20–81.

[26] Gower, *Vox clamantis* 1.2, in *The Major Latin Works of John Gower,* trans. Eric W. Stockton (Seattle: University of Washington Press, 1962), p. 54.

[27] Ibid., 1.21 (p. 94): "So when the peasantry had been bound in chains and lay patiently under our foot, the ox returned to its yoke, and the seed flourished beneath the plowed fields, and the villein ceased his warring."

social ambition: oxen who refuse the plow, asses who claim the right to wear bejeweled saddles. Insofar as the peasants can be said to "want" anything, they seek to imitate and dominate over their masters, but essentially they are irrational. Their anger is without purpose, the manifestation of a degenerate nature released by opportunity. As the uprising proceeds, they become wild animals, even vermin: foxes, swine, owls, flies, frogs. They make furious animal noises—grunts, barking, wails, howls—evidence of orgiastic rage.[28]

The rebels appeared threatening because of their mass. Much as in Froissart's portrayal of the Jacquerie, the English peasants are not well equipped for war. Gower describes the raging peasantry (*rusticitas furiens*) but mocks their loutish weapons (pitchforks, mattocks, even branches and rocks).[29] Similarly in Thomas Walsingham's chronicle their bows are blackened with age, they have only a few arrows, their swords (when they have them), are rusty.[30] That the mob is ineptly outfitted does not contradict the depiction of a terrifying rebellious cataclysm. Peasants, incapable of being knights, are militarily ridiculous. Their farm tools, iconographic emblems of lowly toil, are risible as weapons. As a swarm or herd, however, they are a frightening spectacle. Anger of an instinctive and bestial sort transforms these dull-witted creatures into an enraged throng.

The Hungarian Peasant War of 1514 produced similar images of wild license. In a letter to the Count of Abaúj, dated June 16, 1514, four other Hungarian administrative officials sketched in graphic and panicked tones the rustics' savagery that had boiled over (*efferbuit*).[31] Once again, the anger of the peasants was regarded as a destructive potentiality now unleashed, the act of a malevolent nature. The count of Abaúj was exhorted to aid his fellows to prevent the extermination of the nobles. Rape, murder, and pillage are the standard peasant crimes: "How many homicides, rapes, how much slaughter and burning [have been committed] by the cursed and wicked peasants calling themselves crusaders, who are rather crucifiers of Christ."[32] Another letter from the king of Hungary to Pope Leo X details lurid scenes of torture and murder, including the impaling of the Bishop of Csanád. The king also dwelt on the rape of virgins and

[28] Steven Justice, *Writing and Rebellion: England in 1381* (Berkeley: University of California Press, 1994), pp. 208–9.

[29] Gower, *Vox clamantis* 1.12, ed. Macaulay, 4:44–45.

[30] Justice, *Writing and Rebellion*, p. 204.

[31] *Monumenta rusticorum in Hungaria rebellium anno MDXIV*, ed. Anton Fekete Nagy et al. (Budapest: Akadémiai Kiadó, 1979), no. 73 (p. 116).

[32] "Quot homicidia, quot stupra et adulteria quotque cedes et incendia per maledictos sceleratissimosque crucifixores illos, que se se cruciferos appelabant, sed crucis potius Christi persecutores fuerant" (ibid.). There is a pun on "cruciferos" (crusaders) and "crucifixores" (crucifiers).

matrons whose families were forced to watch the performance of the atrocities.[33]

The German Peasants' War of 1525 also produced apocalyptic denunciations of the supposed bestial savagery of the peasants. Luther's pamphlet "Against the Robbing and Murdering Hordes of Peasants" typifies an imagery of frenzied "hordes" that can be defeated only by righteous anger, by the sword.[34] They are incapable of reasoning and can understand only the fist and the rod.[35] A report of the parson Johann Herolt concerning the murder of nobles at Weinsberg describes the peasants as mad, raging, and possessed by demons. Similarly, nobles who had compromised with the insurrection at its height later explained their conduct by the terror inspired by the mobs.[36]

Chroniclers attributed peasant uprisings to disobedience, a foolish desire for equality and a blind hatred for the nobility. Peasant anger was not portrayed as a response to injustice, much less as a purposeful social movement. Rage was a potentiality inherent in the essentially low nature of the peasantry that could erupt ("boil over") if the rustics were not held firmly in check. Cold, calculated anger, either for revenge or in defense of honor, was considered generally impossible for peasants. Their anger was not a channeling of the "mind's sinews" but an instinct opposed to thought, the most dramatic expression of baseness more commonly evidenced by mere boorishness.

Righteous Peasant Anger

It was just possible for the higher levels of society to imagine purposeful peasant anger, although the examples are hardly numerous. The thir-

[33] Ibid., no. 104 (pp. 141–43). Similarly, the account of Giovanni Vitale of Palermo which shows the peasants (whom he calls "impudent cattle") impaling nobles in front of their wives and children, and the rape of wives before their husbands' eyes; *Monumenta rusticorum*, ed. Nagy et al., no. 200 (pp. 242–245). Forcing relatives to watch or even participate in torture or execution is a recurrent theme in chroniclers' accounts of peasant atrocities, as in the Flemish uprising of 1323–28 and in the Jacquerie. See William H. TeBrake, *A Plague of Insurrection: Popular Politics and Peasant Revolt in Flanders, 1325–1328* (Philadelphia: University of Pennsylvania Press, 1993), pp. 116–17; de Medeiros, *Jacques et chroniqueurs*, pp. 35–36, 50–52.

[34] Martin Luther, *Against the Robbing and Murdering Hordes of Peasants*, in *Luther's Works* 46, ed. Robert C. Schultz (Philadelphia: Fortress Press, 1967), pp. 49–55.

[35] Elaborated in Luther's reply to those who criticized his tract against the peasants: "An Open Letter on the Harsh Book against the Peasants," in *Luther's Works* 46:63–85.

[36] *Quellen zur Geschichte des Bauernkrieges*, ed. Günther Franz (Darmstadt: Wissenschaftliche Buchgesselschaft, 1963), no. 104 (p. 336); *The German Peasants' War: A History in Documents*, ed. Tom Scott and Bob Scribner (Atlantic Highlands, N.J.: Humanities Press International, 1991), no. 87 (pp. 206–8).

teenth-century poet known as "Der Stricker" warned of the ire of peasants against those who oppress them. They can even destroy castles: "Their anger causes castles to fall. However strongly fortified, they will burn or destroy castles just as the people of Kirchling [Kirling, near Klosterneuburg, Austria] have done."[37]

There were also cases in which bad lords were murdered by their tenants with surprisingly little adverse response from neighboring lords. There seems to have been a certain understanding of the limits of abusive lordship and acceptance of its informal regulation by violence as long as this was done relatively discretely, without mass insurrection.[38] Exceptionally an act of anti-seigneurial resistance would be widely celebrated. The villagers of Fuenteovejuna in the region of Córdoba 1476 killed their wicked lord, the commander of the Order of Calatrava, a deed that was long remembered and served as the basis of a well-known play by Lope de Vega.[39]

A rather indirect example of elite observers attributing the possibility of righteous anger to peasants comes from late medieval Hungary. At a time when lords were increasing burdens on tenants and recalling them to servile tenures from the market towns in which they had been established, certain Franciscan preachers denounced this oppression and even taught that it might be licitly resisted.[40] The Polish-born Franciscan Oswald of Lasko (d. 1511), whose career was spent in Hungary, is particularly important in this regard. In two sermons Oswald counseled the peasants to be patient and to bear their oppression as a "sad gift" that gains them merit in God's eyes.[41] Yet because the conduct of lords violates human

[37] Der Stricker, "Beispiel von den Gäuhühnern," in *Märe von den Gäuhühnern*, ed. Franz Pfeiffer (Vienna: C. Gerolds Sohn, 1859), p. 72:

> ir zorn machet bürge val:
> swie groze veste ein burc habe,
> si brennents oder stozents abe
> alss Kirchelinge taten.

See Clair Bauer, *Der Bauer in der Dichtung des Strickers: Eine literar-historische Untersuchung* (Tübingen: Buchdruckerei A. Becht, 1938), pp. 93–103.

[38] Robert Jacob, "Le meurtre du seigneur dans la société féodale. La mémoire, le rite, la fonction," *Annales ESC* 45 (1990): 247–263; Carlos Barros, "Violencia y muerte del señor en Galicia a finales de la eded media," *Studia Historica, Historia Medieval* 9 (1991): 111–57.

[39] Emilio Cabrera and Andrés Moros, *Fuenteovejuna: La violencia antiseñorial en el siglo XV* (Barcelona: Editorial Crítica, 1991), pp. 139–84.

[40] Of fundamental importance for the Franciscans and peasant sentiment on the eve of the Hungarian Revolt of 1514 is Jenő Szűcs, "Die oppositionelle Strömung der Franziskaner im Hintergrund des Bauernkrieges und der Reformation in Ungarn," in *Études historiques hongroises 1985* (Budapest: Akadémiai Kiadó, 1985), 2:483–512.

[41] [Oswald of Lasko], *Sermones dominicales perutiles a quodam fratre Hungaro Ordinis Minorum de Obseruantia compartati Biga salutis intitulati* (Hagenau: Henricus Gran, 1498), sermons 85, 97. I have used the copies of Oswald's sermons preserved at the Franciscan Institute, Saint Bonaventure University. I am very grateful to Fr. Gedeon Gál, O.F.M., Dr. Rega Wood, and Dr. Paul Spaeth for their

equality, for they treat their tenants as if they were animals, they do not merit obedience or tribute so that resistance cannot be condemned.[42]

Although they are never directly linked to his laments over the oppression of the peasantry, Oswald's teachings about anger are contained in these same sermon collections, which were designed, as their author explicitly states, to be the basis for preaching to poor and unlearned rustics.[43] Pious and appropriate anger is clearly to be directed against those who act with evil purpose within Hungarian society. In order to defend truth, bring about peace, or chastise those who offend God it is permitted actively to oppose the wicked. Oswald cites the distinction of Gregory the Great between culpable anger arising from impatience and virtuous anger arising from an eagerness for justice.[44] Oswald actually divides anger into three: culpable, excusable, and laudable. The prophets were justly angry as was even Christ himself (Mark 3:5). Those who withhold anger when faced with injustice are to be condemned.[45]

Oswald did not foresee the uses to which his sermons would be put. Provincial Vicar of the Order on three occasions between 1497 and 1509, he was hardly a deliberate fomenter of revolution. By 1510, however, Franciscan authorities in Hungary were disturbed by wandering friars who preached on texts that opened dangerous opportunities for subversion. It was not the texts themselves but their application that was upsetting. Nevertheless, formulations such as those of Oswald, when interpreted with a degree of immediacy, were indeed perilous.[46]

In the spring and summer of 1514, a peasant revolt arose from what had begun as a crusade against the Turks. The peasants denounced the nobles for their dereliction in face of the enemy and for continuing their subjuga-

---

help with these sermons and with the Hungarian literature concerning the Franciscans. Following an error in Hain's catalogue of incunabula (repeated in Goff's guide to incunabula in American libraries), the sermons in this volume and its companion *Sermones de sanctis* are often wrongly attributed in US library catalogues to Michael of Hungary. It was demonstrated in 1862 that the author of these sermons was Oswald of Lasko and this remains the consensus in Hungary. See Marcell Börörocz, *Ferencesek a középkori Magyar irodalomban* (The Franciscans in Hungarian Literature of the Middle Ages) (Pécs: Katholikus Hirlapkiadó és Nyomda Részvénytársaság, 1911), pp. 113–15; Kálmántól Timár, "Laskai Ozsvát és a bibliográfia" (Oswald of Lasko, Bibliography), *Magyar Könyvszemle* 18 (1910): 122–53.

42 [Oswald of Lasko], *Sermones de sanctis perutiles a quodam fratre Hungaro Ordinis Minorum de Obseruantia comportati Biga Salutis intitulati* (Hagenau: Henricus Gran, 1497), sermon 50: "quia talis fur est et latro et continue est in peccato . . . nec tali domino subditi tenentur obedire et solvere tributum"; sermon 49: "Et etiam adversus suum superiorem posset quis se defendere, dummodo superior iniuriose vult ipsum ledere." Discussed in Szűcs, "Oppositionelle Strömung," p. 508.

43 Szűcs, "Oppositionelle Strömung," p. 506.

44 Oswald, *Sermones dominicales*, no. 85, based on Matthew 5:22.

45 "Omnino non irasci est vituperabile. . . . Qui enim non irascitur, in quibus debet irasci, sequitur, quod non vindicet ea, que debet vindicare, quod est vituperabile" (ibid.).

46 Szűcs, "Oppositionelle Strömung," pp. 493–99.

tion of the countryside rather than rallying to fight to infidel. Franciscans were active as leaders of the revolt, and documents investigating their activities after the war show controversies over social doctrines that date from before 1514.[47]

So far we have looked at peasant anger as conceived by elite observers. Closest to what might be described as a peasant defense of righteous anger is the legend of William Tell, who is remembered as the founder of Swiss liberties. Although it is uncertain that he ever existed (and if he did, exactly what his status was), Tell became a symbol of peasant freedom both to hostile observers and to peasants themselves. A dangerous upstart to the enemies of the Confederation, Tell epitomized for the Swiss a response to seigneurial mistreatment and contempt.[48] In both pro- and anti-Swiss writings Tell represents the unusual claim by the common rural population to possess dignity and exact vengeance on the nobles or their functionaries. As a foundational myth of national formation, Tell also demonstrates the importance of anger as the galvanizing element to action and constitutional change.

The William Tell material appears in a variety of chronicles, plays, and stories written by Swiss anti-Hapsburg authors. The legend turns on the question of who has the right to claim sufficient dignity to be capable of exacting revenge. Gessler, the Hapsburg steward for Uri and Schwyz, set up a hat in the marketplace at Altdorf and required all who passed it to bow. This humiliating and capricious act was designed both to reinforce Gessler's superiority and to emphasize the lowliness of the people. Tell's refusal to perform the obeisance resulted in the sadistic (but in Gessler's eyes appropriately comical) test of the apple placed on the head of Tell's son. The same humiliation implied by setting up the cap was thereby reinforced with the addition of a mock-chivalric ordeal to taunt the claim to dignity. Tell succeeded in shooting the apple and Gessler asked why he had held two arrows in his hand. Tell said that had he missed the apple or hit his son, the second arrow would have been shot to kill Gessler. Such arrogation of a chivalric right of retaliation so enraged Gessler that he

[47] Jenö Szücs, "Die Ideologie des Bauernkrieges," in *Nation und Geschichte: Studien*, trans. Johanna Kerekes (Cologne: Böhlau Verlag, 1981), pp. 345–46; idem, "A Ferences Obszervancia és az 1514 évi parasztháború. Egy kódex tanúsága" (The Observant Franciscans and the Peasant War of 1514: Evidence of a Codex), *Levéltári Közlemények* 43 (1972): 257–60. This is an appendix containing edited records from the codex that report the investigation into Franciscan preaching and the 1514 war.

[48] On William Tell see Jean-François Bergier, *Guillaume Tell* (Paris: Fayard, 1988); "Das Weisse Buch von Sarnen," ed. Hans Georg Wirz, *Quellenwerk zur Entstehung der Schweizerischen Eidgenossenschaft* 3 (Aarau: Verlag H. R. Sauerländer, 1947), 1:14–19; "Das Lied von der Entstehung der Eidgenossenschaft," ed. Max Wehrli, in *Quellenwerk* 3 (Aarau: Verlag H. R. Sauerländer, 1952), 2, 1:21–51; "Das Urner Tellspiel," ed. Wehrli, *Quellenwerk* 2, 3:53–99.

ordered Tell taken to a dungeon. Tell escaped and finally exacted his revenge by ambushing and assassinating the steward.

Tell, if he existed, was something between a wealthy peasant and a small landowner, but he was treated by Gessler as a person lacking honor. The same treatment is meted out to three sets of peasants in a parallel foundation legend, that of the "Three Swiss" who supposedly mobilized the countryside and inspired the original confederation in revenge for seigneurial insults such as confiscating property arbitrarily and, in one instance, molesting the wife of a peasant.[49] Their anger and consequent vengeance took the form of the oath that supposedly established the basis for the alliance of local communities and their casting aside the rule of the nobles.

During the late Middle Ages, the Swiss exemplified a disturbing and anomalous peasant liberty. The actual governance of the confederation and its cantons was less democratic than its later reputation would suggest, but nevertheless, the Swiss did represent peasant freedom and autonomy, both to themselves and to outsiders. They were called peasants by their enemies, and especially in the late fifteenth and early sixteenth centuries they were considered an inspiration for liberty by peasants in the South German regions.[50] The foundational legends depict a people motivated by righteous anger over arbitrary mistreatment who refuse to be taken as servile objects of seigneurial will. To claim the right of deliberate vengeful anger, normally considered the property of nobles, was to perform an act of defiance.

Peasant Piety

If we look for the peasants' own opinion, there is very little in the way of explicit indignation to be found apart from the William Tell legend. There were occasional proposals to kill all priests, as at Niklashausen in 1476 or

[49] "Das Weisse Buch von Sarnen," ed. Wirz, pp. 8–15.

[50] In general see Peter Blickle, "Das Gesetz der Eidgenossen: Überlegungen zur Entstehung der Schweiz 1200–1400," *Historische Zeitschrift* 225 (1992): 561–86. Hostile depictions include those of Felix Hemerli, *De nobilitate et rusticitate dialogus* (written in the mid-fifteenth century, published Strasbourg: Johann Prüss, ca. 1497), c. 33, fols. 129v–131r, and a poem of 1499 in Theodor Lorentzen, "Zwei Flugschriften aus der Zeit Maximilians I," *Neue Heidelberger Jahrbücher* 17, no. 2 (1913): 169–70. On the appeal of the Swiss model see Thomas A. Brady, Jr., *Turning Swiss: Cities and Empire, 1450–1550* (Cambridge: Cambridge University Press, 1985). See also the report of the priest Jacob Unrest (*sic*) of the peasant rising of 1478 in Carinthia concerning the desire of the peasants to imitate the "faithless Swiss customs," in *Quellen Bauernkrieges*, no. 3 (p. 21).

the Tyrol in 1525,[51] but lists of grievances and other denunciations of abuses were almost always framed in tones of pious reproach rather than explicit threats. From John Ball's sermon at Blackheath in 1381 to the broadsides (*Flugschriften*) issued during the 1525 German uprising, the common theme among peasant demands is the abolition of serfdom, an institution that goes against divine law and fundamental human dignity. This demand underlay even practical grievances over the use of common land, seigneurial taxes, and other local disputes, because serfdom in this context meant not just the legal condition of unfreedom but also the ability of lords to dominate their tenants arbitrarily. Thus one finds peasants of such territories as Kent and Tyrol, where serfdom in the formal legal sense did not exist, complaining of their bondage to unjust and capricious demands.[52]

The tone of peasant grievances was more often plaintive than minatory so that righteous anger was not a widely popular theme, but the idea of honor violated by mistreatment was important. Here dishonor was not an affront to individual self-worth but an injustice to a community and against divine law. The prospective agent of vengeance was God, perhaps acting through the peasants, but human anger emerges in these documents as less significant than piety and divine protection.

In their remonstrances peasant spokesmen condemned the conduct of the nobility for violating even the most minimal human dignity.[53] Denunciation was more pointed in texts addressed to rally peasants, such as John Ball's famous sermon at Blackheath or the Cegléd Proclamation in Hungary. In these documents there are at least intimations of possible revenge against ill treatment and nobles' treachery.[54] That the peasants' wrath might descend on the nobles was remembered in England. A number of different ecclesiastical manuscripts written after 1381 include

[51] Klaus Arnold, *Niklashausen 1476: Quellen und Untersuchungen zur sozialreligiösen Bewegung des Hans Behem und zur Agrarstruktur eines spätmittelalterlichen Dorfes* (Baden-Baden: Verlag Valentin Koerner, 1980), pp. 191–96, 215, 262, 281; Walter Klaassen, *Michael Gaismair: Revolutionary and Reformer,* Studies in Medieval and Reformation Thought 23 (Leiden: E. J. Brill, 1978), pp. 91–92.

[52] Justice, *Writing and Rebellion,* pp. 44–45; *Quellen zur Geschichte des Bauernkrieges in Deutschtirol 1525,* ed. Hermann Wopfner (1908; repr., Aalen, Scientia Verlag, 1973), pp. 46–61, 134–35; Joseph Macek, *Der Tiroler Bauernkrieg und Michael Gaismair* (Berlin: Deutsche Verlag der Wissenschaften, 1965), pp. 62–70.

[53] For Catalonia, see the prologue to a document recording the formation of local peasant associations in 1448–49 in Paul Freedman, *The Origins of Peasant Servitude in Medieval Catalonia* (Cambridge: Cambridge University Press, 1991), pp. 224–26; for Germany, see the grievances collected in Scott and Scribner, *German Peasants' War* , nos. 1–11 (pp. 65–95).

[54] For Ball's sermon as reported by Thomas Walsingham, see *Chronicon Angliae,* ed. Edward Maunde Thompson, Rolls Series 64 (London: H.M. Treasury, 1874), p. 321; *Monumenta rusticorum,* ed. Nagy et al., no. 79 (pp. 121–22).

verses that caution lords against the consequences of oppressing their tenants:

> man be war and be no fool
> thenke a pon the ax and of the stool
> the stool was hard, the ax was scharp
> the iiii. yere of kyng Richard[55]

Another warning is implied by the motto of a long pamphlet written in 1525, "On the Convocation of a Common Peasantry" (An die Versammlung gemayner Pauerschaft), whose frontispiece states succinctly: "What makes the Swiss flourish? The nobles' greed!" (Wer meret Schywtz? Der herren geytz!).[56] This is a threat issued by a peasant spokesman rather than (as above) the friendly advice offered by one landlord to another. When we turn to the body of the work, however, there is little sense of righteous anger. Its author instead seeks to counter the accusation of inciting disorder and disobedience by referring to the law of God. He is careful and defensive rather than dramatic and vengeful.

Peasant anger and peasant revenge yield to evocations of piety and righteousness even in songs, popular poems, and other works addressed to peasants (and perhaps composed by them.)[57] Swiss battle songs of the fourteenth to late fifteenth centuries contrast the pious Swiss with the arrogant and reckless foreigners who want to place them under lordship. Their enemies mock them as peasants, but the Swiss apostrophize themselves as "pious members of the common union" (fromen Eidgenossen) who will be granted victory as long as they obey God. A song celebrating the victory at Murten in 1476, for example, likened the Swiss to the children of Israel who bested their seemingly invincible opponents and crossed the Red Sea under God's protection.[58]

[55] Justice, *Writing and Rebellion*, pp. 251–54.

[56] *An die Versammlung gemeiner Bauernschaft: Eine revolutionäre Flugschrift aus dem Deutschen Bauernkrieg (1525)*, ed. Siegfried Hoyer (Leipzig: VEB Bibliographisches Institut, 1975).

[57] Guy Marchal, "Die Antwort der Bauern: Elemente und Schichtungen des eidgenössischen Geschichtsbewusstseins am Ausgang des Mittelalters," *Vorträge und Forschungen* 31 (1987): 757–90; Fritz Martini, *Das Bauerntum im deutschen Schrifttum von den Anfängen bis zum 16. Jahrhundert* (Halle [Saale]: Max Niermeyer Verlag, 1944), pp. 302–10; *Die historischen Volkslieder der Deutschen*, ed. Rochus von Liliencron, 3 vols. (1865–67; repr., Hildesheim: Georg Olms Verlag, 1966), vol. 1, nos. 34, 80, 83, 130, 197; vol. 2, no. 210. For some cautious words on the use of supposedly popular sources for the Swiss see Matthias Weishaupt, *Bauern, Hirten und "frume edle puren": Bauern- und Bauernstaatsideologie in der spätmittelalterlichen Eidgenossenschaft und der nationalen Geschichtsschreibung der Schweiz* (Basel: Helbing & Lichtenhahn, 1992), esp. pp. 150–65.

[58] Liliencron, *Historischen Volkslieder*, vol. 1, no. 144 (p. 102).

The peasants are hardly viewed as passive in these songs; they are represented to the nobles as angry. A song written to commemorate the victory over the Hapsburgs at Sempach in 1386 describes the anger of the men of Uri, whose heraldic symbol is a black bull. Their rage, strong as that of their emblem but purposeful, gives them strength to cleave the helmets of their high-born enemies.[59] War songs express the grim satisfaction that those who try to suppress the peasant will learn to their sorrow what a hard task they have undertaken. In one song from the mid-fifteenth century, the suddenly fearful nobles admit that "the common man cannot be beaten," for the Swiss are ferocious, "wild with anger," ready to murder nobles on the spot.[60] This is peasant anger doubly reflected in the eyes of nobles as imagined by peasants—a pointed and paradoxical return of the theme of savage rage—rather than the peasants' own estimation of their character, which dwells on courage inspired by religious devotion more than anger.

Another unusual free peasant community of the late Middle Ages was Dithmarschen, located in Schleswig-Holstein, a marshland near the North Sea. Here, too, folk songs (in this instance commemorating victories against the Danes and the nobles of Holstein) emphasize piety rather than anger, contrasting God-fearing heroism with overconfident impiety.[61] The Battle of Hemmingstedt in 1500 gave rise to a number of poems in which the arrogance of the Danes is set beside the religious devotion of the men of Dithmarschen. The Danes boast that they will kill these peasants, while the Dithmarschers pray to the Virgin. The Danes recoil from the cross carried by the peasant army and soon seven thousand of the Danish army lie dead, a wonder performed by the common man and God's will.[62] The Dithmarschers express understandable satisfaction at the discomfiture of their enemies. Those who set out against Dithmarschen had better come well armed, warns another Hemmingstedt song-

[59] Ibid., vol. 1, no. 34 (pp. 133–34):

> Darzu die vesten von Uri
> mit irem schwarzen stier,
> vil vester dann ein mure
> bestrittends das grimme thier:
> he in irem wutenden zorn,
> sie schlugend durch die helme
> die herren hochgeborn.

[60] Ibid., no. 93 (p. 433), also cited in Brady, *Turning Swiss*, p. 36.

[61] In general see William L. Urban, *Dithmarschen: A Medieval Peasant Republic* (Lewiston, N.Y.: Edwin Mellen Press, 1991); Walther Lammers, *Die Schlacht bei Hemmingstedt: Freies Bauerntum und Fürstenmacht in Nordseeraum*, 3d ed. (Heide in Holstein: Westholsteinische Verlagsanstalt Boyens, 1982).

[62] Neocorus [Johann Adolfi], *Chronik des Landes Dithmarschen*, ed. Friedrich Dahlmann (Kiel: Königliche Schulbuchdruckerei, 1827), 1:561; also in Liliencron, *Historischen Volkslieder*, vol. 2, no.

poem,[63] but once again quiet resolve and a pious purpose rather than anger bring about victory.

What the Swiss historian Guy Marchal calls "the answer of the peasants" refuted both seigneurial images of cowardice and the portrayal of the rebellious peasant throngs as raging and uncontrollable.[64] In their justifications peasants presented themselves not just as courageous and bellicose but also, significantly, as pious. Their insurrections are represented as a defense of their humanity against those who seek to hold them as serfs in violation of divine or customary law. Especially in 1525, peasant grievance statements accused lords of behaving toward them as if they were cattle or other domestic animals.[65] The impiety of their oppressors was more than the mocking overconfidence depicted in the war songs; it was an injustice inherent in the institution of servitude.

Peasant anger therefore had only a circumscribed space in historical and literary description. At certain moments—for example, in the late tenth and early eleventh century—it was possible to imagine and justify peasant participation in militant movements such as the Peace of God.[66] During the high Middle Ages, however, peasants were usually represented by their social superiors as passive or stupidly violent against each other.

---

116 (p. 447):

> se [the Danish army] repen: "wolan, gi ditmarschen buren
> gi moten (noch alle) van avende sterven!"
> . . . .
> "nu help, Maria du maged rein,
> wi laven di mit gantser truwen:
> beholden wi nu de averhand,
> ein kloster willen wi di buwen!"
> . . . .
> Ein crucifix hadden se all mit gebracht
> dar sik de garde [i.e., the Danish soldiers] so ser verschrak:
> an einer korten ure
> der garde blef söven dusent dod
> dat dede god dorch Ditmarsche buren!

(They say: "Beware you Dithmarschen peasants. You will all be dead by evening." . . . "Now help, Maria, pure maid, we adore you with all our faith. Give to us the victory and we will build you a church." . . . They had brought with them a crucifix before which the Danish troops were greatly frightened; in a brief hour the Danes left seven thousand dead. This is what God did through the Dithmarschen peasants!)

[63] Neocorus, *Chronik*, p. 522; also in Liliencron, *Historischen Volkslieder*, vol. 2, no. 219, (p. 454).

[64] Marchal, "Antwort der Bauern," pp. 757–90.

[65] For the complaints of peasants of Kempten and Salzburg, see *Quellen Bauernkrieges*, nos. 26 (p. 129), 94 (p. 301); for the complaints of tenants of Ochsenhausen, see Horst Buszello, *Der deutsche Bauernkrieg von 1525 als politische Bewegung* (Berlin: Colloquium-Verlag, 1969), p. 17.

[66] Richard Landes, "Between Aristocracy and Heresy: Popular Participation in the Limousin Peace of God, 994–1033," in *The Peace of God: Social Violence and Religious Response in France around the Year 1000*, ed. Thomas Head and Richard Landes (Ithaca: Cornell University Press, 1992), pp. 184–218.

Beginning in the fourteenth century, when insurrections became more common and increased in scale, the peasants came to seem a dangerous mob, the peril they presented being the result of sheer numbers. Their anger, in this respect, transformed them, as in Gower's vision, from docile to violent.

In asserting a right to resist seigneurial authority, the peasants were, at least indirectly, claiming a right to anger, to avenge a wrong. That wrong was not a particular insult to a person's honor but the denial of a common humanity as represented by arbitrary misrule and servitude. That Christ freed all with His blood and that therefore no believer should be owned by another (deprived of the liberty purchased by Christ) is a theme that appears in peasant movements from Bohemia to Catalonia to Swabia, even to Kett's Rebellion in mid-sixteenth-century England.[67]

The peasants in their grievances remonstrate rather than threaten, but even at their most pious, their statements drew much force from the vivid image of an anger that was not merely their own but that of God. The Bohemian Taborite Peter Chelčický invoked Christ's sacrifice as a proof against the morality of owning human beings and warned that the oppressors of the poor would stir God's wrath: "Then will you see the Lord, the avenger of the poor . . . it will go hard in that time with the lords of the earth, who have ridden without mercy on the backs of the laboring poor, whom Christ has redeemed."[68]

To some degree such threats were accepted as plausible by the higher levels of society. A less apocalyptic text written by Queen Maria de Luna of Aragon anxiously describes the danger of violating divine law. In 1402 the queen attempted to have servitude abolished on the estates of the church in Catalonia by appealing to her kinsman, the Avignonese Pope Benedict XIII. Serfdom contradicted divine law and brought infamy to Catalonia, Maria argued. It was detestable and execrable in the eyes of God and man. Christ had liberated all from servitude, an example that the pope was invited to follow.[69]

Peasant piety may have been a more common justification of revolt than peasant anger, but behind admonitions to heed the word of God lay the danger of both human and divine wrath.

[67] Peter Brock, *The Political and Social Doctrines of the Unity of Czech Brethren in the Fifteenth and Early Sixteenth Centuries* (The Hague: Mouton, 1957), pp. 63–64; Paul Freedman, "The German and Catalan Peasant Revolts," *American Historical Review* 98 (1993): 46, 50; Margaret Aston, "Corpus Christi and Corpus Regni: Heresy and the Peasants' Revolt," *Past and Present* 143 (May 1994): 19.

[68] Brock, *Political and Social Doctrines*, pp. 63–64.

[69] Barcelona, Arxiu de la Corona d'Aragó, Canc. reg. 2350, fols. 43r–43v, ed. Antoni Riera i Melis, in "El Bisbat de Girona al primer terç del segle XV: Aproximació al context socio-econòmic de la sèrie sísmica olotina (1427–1428)," *Anuario de estudios medievales* 22 (1992): 199–200.

PART IV

CELTS AND MUSLIMS

C H A P T E R   N I N E

Anger and the Celtic Saint

WENDY DAVIES

One day the blessed Cadog sailed with two of his followers, Barruc and Gualees, from the island of Echni to Barry Island—both off the coast of southeast Wales, not far from the modern city of Cardiff. When they arrived, St. Cadog asked for his special book, but the two disciples had forgotten it and left it on Echni (now known as Flat Holm). Thereupon the saint made them go back and fetch it; burning with anger (*cum furore inurens*), the holy man said "Go, and do not ever return." The men rowed to the island, picked up the book, and set off for Barry again. However, midway between the two islands the boat suddenly overturned and they were both drowned. Fortunately the book was not lost for it turned up in the stomach of a large salmon later that day.[1]

Somewhat earlier, the man of God sent all but two of his community to fetch timber to rebuild his monastery of Llancarfan, in the Vale of Glamorgan, allowing two young men to remain reading. But three of the monastery's officers, seeing the two sitting down, rebuked them for idleness and made them join in the work. When St. Cadog saw them carting timber, he

I am extremely grateful to members of seminars of the History Department, University of Washington (Seattle), and of the Celtic Program, UCLA, for their lively and instructive comments on an earlier version of this paper. They raised issues that could support much further development.

[1] "Vita Sancti Cadoci," c. 29, in A. W. Wade-Evans, *Vitae Sanctorum Britanniae et Genealogiae,* Board of Celtic Studies History and Law Series, no. 9 (Cardiff: University of Wales Press, 1944), pp. 90–92.

was furious (*furore succensus*) and cursed the three officers (*maledictionem inussit*), asking God to bring them the worst of deaths.[2] Then, miraculously, a sudden shower did no damage to the book which the two disciples had left out in the open when summoned to work.

In other cases in the late eleventh-century "Life of St. Cadog," the saint saw to it that a barn burned down with a peasant inside, that a swineherd was struck by God when Cadog disturbed his pigs, that robbers were swallowed up by the earth, and that a range of kings was blinded.[3] This was a saint of power, who used his powers of intercession with the deity to see to it that those who thwarted him either met their end or—if they were powerful enough to have something to offer him and his community—were damaged for long enough for the saint to extract concessions.

This Life is not an isolated example. Saints that curse and cause destruction are characteristic of Celtic material of the early Middle Ages. King Vortigern, all his companions, and his fortress on the River Teifi, in Dyfed, were destroyed through the concentrated attention of St. Germanus, according to a ninth-century Welsh collection.[4] In Ireland, in collections of the seventh century, St. Patrick cursed (*maledixit*) the son of Fíachu for killing some of those traveling with him; cursed a river because it gave him no fish; cursed into slavery the sons of Ercc, who had stolen his horses; cursed a druid (*magus*) so that he was consumed by fire; cursed a fertile field so that it became a permanently fruitless marsh; and saw to it that a horse who disturbed his peaceful place dropped dead.[5] In texts of a few centuries later, St. Mochutu cursed King Blathmac and all his family, and they were quickly wiped out;[6] St. Ruadan had what amounted to a cursing contest with King Diarmaid, which ended with the vacation of the symbolic royal seat of Tara;[7] and many other Irish saints cursed on greater or lesser provocation.[8]

[2] Ibid., 12 (pp. 50–54).

[3] See Hywel D. Emanuel, "An Analysis of the Composition of the 'Vita Cadoci,'" *National Library of Wales Journal* 7 (1951–52): 217–27, for basic textual work; Wendy Davies, "Property Rights and Property Claims in Welsh 'Vitae' of the Eleventh Century," in *Hagiographie, cultures et sociétés IVe–XIIe siècles,* ed. Evelyne Patlagean and Pierre Riché (Paris: Études Augustiniennes, 1981), pp. 518–19, for dating, and nn. 14–16 for discussion of some earlier historiography.

[4] *Historia Brittonum,* c. 47 in *Chronica minora saec. IV. V. VI. VII,* vol. 3, ed. Theodore Mommsen, MGH AA 13:190–93; cf. ibid., c. 71 (pp. 215–16), where lack of respect for a portable altar in a church in Gower brought death and blindness to offenders.

[5] Tírechán, c. 16, 46, 31, 42, in *The Patrician Texts in the Book of Armagh,* ed. Ludwig Bieler, Scriptores Latini Hiberniae 10 (Dublin: Dublin Institute for Advanced Studies, 1979); Muirchú, 1.26, 1.24, in ibid., pp. 108–12.

[6] "Vita Sancti Carthagi sive Mochutu episcopi de Less Mor," c. 58, in *Vitae Sanctorum Hiberniae,* ed. Carolus Plummer (Oxford: Clarendon Press, 1910), 1:193.

[7] "Vita Sancti Ruadani abbatis de Lothra," c. 16–19, in *Vitae Sanctorum Hiberniae,* ed. Plummer, 2:247–49. See also Lester K. Little, *Benedictine Maledictions: Liturgical Cursing in Romanesque France* (Ithaca: Cornell University Press, 1993), pp. 167–69.

[8] See *Vitae Sanctorum Hiberniae,* ed. Plummer, 1:clxxiii–clxxiv.

Scottish material, though very much less plentiful than Irish or Welsh, nevertheless also provides examples of the cursing saint. According to Adomnán's Life, written ca. 700, St. Columba (of Iona)—through prayer—saw to it that a robber, together with his companions, his boat, and the stolen goods, was drowned by a sudden squall in the very calm sea between Mull and Coll. And when a corrupted priest sought to ordain a known killer, Columba pronounced that the priest's right hand would rot and the killer would be killed; both duly came to pass.[9] Breton material has some similarities, although the characteristic curse is not nearly so pronounced as it is in insular Celtic material: like Cadog, St. Machutes (of Saint-Malo) blinded local rulers who encroached on monastic property; and St. Gildas (of Rhuys) turned thieves to stone and made a wicked tyrant's house collapse to the ground, in ninth- and tenth-century texts, respectively.[10] Gildas put a stop to thieving by calling on the name of Christ (*invocato Christo nomine*); Machutes had Hailoch blinded by praying to God (*ad Deum de re exorandum*). Both of these Lives have Irish connections; most early medieval Breton Lives, however, do not exemplify the destructive powers of their saints.

It is also the case that maledictions characteristically terminate both Latin and vernacular charters from Celtic areas:[11] "whoever breaks this will be cursed by God," from south Wales in the ninth century; "he who violates this will be cursed," from south Wales, eighth to eleventh century;[12] "whoever wishes to break or diminish [this], shall be cursed by the God of heaven," from western Brittany in the eleventh century; "he who breaks this freedom shall be anathematized," from Cornwall, ca. 1000; "he who shall change this, shall be anathematized," from central Brittany in the tenth century;[13] "they all gave their curse to every king who should violate it," from Ireland in the mid-eleventh century; "his curse on everyone who shall come against it," from Scotland in the mid-twelfth century. These charters follow a distinctive charter form; the malediction is one of its identifying characteristics, one which differentiates the form from that of continental charters, in which maledictions do certainly occur but are

[9] *Adomnán's Life of Columba* 2.22; 1.36, ed. and trans. Alan Orr Anderson and Marjorie Ogilvie Anderson (London: Thomas Nelson and Sons, 1961), pp. 372–77, 278–83.

[10] "Prima Vita Machutis" = "La plus ancienne vie de Saint Malo," c. 19, 22, in Ferdinand Lot, *Mélanges d'histoire bretonne* (Paris: Honoré Champion, 1907), pp. 318–19; 321–22; "Vita Gildae, auctore monacho Ruiensi," in *Gildae de Excidio Britanniae,* c. 15, 23, ed. Hugh Williams, Cymmrodorion Record Series 3, pts. 1–2 (London, 1899–1901), pp. 344, 358–60.

[11] See Wendy Davies, "The Latin Charter-Tradition in Western Britain, Brittany and Ireland in the Early Mediaeval Period," in *Ireland in Early Mediaeval Europe,* ed. Dorothy Whitelock, Rosamond McKitterick, and David Dumville (Cambridge: Cambridge University Press, 1982), pp. 263–66, 270.

[12] *The Text of the Book of Llan Dâv,* ed. J. Gwenogvryn Evans with John Rhys (Oxford: n.p., 1893), no. 184 and others.

[13] *Le Cartulaire de Redon,* ed. Aurélien de Courson (Paris: Imprimerie national, 1863), no. 277.

far from being characteristic of the entire genre of sixth- to eleventh-century charter writing.[14]

Saintly cursing is evidenced throughout the early Middle Ages in Celtic areas from the seventh to the eleventh centuries. Although there are examples from later Welsh and Irish Lives, the feature becomes somewhat less evident after the eleventh century.[15] This weakening is demonstrated, for example, by the differences between the first Life of Cadog and that written half a century later by Caradog: Caradog used the same material but made Cadog a much milder character, less prone to curse (he therefore omitted the dire end of Barruc and Gualees when he told the Flat Holm story).[16] As for place, saintly cursing is much more strongly evidenced in Ireland and Wales than it is in Brittany, the maledictions of whose saints are but a pale reflection of their insular brothers'.[17] We have very little early medieval material of any kind from Scotland, Cornwall, and the Isle of Man and therefore cannot assess the comparative strength of the practice there; one would expect Scotland, however, to produce some points of close comparison with Ireland.

This, then, is a distinctively (though not exclusively) *early* medieval, pre-twelfth-century, phenomenon. It is a prominent characteristic of Celtic cultures, where it was not confined to ecclesiastical contexts: cursing is common in Irish secular literature, where it is practiced by druids, kings, mothers, witches, and devils among others.[18] The prominence of cursing is paralleled by the strikingly low profile that healing miracles have in

[14] For some of the particular circumstances in which maledictions became popular on the continent, see M. Zimmermann, "Protocoles et préambules dans les documents catalans du Xe au XIIe siècle: Évolution diplomatique et signification spirituelle," *Mélanges de la Casa de Velazquez* 10 (1974): 41–76; and Little, *Benedictine Maledictions*, p. 55.

[15] Our evidence of the Welsh hagiographic tradition does not really begin until the eleventh century, the two earliest full Lives being those of Saints Cadog and David; there are a number of hints of hagiographic activity before that, however, and it is extremely unlikely that the dossiers of Cadog and David actually represent the beginning of the written tradition; see further, Davies, "Property Rights and Property Claims," pp. 517–18. Elissa Henken's very useful study of Welsh saints includes these dossiers but for the most part uses later material: Elissa R. Henken, *The Welsh Saints. A Study in Patterned Lives* (Cambridge: D. S. Brewer, 1991); cf. her motif index of weapons and punishments, pp. 144–46. See also her *Traditions of the Welsh Saints* (Cambridge: D. S. Brewer, 1987), for details of and comment upon the content of the corpus of Welsh Lives. For the dating of the Irish Lives, see Richard Sharpe, *Medieval Irish Saints' Lives: An Introduction to Vitae Sanctorum Hiberniae* (Oxford: Clarendon, 1991).

[16] Davies, "Property Rights and Property Claims," pp. 522–23.

[17] See Little, *Benedictine Maledictions*, p. 182, where he stresses that the Irish practice did not transfer to the continent.

[18] Cf. Stith Thompson, *Motif-Index of Folk-Literature. A Classification of Narrative Elements in Folktales, Ballads, Myths, Fables, Mediaeval Romances, Exempla, Fabliaux, Jest-Books and Local Legends*, 6 vols., 2d ed. (Copenhagen: Rosenkilde and Bagger, 1955–58), especially motifs M400–493, although there are some other pertinent motifs; it is striking that the sources of Stith Thompson's examples are overwhelmingly Irish (and in fact many of them are of saintly cursing).

Celtic hagiography: in Muirchú's Life of Patrick only one of twenty-five miracles concerns healing; in Tírechán's there are none; in the Life of Cadog there is only one of twenty-seven. Healing stories rarely account for more than 10 percent of miracles in early medieval Celtic *vitae.* This contrasts strongly with continental norms, where anything between 50 percent and 100 percent is common.[19]

Does Cursing Arise from the Emotion of Anger?

The examples with which I began—St. Cadog's fury at the followers who forgot his book and at the monastic officials who made his favorite pupils join in the heavy labor—associate anger and cursing. But these examples are unusual; indeed, when Cadog had the barn burned he is explicitly called gentle—*docilis puer.* Anger is not often specified in conjunction with the maledictions of the Celtic saint; in fact, cursing is not normally associated with any emotion on the part of the saint, let alone with anger, and is on the contrary frequently associated with prayer. Our modern approaches to behavior may lead us to suppose that cursing and anger must go together. But when we look at other cultures, earlier or later, we need to be wary of our assumptions and careful about their application. There is no need to assume that behavior which is both surprising and unpalatable to modern tastes—that of selfish, self-regarding, demanding, willful saints (Charles Plummer found them spiteful and vindictive, as did Gerald of Wales in the late twelfth century)[20]—necessarily arose from anger.

How can we assess this? First, what can we perceive of anger in the material I have already cited? There is plenty of anger in these texts, but it is much more usually associated with laymen than with holy men. Kings and aristocrats are suffused with rage (*ira, furor*) when their acolytes are attacked, or when they are refused food or women, or when they decide to rebel.[21] These cases include examples of pure aggressive energy: the rebel who moves against a church or against his lord starts up, moved by rage and fury (*motus ira et furore*). The emotion of anger (*furor* frequently) is more often associated with wicked rulers and aristocrats in this material

[19] Wendy Davies, "The Place of Healing in Early Irish Society," in *Sages, Saints and Storytellers: Celtic Studies in Honour of Professor James Carney,* ed. Donnchadh Ó Corráin, Liam Breatnach, and Kim McCone (Maynooth: An Sagart, 1989), pp. 43–46. See also Henken, *Welsh Saints,* pp. 49–64.

[20] *Vitae Sanctorum Hiberniae,* ed. Plummer, 1:cxxxv; Giraldus, "Itinerarium Kambriae" 2.7, in *Giraldi Cambrensis Opera,* ed. James F. Dimock, Rolls Series (London, 1868), 6:126–32.

[21] For example: Muirchú 1.18 (p. 90), 1.20 (pp. 92–96), 1.23 (pp. 102–6); "Vita Sancti Cadoci," prologue (pp. 24–28), c. 8 (pp. 40–44), 23 (pp. 72–74), 24 (74–78), 43 (112–14), 69; (136–40); *Text of the Book of Llan Dâv,* ed. Evans with Rhys, nos. 125a, 193, 212, 216b, 217, 249, 259. See Catherine Peyroux, Chapter 2 above, on the force of *furor* in some early medieval texts.

than with saints, much less cursing saints.[22] Associated with the wicked, anger is something that good men, religious men, should avoid.[23] Much earlier, in the sixth century, the cleric Gildas had exhorted the wicked Welsh king Cuneglasus to stop his *ira* and abandon the *furor* that brings destruction—or one day he too would be devastated.[24] We find the same picture in the penitential literature from Ireland and Wales (often in Breton texts): here anger (both *ira* and *furor*) is identified as a sin, requiring penance. For Finnian, a wrathful (*iracundus*) cleric is guilty of a capital sin; for Cummean, cursing a brother in anger (*cum furore maledicens*) requires seven days' solitary penance; for Gildas, he who holds anger in his heart for a long time is in a deathlike state; and wrath, Gildas warned, nourishes killing.[25] For religious legislators anger was a bad thing, necessitating penance. Occasionally, however, saints got angry, as did Cadog in the examples above, Patrick occasionally, and one or two bishops. But even Cadog realized that it was bad form to be angry: on hearing that St. David had had the effrontery to summon a synod while Cadog was traveling abroad, Cadog grew furious with David but then fasted for a day and a night; during the night an angel came and reminded him that he who hates his brother is a killer; he then forgave David.[26]

The writers of the *vitae* and other ecclesiastical literature did not condone anger. They berated rulers for their anger, which they associated with secular warfare and violent uprisings. When they rail against rulers for their anger, they are in effect condemning military activity and condemning the energy of the fighting man, energy that drove him to up and fight, to be active, whether justifiable or not. This is a Christian religious perspective on secular virtue, with a hint of conflict between the ecclesiastical and secular ethics. In Irish secular texts anger is a heroic quality (although inappropriate in court or at a sickbed).[27] Cúchulainn's warp-

22 Elissa Henken, *Welsh Saints*, pp. 1–6, argues that the "biographical pattern" of the male Welsh saint is basically a clerical version of the secular hero in international tradition; that is, she equates the clerical and the secular. I think this underestimates the force of some real differences in the patterns and in associated values.

23 We rarely find the topos of the just ruler exhibiting righteous anger in this material. The exception is Salomon in ninth-century Brittany; his cultural world was eastern Brittany, open to influences from the Frankish world: Salomon is portrayed as the wise judge, angry (*iratus*), initially, with the monks of Redon; see *Cartulaire de Redon*, no. 105.

24 Gildas, *De Excidio*, c. 32, in *Gildae de Excidio Britanniae*, pp. 72–76.

25 Gildas "Praefatio de poenitentia," c. 17–18; "Penitentialis Vinniani," c. 29; "Paenitentiale Cummeani" IV; cf. "Paenitentiale quod dicitur Bigotianum," c. 37, 39, 43, IV; all in *The Irish Penitentials*, ed. Ludwig Bieler, Scriptores Latini Hiberniae 5 (Dublin: Dublin Institute for Advanced Studies, 1963), pp. 62, 84, 118–20, 204, 206, 226–32. Cf. also Little, Chapter 1 above, on patristic literature and Richard E. Barton, Chapter 7, on anger as sin.

26 "Vita Sancti Cadoci" 17 (pp. 60–62).

27 Fergus Kelly, *A Guide to Early Irish Law*, Early Irish Law Series 3 (Dublin: Dublin Institute for Advanced Studies, 1988), p. 195; "Bretha Crólige," c. 61, ed. Daniel A. Binchy, *Ériu* 12 (1938): 48–51.

spasm (*-ríastarda*) is to be admired: it is the quality that makes him capable of heroic feats.

> The first warp-spasm seized Cúchulainn, and made him into a monstrous thing, hideous and shapeless, unheard of. His shanks and his joints, every knuckle and angle and organ from head to foot, shook like a tree in the flood or a reed in the stream. . . . Malignant mists and spurts of fire—the torches of Badb—flickered red in the vaporous clouds that rose boiling above his head, so fierce was his fury. The hair of his head twisted like the tangle of a red thornbush stuck in a gap. . . . When that spasm had run through the high hero Cúchulainn he stepped into his sickle war-chariot that bristled with points of iron and narrow blades . . . he drove out to find his enemies and did his thunder-feat and killed a hundred.[28]

In this carefully crafted version of a famous passage of a famous text, Cúchulainn's anger is of course exaggerated and extreme. But the essential qualities of the warrior that are embroidered here feature again and again in less elaborate, and earlier, Welsh and Irish texts. The warriors are "fierce" and "fiery"; they must be "bold" and "fearless"; they lead from the front, "puffed up" and "swollen."[29] These are qualities deemed appropriate in a world where kingdoms were tiny and politics dominated by raiding beyond community boundaries—the world of the seventh, eighth, ninth, and tenth centuries in the far west of Europe. Even as late as 1022, when the Welsh men of Gwynedd fought the Irishman Rhain in Dyfed, they certainly fought bravely but they also pursued the intruder "in rage (yn llidyawc) . . . slaughtering his host and ravaging the land and plundering every place and harrying it as far as the March."[30] The chronicler writes with approval. Anger is to be encouraged; it is a heroic, admirable quality necessary to the successful pursuit of war; it is justifiable in terms of its military effectiveness; there are no moral overtones. It was therefore

[28] *The Táin,* trans. Thomas Kinsella (London: Oxford University Press, 1969), pp. 150–53. These qualities were not of course exclusive to Celtic societies; see the discussion of Scandinavian warriors and the *berserkir* in Peter Foote and David M. Wilson, *The Viking Achievement* (London: Sidgwick and Jackson, 1970), pp. 263–85 (but note Professor Foote's comments on p. 285 that these figures became something of a laughingstock in the late Middle Ages). Cf. P. L. Henry, "Furor Heroicus," *Zeitschrift für celtische Philologie* 39 (1982): 235–42.

[29] For example, frequently in *Canu Aneirin* and *Canu Taliesin;* for recent texts, see Aneirin, *Y Gododdin, Britain's Oldest Heroic Poem,* ed. and trans. A. O. H. Jarman, Welsh Classics 3 (Llandysul: Gomer Press, 1988); *Taliesin Poems,* trans. Meirion Pennar (Llanerch: Llanerch Enterprises, 1988).

[30] *Brut y Tywysogyon or The Chronicle of the Princes, Red Book of Hergest Version,* ed. and trans. Thomas Jones, Board of Celtic Studies History and Law Series 16 (Cardiff: University of Wales Press, 1955), pp. 20–22.

an appropriate kind of mental condition for the rural, bellicose aristocracies that dominated these peasant cultures during the early Middle Ages.[31] It is quite different from the anger that led to the resolution of disputes *by compromise* in the mannered, international world of the central Middle Ages that Richard Barton discusses, or from the courtly attitude to enemies that developed in the highly governed, Anglo-Norman kingdom of England, discussed by Paul Hyams.[32] These were different emotions and different behaviors, appropriate in later worlds and larger states.

Cursing and Honor

Saints did not express anger so much as curse. Where, if at all, does cursing fit into the aggressive state of mind, the battle rage or even the zeal associated with righteous anger in some classic Christian texts?[33] If we consider when and where saintly cursing occurs, we find that it is a response to circumstances like the following: the killing of *peregrini* (holy travelers); a pagan attack on Christians; the theft of holy property; opposition to the word of God; lack of respect for the word and wishes of the saint; failure to provide the saint with something that he wants or needs (fire, fish, etc.); disturbing the saint at rest. Most of these examples could be encompassed within the notion "lack of respect"; in early medieval Celtic terms, they were much more: these were cases of dishonor and therefore of legal insult. Cursing, it would seem, was regarded as an appropriate response to dishonor in ecclesiastical texts from these cultures; it had more to do with outrage than rage.

Irish, Scottish, and Welsh societies in the early Middle Ages were societies in which honor was precisely related to legal distinctions between persons. It had more than personal significance and was much more than a simple moral quality or code of behavior. Every independent freeman had his proper "privilege" (*braint*) in Welsh, "honor" (*enech*) in Irish; these are

[31] For bellicose aristocracies, see Francis John Byrne, *Irish Kings and High-Kings* (London: B. T. Batsford, 1973); Thomas Owen Clancy and Gilbert Márkus, *Iona. The Earliest Poetry of a Celtic Monastery* (Edinburgh: Edinburgh University Press Ltd, 1995), pp. 3–6; Archibald A. M. Duncan, *Scotland: the Making of the Kingdom,* The Edinburgh History of Scotland 1 (Edinburgh: Oliver & Boyd, 1975), pp. 73–77; Wendy Davies, *Patterns of Power in Early Wales* (Oxford: Clarendon, 1990), pp. 18, 80–89.

[32] For Hyams, see Chapter 5 above; for Barton, see Chapter 7. Note Hyams' reference to the contrasting behavior found on the "Celtic fringe." On the other hand, the Anglo-Norman William Rufus in the late eleventh century behaves rather like a Welsh or Irish warrior, ravaging and wreaking havoc; see Stephen D. White, Chapter 6 above.

[33] See Little, Chapter 1 above.

words which refer to a publicly acknowledged status at law (often translated *dignitas* in Latin texts).[34] A measurable value could be put on this status, expressed in terms of goods and valuation called "honor price."[35] A man's capacity to perform legal actions (that is, to be a surety, a party to a contract, and so on) was rated in accordance with honor price; and, if damaged, he was compensated in accordance with its value—that is, for the insult—*in addition* to compensation for the particular offense.[36] Hence, honor price was a very practical valuation with a very practical application. In Irish honor price was *lóg n'enech* (literally "price of his face") or sometimes *díre* (payment); in Welsh *sarhaed,* with its different semantic range (primarily "insult" but also "insult price"), replaced the earlier *wynebwerth,* literally "worth/price of face." (Although there are some hints of status distinctions in early medieval Breton societies, status does not seem to have had the formal, measurable expression that it did in insular Celtic cultures, and that made for a different society and different values.[37])

Honor therefore in practice related to rank, and honor price was in practice a measure of status.[38] Status had other concomitants in these cultures, among them—especially—protection. The Welsh word for a body's power of protection (a well-defined concept in Welsh and Irish law) is *nawdd;*[39] the cognate in Irish is *snádud.* The higher the status of the protector, the greater his legitimate power of protection and the greater the compensation due for violation. High-status holy men could offer protection just as laymen could, and saints were accordingly invoked as

[34] See *Críth Gablach,* ed. D. A. Binchy, Mediaeval and Modern Irish Series 11 (Dublin: Dublin Institute for Advanced Studies, 1941), pp. 84–86; Kelly, *Guide to Early Irish Law,* pp. 7–10 (and p. 125 for the occurrence of *enach/enauch* in medieval Scots law); *The Welsh Law of Women,* ed. Dafydd Jenkins and Morfydd E. Owen (Cardiff: University of Wales Press, 1980), pp. 44–46, 216, 220.

[35] See Neil Mcleod, "Interpreting Early Irish Law: Status and Currency," parts 1 and 2, *Zeitschrift für celtische Philologie* 41 (1986): 46–65; 42 (1987): 41–115.

[36] Cf. the ancient Greek offence of *hybris,* as clarified by Fisher: the offense of insult against a person's honor or status, and also the legal action taken in such cases; N. R. E. Fisher, *Hybris, A Study in the Values of Honour and Shame in Ancient Greece* (Warminster: Aris & Phillips, 1992).

[37] See Wendy Davies, *Small Worlds. The Village Community in Early Medieval Brittany* (London: Duckworth, 1988), pp. 86–87. Some of the Brittonic honor/status words occur in early medieval Breton texts, but they have different meanings; for example, Old Breton occurrences of *wynebwerth* (*enepuuert* in the late ninth century and *enep guerth* in the late tenth) have the meaning "morning gift," Léon Fleuriot, *Dictionnaire des gloses en vieux Breton* (1964; repr., Toronto: Prepcorp, 1985), p. 160.

[38] See Thomas M. Charles-Edwards, "Honour and Status in Some Irish and Welsh Prose Tales," *Ériu* 29 (1978): 130, for the relationship between honor as moral value and honor price as face value determined by status.

[39] Commonly translated into Latin as *refugium* in medieval legal and other texts; see Huw Pryce, *Native Law and the Church in Medieval Wales* (Oxford: Clarendon, 1993), pp. 168–69. This usage of *refugium* is rare outside Celtic Latin.

protectors.[40] "Protection" was by the eleventh century very clearly territorialized, especially in Welsh texts, as we see in the concept of *noddfa* (literally *nawdd* + *ma*, "protection place"), the area within which *nawdd* was exercised. The ecclesiastical *noddfa*, the protected holy place, was therefore a visible, measurable, spatial expression of ecclesiastical status in insular Celtic areas, and compensation was due for their violation.[41]

The places that were violated in the hagiographic texts mentioned at the start of this paper were not therefore notional spheres; they were physical spaces protected by churches, often extending beyond the church building and precinct for some miles; by the eleventh century they were usually clearly defined, publicly known zones.[42] So, when the king's retainer Caradog grabbed another man's wife at the door of the episcopal church of Llandaff in the mid-eleventh century, he had to compensate the church or take the consequences; when the kings of the north came raiding Cadog's land, they were blinded or otherwise confined until they confirmed the monastery of Llancarfan's zone of protection.[43]

Cursing took place when status was not acknowledged or when there was intrusion into protected space; it was appropriate behavior—and the tales cited were appropriate kinds of stories to tell—when status was denied or insulted.[44] It did not spring from anger and has nothing to do with the battle rage of the wicked, and not-so-wicked, laity. In fact, the rare occasions when a saint became angry also arose in circumstances of dishonor, and especially of disrespect for the word of God. Understandable, given the level of insult, they nevertheless represented loss of control and were regarded as sin. Even saints had their weaknesses. Cursing was the more appropriate response—and it was normally distanced from anger.

[40] Cf. the importance of the saint as protector, *lorica*, "breastplate," in many Celtic texts; see, for example, *The Hisperica Famina II: Related Poems*, ed. Michael W. Herren, Stories and Texts 85 (Toronto: Pontifical Institute of Mediaeval Studies, 1987), pp. 76–92.

[41] See Wendy Davies, "'Protected Space' in Britain and Ireland in the Middle Ages," in *Scotland in Dark Age Britain*, ed. Barbara E. Crawford (St. Andrews, Scotland: Committee for Dark Age Studies, University of St. Andrews, 1996).

[42] Cf. Lynette Olson, *Early Monasteries in Cornwall*, Studies in Celtic History 11 (Woodbridge, England: Boydell, 1989), p. 72.

[43] *Text of the Book of Llan Dâv*, no. 261; "Vita Sancti Cadoci" c. 23–25, 69–70 (pp. 72–80; 136–40). The territorialization of protection is stronger in Wales than Ireland, although by the tenth and eleventh centuries the Irish *termonn* had functions comparable to those of the Welsh *noddfa*; see further, Davies, "Protected Space," p. 19 n. 12.

[44] In essence the Celtic clerical perception that cursing was appropriate when status was denied is not at all dissimilar to the continental perception that anger was justifiable in cases of dishonor in eleventh-century France (see White, Chapter 6, and Paul Freedman, Chapter 8 above); the differences in practice lie in the legal force and consequences of honor/dishonor in the two cultures.

The Status of the Highest

If cursing was appropriate when status was denied, then the higher the status that was denied the more appropriate the defense of cursing. Saints were closer to the Christian God than others, brushed with his divinity. God's status was the highest. To curse most strongly in defense of God's honor was therefore entirely appropriate; and being meek and humble was not at all appropriate. Insult to the divine simply was not tolerable. The saintly curse is often explicitly associated with divine force (*divina virtus*), which it served to demonstrate: Patrick cursed the river to "commemorate" (make people mindful of) *virtus;* Cadog cursed the peasant and burned the barn so that *virtus* and divine power would be made manifest to the wicked. And when Patrick called on God to make a pagan druid die quickly, the druid was smashed to pieces and "the pagans were afraid" (timuerunt gentiles).

To deny status, to compete in any way, was to insult. Likewise the gods of Greek antiquity: Apollo killed the piper who outplayed him, and Latona the mother who had more children than herself.[45] It is in the nature of gods to be at the top in everything: it is not safe for a mortal to beat a god or be better at anything. When Gildas related how Eli was punished, having snatched the flesh from the pot before the fat had been offered to the Lord, he emphasized that his punishment was just and was effected through God's mortal anger.[46] This *was* anger such as only gods could rightly express. The Old Testament God of wrath—who "waxed hot" against the people that made the golden calf, who struck Miriam with leprosy for her murmurings against Moses, who destroyed the disobedient and the idolatrous and the unbelieving—is recognizable in the world of the Celtic saint.[47] Punishment was appropriate for those who denied the highest status, although the saint himself was clearly less than God and served as the agent only of punishment.

The value put on status and honor in these early medieval societies is more reminiscent of Old Testament values than the characteristic humility of the Gospels. It cannot be a coincidence that it is the Old Testament, rather than the New, that is particularly influential on Irish ecclesiastical thinking of the seventh and eighth centuries, especially with regard to the framing of aspects of Old Irish law.[48] The formally stratified societies of

[45] For example, Ovid, *Metamorphoses* 6.1–400.

[46] Gildas, *De Excidio* 69, in *Gildae de Excidio Britanniae,* pp. 174–76.

[47] Exod. 32; Num. 12; Deut. 13, 28; Ps. 78.

[48] See Leslie Hardinge, *The Celtic Church in Britain* (London: Society for the Promotion of Christian Knowledge, 1972), esp. pp. 49–51; and much of Irish writing of the last ten years on the

the far west, with their emphasis on status and honor, had high levels of community responsibility and low levels of state activity. As such, they were more like Old Testament than New Testament—Roman—cultures. Celtic societies changed, of course, but until the increasing state development of the later Middle Ages their values had more in common with those of cultures with low levels of politicization.

Approaches to anger in early Celtic hagiographic material are not as inconsistent as they look at first. The texts are consistent in suggesting that the emotion of anger, which leads to violent deeds or cruel words, is a bad thing in itself; it is a characteristic of wicked, violent rulers and is a sin. Occasionally, in circumstances of the greatest insult to the status of God, the saint slips up and gets angry; if he does, like Cadog, he must do penance. Usually, however, when holy status is insulted, the saints employ the appropriate response for matters of honor: they curse.

To the late twentieth-century Western reader, cursing may appear at once comical and distasteful. But in these early ecclesiastical cultures it was a technique for reminding protagonists of the importance of status and honor and of the power of protection that went with them. Cursing was appropriate in a world of highly stratified societies in which honor had a formal place and a compensatable value; in which the apparatus of the state was exceptionally limited; and in which mechanisms for ensuring justice and social stability were community based. Status was one of the key principles in sustaining social order, and the retelling of cursing stories served to emphasize that principle.[49]

As Normans conquered and cultures changed in the twelfth century, honor came to be differently perceived and to have a different social function; and the discourse about honor changed too. Though stories were still told about the cursing saint, they were told to entertain and amuse rather than to instill respect. As the characters dwindled to become an amusing memory of a quaint past, the social function of the curse changed. Cursing continued in Western cultures, as it had flourished in pre-Christian classical cultures, but it lost its close, functional association with legally defined honor.

---

early Middle Ages, for example, Donnchadh Ó Corráin, Liam Breatnach, and Aidan Breen, "The Laws of the Irish," *Peritia* 3 (1984): 382–438. Cf. Freedman, chapter 8 above.

[49] Little, depending on Cáin Adamnáin, has made a good case for ritual ecclesiastical cursing in early Ireland (*Benedictine Maledictions*, pp. 170–71); it is therefore likely that the stories reflect practice.

C H A P T E R   T E N

From Anger on Behalf of God to "Forbearance" in Islamic Medieval Literature

ZOUHAIR GHAZZAL

Western history is usually conceptualized in terms of explicit evolutionary perspectives. The subject matter of this book—anger and its control, viewed from both an ethical and a political perspective and from the standpoint of both the individual and the state—can be understood in terms of the concept of the "civilizing process" of Norbert Elias. This is the process of monopolization by the feudal powers of their territorial divisions that took place in Europe (France represented its "purest" form) roughly between the eleventh and sixteenth centuries.[1] By the sixteenth century, the process of state formation had left only a few players on the scene, most notably the kings of France and England.[2] It was the "court society" of these two countries that in the

I would like to thank Waḍḍāḥ Sharāra (Lebanese University, Beirut) for having helped me in the various stages of the drafting of this paper during my summer 1995 stay in Beirut (May–August 1995) and for pointing out to me the importance of Father Henri Lammens's research on Muʿāwiya I (and Islamic history in general). Although I found all Dr. Sharāra's remarks and suggestions were invaluable, I hold full responsibility for the final draft. This research would not have been possible had Barbara Rosenwein not suggested that I examine the early medieval Islamic period, a period that I "belong" to, I found, more so than the "modern" period on which most of my research has concentrated thus far. This paper is part of a wider research project on the political and anthropological implications of the classical Arab-Islamic literature. I thank Loyola University Chicago for a generous Summer Research Grant (1995), during which much of the work for this paper was completed.

[1] See Roger Chartier's introduction to the French translation of *The Court Society* in Norbert Elias, *La société de cour* (Paris: Champs Flammarion, 1985).

[2] See Norbert Elias, *The Germans* (New York: Columbia University Press, 1996), pp. 8–9: "Com-

sixteenth and seventeenth centuries made possible the evolution of "manners"—a term that embraces several aspects of individual behavior: prestige, status, rank, place, privilege, consideration, position, posture.[3] Thanks to a remarkable set of historical conjunctures, Western societies by the seventeenth century brought the "individual" into prominence, and the works of Elias and Weber, among others, emphasize the actualization and rationalization of the process of modernity that began in medieval times. At another level, Michel Foucault's more recent attempts to link the "classical age" of European society with the Greco-Roman cultures leads him to the notion of the "care of the self" (*le souci de soi*), a notion that converges with other ideas about the human subject and the culture of the "individual" in different societies and periods.[4]

Despite the expansion of Islam around the Mediterranean basin by the end of the seventh century and the creation of a hostile "buffer zone" between Byzantium and the West, Middle Eastern and Islamic societies were radically different in their evolution from the West as a whole. In the first place, and this applies to all Islamic empires, there was no such thing as a "court society" where the "bourgeois" strata of the population integrated with aristocratic groups and new "manners" were imposed and experimented with. Above all, the notions of "individualization," "subjectification," and the "care of the self," which were the cornerstones of the court society and the civilizing process in Europe, were not common in Middle Eastern and Islamic societies.[5]

Ibn Khaldūn, a fourteenth-century Arab historian from North Africa, described the process of power formation as one where a dominant "group feeling" (*ʿaṣabiyya*) assumes political power by force, imposes itself as the

---

pared with other European societies, for example the French, British or Dutch, the development of the state in Germany shows many more breaks and corresponding discontinuities. . . . Elsewhere, I have examined with some precision the process of state-formation in France. It is astonishingly continuous and direct. The central rulers of the embryonic French state had to contend with few defeats."

[3] See Claudine Haroche, "Égards, respect, considération: Les formes de souci de l'autre," *Magazine littéraire* 345 (July–August 1996): 33–36.

[4] Michel Foucault, *Histoire de la sexualité,* vol. 3, *Le souci de soi* (Paris: Gallimard, 1984).

[5] Western societies take for granted the historical and conceptual separation between church and state, a process which was described in Marc Bloch's *Les rois thaumaturges* and Kantorowicz's *King's Two Bodies.* In Byzantium, however, the king shared the functions of priesthood, and it was legitimate for the temporal power of the state to meddle in the affairs of the church. See Gilbert Dagron, *Empereur et prêtre: Étude sur le «césaropapisme» byzantin* (Paris: Gallimard, 1996). The Islamic tradition, which also does not separate between political and religious powers, could indeed have picked up the concept from the much older Byzantine tradition and modeled it according to its own perspective. What is of interest to us, together with the concepts of the "court society" and "individualism," is to see how these societies operated quite differently from Western ones, or in other words to determine the roots of their "otherness."

ruling dynasty, and then renders other group feelings subservient.[6] But unlike Elias's concept of monopolization, which assumes a process of political and cultural "integration" (through "court society") of those who are dominated, Khaldūnian "subservience" (*istitbāʿ*) operates only by keeping the various group feelings intact and maintaining their "mechanical and organic identity," to use Émile Durkheim's terminology. Thus, Islamic dynasties, whether of Arab, Persian, or Turkish origin, were like closed systems, which had no "manners" as such to impose and which dominated and ruled over others by maintaining a great deal of their internal cohesion intact.

As the following pages will show, the Arab-Islamic literature of the ninth century and later was indeed concerned with modes of behavior and a care for religious ethics and morality; but these are not to be confused with the notions of individualism and care of the self, which are unique to the Western experience.[7] What was rather at stake during the second century of ʿAbbāsid rule, was the survival of the ruling dynasty as such, a process that would repeat itself, under different historical conditions, in the centuries to follow. In short, the ʿAbbāsids were concerned with both religious and secular forms of legitimation, which led them to look at the first two centuries of Islamic experience in terms of their *own* political and social problems. This was needed both for their internal cohesion and for their unsuccessful attempts to bring other groups under their political hegemony. (For the dates of key events as well as of the persons and texts discussed in this chapter, see Chronological Table.)

Chronological Table[8]

622	Hijra (migration) of the Prophet Muḥammad from Mecca, where he was born and where his Banū Hāshim "relatives" were located, to Medina: beginning of the Islamic era
630	Muḥammad conquers Mecca after having already conquered—"opened"—most of the Arabian Peninsula
632	Death of Muḥammad; Abū Bakr becomes the first caliph
633–37	Arabs conquer Syria and Mesopotamia

[6] Ibn Khaldūn, *The Muqaddimah: An Introduction to History* (Princeton: Princeton University Press, 1967).

[7] Concepts like "individualism," "care of the self," "subject," and "court society" are used throughout this chapter with great caution. Not only did such notions originate in the Western experience that made modern civilization possible, but, more important, they are not properly rooted in the Arab and Islamic cultures.

[8] The following chronology is restricted to the events, authors, and works extensively used in this chapter. For a broad survey of Islamic history, see Marshall Hodgson, *The Venture of Islam*, 3 vols. (Chicago: University of Chicago Press, 1974); Bernard Lewis, *The Middle East: A Brief History of the Last 2,000 Years* (New York: Scribner's, 1995).

661	Murder of the fourth caliph ʿAlī, Muḥammad's son-in-law, and founder of Shīʿism; beginning of Umayyād dynasty with Muʿāwiya I as the fifth caliph
750	Fall of Umayyāds, accession of ʿAbbāsids
800–870	**Ibn Ḥanbal:** founder of one of the four legal schools, collector of ḥadīths, and author of the *Musnad*
810–70	**Bukhārī:** one of the first systematic collectors of ḥadīths, his *Ṣaḥīḥ* (Sound) became an authority in Islamic literature
817–65	**Muslim:** like Bukhārī, a collector of ḥadīths; his *Ṣaḥīḥ* became a second major authority
833–42	Reign of the ʿAbbāsid caliph al-Muʿtaṣim: beginning of Turkish domination and of the slow decline of the centralized Empire
c. 775–868	**Jāḥiẓ:** leading figure of the belles-lettres (*adab*) movement
889	Death of **Ibn Qutayba,** theological and literary critic of the *adab* movement
860–940	**Ibn ʿAbd Rabbih:** from Cordoba (al-Andalus, Spain, which remained under an Umayyād dynasty), another contributor to the *adab* movement
923	Death of **Ṭabarī,** historian and interpreter of the Scriptures
957	Death of **Masʿūdī,** historian
1258	Mongols capture Baghdād; end of the ʿAbbāsid Empire, already consumed by its internal divisions and the satellite dynasties active since the ninth century

Anger is definitely not a theme that occurs frequently in Islamic medieval literature: no systematic treatise was ever written on anger, and books on ethics said little on the subject. Examining anger in a coherent way poses difficulty because references to it, whether direct or indirect, are scattered among a great variety of sources, from the very religious to the secular and profane.

In the Qur'anic text, anger was always depicted as God's anger, and it was usually oriented toward the Jews (seldom toward the Christians as their "companions").[9] The Hebraic religion created God's anger in order to explain the misfortunes and social and political problems that had be-

[9] See for example the following Qur'anic verses: 2:61, 3:112, 7:70, 7:151–2, 7:153, 8:16, 16:106, 20:81, 20:86, 24:9, 42:16: all those verses, and many others, represent only a divine anger; one should also perhaps add the "Opening" (*Fātiḥa*) of the Qur'ān (1:5) which describes those who were not the object of God's anger (*ghayri al-maghḍūbi ʿalayhim*). The political and social status of Christians and Jews within the protected boundaries of an Islamic *umma* is quite ambiguous: by referring to the Christians and Jews as the *ahlu-l-kitāb,* commonly translated in its literal meaning as the "people of the Book," the Prophet implicitly recognized the "superiority" of the Judeo-Christian tradition because of its focus on a set of *written* codes and values very different in this respect from the honor strategies of *murūʾa* and *shahāma.* For this reason, as Henri Lammens pointed a long time ago, the implication behind the *ahlu-l-kitāb* is that of the "people of writing" (*gens de l'écriture*); thus the focus on *kitāb* is an explicit emphasis on the original derivative and the act itself, *kataba,* to write, while "Qur'ān," from *qaraʾa,* refers to the acts *reading* and *listening,* closer in this respect to the pre-Islamic poetry in all its forms, which were primarily oral.

fallen the Jewish community;[10] the Prophet Muḥammad did nothing more than pick up a theme which was already there in the first monotheistic religion and create a *strategy of differentiation* out of it. Thus the Qur'ān lavishly recaptured many of the episodes in which the Jews were subject to God's anger for having perversely played with the meaning of His signs and words. Roughly, one-third of the Qur'anic text is devoted to the "People of Moses," and this in itself is a sign of how much the Prophet feared the competition from Jewish monotheism. The verses dealing with God's anger were therefore included not simply to show the misfortunes that had befallen the Jews, but, more important perhaps, to deliver a message to the Muslim community, the *umma,* which had not been subjected yet to God's anger. There are even verses showing that the *umma* did in fact so well (for example, in the battle of Badr)[11] that it got its just reward from God. Ironically, because the Jews had already emphasized the theme of God's anger with the community of believers who betrayed His message, the Qur'anic text made limited use of the theme. In fact, beyond this strategy of differentiation between Islam and the two other monotheistic religions, anger was used in a very conservative manner in the Qur'ān: only God gets angry—and even His Messenger does not have the luxury of such an opportunity.

The words of the Prophets were usually orally transmitted: this ensured by itself that the uniqueness of their charismatic authority could not be reproduced. It also meant that the "routinization" of their message and religious authority *in a written form* would need a great deal of work before it could finally become the source of legitimation for the priestly class (*ʿulamā'*). In Islam, this process took place at an incredible speed since the decision to "edit" the Qur'ān and transmit it in the form we are familiar with goes back to the second caliph, ʿUmar. But another source of tradition was soon to be added to the Qur'anic text in the form of the ḥadīths, the sayings and doings of the Prophet.

[10] Cf. Max Weber, *Economy and Society* (Berkeley: University of California Press, 1978), 1:437: "This made possible the assumption that when enemies conquered or other calamities befell one's group, the cause was not the weakness of the god but rather his anger against his followers, caused by his displeasure at their transgression against the laws under his guardianship. Hence, the sins of the group were to blame if some unfavorable development overtook it; the god might well be using the misfortune to express his desire to chastise and educate his favorite people. Thus, the prophets of Israel were always able to point out to their people misdeeds in their own generation or in their ancestors', to which God had reacted with almost inexhaustible wrath, as evidenced by the fact that he permitted his own people to become subject to another people that did not worship him at all."

[11] The battle of Badr took place in 624, two years after Muḥammad's *hijra* (migration) to Medina. The Prophet, who had to fight a large Meccan army with a small number of followers, won a decisive victory over his enemies.

Even though the process of ḥadīths transmission began during the first two centuries of the Islamic era (the seventh and eighth centuries A.D.), the first transmissions might have been as early as the Prophetic period itself. However, the systematic compilation of ḥadīths dates from the middle of the ninth century, that is, the second century of ʿAbbāsid rule, when state power had already started to decline and slowly deteriorate.[12] Naturally, the question has often been posed as to how many of these ḥadīths were genuine and how many were pure fabrications of the ʿAbbāsid or earlier periods.[13] Despite the importance of questions relating to the authenticity of ḥadīths, their transmission, internal organization and logic, and relation to Islamic law, such issues are beyond the scope of this paper. It would even be extremely difficult to date with any degree of precision the few ḥadīths interpreted below. We have to assume, however, that whether they were fabricated during the first century of ʿAbbāsid rule or much earlier, they reflect the needs and aspirations of both the ʿAbbāsid ruling élite and its *ʿulamāʾ* class (learned men of Islam). Beyond that, it is difficult to be more specific as to why anger as a theme (or any other theme for that matter) was represented in one way rather than in another. Our study simply assumes that, whether those ḥadīths were genuine or fictitious (or even a combination of both), they reflect the *épistémè* of the second century of ʿAbbāsid rule rather than the historicity of the previous periods. So, we will be studying the anger-related ḥadīths textually as part of the ʿAbbāsid ninth-century religious and profane literature rather than contextualizing them within the historical periods to which they were supposed to refer (most of them directly relate to the two decades or so of the Prophetic mission).

The same applies in essence to the belles-lettres (*adab*) traditions of the ninth century, which we shall extensively examine in the last part of this chapter. Even though these sources are more profane than the ḥadīth collections, they are based on the same principle of accumulation through a "chain of transmitters" (*isnād*), and hence a textual analysis of their contents, in particular for a theme like anger, proves to be more important than the historical verification of the factual information they contain.

[12] The ʿAbbāsids were the second Islamic ruling "dynasty" and took control after the fall of the Umayyāds in 750. Like the Umayyāds, they had close ties with the Prophet's clan of Banū Hāshim and they were all part of the Quraysh tribe.

[13] The first major insights into the organization of the ḥadīth literature go back to Goldziher and Schacht (see the following section); for a more recent study concerning the present status of ḥadīth research, see Michael Cook, "Eschatology and the Dating of Traditions," *Princeton Papers In Near Eastern Studies* 1 (1992): 23–48.

A Triangle of Anger

By the ninth century, the literature known as the ḥadīth, which brought together all the sayings and doings of the Prophet, had been canonized thanks to the works of Muslim and Bukhārī.[14] For our theme here, that of anger in early medieval literature, the ḥadīths turn out to be one of the richest sources. There are in fact close to a hundred references to *ghaḍab* (anger) and all its other derivatives in the *Ṣaḥīḥ* (Sound) of Muslim alone, and a dozen more (albeit similar ones) in the *Ṣaḥīḥ* of Bukhārī, while the *Musnad* of Ibn Ḥanbal[15] has even twice as many ḥadīths related to "anger" than both Muslim and Bukhārī. But since many of these ḥadīths overlap, I will limit myself mainly to the *Ṣaḥīḥ* of Muslim, since he, like Ibn Ḥanbal, offers the greatest variety of *ghaḍab*-related ḥadīths.[16] In fact, after the austerity we have encountered in the Qur'ān, the ḥadīths offer a much greater variety of kinds of anger. In addition to God's anger, there is also the anger of the Prophet and his wives, disciples, and friends, and of ordinary men and women as well. Because of the importance of the ḥadīths for our topic and the controversies which have surrounded their "authenticity," it would be a good idea to establish first the nature and essence of ḥadīth literature.

[14] Al-Ḥajjāj b. Muslim (817–65), born in Nīsāpūr (capital of Khurāsān), traveled extensively to the Arabian Peninsula, Egypt, Syria, and Iraq, where, according to legend, he collected close to three hundred thousand ḥadīths, out of which he selected roughly one-tenth for his *Ṣaḥīḥ Muslim*, 5 vols. (Beirut: Mu'assassat 'Uzz al-Dīn, 1987). Muḥammad al-Ja'fī al-Bukhārī (810–70), collected at one point close to six hundred thousand ḥadīths and included a carefully edited selection in his *Ṣaḥīḥ Bukhārī*, 6 vols. (Beirut-Damascus: Dār Ibn Kathīr, 1993). The present section, on the representations of anger in the ḥadīths, would not have been possible without the pioneering work of A. J. Wensinck and his collaborators in indexing the nine major ḥadīth sources in Islamic literature; see *Concordance et indices de la tradition Musulmane*, 2d ed., 8 vols. in 4 (Leiden: E. J. Brill, 1936–1992); on *ghaḍab* and its derivatives, see 4:520–526.

[15] The Imām Aḥmad b. Ḥanbal (800–870), born in Baghdād, was the founder of the Ḥanbalī sect of Fiqh (jurisprudence) and the author of the *Musnad*, in which he collected thirty-thousand ḥadīths.

[16] An inspection of the content of a great number of ḥadīths from nine major sources—Muslim, Bukhārī, Abū Dāwūd (d. 275/888), Tirmidhī (d. 279/892), Nasā'ī (d. 303/915), Ibn Māja (d. 273/886), Dārimmī, Mālik, and Ḥanbal—shows there is no such thing as only one ḥadīth (in the same sense that there is only one Qur'ān). Instead we find a multiplicity of sets of ḥadīths that were gathered and edited (or "textualized") according to the particular needs and aspirations of individuals in specific sociohistorical contexts. Bukhārī, for example, was primarily concerned with a set of ḥadīths that would be useful within a legal framework, while Muslim was more interested in establishing a tradition of the Prophet that would form a continuum with what the Qur'ān had already established. Ibn Ḥanbal, who established with his disciples what became known as the Ḥanbalī sect of jurisprudence, had, like the *khawārij* and Shī'īs, an antistate view of things which was reflected in his own collected set of ḥadīths. Because the ḥadīths were a "literary creation" of primary importance, designed in the first place to create a new set of normative rules, customs, habits, and modes of behavior, their "historical truthfulness," to which historians have devoted so much attention, might not be their most interesting and promising side.

Muslim's *Ṣaḥīḥ* became, together with Bukhārī's *Ṣaḥīḥ*, the second most important source after the Qur'ān for the Sharīʿa (holy law) and fiqh (jurisprudence). Thus, if the Qur'ān is silent on a particular matter, a student of Islam should turn to the ḥadīths. If the ḥadīths are silent, too, one is left with one's own personal *ijtihād*, that is, the tortuous path of knowledge (*maʿrifa*) based on the Qur'ān and ḥadīths. Because of the crucial importance of the ḥadīths, the authenticity of each one of them became a crucial issue in Islamic literature. Very briefly, for each ḥadīth, there is a chain of transmitters, a process known as *isnād* (from *asnada*, "to refer to"): a ḥadīth is referred to X, who refers it to Y, who in turn refers it to the original source Z; Z should be the one who allegedly heard or saw the Prophet performing something worth reporting. The *isnād* system therefore rests on the trustworthiness and prestige of each one of the individual transmitters. Thus, even though there were hundreds of referees (*ruwāt*), the bulk of the ḥadīths originated from a small group of people among the "closest" to the Prophet, that is, his Companions (*ṣaḥāba*).

Literally, *ḥadīth* means "new," and it is the novelty of a saying or a deed that is at stake here: the ḥadīths could therefore be considered an agglomeration of "reports" of the Prophet in action. More important, the ḥadīths in their content and form structured all discourses of jurisprudence (fiqh) to come; it became the norm in any treatise on law and jurisprudence to touch upon all aspects of action in society. In fact, the fiqh was never limited to what could be described as public matters such as contract, rent, and property; rather, like the ḥadīths, it dealt mostly with private normative values: faith (*īmān*), belief, prayer, fasting, eating and drinking, divorce and marriage, to name only a few of the many topics typically covered in both ḥadīth and fiqh. Like the Qur'ān, the ḥadīths provided believers with the normative values they needed: there is a numerical preponderance of the ḥadīths on ritual matters, in contrast to the "punishments" (*ḥudūd*) and "issues of governance" (*aḥkām*). The crucial issue here is to see what type of process these normative values created at the *individual* level. What needs to be examined is how much these normative values left for the individual self to decide, and what kind of dynamism is established between the self and others (individuals, society, politics, etc.).

Because of the parallels in structure between the ḥadīth and fiqh literature, it has often been assumed that one followed from the other: the fiqh emerged from, elaborated upon, and provided a legal interpretation of the ḥadīth. Progress was made in ḥadīth and fiqh scholarship when Joseph Schacht, basing his work on Ignaz Goldziher's discoveries, argued convincingly that the bulk of the ḥadīth was canonized in the ninth-century—

the same time that the fiqh literature became established on what henceforth came to be known as the four major schools of Sunni jurisprudence.[17] The ḥadīths were thus organized and canonized at a time when the legal field was faced with its own set of problems; in particular, a reorganization of the ḥadīths became necessary after some jurists made them the building blocks of the fiqh.

The discursive method considers that individual statements are in themselves neither false nor true because they are part of a discursive totality that provides them with poetic strength and ideological meaning. Discursive practices are a construct of the imagination; they provide a society with the ideas, ideologies, and norms it needs to function. This is why it is more important to see *how they are constructed as discourses* than to limit them by some reality principle. Goldziher was perfectly right (and ahead of his time) when he described the ḥadīths as "one of the greatest and most successful literary fictions." "Fiction" has here the sense of "textualist history," that is, a set of practices (things originally *said* and *done*) that have been textualized and given their politico-religious legitimacy through a chain of transmitters. As such, this literature served as the backbone for all politico-religious power to come.[18] Thus, whether or not individual ḥadīths directly conform to *acts* performed by the Prophet does not matter much from our perspective since the issue here is the process of textualization of performative utterances and their canonization into discursive practices.

In what follows, I will therefore consider individual ḥadīth statements as part of a much larger discursive totality which needs to be reconstructed. On the theme of anger in particular, our question is how a discourse on anger was constructed.

The ḥadīths are mainly about the Prophet and his entourage, and the image of God's Messenger depicted in this part of the Islamic tradition is that of a "simple man," someone like any ordinary human being, who at times could get angry. Yes, the Prophet did occasionally get angry and his anger seemed much more manlike than godlike. The following ḥadīth was first narrated by Anas b. Mālik.[19]

17 Joseph Schacht, *The Origins of Muhammadan Jurisprudence* (Oxford: Clarendon, 1950), pp. 4–5: "a great many traditions in the classical and other collections were put into circulation only after Shāfi'ī's time; the first considerable body of legal traditions from the Prophet originated toward the middle of the second century, in opposition to slightly earlier traditions from Companions and other authorities, and to the 'living tradition' of the ancient schools of law."

18 Ignaz Goldziher, *Introduction to Islamic Theology and Law* (Princeton: Princeton University Press, 1981), pp. 37–44.

19 I will be referring only to the "original" narrator who allegedly directly witnessed the act of saying or doing from the Prophet himself. In its reverse order, the above chain of narrators goes as follows: Zuhayr b. Ḥarb and Abū Ma'an al-Raqāshī, 'Umar b. Yūnis, 'Ikrimatu b. 'Ammār, Isḥaqu b. Abī Ṭalḥa,

> Umm Salīm had an orphan by the name of Umm Anas. God's Messenger saw the orphan and said to her, "That's you? You've grown older. You should not grow older." The orphan went back to Umm Salīm weeping, so she asked her, "What's wrong, my child?" The young girl (*jāriya*, "maid") replied, "God's Messenger has prayed for me (*daʿā*) not to grow older anymore. So from now on I won't grow older anymore."
>
> Umm Salīm left in a hurry, covering her face with a scarf, till she saw God's Messenger, who asked her, "What's up, Umm Salīm?" She replied, "O Prophet of God! Did you wish anything on my orphan?" He said, "And what's that, Umm Salīm?" She said, "She claimed that you prayed for her so that she wouldn't grow older anymore." God's Messenger laughed and said, "Umm Salīm! Don't you know that I've put only one condition on God (*sharṭī ʿala rabbī*) and said: 'I am a human being (*anā bashar*), and I am satisfied like the rest of humans, and *I get angry like the rest of humans.*' So whenever I pray for (*daʿautu*) someone from my *umma*, [my action] is not aimed at anyone in particular (*laysa lahā bi-ahl*), and its purpose is to purify and perform a good deed (*qurba*) so as to make it easier [for the person in question] during the Day of Judgment (*yawmu al-qiyāma*)."[20]

Even though there are many ḥadīths depicting the Prophet in a state of anger, this seems to be one of the very few passages in which he says expressly that he is in fact like any other human being (interestingly, such a claim was based almost exclusively on an *attitude toward anger*—an attitude that at the time, the ninth century, might have been considered proper). That the Prophet *was made* to express anger—the anger of all mortals—to show his commonality with others could be a sign that anger and its negation, its *control*, depicted the essence of a man's (or a woman's?) qualities. Abū Hurayra reported God's Messenger as saying—and this is from a ḥadīth in both Bukhārī and Muslim: "The strong man (*al-shadīd*) is not the good wrestler (*aṣ-ṣuraʿa*); the strong man is only he who controls himself when he is angry."[21] The Umm Anas ḥadīth, however, is far from clear (and this lack of clarity is common to many ḥadīths). For one thing, anger does not seem to be the main theme here: it is as if it were brought in to prove that the Prophet was indeed a common man (whatever that may mean)—a qualification which might have been useful to portray later caliphs, who assumed the role of the Prophet in the politi-

---

and Anas b. Mālik.

[20] Muslim, *Ṣaḥīḥ Muslim*, bk. 45, ḥadīth 95 (emphasis added); henceforth abbreviated as M 45:95. All translations from Muslim and other Arabic sources (except the Qur'ān) are mine.

[21] Bukhārī, *Ṣaḥīḥ Bukhārī*, 81:5763; 45:107.

cal and religious leadership of the *umma,* and who were also subject to common human error and passions (the implications of all this though are far from clear). Then there is Umm Anas's problem: clearly she took the Prophet's words as an offense and the implication behind it (which seems to be "hidden" beneath the text): having grown older, Umm Anas has become less attractive. So the whole Umm Anas episode could have been placed at the beginning simply to portray the Prophet "making a mistake" by offending a woman of lower status (an orphan and maid) and then withdrawing with some kind of "generic" apology in terms of his "weaknesses."

Knowing that everything the Prophet did and said became part of the holy tradition, what then does his claim that he is like any other human being mean? The Prophet's commonality could be part of the many strategies deliberately deployed to make the ḥadīths even more acceptable to the common believers and to negotiate the Prophet's status in society: if the Prophet—this common man—can perform such a thing, then I should myself be capable of doing so. (Interestingly, the commonality of the Prophet was first introduced in the Qur'ān as a way to differentiate between Christianity and Islam on the issue of the divinity of Christ.)

On the other hand, the ḥadīths abound with descriptions of the Prophet in states of anger. Here is one narrated by ʿĀysha, one of the Prophet's wives.

> Two men came to God's Messenger and talked to him about a matter; I couldn't figure out what it was. They made him angry and he cursed and insulted them (*laʿanahumā wa sabbahumā*). When they left, I said to him, "O Messenger of God! A person who aims toward goodness would not do such a thing." "What's that?" he asked. I replied, "You've cursed and insulted them." Then he said, "Don't you know about the deal I made with God? I said: 'O God! I am a human being, so that for any of the Muslims I've cursed or insulted, I'll create a *zakāt* [tax for the poor] and a reward (*ajr*).'" (M 45:88)

This ḥadīth fits well with the previous one; the two express both the human, down-to-earth side of the Prophet and the dark, offensive side of him that irritated people. This ḥadīth, however, adds another aspect: the Prophet here not only grows angry, he also curses and insults his visitors (the offense is here stated explicitly). But the interesting point in both ḥadīths is the Prophet's claim that he made a "deal" with God—which the Umm Anas ḥadīth refers to as *sharṭ* (condition), a "stipulation" that implies some sort of covenant between the Prophet and God regarding the Prophet's personal behavior and qualities as a human being. But the

Prophet is no ordinary human being since he is the "heroic figure" of both the Qur'ān and ḥadīths. Being God's Messenger, he enjoys no creative powers of his own, and it is only in the ḥadīths that we begin to contemplate a Prophet acting "on his own"—thanks to this "deal" of his, his only covenant with God. Keeping in mind that in "heroic societies," as Marshall Sahlins likes to call traditional Polynesian cultures, the "social structure is the humanized form of cosmic order,"[22] the anger of the Prophet is what makes this "humanization from the top" possible. The Prophet's insistence that he is common and ordinary—and that God gave him permission to become angry for anything at any time—encourages men and women to look at their own actions as a humanized form of the Prophet's behavior. Anger is therefore one of those attitudes through which the heroic image of the Prophet is constructed.[23]

In both ḥadīths, women act as mediators to the Prophet's anger by questioning him about his offensive attitudes. At the same time, these women—and in particular the wives of the Prophet—themselves get angry, or at least upset and frustrated, and we see their frustration expressed in the ḥadīths. It is indeed a dissatisfaction often turned toward the Prophet himself: these women are sometimes portrayed as angry with him for one reason or another, or with his entourage, the Companions, who often disapprove of what the Prophet's wives do in public.[24] And finally, theirs was an anger turned toward society in general. The ambiguity of the women's attitudes, in particular some of the Prophet's wives, and the resulting tensions within the Prophetic household prompted a divine intervention in the form of a Qur'anic verse (66:1) in a chapter entitled "The Forbidding" (*Al-Taḥrīm*):[25]

> O Prophet, why forbiddest thou what God has
> made lawful to thee, seeking the good pleasure

[22] Marshall Sahlins, *Islands of History* (Chicago: University of Chicago Press, 1985), p. 58.

[23] In a ḥadīth reported by both Muslim and Tirmidhī, who classified it as sound, 'Āysha, one of the Prophet's wives, was reported to have said: "One night, I missed God's Messenger in my bed, and so went to look for him. I put my hand on the bottom of his feet while he was praying and saying: 'O God, I seek refuge in Your pleasure from Your anger, and I seek refuge in Your forgiveness from Your punishment, and I seek refuge in You from You. I cannot praise You as You have praised Yourself.'" This ḥadīth, like many others, combines in a single text the intimate—the Prophet's wife missing him in bed—with the divine. But it probably does more in establishing the boundaries between the divine and temporal: God as the Being of beings gets "pleasure" from His anger—a luxury only God could afford—and He forgives and punishes at the same time. Thus, even though the Prophet was depicted at times in states of anger, they were portrayed neither as "acts of pleasure" nor as something the Prophet was proud of; as a matter of fact, someone (usually a woman) would point out to him that he acted badly, in a way which dishonored his role as God's Messenger.

[24] The Qur'ān was already critical of a few of the public attitudes of some of the Prophet's wives.

[25] All the Qur'anic translations are from Arthur J. Arberry, *The Koran Interpreted* (London: Oxford University Press, 1964).

> of thy wives? And God is All-forgiving,
> All-compassionate.

and a couple of verses later (66:5):

> It is possible that, if he divorces you,
> his Lord will give him in exchange wives
> better than you, women who have surrendered,
> believing, obedient, penitent, devout,
> given to fasting, who have been married
> and virgins too.

In a Muslim ḥadīth (18:34), the mystery behind these verses is at least partially explained in a manner that is revealing for our subject of anger. The narrator, a certain Ibn ʿAbbās, asked ʿUmar b. al-Khaṭṭāb (who later became the second caliph) about the two wives of the Prophet who apparently were the subject of the above verses. ʿUmar, after conceding that one of the wives was his own daughter, Ḥafṣa, and the other was ʿĀysha, said: "We, the tribe (*maʿshar*) of Quraysh, were a people who prevailed over their wives (*qawman naghlibu an-nisāʾa*).[26] But when we came to the city, our women began learning from theirs. . . . One day I got angry at my wife, so she withdrew from my presence (*turājiʿunī*) on her own; and then I complained to her for having withdrawn." She said, "You are complaining that I have withdrawn? Don't you know that the wives of God's Messenger withdrew from him and left him (*hajara*) all day till night." And ʿUmar added, "I went to see [my daughter] Ḥafṣa and asked her whether she ever withdrew from [her husband], God's Messenger, and she replied positively. I then asked her whether any of [the Prophet's wives] ever left him all day till nightfall, and she replied positively. So I said to her, 'Those of you who are doing this will be disappointed and will be losers. Would any of you like to provoke God's anger because of His Messenger's anger? . . . Don't withdraw from God's Messenger and don't demand anything of him, but demand of me whatever you like. Aren't you aware that [ʿĀysha] is more attractive (*awsam*) than you and more lovable to God's Messenger?' " The conversation between ʿUmar and his daughter ended at this point and the narration shifted to the Prophet's own attitude vis-à-vis his wives and the specific problem of withdrawal that he encountered with Ḥafṣa and ʿĀysha in particular. The connection between the first part of the ḥadīth, about Ḥafṣa's withdrawal, and the next part, about the Prophet's reaction,

[26] *Ghalaba,* translated as "prevail over," could also mean to defeat, beat, triumph over, conquer, subdue, overcome, overpower, etc., all of which could well describe gender relationships in the "society" of Quraysh.

was established by a report by ʿUmar in which he claimed that at one point a friend of his came to him in the evening and told him, "Something important happened. . . . The Prophet divorced his wives," to which ʿUmar replied, "Ḥafṣa got disappointed and lost." ʿUmar then sought to meet the Prophet himself and asked him about his alleged "divorce." But the Prophet denied that he had divorced any of his wives. After a recapitulation of the conversation between ʿUmar and his daughter, and after ʿUmar requested an explanation of the above Qur'anic verses, the Prophet replied that because of the anger that his two wives had provoked in him, he had committed himself not to come to them for a month. The next ḥadīth (18:35) was even more specific: the Prophet kept himself away from his wives for exactly twenty-nine days.

In the ḥadīths that recount the withdrawal of two of the Prophet's wives, a *triangle of anger* comes through as a coherent whole (in the previous ḥadīths, the images of anger were portrayed as dualistic): God's anger, that of his Prophet, and that of the Prophet's wives. It was the anger of the wives that led to their withdrawal, an act that triggered the Prophet's anger and forced him into a voluntary twenty-nine-day withdrawal of his own; and God himself, probably out of fear that the Prophetic mission might be disrupted, urged Muḥammad to go back to his wives and summoned the latter to "obey" the Prophet with an explicit threat that God's Messenger still had several marital opportunities open. A similar triangle of anger structures many representations of anger in the ḥadīths, creating an interplay between the persons involved. Within this triangle, the Prophet is often portrayed with some degree of anger; God is often but not always present (one should keep in mind that the ḥadīths are primarily about the Prophet); and finally, a third party is involved in one way or another: wives of the Prophet or their friends, ordinary men or women, judges and officials, and the like. What this ḥadīth shares with the other two is a humanization of the Prophet's anger, in this case turned against his wives; but here the heroic aspect of the Prophet's life is restored through a reminder from God. In kin-based societies where marriages, arranged through an "exchange of women," often function as political alliances between families and clans, the Prophet's anger could well be interpreted politically (at least at a certain level) as the means whereby he negotiates his power and status with various factions of the kin group (again, all this needs to be seen through the eyes of the caliphs to come).

In one of the longest ḥadīths in Muslim's collection (49:53), primarily dealing with those followers of the Prophet who assisted in the conquests (*ghazwa*) or who participated in one conquest but who "missed" (*takhallafa*) others, a hierarchy (*tarātub*) was established among the *anṣār* (Companions of the Prophet), the criteria of which were determined by the

Prophet himself. This was done on a personal basis, between the Prophet and each one of his *anṣār,* a process which established hierarchically organized networks along lines of devotion to the Cause. In one case, Kaʿb b. Mālik,[27] who was also the narrator of this ḥadīth, claimed to have absented himself (*takhallafa*) from the conquest of Tabūk,[28] even though he never missed any prior conquest organized by the Prophet except Badr.[29] Kaʿb also claimed that the Prophet did not reproach (*ʿātaba*) anyone who absented himself from Badr, and then went on to find an excuse for having "accidentally" missed Tabūk: he was preparing himself for the conquest, but the *anṣār* rushed through so suddenly and at such an unexpected moment that he found himself unprepared.

If, as Kaʿb says, the Prophet seems to have been easy on those who missed Badr, this was not the case for Tabūk: the Prophet in fact inquired about him personally: "Where was Kaʿb b. Mālik?" This question precipitated feelings of guilt in Kaʿb's already troubled conscience. Looking back at his state of mind prior to Tabūk, he abandoned his hesitations: "I said to myself that I can do it if I want to." But this was not enough to release the tension in him, and he chose to confront the Prophet directly, face to face: "As I was told that God's Messenger was on his way [from Tabūk], I felt somewhat relieved since I knew I could not avoid him anymore, so I decided to see him."

The Prophet, who was devoting some of his time to receiving and asking God's forgiveness on behalf of those eighty or so men, the *mukhallafūn,* who had managed to avoid the latest conquests, noticed Kaʿb in the crowd; and when Kaʿb approached him, the Prophet smiled at him—"the smile of an angry man" (*tabassum al-mughḍib*)—and asked him, "What is it that forced you to absent yourself?" To which Kaʿb replied, "I had no excuse, and, O God! I was strong and well enough when I absented myself from you." And the session ended with this brief word from the Prophet: "He said the truth (*ṣadaqa*). Stand up till God decides (*yaqḍī*) about you." Because the Prophet left him in this suspended position without relieving his mind once and for all, the period that followed was for Kaʿb even more atrocious than the previous one: he was riddled with anxieties, self-doubts, and uncertainties. He was slightly relieved when he discovered that there were two other men in the same situation who were also "left behind." But thereafter he stayed at home most of the time, and when he did go out to the marketplace (*sūq*), no one ever talked to him. Whenever he saw the

[27] A poet and Companion to the Prophet from Medina (d. about 660).

[28] An oasis in the Ḥijāz, on the pilgrimage road between Damascus and Medina, which the Prophet conquered in 630 to convert the Arabs of the North to Islam.

[29] See n. 11. Because of the much larger number of the Meccans, the battle of Badr became one of those "signs" for the *umma* of the Prophet that God was on their side.

Prophet, he would say to himself: "Did he move his lips in a gesture of forgiveness?" He would then sit close to him for praying so that he would be able to glance at him from time to time.

At some point, things became even worse. One day, as he was walking, he saw his cousin, one of the people closest to him. This cousin refused to talk to him, a sign that even his family felt that it should distance itself from someone who betrayed God's cause. Then forty days after the Prophet had left him with the ambiguous message, and while he was still waiting for a sign of God's forgiveness, the Prophet asked him to leave his wife—to simply leave her (*iʿtizāl*) without divorcing her. The Prophet then, upon being requested by a certain woman from the Banū Umayya clan (whose husband was in the same difficult position as Kaʿb), permitted him to take this woman as a servant with strict orders not to come "close" (*qarraba*) to her.

Fifty dark and troubled nights had already passed before people came to him (and to his other two friends who were in the same perilous situation) and greeted him with the good news that the Prophet had finally forgiven him. He therefore rushed to see the Prophet who greeted him with "a face shining from happiness"; once the Prophet was happy, "his face would shine as if it were part of the moon." God had sent through his Messenger the following signs (9:117–18):

> God has turned towards the Prophet and the Emigrants
> and the Helpers who followed him in the hour of
> difficulty, after the hearts of a part of them
> wellnigh swerved aside; then He turned towards them;
> surely He is Gentle to them, and All-compassionate.
> And to the three who were left behind, until,
> when the earth became strait for them, for all its
> breadth, and their souls became strait for them, and
> they thought that there was no shelter from God
> except in Him, then He turned towards them, that
> they might also turn; surely God turns, and is
> All-compassionate.

Despite the differences between Kaʿb's ḥadīth and the one narrating Ḥafṣa's and ʿĀysha's story, there is nevertheless an overlap in the content. Both show a similar pattern: someone first commits a wrongful action which is immediately followed by an angry reaction of ambiguous disapproval from the Prophet; then, as punishment, those who committed the wrongful action must endure a period of physical seclusion and mental torture; and finally, the wrongdoers are forgiven, forgiveness always coming from God in the form of Qur'anic verses stating—in a magic code that only those who have been patiently waiting for are able to decipher—that their repentance has been accepted.

On the other hand, the differences between the two ḥadīths are just as important as the similarities. Thus, whereas Ḥafṣa's and ʿĀysha's "internal states of consciousness" are hardly known and their "voices" are absent throughout the ḥadīth, Kaʿb b. Mālik's "monologue" is an essential part of the narration and enriches considerably the triad of sin, repentance, and forgiveness found in all religious discourses.

The "stream of consciousness" starts right from the beginning when Kaʿb b. Mālik reviews in his mind the Prophet's conquest policy. Three phases structure the narrative, but it is the middle one, in which Kaʿb recounts his decisive meeting with the Prophet who receives him with a "smile of anger," that gives shape to the entire narrative. Kaʿb ends up with a guilty conscience because of the Prophet's angry reception, and the angry smile triggers a response in which he severely questions his attitude toward the Prophet's conquests. Kaʿb's conscience, however, riddled with guilt and anxiety, never undertakes a free Socratic process of "knowing thyself"; instead of transforming the guilt into a self-reflective process, Kaʿb always keeps an eye on the Prophet, to the point that when he is in physical proximity with God's Messenger, he sets himself at an angle so that he might observe from a distance the movement of the Prophet's lips. The Prophet, in turn, is waiting for God's judgment on the matter of the three men: a circle of dependence is established, which prevents each of the actors from freely engaging in acts of introspection. The Prophet's anger, rather than establishing itself in its purely *human* dimension, becomes anger on behalf of God; and it is God's forgiveness that everyone anxiously waits for throughout the ḥadīth. The Prophet's anger, as anger on behalf of God, is an act that creates cultural identities and differences among the Prophet's followers (*anṣār*): it signals a danger, or a weakness in the path they are taking. In this respect it represents an evolution from the anger of God in the Qur'ān. The ḥadīths in fact are less concerned with the other monotheistic religions and concentrate more on the *internal* relationships of the immigrants and followers of the Prophet. In this, they are probably the first systematic textual construct of a detailed set of normative rules to be followed by the *umma*.

The limitations imposed by the Qur'ān and ḥadīths on individual behavior and thought are enormous, and in the ḥadīths, the Prophet's anger on behalf of God is the *sign* that establishes the borderlines between toleration, misbehavior, and heresy. In a ḥadīth in *Ṣaḥīḥ Muslim* (47:2), the Prophet reportedly grew angry when he overheard two men quarreling over the interpretation of a verse. He said: "Those who were before you quarreling over [the meaning of] the Book shall perish (*halaka*)." In another ḥadīth (43:159), a Jew complained to the Prophet that one of the *anṣār* had hit him on the face because he had loudly proclaimed that "Moses was selected as Prophet over all people (*al-bashar*)," and the Prophet in a visible mood of anger—"he had anger all over the face"—said: "Do not favor (*faḍḍala*) one Prophet of God over another." And in still another ḥadīth (4:182), a man came to the Prophet and told him that he would be late for the morning prayer because he was preoccupied with someone in a reading session, which, according to the narrator, "got the Prophet in a mood of anger I have never seen him in before," and he said: "O people! Some of you are really repulsive (*munaffirīn*). Those who have to conduct prayers should keep [their reading sessions] short; you might have left behind you the elderly, the weak, and the needy."

Before we close this section on anger in ḥadīth literature, we need to see whether ordinary men and women also had the right to get angry, and if so, how their anger differed from anger on behalf of God. Some people, such as the judges, did not have the right to get angry, particularly when they were on duty, and in a ḥadīth reported by both Bukhārī and Muslim, the Prophet said that "no one should decide on a ruling between two persons when he is angry" (*lā yaḥkum aḥadun bayna ithnayn wa huwa ghaḍbān*)."[30] In another ḥadīth (M 27:32), a person by the name of Suwayd grew angry when he saw someone hitting a maid on the face for having offended him with a spoken word. Suwayd, upset by his anger, justified it by telling his friends that the Prophet had ordered a group of men to free a maid who was working for them because the youngest among them had hit her on the face. What these two stories show us is that even when ordinary individuals are represented in moods of anger—and such ḥadīths are much fewer than those involving God and His Messenger—their anger does not have an autonomous path of its own but is usually mediated by a saying and deed of the Prophet's.

There is a common message in all three ḥadīths and in other similar ones: give yourself entirely to the Common Cause, that of God and his Messenger, and concentrate your thoughts, actions, and passions on it. Individualistic actions are not encouraged, and even quite often prohibited. The battle here is against individualism and subjectivism: this is what unites together in a single stroke (1) the two persons who were attempting their own interpretation of the Qur'ān, (2) the Jew who was declaring Moses as his prophet (while Muḥammad wanted *all* prophets at the same level), and (3) the man who seemed more interested in reading (a

[30] 30:16;, Bukhārī, *Ṣaḥīḥ Bukhāri* 97:6739. In Bukhārī, there is a slight variation in the structure of the sentence: *lā yaqḍiyanna ḥakamun bayna ithnayni wa huwa ghaḍbān*.

purely subjective act which involves the mind) than in praying (a ritualistic act, which in Islam relies on several bodily movements), whereas the Prophet summoned him to do the reverse. Anger is the sign that reestablishes "the order of things" into an objectively more coherent world, that is, a world in which the Prophetic mission guides all mankind, and where individuals, groups, and clans are rewarded to the degree that they support the Prophet and his *anṣār.*

The Anger Beneath

Already from the first century of ʿAbbāsid rule, the Sharīʿa became the ideological foundation of the absolutist state. It is no surprise then to find that the various branches of knowledge (*ʿilm*) related to the sciences of religion (*ʿulūm al-dīn*)—in particular the ḥadīth, fiqh (jurisprudence), and *tafsīr* (interpretation) of the Qur'anic text—matured a great deal by the ninth century.[31] But what gave ʿAbbāsid absolutism the cultural prestige and power it needed was a mixture of literary profane genres, from history to story telling (the *Thousand and One Nights* is definitely the most well known, but this literature also includes the much more complex *Al-Aghānī,* the Book of Songs, by Abū Faraj al-Aṣbahānī), to poetry, literature, and art, all of which represented various categories within belles-lettres (*adab*) culture. The importance of this literature stems primarily from the balance established with the "sciences of religion," which were narrowly focused on the scriptures, the origins of Islam, and the axis of Mecca and Medina. In addition the *adab,* which also had greatly matured by the ninth century, established another balance by integrating elements of the Persian (and Zoroastrian), Judaic, and Christian, cultures with the Islamic. It was also more open to crucial issues such as the Sunnī-Shīʿī split, the abuse of political power, manners, good behavior, and sexuality. It thus considerably broadened the horizon of ʿAbbāsid political power and gave ʿAbbāsid societies the depth they needed to integrate the previous two centuries of Islam and the other non-Islamic or non-Arab cultures as well.

There are many key representative *adab* figures for the ninth and tenth centuries, but the material for this third part concentrates on four main sources: Jāḥiẓ (d. 868), a Muʿtazilī[32] theologian who mastered a satirical Arabic prose essay genre; Ibn Qutayba (d. 889), a grammarian, a theologi-

[31] On the complex relationships between the various literary "historiographical" genres of the ninth century, see Muhammad Qasim Zaman, "*Maghāzī* and the *Muḥaddithūn:* Reconsidering the Treatment of "Historical" Materials in Early Collections of Hadith," *International Journal of Middle East Studies* 28 (1996): 1–18.

[32] The Muʿtazilīs were a group of piety-minded intellectuals of the late Umayyād period who stressed human free responsibility and divine justice.

cal and literary critic, and a prose writer in the spirit of *adab*; Ṭabarī (d. 923), the best-known historian of Islamic history and master interpreter of the ḥadīths and Qur'anic text; and Mas'ūdī (d. 956), a historian.

Despite the wide variety of these sources, they present us with the same type of methodological difficulties as the ḥadīths. A great deal of the *adab* literature was constructed on the same verification principle as the ḥadīth (it should be kept in mind that the ḥadīth literature was exclusively devoted to the Prophet, and hence was sacred and part of the Scriptures, while *adab* was much more general and open to various aspects of the *Lebenswelt*): that is, there was a chain of transmitters for a particular "story." This, again, raises the question as to whether we should be primarily concerned with the authentication of these stories and the approximate date of their creation, or whether we should look at them through their textual construction. Since it would be naive and absurd to presuppose that the ḥadīths, *adab* stories, and similar short narratives were reported as they exactly occurred, the problem is to determine with some degree of exactitude when they were created and for what purposes (cultural, political, or economic). But the fact that they were collected and textualized for the most part by the ninth and early tenth centuries does not imply either that they were *created* at that time. Undoubtedly, some of these stories were created by the eighth century under different political and cultural circumstances and were later picked up and possibly remodeled. One way to move outside these layers upon layers of tradition is simply to presuppose that *as a totality* the stories should reflect the period in which they were textualized. But this contextualization presents another set of problems. Which groups, social classes, or political and cultural factions did each text represent? Which institutions or trends were they supposed to protect? For simplicity, we shall speak of 'Abbāsid culture as a totality and not explore its variations, keeping in mind that in a "heroic culture," history necessarily reflects the well-being and misfortunes of the ruling factions.

As with the ḥadīths, a great deal of the *adab* literature focuses on political and social representations of the previous periods, the Umayyāds in particular. Although the 'Abbāsids came to power in 750 after a violent revolution against the Umayyāds that destroyed their Damascus dynasty (they nevertheless kept their dynasty in Spain), 'Abbāsid representations of the Umayyād period are complex—to the point that in some versions they even show some admiration of some of the Umayyāds' rulers, and in particular the fifth caliph Mu'āwiya.

If Elias was right about the political and social implications of a "society of manners" created by a court system,[33] then it is fair to say that the new

[33] Norbert Elias, *The History of Manners* (New York: Pantheon, 1978).

"manners" imposed by Muʿāwiya in his court—as we might look back upon them after the periods of bloody ʿAbbāsid rule—were primarily constructed by later belletrists (*udabā'*) from common perceptions of the political changes created by Muʿāwiya's feud with ʿAlī, and more generally with the Shīʿīs and Ḥijāzīs. But such a theory, even though it has proved useful in the context of medieval and modern Europe, fails to take account of the intricacies of the Umayyād and ʿAbbāsid dynasties. For one thing, in the context of Arab-Islamic history, there were neither "court societies" nor courtly "manners" (both terms should be used very cautiously). The hegemonic group which ascended to power because of a strong "group feeling" was more concerned in keeping its own cohesiveness intact than in working out a vertical policy of integration and assimilation for other groups.

Among the new "manners" created by the Umayyāds was the ambiguous notion of *ḥilm,* which became totally associated with Muʿāwiya's character as the caliph of a politically divided *umma.*[34] Let us see first how Muʿāwiya, as reported by Ibn Qutayba, expresses to his niece the implications of the new policy of the Umayyāds:

> My brother's [ʿUthmān] daughter: people gave us [their] obedience (*ṭāʿa*) and we gave them security (*amān*), and we showed them forbearance (*ḥilm*) with anger beneath (*ḥuluman taḥtahu ghaḍab*), and they showed us obedience with grudge (*ḥiqd*) beneath, and every human being [keeps] his sword while he checks on the place of his supporters (*anṣār*). If we break our commitment (*nakatha*) to them, they will do the same; and we don't know whether this will be in our favor or not. Being the daughter of the caliph's (*amīr al-mu'minīn*) uncle is better (*khayr-un*) than being an ordinary woman among common Muslims (*ʿurḍu al-Muslimīn*).[35]

Such was Muʿāwiya's direct and Machiavellian tone. (It was reported by the historian Ṭabarī that Muʿāwiya's main political foe, ʿAlī, said of him: "You remember Khusro and Caesar and their sharpness [*dahā'-ahumā*]? And now you've got Muʿāwiya!")[36] The major difficulty in conceptualizing Muʿāwiya's notion of *ḥilm* is in being able to determine how much of the ethos the text claims he imposed upon himself was due to pure political conjunctures and the difficulties he encountered in imposing his rule,

[34] On the notion of *ḥilm,* see Henri Lammens, "Le «ḥilm» de Moʿâwia et des Omaiyades," in *Études sur le règne du calife omaiyade Moʿâwia Ier* (Beirut: Université Saint-Joseph, 1908), pp. 66–108.
[35] Ibn Qutayba (Muḥammad ʿAbdullāh b. Muslim), *Kitāb ʿUyūn al-Akhbār* 1 (Beirut: Dār al-Kitāb al-ʿArabī, 1925), p. 14. Reprinted from Dār al-Kutub al-Maṣriyya (Cairo).
[36] Ṭabarī, *Tārīkh al-Umam wal-Mulūk,* vol. 3 (Beirut: Dār al-Kutub al-ʿIlmiyya, 1988), pp. 264–65.

and how much went back to deeper philosophical and personal convictions. The question is important from at least one viewpoint: to check whether the practice of *ḥilm* implied a zealous and righteous character or simply a Machiavellian *virtù*—that is, knowledge of how to handle the contradictions of politics and turn them to one's advantage by creating an external facade or a mask of good behavior.

In its most straightforward meaning, *ḥilm* could mean patience, forbearance, long-suffering, meekness, tolerance, and indulgence in addition to qualities linked to "reason" and "insight" (*tabaṣṣur, taʿaqqul*) such as discernment and prudence. But these qualities, whether combined or taken separately, do not describe well enough what the *udabāʾ* thought Muʿāwiya's *ḥilm* was all about. Let us look more closely at the passage quoted above from Ibn Qutayba. Muʿāwiya is reported to have acknowledged to his niece that the *ḥilm* of the Umayyāds had anger buried beneath it. In Muʿāwiya's view, the obedience manifested by the majority of their subjects was only the surface of things: grudge (*ḥiqd*) lay beneath this shallow layer of obedience. Here we are in the presence of a politics of layers, where what shines beautifully at the surface is the historical result of its opposite. This is not to imply, however, that the surface—the visible—is shallow while what is beneath it is the deeper reality: we are not into some kind of signifier-signified opposition where the signified is the content of an otherwise empty sign; or into a Freudian ego-id dualism. *Ḥilm* was not a politics of shallowness, hiding something more important beneath, such as the anger and grudge of ordinary people. *Ḥilm* cannot be "explained" by means of the anger hiding beneath, nor is the "truth" about *ḥilm* revealed from anger. For Muʿāwiya, *ḥilm* was simply a *tactics or strategy of survival* through which he contained the anger of his opponents and neutralized it for a moment; he then had to start all over again. But such a strategy in the long run constructed a form of "righteousness" (*ḥaqq*) in the behavior of the caliph.

Thus far, *ḥilm* implies suspicion of one's opponents and even of one's best friends. Asked whether it was a good idea to reveal to others one's deepest secrets, Muʿāwiya was reported to have replied without hesitation: "Whenever I gave my secret to someone, I felt a deep regret (*nadam*) and a lot of disappointment, but whenever I kept it to myself within my own ribs, I gained glory (*majd*) and good memory, sublimity (*sanāʾ*) and highness (*rifʿa*)." Then asked whether he would not even share his secrets with his most loyal friend, ʿUmaru b. al-ʿĀṣ,[37] he was said to have replied, "Not even to al-ʿĀṣ," and he added: "What you've hidden from your enemy, you

[37] ʿUmaru b. al-ʿĀṣ, commander of the Arab forces under Muʿāwiya, conquered Egypt and died in 664.

should also hide from your friend."[38] Thus the person who practices the *ḥilm,* the *ḥālim,* should be always suspicious of everyone and everything. He is connected to those he rules by a very thin layer of convenient trustworthiness which can be broken at any moment. Muʿāwiya was reported as saying, "I never use my sword whenever my whip (*sawṭ*) is enough, and never use my whip when my tongue is enough. And if there's only a hair left connecting me to people it wouldn't break. . . . Whenever they extended [the hair] I would hold on to it, and whenever they held on to it I would extend it (*madadtu-hā*)."[39] The suspicious attitude of the *ḥālim* was in a permanent state of delicate equilibrium. The point is to avoid unnecessary violence: not to rule by force at any price, but to keep one's eyes—and ears—open all the time in order to seize any opportunity for strengthening one's relationship to the people (the governed). But the process may be long and tedious, and, more important, it is not necessarily cumulative, as if one set of tactics leads to another. The noncumulative aspect of the process does not mean that the *ḥālim* proceeds in empty circles, but rather that he may be back to square one at any time.

Compared to the happy strategies of anger in early Islam, *ḥilm* seems a much more complex and tortuous process, since *ḥilm* was a layer deployed above anger in order to contain it. The *ḥālim* had to neutralize his opponent's anger and contain his own anger as well; showing signs of anger in front of an opponent was bad behavior and a sign of weakness. By means of this layer of *ḥilm,* Muʿāwiya wanted to break with the ethos of early Islam and with the Banū Hāshim in particular. By breaking the fundamental rule that gave political priority to the Banū Hāshim (the clan of the Prophet and part of the wider agglomeration of Quraysh to which the Umayyāds also belonged), Muʿāwiya committed, in the eyes of his contemporaries, an unforgivable sin. It is as if Muʿāwiya had broken the divine order of things and replaced it with a new sociohistorical order.[40]

[38] Jāḥiẓ (Abū ʿUthmān ʿUmar b. Baḥr al-Jāhiz), *Al-Maḥāsin wal-Aḍḍād* (Beirut: Maktabat al-Hilāl, 1991), p. 46.

[39] Ibn Qutayba, *Kitāb ʿUyūn al-Akhbār,* p. 9.

[40] In a set of questions to the Banū Hāshim, Muʿāwiya, in his usual witty style, was reported to have played on the ambiguity of what the fundamental "rule of succession" is all about:

> O Banū Hāshim, aren't you going to tell me about your claim for the caliphate [for yourself] while [excluding] Quraysh: How do you get it to yourself? Is it by accepting you (*riḍā*) or by a consensus (*ijtimāʿ*) around you without taking into consideration kinship factors (*qarāba*)? Or is it kinship without the group (*al-qarāba duna al-jamāʿa*), or is it both together? If it were only a question of accepting (*riḍā*) a group (*jamāʿa*) without [taking] kinship (*qarāba*) [into consideration], I don't see that kinship [on its own] has established any right (*ḥaqq*) nor has it established any [political] authority (*wa-lā assasat mulk-an*). And if it were kinship without the group and its acceptance [that is, consensus over the (ruling) group], what was it that forbade then al-ʿAbbās—the uncle of the Prophet, his inheritor (*wārith*), and the guardian of the pilgrims and the orphans—from

Having broken the sacred ambiguous rule, which up to Muʿāwiya had been practiced but never officially stated as such (even though it was the subject of many controversies since the *bayʿa*—process of political endorsement—of Abū Bakr), Muʿāwiya realized that his political legitimacy could no longer rest on much support from Quraysh (or the Shīʿīs, for that matter). Hence the primordial importance of the *ḥilm* strategy in establishing this missing link with the majority. The *ḥālim* could not show his anger publicly, as the Prophet did, because he was already confronted with a situation where too many people angrily refused his *bayʿa.* Muʿāwiya ended up creating a complex give-and-take: because suspicion is the main *état d'esprit* of the *ḥālim,* one needs to test opponents and friends on a permanent basis and listen to their ideas, thoughts, complaints, dreams, and opinions before one reveals anything to them.[41] The available literature[42] shows that many of Muʿāwiya's interlocutors—and the majority were political opponents whom he summoned to his palace in order to "listen to them"— scourged him with insulting remarks and opinions about his past and present (his pagan past "till the last moment" and his "betrayal" to ʿAlī in particular). Muʿāwiya would sit down, listen carefully to his interlocutor(s), show no anger at all (at least he seldom did), and when his visitor was on the verge of leaving, he would ask him/her whether she or he was in need of anything: Any specific purpose for your visit? Do you need any money?

By playing the perfect host, Muʿāwiya instituted a *hermeneutics of suspicion.* In fact, this process of direct confrontation was multilayered. At one level, its intent was purely and simply to "let everything go out

---

> requesting [the caliphate], considering that Abū Sufyān b. ʿAbd Manāf [father of Muʿāwiya] had already given him support? And if the caliphate were the combination of contentment (*riḍā*), together with group [feeling] and kinship, then kinship would only be part (*khaṣla*) of the Imāma [that is, the caliphate] and would not be exclusive to the Imāma as you have been claiming. We say: The one who deserves it the most from Quraysh is the one towards whom people have stretched their hands through the *bayʿa* system, and came with their feet to him because they desire him.(ibid., p. 5)

Muʿāwiya's main question, the *political legitimacy* of the caliphate, haunted him all his life and kept the Umayyāds busy throughout their political career. Taking into consideration the three elements which traditionally constituted the legitimacy of the caliphate—consensus, group feeling, and kinship—Muʿāwiya was concerned whether there was any hierarchy of priorities between those elements in a way that made sense of past and present history. If kinship (*qarāba*) was the most important element in determining the right over the caliphate, then why was Abū Bakr chosen over al-ʿAbbās, the Prophet's uncle? Muʿāwiya was thus playing upon what he saw as the "inconsistencies" of the caliphate in order to widen the traditional pool of candidates to Quraysh as a whole, and he suggested as a solution to this "crisis" a fair play among potential candidates through the *bayʿa* system.

41 For a historical and anthropological look at the notions of property, violence, status, and honor in a modern context, see Michael Gilsenan, *Lords of the Lebanese Marches: Violence and Narrative in an Arab Society* (Berkeley: University of California Press, 1996).

42 This comes mainly from entire chapters of *Al-ʿIqdu al-Farīdu* (see following note) where Muʿāwiya is portrayed as listening carefully to some of his most hostile visitors.

from the heart" on the basis that anger weakens through a genuine communicative process. At another level, by letting his political opponents express their grievances, and through a set of semi-Socratic lines of cross-examination, Muʿāwiya hoped that his opponents would at least no longer take their opinions for granted. He surely was not hoping to convert them to his way of thinking overnight, but he thought he would at least provoke them and make them suspicious of what they were saying and doing. Thus, the irony was that Muʿāwiya was hoping to transfer the feeling of suspicion, from which he was cruelly and unjustly suffering, to his visitors, who, in turn, were the original source of his suspicion and suffering—the ḥālim's perfect Machiavellianism!

The ninth and tenth centuries also witnessed other literary genres, which were neither devoted to a particular topic nor cared much about tying together the wide range of items they included. The *Al-ʿIqdu al-Farīdu* is one example among several of a literature that became encyclopedic and diverse. Thus it is no surprise to find that the *ʿIqdu* devotes a short chapter of only few pages to *ḥilm,* as one of the twenty-five "jewels" (*jawhara*) discussed in the book's twenty-five chapters— in addition to several others recounting episodes of Muʿāwiya with his guests. (One should keep in mind, however, that the author, Ibn ʿAbd Rabbih [860–940], was from Cordoba, and that Andalusia remained under an Umayyād dynasty even after the ʿAbbāsid revolution in 750.)

According to a common legend reported in the *ʿIqdu,* Aḥnaf b. Qays was the one who showed *ḥilm* qualities most. Asked to define what *ḥilm* was all about, Aḥnaf replied—and this was his first attempt at an answer—that it is about "humiliation" (*al-dhull*) which you need to be "patient" about: "humiliation" and "patience" (*ṣabr*) are therefore the first two qualities of a *ḥālim.* Aḥnaf then added: "I am not a *ḥālim* but I practice the *ḥilm* (*lastu ḥalīm-an wa-lakinnī ataḥālam*)." Could this simply mean that the *ḥilm* was an ideal (like honesty and piety) that no one could match, that it was beyond what common mortals could achieve? Or is it that *ḥilm* could be actualized only by the sultan (caliph) while ordinary human beings could only practice it without ever being able to embody the qualities of a *ḥālim?* The next question addressed to Aḥnaf—Who was a better *ḥālim,* he himself or Muʿāwiya?—adds even more to the puzzle. Aḥnaf replied that the difference was so great that he could not possibly be compared to Muʿāwiya: "Muʿāwiya is capable and he therefore practices the *ḥilm,* while I practice the *ḥilm* without being capable" (*Muʿāwiya yaqdir fa-yaḥlam, wa-anā aḥlam wa-lā aqdir*)."[43] What is it that

[43] Ibn ʿAbd Rabbih (Shihāb al-Dīn Aḥmad), *Al-ʿIqdu al-Farīdu,* vol. 1 (Cairo: al-Maktaba al-Tijāriyya al-Kubra, 1935), p. 291.

Muʿāwiya was capable of and Aḥnaf not? Here I am translating *qadira* as "be capable," but it could also mean "be able or be in a position," "have or possess the ability or power," "be or become possible or feasible," or "afford or manage"; and in the context of Aḥnaf's comment, Muʿāwiya was "in a position" to practice *ḥilm* as a full-scale experience, while Aḥnaf practiced *ḥilm* without being in a position to do so. Does this mean that *ḥilm* needs political power to become fully actualized? We are told, in the same chapter of the *ʿIqdu,* that "there are three qualities which are known only [in conjunction] with three situations: *ḥilm* is known only at the moment of anger; the courageous person is known only during war; and you know your brother only when you need him." The essence of *ḥilm* reveals itself therefore in conjunction with anger or at the moment of anger; and in the passage where Muʿāwiya is discussing his polity with his niece, he tells her that *ḥilm* is like a layer which conceals and acts upon the anger hidden beneath: the sultan (or caliph) is the one who is really confronted with anger from many different places; and such a confrontation is much harsher for someone of this status than for those ordinary men or women who might be occasionally confronted with situations of anger with no political consequences at all. Aḥnaf might be right therefore in not seeing his practicing of *ḥilm* as being as extraordinary as that of Muʿāwiya—an indication of how much this kind of ethics denies the "universal" and creates barriers between individuals, groups, and the rulers and ruled.

Not only was *ḥilm* one of those qualities that no one could satisfactorily pursue, but, more important, *ḥilm* was an exercise of social status, constraint, and power.[44] The historian Masʿūdī reports extensively on a sort of dialogue between Muʿāwiya and ʿAlī's companions,[45] a debate that required full attention and shrewdness in order to find *le mot juste* and, at the same time, complete distance and control of oneself as if nothing was happening, as if all the insulting remarks were not even worth replying to. In this debate among men (a woman could not be a *ḥālim*), the purpose was to intimidate, humiliate, and destroy the self-esteem of your adversary *without showing any of your anger:* you needed to humiliate your adversary, who was angry at you and was insulting you, by not showing your anger. It is as if you were telling your opponent that he or she (since

[44] It seems that at least some of the *ḥilm* qualities survived with the Ottoman sultans; see Leslie Peirce, *The Imperial Harem* (New York: Oxford University Press, 1993), p. 177: "As Tursun Beg argued in the introduction to his late-fifteenth-century history, the sultan's principal means of ensuring order was the judicious application of summary punishment (*siyaset*); this right of the sultan over the lives of his subjects was itself a source of tyranny, however, if it was not exercised within the confines of the holy law, and not tempered with forbearance (*ḥilm*)."

[45] Masʿūdī, *Murūj al-Dhahab wa-Maʿādin al-Jawhar,* vol. 3 (Beirut: Publications of the Lebanese University, 1970), pp. 229 ff.

many of Muʿāwiya's interlocutors were women) is so ignorant that nothing matters anymore to the point that it is not even worth lowering yourself to his or her standards. Another aspect of *ḥilm* was closely connected to kin and clan strategies. Indeed, it is reasonable enough to consider *ḥilm* strategy as totally unthinkable without all the clan factionalism of that period: it was something that you deployed against another tribe or clan, but never against your own.[46]

It is difficult with a literature like the one we have been examining—a literature that mainly includes sets of canonized religious texts and several belles-lettres traditions, that was composed for the most part in the ninth century, but that refers extensively to earlier periods—to see what "went on" in those first two centuries of Islamic rule when we seem to be endlessly trapped in layers upon layers of traditions. The approach that we have been following throughout presupposes that it is more important to follow *how this literature is constructed* than to proceed by a systematic empirical verification of the material in question. More specifically, we have looked upon the theme of anger and the virtues of its control for the first two centuries of Islamic rule as they were looked upon in the eyes of ʿAbbāsid historians and generations of belletrists. Once we accept such presuppositions, however, we are faced with a host of new problems. It is certain that the presupposition that such texts, by virtue of their belonging to the ʿAbbāsid period, should also ipso facto "make sense" within a more global "ʿAbbāsid culture" is an oversimplification. Such a view necessarily and overwhelmingly oversimplifies the complexity of intellectual traditions because it falsely presupposes that all those individual intellectuals were part of a single culture or that they were all working for the ideological state system as promoted by the ʿAbbāsid ruling élite. Needless to say, they were part of different strata of the populations in various areas of the ʿAbbāsid Empire, and their writings therefore reflected the tensions inherent in the fields of cultural production. Those different intellectual figures need therefore to be situated within these fields, and their works should undergo a process of sociohistorical contextualization only then can we understand how they were able to operate within the broader culture of ʿAbbāsid institutions. Such a study would be long and complex; I have limited myself to a much simpler task while keeping in mind that the notion of "ʿAbbāsid culture" should be used cautiously.

[46] Cf. Lammens, "Le «ḥilm» de Mo'âwia," pp. 74–75: "Tout dépend de la situation du «ḥalîm», de sa position sociale: vertu, s'il se sent fort, indépendant; s'il est roi, à tout le moins, saiyd incontesté; faiblesse, si sa condition lui interdit de se faire craindre, de nuire surtout. Mais principalement le ḥilm doit savoir céder aux intérêts, aux caprices même de la parenté et du clan. Ce serait un crime de lèse-tribu de le pratiquer contre l'assentiment des siens."

What does this culture tell us then about the significance of anger in ʿAbbāsid society or in earlier periods? A great deal of the selected literature was looking for modes of appeasement and reconciliation (with the other, with opponents and enemies, etc.); primarily it was searching for forms of governing. In a period of complex state formation, intellectuals were looking at the first two centuries as a source for inspiration primarily in terms of government: how did the Prophet govern and how did he conduct the affairs of the early Muslim state? There was definitely a parallel drawn, in this ninth-century literature, between the role of the Prophet as leader of his *umma* and the Umayyād caliphs, on the one hand, and the role of the ʿAbbāsid caliphs on the other. Considering the historical and long-term hostility between the Umayyāds and ʿAbbāsids, it seems surprising that much of ninth-century literature portrayed Muʿāwiya with a cool eye. But this could be less the outcome of a desire for "objectivity" than a perception of Islamic history as a continual flux of mini-narratives whose chain of referees (*ruwāt*) was what established their legitimacy. With such an epistemological horizon in mind, the narratives on anger could be perceived as part of the "rules of behavior" (*adab*) that an enlightened caliph should follow within the framework of a Sharīʿa-oriented state. Beyond the person of the caliph himself, there is not much to suggest that those rules of behavior were destined to become "etiquette" for his court. The body of the caliph, after all, represented his court and society as well.

PART V

CONCLUSIONS

CHAPTER ELEVEN

Controlling Paradigms

BARBARA H. ROSENWEIN

Infants are harmless out of weakness of body, not mind. I once knew an envious baby: it could not yet speak, but it became pale and looked bitterly at a child sharing its milk. Who doesn't know this?

—Augustine, *Confessions* (ca. 400)

Emotional schemas are the internal representation of social norms or rules.

—James R. Averill (1986)

In the medieval West, anger posed a conceptual dilemma for anyone who thought about it. On the one hand, it was out of control. Thus Alcuin, echoing the Stoics, noted with disdain how anger "took over," crowding out forethought and judgment. On the other hand, it was entirely under control. When God was angry, His anger was not uncontrolled. It was, indeed, the opposite: meted out in proper measure, perfectly just.[1] Nor was His anger "incidental"; it was integral to Jewish and Christian theology (and, partly for that reason, *not* so important in Islam). Especially in the Psalms—read over and over again by monks and, later in the Middle Ages, by laypeople as well[2]—God's wrath loomed large: "The kings of the earth stood up, and the princes met together, against the Lord, and against his Christ / . . . Then he shall speak to them in his anger (ira sua), and trouble them in his rage (furore suo), (Ps. 2:2–5, Vulgate ed.). Or, at the beginning of the sixth Psalm, "Lord, rebuke me not in your fury (furore tuo) nor chastise me in your anger (ira tua)."[3]

For helpful critiques of this essay, I am grateful to the contributors to this volume. I thank Ian Wood, who helped me think about anger in the early Middle Ages. Robert Rosenwein supplied me with a useful preliminary bibliography on the theory of anger. I want also to thank Bryon White, my research assistant.

[1] The idea of just anger, both divine and human, was already being worked out in the fourth century; see Ermin F. Micka, *The Problem of Divine Anger in Arnobius and Lactantius* (Washington, D.C.: Catholic University of America Press, 1943), esp. pp. 128–32.

[2] Benedicta Ward, *Bede and the Psalter,* Jarrow Lecture, 1991 (Newcastle-upon-Tyne: n.p., 1992). I thank Paul Hyams for this reference.

[3] This verse formed part of Bede's very popular "Abbreviated Psalter," as discussed by Ward, *Bede*

God's anger, therefore, presented a comforting paradigm to counter and neutralize the monster of uncontrolled anger: His was willed anger, properly felt, and with just consequences. This controlled and controlling paradigm, as we see from the present essays, had as rich a history as that of anger "out of control." Lester K. Little and Richard E. Barton have elucidated here the "twofold definition of anger" created by both medieval theologians and rulers. On the one hand was the anger that was out of control; it was unreasonable, sinful, animal. On the other was the anger directed at extirpating sin or punishing evildoers: it was reasonable, just, useful, controlled. It was anger with a moral dimension.

A "Method" to the Madness

Not surprisingly, a similar bifurcation appears in more recent scientific and social scientific thinking about anger. For modern scientists the debate focuses on whether anger is "pneumatic," welling up irrepressibly like water from a spring, or purposive and rational.

For Darwin, who had already discovered rational laws behind the riot of living forms, emotions were under control. Or rather, he was less interested in emotions than with the twitches, movements, and gestures that manifested them. (At about the same time, William James argued that "bodily symptoms" *were* the emotions.)[4] Twitches might seem arbitrary, but they were not so for Darwin: excitations of the nervous system, induced from both outside and within the organism by desires or pains, led to adaptive muscle movements.[5] Practiced over and over, gestures were habitual and heritable. In their original context, they made good sense; under changed circumstances, of course, they might seem irrational.

Such was the case with anger, or as Darwin termed it, rage. The gestures associated with it (ears pulled back, canine teeth bared) "represent more or less plainly the act of striking or fighting with an enemy."[6] In this way, rage's outward manifestations were perfectly useful. Enraged animals—and for Darwin, human beings belonged in the animal category—were not "out of control" but, on the contrary, precisely in control of the survival of their kind: "The males which succeeded in making themselves appear the

---

and the Psalter, pp. 11–13, 18. See "Collectio Psalterii Bedae," in *Bedae Venerabilis Opera,* pts. 3–4, Corpus Christianorum Series Latina (Turnhout: Brepols, 1955), p. 453.

[4] William James, "What Is an Emotion?" *Mind,* o.s. 9 (1884): 194: "whatever moods, affections, and passions I have, are in very truth constituted by, and made up of, those bodily changes we ordinarily call their expression or consequence."

[5] Charles Darwin, *The Expression of the Emotions in Man and Animals* (New York: D. Appleton, 1896), chap. 3.

[6] Ibid., p. 74.

most terrible to their rivals, or to their other enemies, if not of overwhelming power, will on an average have left more offspring to inherit their characteristic qualities."[7]

Darwin might be seen as a modern, secularized counterpart to the medieval theoreticians of righteous, purposeful anger. Freud was more complicated. He certainly adopted a pneumatic model of affects that emphasized their unconscious source, their force, irrationality, autonomy, and wantonness. In this sense, they were out of control. At the same time, however, he understood affects to be the building blocks of the mind, the life forces that, transmuted by the external reality principle, metamorphosed in some small measure into the ego and superego. In this sense they became the agents of their own control.

Anger, like other "named" emotions, interested Freud very little per se.[8] But after he postulated the formation of the superego (in 1914), he became very interested in aggression: the "death instinct" that took out its wrath on "enemies" both without and within.[9]

In the 1970s anthropologists' and others attacked both the Freudian and Darwinian models. The "old" view of emotions implied by those models was termed "positivist" and "universalist." The critics complained that the diverse literature based on them assumed, first, that affect was universal and second, that emotions were real, material, and biological entities, hard-wired (as it were) into the organism.[10] In the 1960s and 1970s these

[7] Ibid., p. 104.

[8] Sigmund Freud, "The Unconscious" (1915), in SE 14:178: affects (emotions) are the aspect of instincts that "correspond to processes of discharge, the final manifestations of which are perceived as feelings." For Freud's forty-one—surely, rather few—references to "anger," see Samuel A. Guttman, *The Concordance to the Standard Edition of the Complete Psychological Works of Sigmund Freud,* 6 vols. (New York: International Universities Press, 1984).

[9] The idea of the superego was first set forth in "On Narcissism: An Introduction" (1914), where it appeared as the "ego-ideal"; see SE 14:69–102. The theory of the aggressive instinct was introduced, but only tentatively, in 1905 in Freud, "Three Essays on the Theory of Sexuality," in SE 7:157–60. It became the "death instinct" in "Beyond the Pleasure Principle" (1920), in SE 18:52–55.

[10] A wide-ranging bibliography and a survey of theories of emotions and the categories for criticism are given in Catherine Lutz and Geoffrey M. White, "The Anthropology of Emotions," *Annual Review of Anthropology* 15 (1986): 405–36. For work published thereafter, see Thomas J. Scheff and Suzanne M. Retzinger, *Emotions and Violence: Shame and Rage in Destructive Conflicts* (Lexington, Mass.: D.C. Heath, 1991), which argues that shame lies at the core of twentieth-century American guilt; Paul Ekman and Richard J. Davidson, *The Nature of Emotion: Fundamental Questions* (New York: Oxford University Press, 1994) takes a largely functionalist approach to emotions.

On "primary" emotions, of which anger is almost always one, though others in the pantheon may vary, see Robert Plutchik, *The Emotions: Facts, Theories and a New Model* (New York: Random House, 1962); on p. 42 he speaks of "pure and primary emotions." The idea of such emotions rests on universalist and materialist hypotheses, and it is thus contested by some social constructionists, as for example Robert C. Solomon, "Getting Angry: The Jamesian Theory of Emotion in Anthropology," in *Culture Theory: Essays on Mind, Self, and Emotion,* ed. Richard A. Shweder and Robert A. LeVine (Cambridge: Cambridge University Press, 1984), pp. 238–54, esp. pp. 242–43; James Averill surveys various theories of basic emotions and discusses their generally biological foundation in "A Constructivist View of Emotion," in *Theories of Emotion,* vol. 1 of *Emotion: Theory, Research, and*

assumptions seemed less scientific than political; they upheld a status quo crying out to be challenged. The critics sought to downgrade claims of Western superiority, eradicate racism, and to open up the canon; they questioned, for example, the way "emotion" had been used as a code word for "female."[11] "Cognitive" or "cultural" anthropologists were dismayed at the privileging of Western culture, its categories, and its "universalized" constructions. How could Western students of humankind be sure that emotions—their emotions—were universal? Rather, the claim of universality was a convenient smoke screen behind which Westerners could judge and condemn the mental health of entire cultures. Assumptions about the internal wellsprings of emotions were the products not of objective observation but of Western culture's bias in favor of the "autonomous individual." Clifford Geertz declared that "not only ideas, but emotions too, are cultural artifacts."[12] Catherine Lutz called emotions "unnatural"; she meant that they were "learned" as one negotiated life within society. By 1986 Rom Harré could edit an entire book entitled *The Social Construction of Emotions.*[13]

Presenting a philosophical "take" on the social constructionist view in Harré's collection, Errol Bedford found numerous problems in the kind of observation signified by the statement "he is angry." For, contrary to common assumptions, just because he "is" angry (observed on the basis of his behavior) does not mean that he "feels" angry. In fact, for Bedford, emotion words describe all sorts of things *except* feelings, and even "if an emotion were a feeling no sense could be made of [it] at all."[14] Emotion words and emotion statements functioned largely to make judgments about behavior in specific social contexts.

In the same collection, C. Terry Warner went further and spoke of

---

Experience, ed. Robert Plutchik and Henry Kellerman (New York, Academic Press, 1980), pp. 326–29. For less "strong" social constructionist views, see Keith Oatley, "Social Construction in Emotions," in *Handbook of the Emotions,* ed. Michael Lewis and Jeannette M. Haviland (New York: Guilford Press, 1993), pp. 341–52. Elizabeth A. Lemerise and Kenneth A. Dodge identify six "primary human emotions" as standard: joy, surprise, fear, disgust, distress (or sadness), and anger; see their "Development of Anger and Hostile Interactions," in *Handbook,* ed. Lewis and Haviland, p. 537. For biological and neurophysiological approaches to the emotions, see *Handbook,* pp. 87–222.

[11] Catherine A. Lutz, *Unnatural Emotions: Everyday Sentiments on a Micronesian Atoll and Their Challenge to Western Theory* (Chicago: University of Chicago Press, 1988), p. 16, says this explicitly.

[12] Clifford Geertz, "The Growth of Culture and the Evolution of Mind," in *The Interpretation of Cultures* (New York: Basic Books, 1973), p. 81. Already at the end of the 1950s Hildred Geertz, "The Vocabulary of Emotion: A Study of Javanese Socialization Processes," *Psychiatry* 22 (1959): 225–36, had argued (p. 225) that "the range and quality of emotional experience is potentially the same for all human beings. . . . In the course of the growth of a given person, this potential range of emotional experience becomes narrowed, and out of it certain qualitative aspects are socially selected, elaborated, and emphasized."

[13] *The Social Construction of Emotions,* ed. Rom Harré (Oxford: Blackwell, 1986).

[14] Errol Bedford, "Emotions and Statements about Them," in *Social Construction,* ed. Harré, p. 25.

emotions themselves as "conduct—as manoeuvres or 'moves' in largely institutionalized social interactions." He called anger a "delusion," albeit one abetted by Western culture which, for various reasons, found it useful to adopt the stance that feelings are caused and, once provoked, are beyond restraining.[15] In other words, Western culture capitalized on the pneumatic model, and that explained why it maintained and clung to the notion of emotion out of control, deluded into thinking that it was "scientific."

Nevertheless, in the same book, these views were dubbed "strong" social constructionism by Claire Armon-Jones, whose own version, the "weaker thesis," conceded "a limited range of natural [i.e., not learned, not socially constructed] emotion responses."[16]

Thus, weakly and strongly, influential psychologists and anthropologists in the 1970s and 1980s contested the idea that emotions were out of control; on the contrary, they argued, emotions were (largely) products of control and under control.

Historicizing the Superego

The anthropological critiques of the 1970s and 1980s had two related goals: to propose a new scientific theory of emotions and to challenge the Western-centeredness of the prevailing theory. Historians, whether of the West or elsewhere, did not immediately take up the implications of the anthropologists' agenda, however. This was in part due to the rediscovery in the 1980s of Norbert Elias's concept of "the civilizing process," which he had expounded in 1939 in *Über den Prozess der Zivilisation.*[17] Briefly, Elias argued that in the sixteenth century, members not only of the elite but of the middle class as well came to repress their anger and other emotions, adopting instead the delicate and refined manners of the court as the price of flourishing in the modern state. His book thus combined elements derived from Freud's notion of the id with a more rational, nearly social-constructionist view of *learned* emotions that changed with the culture, all incorporated into a historically mediated process of emotional change. The result was dazzling and seductive.

Nevertheless, it was not hard to find faults and weaknesses in Elias's book. Even in 1939 its history was out of date and its handling of theories

[15] C. Terry Warner, "Anger and Similar Delusions," in *Social Construction,* ed. Harré, pp. 135–66. Compare James R. Averill, *Anger and Aggression: An Essay on Emotion* (New York: Springer, 1982), where he shows the social uses of anger in our own culture, including its role in a legal defense to mitigate the charge of murder (pp. 112–16).

[16] Claire Armon-Jones, "The Thesis of Constructionism," in *Social Construction,* ed. Harré, p. 38.

[17] Norbert Elias, *The Civilizing Process: The History of Manners and State Formation and Civilization,* trans. Edmund Jephcott, 2 vols. (Oxford: Blackwell, 1994).

superficial. From history, for example, came Elias's idea of the Renaissance as a turning point, a watershed between the "medieval" and the "modern" worlds. But his notion of the Renaissance went back to the nineteenth-century historian Jakob Burckhardt rather than to the twentieth-century Charles Homer Haskins.[18] From sociology, especially Max Weber, came the connection between state formation and rationalization. Yet Elias's sociology had none of Weber's religious dimension. From Freud came the notion of repression and the development of the discontents of the super-ego. But Elias's "repression" derived largely from an argument about "social control"[19] rather than from Freud's internal and irrational superego, the product of early episodes of unconscious rivalry and hostility that retained parental power in its domineering vigilance over the self.[20]

For these and other reasons, the endorsement of Elias was qualified. His pervasive practice of speaking of the "primitive," "childlike" emotional life of the Middle Ages, at about the same time as Marc Bloch was writing about its "emotional instability" and "impulsiveness," for example, was one that few scholars in the 1980s and after could swallow. As Robert van Krieken remarks, "the image of undisciplined, impulsive medieval personality structure smells just a little, reminiscent of how many used to view 'primitive' culture."[21]

Despite these drawbacks, many historians accepted Elias's notion of a turning point in the Western personality, though some tinkered a bit with the details. C. Stephen Jaeger, writing in 1985, saw the courts of the Ottonian world—not the sixteenth century—as the crucible for "civilizing trends"; the moment when civic activity became a "work of art" occurred in the period 939–1210 rather than during the Burckhardtian High Renaissance of Elias's study.[22] Jaeger thus changed Elias's periodization, but the issues were similar. For Jaeger the warrior—impulsive, violent, hot-

[18] Jakob Burckhardt's *Die Kultur der Renaissance in Italien* was first published in 1860. For Haskins, see Charles Homer Haskins, *The Renaissance of the Twelfth Century* (Cambridge: Harvard University Press, 1927).

[19] Elias, *Civilizing Process,* p. 64.

[20] See, for example, Freud, *The Ego and the Id* (1923), in SE 19:53–58. Elias, *Civilizing Process,* pp. 101–20, apparently thought he was following Freud; yet his insistence on a turning point in human society led him to postulate even "a change in the structure and drives of emotions" via the civilizing process (p. 103). For further discussion of Elias and his sources, see Christopher Lasch, "Historical Sociology and the Myth of Maturity: Norbert Elias's 'Very Simple Formula,'" *Theory and Society* 14 (1985): 705–20, esp. pp. 710–13. I am grateful to Zouhair Ghazzal for references to critics of Elias.

[21] Robert van Krieken, "Violence, Self-Discipline, and Modernity: Beyond the 'Civilizing Process,'" *Sociological Review* 37 (1989): 193–218.

[22] C. Stephen Jaeger, *The Origins of Courtliness: Civilizing Trends and the Formation of Courtly Ideals, 939–1210* (Philadelphia: University of Pennsylvania Press, 1985), esp. p. 13.

headed—was "tamed" by the "educator/statesman," that is, the courtier, who learned "restraint, moderation, self-control, the subjection of passion to reason."[23] Around the same time as Jaeger was writing, Charles Radding published a book that said little about emotions but which, by focusing on cognitive transformations, suggested that a major mental shift took place in the twelfth century: to "thinking in terms of intention and consent instead of hierarchy and obedience."[24] Clearly in these works the moment of "civilizing"—however defined—was being pushed back.

Other historians were pushing the date forward. A year after Jaeger's and Radding's studies appeared, Carol and Peter Stearns argued—in a book focused explicitly, and for the first time, on the history of anger—that the "civilizing" transformation came in the eighteenth century, when a "new view of anger" arose: "the anger-control effort constituted an important shift in emotional values, a new effort at emotional restraint. We cannot say with any certainty how widely this reevaluation spread, in any of its forms, before the nineteenth century."[25] The Stearnses introduced the word "emotionology" into the discussion to denote the "conventions" and "standards" of emotional expression rather than emotions themselves.[26] In their view, when the standards changed, the emotions (internal, biological, pneumatic, but malleable) followed slowly in their wake.[27]

Thus historians found new turning points for a transformation still largely defined in Elias's terms. Rather more recently, however, Edward Muir has reclaimed the sixteenth century. In a detailed analysis of vendettas and feuding in Renaissance Friuli, he saw the Cruel Carnival of 1511 as marking an important end to one kind of culture and the beginning of another: "one of the great transformations in the history of emotions, which had [already] taken hold in the social hothouse of the Renaissance courts, appeared among some Friulan aristocrats, a transformation from externalizing anger . . . to internalizing it by adopting the self-control of good manners."[28]

In the present volume, some historians have found new *locations* for

[23] Ibid., p. 12.

[24] Charles M. Radding, *A World Made by Men: Cognition and Society, 400–1200* (Chapel Hill: University of North Carolina Press, 1985), p. 259.

[25] Carol Zisowitz Stearns and Peter N. Stearns, *Anger: The Struggle for Emotional Control in America's History* (Chicago: University of Chicago Press, 1986), pp. 30–31. See also Peter N. Stearns, "Historical Analysis in the Study of Emotion," *Motivation and Emotion* 10 (1986): 185–93.

[26] Stearns and Stearns, *Anger*, p. 14.

[27] Ibid., p. 15: "In the long run, emotionology, by shaping articulate expectations, does influence actual emotional experience."

[28] Edward Muir, *Mad Blood Stirring: Vendetta and Factions in Friuli during the Renaissance* (Baltimore: Johns Hopkins, 1993), p. xxvi.

the civilizing process. In Chapter 1, Lester K. Little has called attention to the monastery.[29] Paul Hyams's chapter has suggested yet another shift in place, from the princely court to the law court: "Royal justices liberated by their minimal investment in the politics of a particular lordship easily dismissed seignorial anger as an irrelevancy, certainly no excuse for violence, now simply proscribed as unjust and illegal." In general, then, historians of the West have accepted the thrust of Elias's model. Indeed, in an e-mail message to the authors of this book, Hyams wrote: "A (the?) central theme of this book is/ought to be the emergence of the Western Superego, right?"

Rifts and Convergences

But as it turns out, the answer is: not necessarily. For this theme, far from being a leitmotif, is the source of the most serious rift within this book. And insofar as this is so, the chapters herein challenge the easy acceptance of Elias which has heretofore characterized the historiography of emotion in general and of anger in particular.

Once again, the "controlling paradigms" lie behind the split. On the one hand are the chapters that emphasize the explosive force of anger. Wendy Davies' saints, for example, were hardly ever "angry"; but her laymen certainly seethed: "Kings and aristocrats are suffused with rage (*ira, furor*)." Their rage was admirable, secular, and essential: it got them up and going; it was "pure aggressive energy." The "unrestrained violence" of Little's *milites* was similar; and so was the anger of the lords in Hyams's piece, before the king's justices quashed it with the law.

In these images of the medieval emotional universe, there is a civilizing process. The counterpart to the frenzied hag *Ira* is the controlled, clamoring monk, "drained" of anger; or the triumphant, elegant lady Deboneretê, whose origins are in clemency and self-restraint. The uninhibited expression of anger is checked when, for example, the penitentials name the sin of *ira*. In the monasteries the monks practice patience as they curse; and their "decorous" liturgical clamor brings "about a change of behavior in the *potentes*." In the thirteenth-century confessional, priests tell kings about the Seven Deadly Sins; and the friars elaborate a new sort of Mirror of Princes, as thorough as any summa, which takes up the vices one by one.

However, stoutly challenging the notion of the civilizing process, at least on Elias's terms, several chapters in this collection have suggested an

[29] See also his *Benedictine Maledictions: Liturgical Cursing in Romanesque France* (Ithaca: Cornell University Press, 1993).

entirely different paradigm. Taking to heart much of the critique of the cultural anthropologists (and unimpressed by Elias's brand of cultural construction), Stephen White and Richard Barton insist that, in general, medieval lay anger was not "out of control." White, for example, argues that the emotional life that Elias (and Bloch) characterized as "basic," "primitive," and "impulsive" in fact adhered to an implicit ethic: lordly anger was unleashed to avenge dishonor. The anger of *milites* had conventions, rules, and well-understood and justifiable causes. It was sometimes but by no means always—or even often—emotion out of control; it was (in the view of the time) a proper and sane response to a wrongful act. Its "irrationality" had a rational function within a feuding culture. Barton's chapter shows anger's centrality in processes of disputing. This was a society that relied upon compromise, mediation, and local pressure groups to get men and women to come to amicable terms. Anger was part of this system. It may have looked furious, but it was in fact "restrained"—because understood and constructed—by the culture in which it was expressed.

Freedman's chapter makes a different sort of argument that nevertheless similarly challenges the "civilizing" schema. For he has shown how ideas about peasant anger "out of control" were created by an aristocratic elite who regarded their own anger as laudable and that of peasants as comical or frightening. Because their characterizations were so transparently self-serving, these texts suggest to the modern scholar an interpretive strategy contrary to the one Elias used with medieval source materials. Elias took them at their word. Freedman's essay shows that primary sources about violent, impulsive, bestial men cannot be taken at face value.

Gerd Althoff's chapter makes a similar point differently: the extravagance of medieval representations of emotion was due not to any primitive lack of restraint but to its public, "theatrical" mode of communication.

What is the collective import of these four chapters for the notion of the civilizing process? It is, I submit, to suggest that historical change takes us from one set of conventions and restraints to another rather than through a process of civilizing. The "violent" eleventh century, then, becomes as "civilized" as the sixteenth, if civilized means having and largely following delimiting rules of behavior and social codes. In this view, the triumph of Deboneretè would mean that a *new* set of restraints had come to the fore, not that restraint had replaced wantonness.

Not that Hyams, for one, would necessarily disagree with such a hypothesis. For Hyams is extraordinarily sensitive to perspectives—he is asking, after all, what King Henry might actually have seen while lying in bed awaiting the torpor of sleep—and he speaks in his essay largely from the perspective of Henry's practical royal counselors, who were as eager to avoid a *rex inutilis* as they were a *rex furens.* (Althoff suggests some of the same practical considerations at Barbarossa's court.) Royal advisers never wanted the king to be wholly without anger; but the anger that they wanted had to be tempered. It had to be a "certain kind" of anger.

In fact, none of the chapters in this book has accepted the easy notion that emotions in the Middle Ages were the same as—if more loudly expressed than—our own. This view again breaks with the historiography of the subject, though it picks up on the work of the anthropologists.[30] In the first place, all the authors here are concerned with the nuance of language. Catherine Peyroux, for example, points out that "both from place to place and from era to era, words signifying anger reside in different semantic fields, and expressions of anger take place and are received in ways that differ." She has shown how, in the seventh century, the meaning of a young female saint's rage was nothing whatever like that of a twentieth-century child's temper tantrum.

In the second place, all the chapters challenge Elias's scheme by refusing to characterize medieval culture in exclusively negative terms; the Middle Ages were more than just the centuries before state formation. Davies, for example, has emphasized the way in which cursing saints vindicated status in a highly stratified society. She stresses the very material, practical, and legal meaning of honor, which was related to rank, and the important fact that God's honor was ranked higher than any other. Little, dealing with cursing in monastic communities, calls attention to a "shared culture of speech acts" in which words and gestures were efficacious not as ideas but as transformative enactments. Althoff makes a similar observation when he speaks of the importance of "signals" and "stage productions" in medieval communication. Barton notes the role of personal bonds in expressing and enforcing relationships of power. White emphasizes the aristocratic feuding culture of medieval lords, in which honor and shame characterized a "distinctive political structure." Yet Althoff, Geneviève Bührer- Thierry, and Hyams remind us that this same culture was not entirely acephalous; it had institutions (or, at least, memories of institutions) of law, centralization, and legitimate (indeed, divinely sanctioned) royal and imperial power.

Within so complex a society, it is perhaps a mistake to look for clear "turning points" in a "civilizing process." The chapters here suggest that an entire repertory of conflicting norms persisted side-by-side throughout

[30] For example, though in *Unnatural Emotions* Lutz could use the English emotion word "anger" in her discussion of the emotional life of the Ifaluk, she hastened to show how inadequate it was to understanding "hot-tempered" behavior (Ifaluk: *sigsig*), "righteous anger" (Ifaluk: *song*), or the many other "anger" words in the Ifaluk vocabulary.

the Middle Ages.[31] Some of these condemned anger outright; others sought to temper it; still others justified it. The job of the historian then becomes—the authors here have already marked the path—to discover the particular norms adhered to at a given time and to understand the complex of social, political, religious, and cultural forces responsible for or at least influencing those norms.

Let us sketch very provisionally what has emerged, for example, on the issue of royal anger. Contrary to the model put forth by Elias, or even Jaeger's modification of it, Althoff's new periodization pushes the date for an anti-anger stance back to the Carolingian era. Behind royal restraint was "growing ecclesiastical influence on the ruler." This influence did not let up; indeed, we see it flourishing in the time of Henry III. But a thirteenth-century English king could afford to be debonaire—and indeed to some extent he *had* to be, given the restraints imposed on him by Magna Carta. Henry III is known largely for his political weaknesses. Yet he had strengths as well, among which was his ability to manipulate relatively new instruments of state power—the imposing edifice of royal justice, the services of an educated proto-bureaucracy, a burgeoning economy—which obviated the need to be (or seem) impulsive or heroic.[32]

At the same time, even as early as the Carolingian era, the notion of "just anger" was making its own headway. Alcuin and Hincmar, members of those coteries of "courtly intellectuals" that constituted the Carolingian Renaissance, discussed it theoretically. But "just anger" was being worked out in practice as well, and at about the same time. Bührer-Thierry has shown how blinding—an act formerly interpreted as an impulsive, heinous abuse of power—came to be associated with a just and even merciful imperial judgment. Indeed the formerly "angry" act of blinding became integral to the very definition of the emperor's rule, part of his control over the splendor and light that suffused his court. That Barbarossa's ecclesiastical counselors could praise him for the wars and executions born of his anger was thus not necessarily a turning point in ideas about anger; it was just possibly the flowering (so to speak) of a tradition. Barbarossa controlled far fewer institutions of power than did his contemporary the English King Henry II (let alone Henry III); he could be either glorious (like Carolingian emperors) and heroic (like avenging *milites*) or very weak

[31] For the coexistence of conflicting norms concerning gift giving, see Stephen D. White, *Custom, Kinship, and Gifts to Saints: The "Laudatio Parentum" in Western France, 1050–1150* (Chapel Hill: University of North Carolina Press, 1988), p. 73.

[32] On Henry III, F. M. Powicke, *King Henry III and the Lord Edward: The Community of the Realm in the Thirteenth Century,* 2 vols. (Oxford: Oxford University Press, 1947), is the classic account; see Robert C. Stacey, *Politics, Policy, and Finance under Henry III, 1216–1245* (Oxford: Clarendon, 1987), for an assessment of the resources of Henry's reign prior to the baronial revolt.

indeed.[33] But it may also be that grand generalizations about the political institutions available to medieval rulers (such as those I have just made here) are less important than particular moments in each reign—the context would need to be studied with care—that demanded or made possible the adoption of one norm over the other and determined how it would be manifested in both theory and action.

Bührer-Thierry's chapter shows how the condemnation of anger could become transformed into its celebration. In Zouhair Ghazzal's chapter human anger is somewhat similarly transmuted into anger on behalf of God in the entirely different context of a multilayered tradition of exemplary stories about the Prophet and his followers. When the Prophet gets angry, even irrationally, his anger is converted into a source of good; it is anger on behalf of God. Somewhat differently, the caliph's anger, lying "underneath" his patience, allows him to practice virtue: *hilm,* as the combination of anger and courtesy, does not "repress" anger but incorporates it into a mode of communication between caliph and subject.

Orders and Categories

This book has been structured by an obvious set of social categories; it remains to be seen how illuminating these categories are and whether there are others that might be equally fruitful. In a society that often thought of itself as composed of three orders—those who pray (*oratores:* monks), those who fight (*bellatores:* kings, lords, and their henchmen), and those who work (*laboratores:* peasants)—the partitioning that obtains here makes considerable sense.

Lords could be—indeed, were often supposed to be—angry: expressing anger was intimately bound up with their status and honor. This point is never so clear as when it is made in the context of the *laboratores.* For the written sources largely succeeded in making anger the monopoly of lords. They refused to credit peasants with the righteous anger that was granted the *bellatores.* Peasants (in their view) had no honor to avenge; they were simply out of control. This view would continue for a very long time; only in the 1970s was the alternative paradigm fully worked out, with commentators insisting on the rationality of peasant behavior. James Scott, for example, emphasized the logic behind what appeared on the surface to be

[33] For some of the resources and strategies of exploitation available to Barbarossa, see Evamaria Engel and Bernhard Töpfer, *Kaiser Friedrich Barbarossa: Landesausbau—Aspekte seiner Politik—Wirkung,* Forschungen zur Mittelalterlichen Geschichte 36 (Weimar: Böhlaus, 1994).

impulsive bursts of modern peasant rebellions or self-destructive spells of foot dragging and limit testing.[34]

Monks, like lords (from which class they were largely drawn), were considered perfectly capable of real anger; but, as befitted their conversion, their heroism consisted in being free of it. "Monastic anger" was in effect an oxymoron: despite a set of theories composed by churchmen which justified certain kinds of anger, monks had no virtuous outlet for fury. Their ritual curses both "contained" emotion and distanced them from it.[35]

Kings presented a special case, somewhere between lords and monks. Althoff and Hyams have demonstrated how theories about patience and anger, parsed into almost infinitely fine variants by the thirteenth century, were applied with enormous ambivalence to kings whose royal anger was at once desired and detested. Bührer-Thierry has shown how sometimes the theoreticians could even turn "iniquitous anger" into its precise opposite.

Davies's and Ghazzal's chapters depart from the scheme of the three orders. Is it helpful to have a section such as this, meant to invite comparisons? Certainly: a precise legal status connected with honor existed only in Celtic societies; and therefore the precise meaning of cursing there was different than it was in the Latin West. Similarly, only in the Islamic world do we see a ruler whose anger quite consciously undergirded his courtesy.

Yet it would be useful to have far more than two comparative essays. Indeed, a set of studies firmly pitched to inquire about regional variants would be enormously valuable to make clear which differences in the uses and meanings of anger were basic and which cosmetic.

Other categories might well be explored. Gender is one. Can we, for example, speak of "female anger" as opposed to "male anger"? At first it seems we cannot. Lutz revealed that her study of Ifaluk emotion was born in part of her dislike of the way contemporary Western society constructed women to be (or rather, seem) more emotional. If societies construct emotion, and if men and women live in the same society, then there is no "essential" difference in emotion, only in the way society engenders

[34] See James C. Scott, *The Moral Economy of the Peasant: Rebellion and Subsistence in Southeast Asia* (New Haven: Yale University Press, 1976); idem, *Weapons of the Weak: Everyday Forms of Peasant Resistance* (New Haven: Yale University Press, 1985); idem, *Domination and the Arts of Resistance: Hidden Transcripts* (New Haven: Yale University Press, 1990); and the collection of articles inspired by Scott, *Everyday Forms of Peasant Resistance,* ed. Forrest D. Colburn (Armonk, N.Y.: M. E. Sharpe, 1989).

[35] Compare Thomas J. Scheff, "The Distancing of Emotion in Ritual," *Current Anthropology* 18 (1977): 483–505.

it. The alternative would be the largely unacceptable one of postulating two truly different, presocial emotional lives for men and women.

Yet we are justified in speaking of male and female anger if by that we intend to understand how gendered emotion is constructed. Peyroux's chapter, the only one here to focus on a woman, shows two children getting angry at almost the same moment. One is a girl—a saint—enraged when offered a husband. The other is her rejected male suitor. *His* feeling is unproblematic: like Queen Brunhild in the *Life of St. Columbanus,* he is enraged by an insult to his person, his family, and his (potential) descendants.[36] There is nothing gendered about this sort of anger in the seventh century. But the precise context, and therefore content, of the *girl's* anger is exclusively female. If Christ is "the spouse of highest status in the marital economy," then only a female can be in the position of furiously rejecting other suitors on His behalf, and of anticipating the consequences of adultery (in this case to be meted out by God) if she does not. Thus gender is indeed a category in need of exploration.

Similarly, differentiation by time period would be useful. The essays here cut across periods as though there was one Middle Age rather than many: they blur distinct moments of medieval cultural construction. Peyroux's chapter is about seventh-century female anger; it is almost certainly not about angry women in the twelfth or fourteenth centuries. The anger that moved Celtic warriors had little to do (as Davies points out) with the anger that led lords to compromise in the twelfth century. Henry III's Deboneretė could never have decorated the apartments of a pre-Conquest English king, and not only because of her French origins. Peasant anger was valued in the tenth century (as in the Peace of God movement), but it was roundly condemned as violent and irrational in the later Middle Ages.[37] There were many Middle Ages, and it would be well to explore anger in all of them. The "research agenda" of anger studies was not easy to come by, as I suggested in the Introduction; but in the wake of these essays, it begins to define itself.

The Return of the Repressed

This book has been about the social uses of anger, and that focus in large measure determined its thrust. Had it been about anger as one of the deadly sins, it would have concentrated on a different set of problems. It

[36] Jonas, *Vita Columbani* 1.19, MGH SSrerMerov 4:87. Brunhild was enraged (*furens*) when Columbanus refused to bless her grandchildren.

[37] For the Peace of God, see *The Peace of God: Social Violence and Religious Response in France around the Year 1000,* ed. Thomas Head and Richard Landes (Ithaca: Cornell University Press, 1992).

would have had to focus on images, beginning with the harridan *Ira* and the agitated Devil of Lester Little's piece and continuing with representations of anger out of control, whether in penitentials or confessionals, whether in royal courts, peasant fields, or inquisitional tribunals. It would have had to look at punishments, penances, ideas about intention, and belief systems.[38] Had the book been about anger as vice, it would have invoked civic traditions and the intellectual distinctions of the schoolmen. Had it been on the literary functions of anger, it would have followed Barton's discussion of anger's role in structuring the narrative *Raoul de Cambrai* with similar inquiries concerning other vernacular poems.

Since it is about the social uses of anger, however, this collection emphasizes rationality. Even if the social constructionists are not *entirely* right, they are right enough to focus our attention on the strategic, calibrated aspects of anger—and, by association, other emotions—in the Middle Ages.[39] This is absolutely proper, and a salutary corrective to the Bloch-Elias model of medieval affect. Yet it would be wrong to end with everything under control. Neither the social construction of anger nor the social *uses* of anger constitutes the whole story, as every writer represented in this book—and surely every reader perusing it—is aware.

[38] For cursing, anger, and inquisitorial punishment in a slightly later period, see Maureen Flynn, "Blasphemy and the Play of Anger in Sixteenth-Century Spain," *Past and Present*, no. 149 (1995): 29–56.

[39] On assessing the social constructionists, see Oatley, "Social Construction in Emotions"; and William Ian Miller, *Humiliation and Other Essays on Honor, Social Discomfort, and Violence* (Ithaca: Cornell University Press, 1993), pp. 196–97.

Contributors

GERD ALTHOFF is Professor of History at the University of Münster (Germany). He is the author of *Das Necrolog von Borghorst* (1978), *Adels- und Königsfamilien im Spiegel ihrer Memorialüberlieferung* (1984), (with Hagen Keller) *Heinrich I. und Otto der Grosse* (1985), *Verwandte, Freunde und Getreue* (1990), *Amicitiae und Pacta* (1992), *Otto III.* (1996), *Spielregeln der Politik im Mittelalter* (1997), and he is the editor of *Die Deutschen und ihr Mittelalter* (1992).

RICHARD BARTON completed his Ph.D. at the University of California, Santa Barbara, in 1997 under the direction of Warren Hollister. His dissertation is entitled "Lordship and Power in Maine, 890–1110," and he is the author of "Lordship in Maine: Transformation, Service, and Anger," *Anglo-Norman Studies* 17 (1995): 41–63. He is currently working on the practice and cultural expression of lordship from the end of the Carolingian empire through 1200.

GENEVIÈVE BÜHRER-THIERRY received her doctorate in medieval history and is currently *maître de conférences* at the University of Marne-la-Vallée. Her study of the political role of the episcopacy in the Carolingian and Ottonian kingdoms has been published as *Evêques et pouvoir dans le royaume de Germanie, 876–973* (1997). Currently she is working on manifestations and forms of power in the ninth and tenth centuries, for which she has written "La reine adultère," *Cahiers de Civilisation Médiévale* 35 (1992): 299–312.

Wendy Davies is Pro-Provost of University College London and a Fellow of the British Academy. She has published *Small Worlds: The Village Community in Early Medieval Brittany* (1988), *Patterns of Power in Early Wales* (1990), and with Paul Fouracre she has co-edited *The Settlement of Disputes in Early Medieval Europe* (1986) and *Property and Power in Early Medieval Europe* (1995). Her most recent book, entitled *A Breton Landscape,* is a systematic interdisciplinary study of two thousand years of land use in eastern Brittany.

Paul Freedman taught at Vanderbilt University from 1979 to 1997 and is currently Professor of History at Yale University. He has published *The Diocese of Vic* (1983) and *The Origins of Peasant Servitude in Medieval Catalonia* (1991). A book entitled "The Image of the Peasant in the Middle Ages" is forthcoming.

Zouhair Ghazzal is Assistant Professor of History at Loyola University Chicago. He has published *L'Économie politique de Damas durant le XIXe siècle. Structures traditionneles et capitalisme* (1993) and is completing a book on the Ottoman religious courts of Beirut and Damascus, "The Ethnography of Court Documents." He is also preparing a legal study of crime and punishment in contemporary Syria and Lebanon.

Paul Hyams was for twenty years a Fellow of Pembroke College, Oxford. Since 1989, he has been an Associate Professor at Cornell. He has followed his book, *King, Lords and Peasants in Medieval England: The Common Law of Villeinage in the Twelfth and Thirteenth Centuries* (1980), with a series of papers exploring the social and cultural implications of various aspects of English law seen in its European context. His book in progress, "Rancor and Reconciliation in Medieval England," is a study of the various responses to perceived Wrong, legal and extralegal.

Lester K. Little is Dwight W. Morrow Professor of History at Smith College. He is author of *Religious Poverty and the Profit Economy in Medieval Europe* (1978), *Liberty, Charity, Fraternity: Lay Religious Confraternities at Bergamo in the Age of the Commune* (1988), and *Benedictine Maledictions* (1993). He has recently been visiting professor at Yale University and the École des Hautes Etudes en Sciences Sociales in Paris and Resident in Postclassical Studies at the American Academy in Rome.

Catherine Peyroux is Assistant Professor of History at Duke University. She has written articles on the historical imagination of women's sacral authority in early medieval Europe, on women and the holy in early medieval Ireland, and on Frankish canonists' legislation about nuns. She is currently completing a comparative study of dual-sex monasteries in early medieval Spain, Ireland, England, and France.

Barbara H. Rosenwein is Professor of History at Loyola University Chicago. She has published *Rhinoceros Bound: Cluny in the Tenth Century* (1982) and *To Be the Neighbor of Saint Peter: the Social Meaning of Cluny's Property, 909–1049* (1989) and has recently completed a book on early medieval political culture and strategies, "Negotiating Space: Early Medieval Immunities and Other Entry Prohibitions."

Stephen D. White is Asa G. Candler Professor of Medieval History at Emory University. He is the author of *Sir Edward Coke and "the Grievances of the Commonwealth," 1621–1628* (1979), *Custom, Kinship, and Gifts to Saints* (1988), and *Feuding, Peacemaking, and Law in Early Medieval France* (forthcoming). He is currently writing a book entitled "Imaginary Justice: The Representation of Judicial Processes in Old French Romances and Epics."

Index

evidentiation
communication

plausible

formulaic
language

physical v. / notional
spheres

Not confined to the P's

Use Gertrude as eg.